Programed Instruction

A Guide for Management

With chapters by

Joseph A. Tucker, Jr. and Jerome P. Lysaught

and case histories of programed instruction in:

Aerojet–General Corporation
American Bankers Association
American Telephone and Telegraph Company
The Atlantic Refining Company
Burroughs Corporation
Chemical Bank New York Trust Company
Dartmouth Medical School
Elmhurst National Bank
First National City Bank of New York
First Pennsylvania Banking and Trust Company
General Electric Company
The Headquarters Air Force Control System (473L)
International Business Machines Corporation
Liberty Mutual Insurance Company
Life Insurance Agency Management Association
Martin Company, Denver Division
Michigan Bell Telephone Company

Montgomery Ward
National Institutes of Health
Northern Natural Gas Company
Northrop Norair
Pfizer Laboratories, Inc.
The Quaker Oats Company
Schering Corporation
Southwestern Public Service Company
Sperry Polaris
Title Insurance and Trust Company
Trans World Airlines
Union Carbide Chemicals Company
United Services Automobile Association
U.S. Industrial Chemicals Company
University of Illinois College of Medicine
University of Miami School of Medicine
University of Washington School of Medicine, Department of Pharmacology
Varian Associates

Programed Instruction

A Guide for Management

By GABRIEL D. OFIESH

Colonel, United States Air Force

American Management Association, Inc.

For
Bess,
my wife

Preface

TRADITIONALLY, EDUCATION AND TRAINING HAVE BEEN CATEGORIZED within the realm of the arts; they have not been classified as sciences. Yet, in an age of atomic energy and aerospace, of electronics and technology, we have been content to grapple with the correlative problems of education and training using "horse and buggy" education and training systems—or non-systems. The effort to apply what we know about learning to the art of teaching has been a colossal failure in terms of what should have been done and what merits immediate action.

Attempting to meet the challenge of the technological revolution in our society have been the four major educational and training institutions: the government, the military, the public and private sector, and American industry. Industry, probably more than the others, is beginning to recognize that a technological revolution in education and training to parallel the new "industrial revolution" is necessary if our society is to avoid retrogression—indeed, if it is to survive. Industry is increasingly aware that the forces at work in the economy today are reshaping our manpower requirements. So are the educational associations, for the National Asssociation of Public School Adult Educators recently pointed out that "our educational climate must be attuned to these new requirements (millions of under-educated adults and unemployable citizens) and provide the kind of training that will give workers skills to match modern-day jobs." Automation can be a blessing for our society, but it exacts a high social price. "It eliminates thousands of lower level jobs and requires better education and training for the new jobs it creates."

Every day there is more to learn, yet there is less time for learning it. This crucial time constraint must be the mandate for a new education and training technology, for an educational *process* responsive to, and consistent with, late 20th century challenges. Educational technology seeks to develop a set of axioms to support what must inevitably become a science of education. Technology is the application of what we know—a science replacing an art. Technology is producing a broadly based shift from a blue-collar to a white-collar labor force. The stresses attendant upon this

7

shift can be eased only if the problems created by technology are in turn solved by technology. It is likely that American industry, because it recognizes the problem, will produce the innovative leadership which in turn will help to develop those models of education and training systems.

A thriving, robust educational technology must inevitably lead to the development of new, effective, efficient educational systems made up of integrated materials and elements designed to perform specific educational tasks with a high degree of reliability for a particular group of students.

Geary A. Rummler, director of the University of Michigan Center for Programmed Learning for Business, has said, "The industrial educational system [is] in the forefront in producing educational innovations, [and] continued technological change in industry makes this the most aggressive and progressive educational system we have." If this is true, then it behooves educational leaders to take note of industry's exploratory efforts in programed instruction. It is in programed instruction that industry and other educational and training institutions in our society will find the basis for the needed revolution in education and training.

This book is intended largely as a guide to senior management. There is no claim in this book that the dynamic change taking place in education and training is over or has even made a significant start. The beginning seems to be here: slow and timid, an unborn entity with fragile heartbeat detectible only by stethoscope. This is pathetically far from the roar of a revolution.

It is likely that in another ten or twenty years educational and training innovations will have become massive and will be coming fast, and automated instructional systems will have become as common as TV sets and automobiles, providing ideal instruction for every student on an individual basis. If this occurs, its origins will be directly traceable to the innovative murmurs that are described in the representative case histories contained in this book. With top management support and understanding, and with the favorable climate for innovation which only senior management can create, the contributions that industry can provide to the educational community could well rival those of the industrial and technological revolutions.

Many of the cases in this book testify that programed instruction in industry is no longer a fad. This concept of instruction, born no more than a decade ago out of the laboratory of the behavioral psychologist, has been steadily maturing. Yet, it bears repeating, no claim is made that it is fully grown and that no problems remain. A cardinal principle in human development is that there is no growth without conflict. There are now, and for a long time to come there will continue to be, much discussion and controversy about programed instruction; but the healthiest sign is the willingness to continue trying, to keep experimenting, and to resent and be dissatisfied with the status quo.

Acknowledgments

ACKNOWLEDGMENT IS DUE TO MANY WHO HAVE HELPED TO MAKE this book a reality. The original suggestion came from J. R. "Bob" Johnson of Britannica Press, and further encouragement was received from Charles Schwep, educational consultant for the American Management Association. His support and encouragement were constant throughout the effort. The outline of the book was reviewed in detail by Charles Adams, Roger Kaufman, Robert Corrigan, Gus Rath, Jean Moye, Winn Smith, and William Deterline. Their suggestions were extremely helpful and not only led to revisions of the outline but established the basic approach. More than 200 people in industry, business, and government were contacted for potential case material, and more than 100 case studies were secured. Thirty-five were selected because of the types of situations and the variety of problems and applications which they portrayed. I would like to acknowledge the contributions that were made by the many who provided data which, although not used directly, did provide insights that could not otherwise have been brought to bear in writing the chapters.

A number of people read major portions of the manuscript and made very helpful suggestions; some of them reread several drafts of portions of the manuscript and discussed them at length with me: Charles Adams, Rose Clavering, Irving Goldberg, Walter Hirsch, Robert Mager, Stuart Margulies, Susan Meyer Markle, Leonard Silvern, and Frances Waxman. Although many of the suggestions made by these various fine friends were adopted, responsibility for the final draft is mine.

I also would like to express my appreciation to Patricia Zinsmeyer and Marie DeToto for their stenographic and clerical assistance. I am in deep and sincere debt to Virginia H. Britton for her untiring efforts during the preparation of this volume. She worked many long hours under particularly difficult conditions in preparing the manuscript.

Further my appreciation to the editorial staff of the American Management Association. Without the constant prodding and encouragement of Elizabeth Marting and the patient and detailed editorial assistance of

Robert E. Finley, writing this book would have been more a task than the pleasure it was.

Finally, to Bess, my wife, my gratitude for her emotional support, her understanding, and her tolerance of my having to meet deadlines, to travel so extensively, and to write so much material during the preparation of this book.

Contents

Part I

The Development of Programed
Instruction Based Training Systems

Chapter 1

Why We Must Evolve Instructional Technology

We have been told time and time again that information is accumulating so rapidly in almost every field of endeavor that we are forced to seek out new methods to cope with merely the acquisition, assembly, analysis, and dissemination of the new knowledge that crowds upon us. We may well ask, when we consider the explosions in knowledge, population, and technology, where is the explosion in education and training that will enable us to keep pace with them in our private lives and in our work?

THE CURRENT STATE OF EDUCATION AND TRAINING

In spite of the numerous predicaments in education and training confronting us today, we have made no significant effort to provide hopeful solutions. The problems are too numerous to mention, too difficult to comprehend fully. During the past few years several million lost and bewildered youngsters have left school before graduation and entered a world which really has no place for them. Dr. Daniel Schreiber, Director of the School Dropout Project of the National Education Association, characterized these youngsters as "constantly running from work half-done, from school half-completed, . . . truly fugitives from failure."

Dr. James B. Conant has pointed to the "social dynamite" inherent in millions of *unemployable* youths. Throughout the country in the past year the demand for jobs for late adolescents has increased nearly seven times, whereas the supply of jobs has only doubled. Cities throughout our nation are reporting drastic decreases in jobs available to 16- and 17-year-olds.

There must be no saturation point on learning itself, nor on educational opportunities. Educational and training circles are in a ferment. We hear much talk about new methodologies, new devices, new tools, new organization of curricular content, and so on. Maybe out of all of this talk will come something intelligent, but no "crash program" can possibly deliver us from our predicament.

Our teacher-training programs have an ultimate influence on training itself. We are a nation with a shortage already of 150,000 teachers. Many that we do have are not college graduates and have substandard credentials. The number of able and master teachers among those who have paper qualifications and college degrees is woefully low. Teachers as a group still have a long way to go in developing a high professional status, largely because they lack, at present, a true instructional technology. Many work under impossible conditions (as do trainers in industry) which prevent them from making the most effective use of their talents and skills.

The situation will get worse, not better. Within a mere three years we will increase our present school enrollment by five and one-half million students. Our teacher shortage will keep increasing. Just to maintain the status quo, more than one-half of all our college graduates during the next five years would have to become teachers, which is a most unlikely prospect. One of our Midwestern states anticipates a 45 per cent increase in college enrollment during the next two years. We are all too likely to react to this problem by stressing quantity over quality and by reducing still further our teachers' qualifications.

President John F. Kennedy, in his message to Congress in 1962, emphasized that

> No task before our nation is more important than expanding and improving the educational opportunities of all our people.
>
> Education is both the foundation and the unifying force of our democratic way of life—it is the mainspring of our economic and social progress—it is the highest expression of achievement in our society, ennobling and enriching human life. In short, it is at the same time the most profitable investment society can make and the richest reward it can confer. Educational failures breed delinquency, despair, and dependence. They increase the costs of unemployment and public welfare. They cut our potential national economic output by billions. They deny the benefits of our society to large segments of our people. They undermine our capability as a nation to discharge world obligations. All this we cannot afford—better schools we can afford. . . .
>
> We must provide facilities for fourteen million more elementary, secondary school, and college students by 1970, an increase of thirty per cent. . . . We must find the means of financing a seventy-five per cent increase in the total cost of education—another $20 billion a year for expansion and improvement—particularly in facilities and instruction, which must be of the highest quality if our nation is to achieve its highest goals.

Here again, although all the measures mentioned by the late President are undoubtedly necessary, they will most certainly fall short unless some means is provided for making a breakthrough in the processes by which the few must teach and the many must learn. If an infinitesimally small part of the effort he recommended were to be expended in developing a genuine, comprehensive educational technology, then the tools might be forged—and distributed—for breaking the chronic, stifling impasse in education.

In his message of January 12, 1965, to the Congress concerning "Full Educational Opportunity," President Lyndon B. Johnson said:

> Specifically, four major tasks confront us:
>
> *1.* To bring better education to millions of disadvantaged youths who need it most.
>
> *2. To put the best educational equipment and ideas and innovations within reach of all students.*
>
> *3. To advance the technology of teaching and the training of teachers.*
>
> *4.* To provide incentives for those who wish to learn at every stage along the road to learning.[1]

Again, in the section of his message dealing with "regional education laboratories," the President said:

> I recommend the establishment under the Cooperative Research Act of educational laboratories which will undertake research, train teachers, and implement tested research findings. I further recommend amendments to the act to—
>
> Broaden the types of research organizations now eligible for educational projects.
>
> Train educational research personnel.
>
> Provide grants for research, development of new curriculums, dissemination of information, and implementation of educational innovations.
>
> Support construction of research facilities and the purchase of research equipment. . . .
>
> We are now embarked on another venture to put the American dream to work in meeting the new demands of a new day. Once again we must start where men who would improve their society have always known they must begin—with an educational system restudied, reinforced, and revitalized.

---

[1] Italics supplied.

Two Presidents of the U.S. have spoken. National policy and national objectives for education have been clearly enunciated. The call for action has been sounded. But it still remains to be seen whether it will continue to take almost 50 years for an educational innovation, or a major change in teaching methods and curricula, to work its way into schools and colleges on a substantial scale.[2]

The necessity for change in our educational institutions has more pertinence today and a more compelling quality than it ever has had in the past:

> Assessment of American education is today a matter of great public concern. Debate on educational issues is not new in America. The current debate, however, is animated by a new spirit of urgency due to an unprecedented foreboding about the future and an unprecedented awareness of human potential for progress. Man's destiny appears to depend upon his acquisition and use of knowledge. Public concern is based, in short, upon a new sense of the relationship between the quality of education and the future of America.[3]

An article in *Fortune* in April 1961 by Charles E. Silberman succinctly stated that "the feeling has been growing that the educational system we have is not 'right' for the future needs and responsibilities of American society." In this same article Silberman quotes Phillip H. Coombs of the Ford Foundation as putting the verdict this way:

> Almost everything that the schools and colleges are doing today is obsolete and inadequate. This applies to the curriculum, to the arrangements for teacher training, to textbooks, to organization, to methods of teaching and learning, to school architecture. Education's greatest need is not for more money from the outside, but for sweeping changes on the inside.[4]

Nor is obsolescence our only problem. Not only have we been educating increasing numbers of young people each year, but our schools have also been holding higher proportions of them for longer periods. Twenty years ago about half the 17-year-olds graduated from high school; now around 70 per cent do. We have been building 65,000 to 72,000 classrooms a year, well above the rate a decade ago. It is anticipated that elementary and secondary

[2] See Henry Chauncey, "Report of the President, Educational Testing Service Annual Report, 1962–1963," Princeton, New Jersey.

[3] *An Essay on the Quality in Public Education*, Educational Policies Commission, National Education Association, Washington, D.C., 1959, p. 5.

[4] Charles E. Silberman, "The Remaking of American Education," *Fortune*, April 1961, pp. 126–127.

school enrollments will jump from 36 million now to 44 million by 1970. This means that we will require more than 500,000 new classrooms by 1970, a far greater number than will be produced at the current rate, as high as it is. Also, it is argued, we will need 400,000 additional teachers in the next five years. We will need more and better counselors; stronger programs for gifted students; improved curricula for average youngsters; increased research and experimentation in reading, testing, and learning; more modern vocational programs; and so on. Increasing school taxes are not likely, since World War II state and local tax payments have increased by 220 per cent, as compared to an increase in Federal taxes of 85 per cent. At the same time, state and local bonded indebtedness has risen more than 300 per cent, compared to a Federal debt increase of about 12 per cent.[5]

THE NECESSITY FOR AND PURPOSE OF AN INSTRUCTIONAL TECHNOLOGY

The master teacher or trainer not only has a firm grasp of the knowledge and skills that he wants to impart to others, but also he is able to structure learning experiences for them out of which, he hypothesizes, learning will emerge and knowledge and skills will accrue.

The teacher or trainer is essentially a generator of hypotheses. When he generates a hypothesis, his next step is to test it. The failure to test has kept instruction a nebulous art rather than permitting it to develop as a science. We have been content simply to make educated guesses about the things we do as teachers. If the teacher were to test his hypothesis and find it wanting, then his only alternative would be to modify it and try it again, and again, and again—*ad infinitum*. This takes time, more time than any one teacher has. But we can hope, as we shall presently see.

If an instructional technology is ever developed, it must of course be subject to verification of its adequacy. Many teachers believe that the most useful part of their training was practice teaching, or experience, rather than courses in professional education. What is it about practice teaching that gives rise to this belief? To what extent does it provide the most effective training for the would-be teacher? Why do the usual courses in professional education give the impression, valid or not, that they do not have enough substance to train teachers in the skills of pedagogy? All these questions may equally be asked about training people to train others.

---

[5] The facts in this paragraph come from "The Fight over Federal Aid to Schools," *Changing Times, The Kiplinger Magazine*, February 1965, p. 43.

We cannot determine how any particular process, procedure, or course will improve training ability until we are able to define in precise terms what are the specific skills of pedagogy and how they can be validated. We must be willing to measure teaching ability not by what the teacher does but by what happens to the student and how he ultimately performs. It is for the student that we must structure the experiences out of which, we hope, he will learn. *It is, therefore, the student's performance that we must observe both prior to and following his instruction.* It is observing and evaluating performance and behavior, and only this, that will help us to determine how successful we have been as teachers.

We do not lack methods, ideas, procedures, or subject-matter knowledge. What we do lack is something substantive in the training of would-be teachers to validate those skills which are successful in modifying the behavior of students. We need both quantitative and qualitative measures of what happens to the student and how he performs. *An instructional technology of any significance would be able to assess the difference between a successful learning experience and a relatively unsuccessful one.* It would do even more. It would delineate several possible explanations of why one experience was successful and another unsuccessful. The professional instructor and trainer must accept the commitment to and accountability for the results of the learning experience.

An instructional technology worthy of its name, then, assists instructors in analyzing the structured learning experiences which fail to teach students. William A. Deterline provides us with some insight into the possible reasons why many instructors find this difficult to do:

> In many cases even an experienced and skillful instructor will not be able to identify those subtle causes of a breakdown in instructional communication. . . . Most instructors, whether they are aware of it or not, make use of technical expressions, technical words, complex grammatical structures, and ambiguous or too-terse statements at a level of complexity that is not appropriate for the students. . . . One difficulty is that the instructor is often unaware of the cause of the breakdown of communication and the basis for confusion. . . . Most instructors who are proficient in the subject matter . . . often are ineffectual in their instructional presentations because they do not know the material from the point of view of effective sequencing for instructional purposes, and/or are unable to be consistent in presenting the material at a technical level that is understandable, and in doing so in small enough steps with adequate repetition, examples, clarifying analogies familiar to the student, and so on.[6]

---

[6] William A. Deterline in a letter to the author, March 1, 1963.

Teachers who know how to teach and do not know what to teach are as common as teachers who know what to teach but who do not know how to teach it. Both are equally deficient. A scholar who cannot communicate his wisdom is just as inadequate as a pedagogue who has no wisdom to communicate.

Out of the learning experiences which we build for the student, what really happens? How has his behavior changed? How did he behave before he came to us, and how does he behave after he leaves us? What is the real value of the learning situation created by the teacher for the student? What knowledge, skills, and attitudes does the student now possess that he did not have before he met the teacher? Until we evaluate our teaching effectiveness by the product instead of the process, by what happens to our students and how they subsequently perform rather than by secondary criteria, we will never get to the reason why we are failing to instruct or train while doing what we know how to do in the best way we can.

Educational and training technology has not been able to keep up with the innovations of technology itself. We must turn with hope to the conviction that the problems created by technology will be solved by technology. Can training truly become a science? Is a science of instruction possible? Can the science of learning be applied to the art of pedagogy? Technology is the application of science to art. Can the studies of the behavioral scientist concerning the fundamental processes of learning be applied to training and education? If training will always remain an art and never become a technology, what is our alternative? And ultimately, will our desperate need for an instructional technology be sufficient in and of itself to create a breakthrough?

THE CHALLENGE OF AUTOMATION

Automation challenges education as it has never been challenged before. It certainly is going to have a deep impact upon our current training procedures. How are we going to use it constructively? What program will we develop to make us more capable of exercising to their utmost the skills inherent in our society?

The problems springing from technology and automation bombard us from all points of the cultural compass. We have a seemingly chronic state of oversupply in our unskilled labor ranks and undersupply in our skilled trades. How we solve such problems will in all likelihood determine our future as a nation.

The recent Administrations have shown an awareness of the demand for retraining created by the onslaught of automation. The problems of retraining are more easily stated than solved, however. They are not going to be solved by simply cataloguing the number and types of jobs which need to be filled with skilled workers and then establishing training programs for the unemployables to enable them to fill these jobs.

Through the Manpower Retraining Program the Federal Government made a commitment to help raise the skills, the literacy, and the abilities of the average American citizen. We must do something to help soften the impact of automation. We must make every effort to lessen the costs and debilitating effects of our welfare rolls, our unemployment lines, our undeveloped human resources. The problems of training and retraining are basically the same as those of other types of education. A technology suitable for classroom instruction would be equally valuable in our training workshops. The challenge to industrial training and the challenge to education are the same—the development and universal application of an instructional technology which will replace all the current outmoded methods.

THE HOPE OFFERED BY PROGRAMED INSTRUCTION

What has all this grim reality to do with programed instruction? Just that no development has provided as hopeful a sign for the revolutionary emergence of education and training technology as that started by the efforts of Dr. Sidney Pressey some 35 years ago, temporarily dropped, and so dramatically started again by Dr. Burrhus F. Skinner a few years ago at Harvard. It is this development which has been referred to as programed instruction or automated teaching. And so, while automation poses a threat to current skills and demands retraining of large segments of the workforce, it may also provide a way out of the quandary.

In 1962 the American Management Association published a book which heralded this revolution in education and training technology. The book, called *Revolution in Training*, was a description of the application of programed instruction technology to a variety of training problems in industry. That promising note, "revolution in training," has been sounded very often in the past few years, particularly in the research and development of programed instruction technology. Today, however, as we run down the list of educational and training demands confronting us, we find ourselves marooned on an island of problems surrounded by a sea of despair. It is likely, moreover, that this new technology will be more often applied to industrial and governmental training problems than to those of educational institutions.

Both industry and the military have a history of being receptive to new developments in learning methodology, largely because training and education in these establishments have always required results. Inefficient education and desultory training methods are luxuries that they cannot afford. It is not surprising that they have both looked very hopefully and with intense anticipation to an instructional principle that will help to alleviate the new problems which have accompanied the developments of scientific technology and automation.

John Gardner, president of the Carnegie Corporation, in his 1962 Annual Report made the following comments about innovations which are pertinent to education:

> The young organization is willing to experiment with a variety of ways to solve its problems. It is not bowed by the weight of tradition. It rushes in where angels fear to tread. As it matures it develops settled policies and habitual modes of solving problems. In doing so it becomes more efficient, but also less flexible, less willing to look freshly at each day's experience. Its increasingly fixed routines and practices are congealed in an elaborate body of written rules. In the final stage of organizational senility there is a rule of precedent for everything. Someone has said that the last act of a dying organization is to get out a new and enlarged edition of the rule book.
>
> And written rules are the least of the problem. In mature societies and organizations there grows a choking underbrush of customs and precedents. There comes to be an accepted way to do everything. Eccentric experimentation and radical departures from past practice are ruled out. The more pervasive this conventionality, the less likely is the innovator to flourish. The inventor of the Bessemer process for steel making, Sir Henry Bessemer, wrote: "I had an immense advantage over many others dealing with the problem inasmuch as I had no fixed ideas derived from long established practice to control and bias my mind, and did not suffer from the general belief that whatever is, is right." [7]

The reference to Bessemer is well taken. We must do for education and training what he did for steel. It is time that we gave serious consideration to the *process* of learning itself. Let us (as Gardner says) concern ourselves with "whether things are done" as intensely as with "how they are done," and probably more so.

Teaching today is not a profession. It is, at best, a quasi-profession. It will not become a true profession until it develops an educational and instruc-

---

[7] John Gardner, *Renewal in Societies and Men*, Annual Report, Carnegie Corporation of New York, 1962.

*tional technology based on a science and theory of instruction rather than a
set of theories and vague methods and practices which often are a poor and
only in very rare moments an excellent art.*

*The best hope for the emergence of instructional, training, and educa-
tional technology lies in the fullest exploration of the concept and system of
programed learning and in the developing automation procedures.*

Until the field of education develops a scientifically based technology, it
will not become a profession in the full meaning of the word. We have never
yet had a science of learning that has given us much that we can use as
teachers. Through programed instruction and teaching machine technology
we have found a vehicle which permits us to study the education and training process and to isolate the significant variables which will lead to further
study. Programed instruction and the accompanying teaching machine technology can provide a heuristic model for the development of instructional
technology. L. M. Stolurow points to this possibility in mentioning their
advantage for experimental and demonstrational purposes:

> One of the advantages which the teaching machine has over conventional
> instruction is that it freezes the instructional process during a study in a
> way which permits it to be used with many individual students. Further-
> more, it isolates the instructional material and its plan of organization
> from the personality and related factors which heretofore have always
> appeared in an inseparable combination with the teaching method. The
> combination now can be studied as separate components to determine
> the relative effectiveness of the method independent of those other fac-
> tors. Later, research studies can combine programing and presentation
> methods with the other factors, such as teacher personality, to determine
> how they interact with one another. Thus, we see the possibility of mak-
> ing genuine progress, and, in fact, of using a truly scientific approach to
> study instruction. Through such an approach one should be able to
> develop a theory of teaching which could guide the classroom teacher,
> as well as the writer, in developing educational materials along more
> effective lines.[8]

Programed instruction is the first valid system of educational and instructional technology that our society has ever had. It is patently in error to
categorize it, as has so often been done, as simply another teaching medium
or technique or to classify it along with the teaching machines, which is to
house it among the various audio-visual devices. It is much, much more than
this. Oron P. South, educational advisor at the USAF Air University, has
pointed out that

---

[8] L. M. Stolurow, "Teaching Machines and Programed Instruction," *The American Behavioral Scientist*, Vol. VI, No. 3, November 1962, pp. 43–45.

Continuous change introduces new dimensions into the problem of education and training. Whereas in the past we learned from stable systems, now we have to learn from rapidly and continuously changing systems. Old ways of learning and old patterns for learning may no longer be appropriate.

When change comes slowly and almost imperceptibly, one can be clear as to both the process and content of education and training, as these are worked out over a long period of time. The relevance of what is taught, to whom, and how, is matched against reality. What is dysfunctional is dropped.[9]

Programed instruction, like no other approach to teaching that we have had, is dropping essentially "what is dysfunctional" and developing what is truly functional.

Many of the questions asked regarding programed instruction have been raised in the past in many other contexts. We have frequently heard the comment that it is not new, that we have had it for years. Of course many of its characteristics, independently considered, are not, in and of themselves, new. Programed instruction, however, has emphasized these characteristics with a lucidity and force that no other instructional technique has to date. It has by no means provided all the answers to the ultimate development of an instructional technology worthy of the name. *Through* it, however, we can see the first signs of a true instructional and training technology. In essence, it is an instructional technology which will seek to apply what we know of the science of learning, along with what we are finding out about the science of instruction, to the arts of teaching and training.

Programed instruction, at best, forces us to face many of the questions which we have raised. This is not to say that it will provide all the answers; nor is it to say that it is in and of itself the instructional technology that our society needs. It does mean, however, that its adherents have concerned themselves with testing the experiences which they hypothesize will lead to successful learning. That is, they do not fail to test their hypotheses. As we have seen, it is failure to do so which limits the usefulness of conventional instructional methods. Programed instruction has raised questions regarding the adequacy of current measures of learning experiences. It has deepened our concern with retention of learning and with the sequencing of instructional content, to mention only a few issues.

Through programed instruction we are starting to think about applying engineering to solving educational and training problems, not to mechanize education, but rather to develop educational technology to the point where

---

[9] Oron P. South, unpublished remarks, 1963.

we can shoot with a bullet instead of a shotgun. Programed instruction has forced us to ponder what it is we are about and to establish quality control for the processes we call education and training.

Try-out students for programed materials are sought in the circles of rehabilitation, delinquency, drop-outs, and reform schools and penitentiaries. Adherents of programed instruction have in effect said to school administrators, "Give us your failures. Let us try out our programs on the students who have failed to learn." A refreshing change. This attitude, this commitment will, more than anything else, spur the development of instructional technology.

Programed instruction is not going to replace teachers and trainers, except those who are unfit for their profession, nor is it going to provide a panacea for all of our educational problems. Not even the most ardent adherents of programed instruction believe these things will happen. However, it can attempt more significant and more hopeful solutions to many more problems than can any other system of instructional technology we have had to date.

OVERCONCERN WITH TEACHING MACHINES

We have seen an understandable concern with the procedures and techniques of programed instruction itself and of the accompanying teaching machines. If we concentrate, however, on the specific features of this innovation in its present very primitive and crude form and process instead of on its underlying concepts, then we are not likely to find in it the solutions to our problems of developing an adequate educational and training technology. Its possibilities as an incipient technology of instruction are more important to us than the excessive deliberations about such temporary specific features as linear versus intrinsic programing, overt versus covert responses, teaching machines versus programed textbooks, and so on and on.

The interest in programed instruction has been accompanied by much apprehension, anxiety, and talk about automation, automated instruction, and teaching machines. George Kneller, in his address before the American Psychological Association (1961), stated the issue very succinctly:

> Whether we like it or not, automated teaching is here to stay. Merely to oppose it is futile. Education must mirror the age it strives to improve. It cannot isolate itself from automation any more than from other social or economic changes. For automated teaching is one more of the applications of technology to human life. The question to be asked is not, "Do we accept automation?" but, "How much of it and under what conditions?"

Present-day teaching machines have little to offer that would give them an advantage over programed text. In many cases they present the material and the "program" in the same manner that the programed text does. They have been called electronic page turners, with some justification. They have not been adaptive to the idiosyncrasies of the student. They have had temporary motivational value, particularly with children, but they have not justified their cost. This is not to deny that a few teaching machine systems presently on the drawing board and a few others in various stages of engineering development will in time truly adapt their content to each individual student and provide an ideal tutor for every student. When this happens, the teaching machine will be a useful cybernetic system. Its design and development, however, will be based upon the principles of programed instruction. At that time all the processes that are described as education and training will be radically reconsidered and restructured. The focus, however, must be on providing learning efficiently for individual students rather than accelerating through the machine our present educational and training practices. Rather than, say, inventing a machine to lay bricks automatically, it is more likely, as someone has pointed out, that houses will be designed so that the bricks will not be necessary and therefore do not need to be laid at all. We may restructure the very process of education itself as long as whatever process we evolve in its place circumvents the previous inefficient procedures and develops acceptable new ones, regardless of what they may be, and as long as it teaches well.

THE DREAM OF CYBERNETIC SYSTEMS IN TEACHING AND TRAINING

What is the implication of automation for education? If by automation we mean completely cybernetic systems, then we can talk about an instructional system which will perform its task with a precision and a rapidity now unmatched in human beings. We would be doing things which are distinctly unhuman or nonhuman by machines, thus freeing instructors truly to humanize man.

Cybernetic teaching machines will perform in a manner which is impractical or impossible for human instructors to duplicate. They can be designed so that they will not make the errors of human instructors. They will detect and correct errors in their own performance. They will indicate to their designers which of their components are producing the errors so that they can be removed and replaced. They will be able to make judgments of an instructional nature. They will be able to tabulate appropriate data and search their memories for significant information which either has been programed into them along with their instructions or has been acquired in the process of manipulating new data. They can be so designed that they can learn from past experience with their environment.

Ulric Neisser points out that machines can be designed to

> . . . behave intelligently and purposively. Such a direct use of these terms may be surprising. Is not a machine something made out of simple and unintelligent pieces? Indeed it is, but here as elsewhere the whole is more than the sum of its parts. Out of many thousands of simple operations by relays or transistors can come something unpredictable and adaptive: perhaps a new proof for a logical theorem, or persistent search for an elusive target.

Neisser then goes on to describe an example of what he means:

> In a program written by Gelernter, a computer can be set to seek the proof of a theorem in geometry—the same sort of problem that might give a bright high-school student considerable food for thought, and cause a less gifted one to give up entirely. The computer (or perhaps one should say, the program) will begin by trying some simple rules of thumb. Should these fail, the computer will formulate some conjecture which would advance the solution if it could be proved true. Having made such a conjecture, the computer will check its plausibility in terms of an internal diagram of the situation. If the conjecture is plausible, its proof is sought by the same rules of thumb as before. Once proved, the conjecture will serve as a stepping stone to the desired theorem. If the conjecture is rejected as implausible or unprovable, others will be tried along promising lines, until one has succeeded or the computer's resources are exhausted. Not even the programer knows in advance whether the machine will succeed in proving any given theorem. The number of steps involved is so great that their endpoint cannot be predicted.[10]

Computers have been programed to write TV dramas, although admittedly not of a very high level, to develop musical scripts, to translate from one language to another, and to simulate other logical brain processes such as playing chess and solving puzzles. We may well ask why a computerlike instructional machine could not handle intellectual problems on a great level of sophistication in philosophy, logic, politics, social issues, the social sciences such as economics, behavioral sciences, and the physical sciences.

Why can't a computer-augmented instructional system analyze the stu-

---

[10] Ulric Neisser, "Computers as Tools and as Metaphors" (an address delivered at the Georgetown University Conference on Cybernetics and Society, November 20, 1964).

dent's inputs and responses to a particular set of problems and thereby determine the "critical path" that will lead the student to the next proper item or step in the learning sequence? With the assistance of such cybernetic devices we may even be able to determine the ideal learning sequence for a specific student on the basis of a series or pattern of his responses which will guide the system, the machine continuously correcting itself accordingly.

For if computers can issue instructions for playing "war games," why can we not also develop procedures for coping with political and psycho-social issues in the classroom? In fact, would not the use of such machinery raise the serious question of why we have relied so heavily on human instructors? As the late Norbert Wiener pointed out in 1960:

> The present level of these learning machines is that they play a fair amateur game of chess but that in checkers they can show a marked superiority to the player who has programed them after ten to twenty playing hours of working and indoctrination. They thus most definitely escape from the completely effective control of the man who has made them. Rigid as the repertoire of factors may be which they are in a position to take into consideration, they do unquestionably—and so say those that have played with them—show originality, not merely in their tactics, which may be quite unforeseen, but even in the detailed waiting of their strategy.[11]

The flight simulators used in the training of pilots in the United States Air Force were in many ways the first models of a cybernetic automated teaching system. The more advanced simulators have left these original models far behind. The Air Force, for example, has had developed an international relations simulator. This "man-computer model" of the international system is a war game arrangement on a grand scale. It is described in the *Air Force Times* as follows:

> Almost any number can play and . . . it is just the thing for training personnel entering the international arena (students from the service academies, staff colleges, foreign service, etc.). . . .
>
> Set up something like a fantastically overgrown parlor game, the Inter-Nation Simulation begins with from five to nine hypothetical "nations." Each nation has different characteristics so there is a mixture of small and large, well established, newly emerging, rich and impoverished, etc. Some have conventional weapons and others have a full array of nuclear and traditional military power.

---

[11] Norbert Wiener, "Some Moral and Technical Consequences of Automation," *Science*, May 6, 1960, p. 1356.

Its instructional potential is illustrated by the following:

> The decision-makers exchange notes and hold conferences and work out treaties and alliances. Through simulated mass media, they make statements which praise or denounce each other.
>
> At various points, the instructor running the simulator slips the players in each nation "intelligence reports" about the others. Simulated world organizations may be set up for political purposes or narrow banking operations.[12]

According to the Air Force Office of Aerospace Research, this simulation project was started at Northwestern University and is today being used at the University of Michigan in its International Relations course and at Ohio State in graduate seminars.

The knowledge we gain from programed instruction will provide the basis for information with which we will program our cybernetic teaching systems. It is difficult to anticipate the form that programed instruction will assume in the years to come. We are at present in its first primitive and crude stages. However, the potential of an instructional technology is beginning to emerge.

Someone has said that the greatest block to communication is the illusion that it has been achieved. Programed instruction has begun to dispel this illusion; instructional technology eventually will dispel it once and for all.

Industry, the government, and the military establishment cannot afford to wait for academic patterns to change. Nor can they afford to wait for developments in the laboratories of learning theorists and psychologists. Problems are accumulating too rapidly. The need for solutions is too acute. Effort must be made to innovate with very little in the way of theoretical guidance. What industry has been able to demonstrate empirically in the actual operational training situation should be observed and studied by the behavioral psychologist, the would-be educational scientist, and professional educators in general not only for spin-off benefits but also for suggestions for theoretical formulation which may in turn accelerate both the creativity and productivity of pedagogical research.

The Wright Brothers' first successful aircraft flew only 40 seconds. But it did fly. So if by programed instruction we are flying for only 40 seconds, let us realize that—if we are imaginative and deliberative enough—we may someday be able to engineer those training and educational systems which will parallel in accomplishment man's flight into space.

---

[12] *Air Force Times,* February 3, 1965, p. 16.

Chapter 2

What Is Programed Instruction?

Narrow concentration on the specific features of a newly developed technique, to the exclusion of its underlying concepts, can focus attention on the tool to the neglect of the problems it is meant to solve. Programed instruction is not in this kind of immediate danger, although it will be in a few years if research and development of the concept are not pursued while development of the mechanics, that is, of the teaching machines, is pursued.

The significant implications of programed instruction for training and training research and development can be summarized as follows:

1. The potentiality of programed instruction is of primary importance, not its present crude implementation.
2. Programed instruction is a step in the engineering application of science to educational practice.
3. As a technological application, programed learning is required to make a practical contribution to education or to give way to some other technique that will.
4. The attempt to alter the process of human learning will feed back to the behavioral scientist and open up many basic research questions.
5. Programed instruction focuses attention more than ever before on the essential ingredients of training—learning and student behavior.
6. Programed materials can increase the effectiveness of training because as tangible, reproducible devices they can be severely tested, evaluated, improved, and redesigned.

Programed instruction is not a tool of teaching, it is not an aid, it is not another method, it is instead probably the first complete system of instruction which has evolved in the art of pedagogy. It may possibly eventually embrace all instructional techniques, media, aids, equipment, and so on which are necessary to attain a specific instructional objective. It is a system designed to effect the most efficient learning possible. We can say that learning is most efficient when it is attained with the minimum expenditures of time, effort, energy, money, and resources. From this point of view, therefore, programed instruction is not synonymous with programed learning materials, or programed texts, or a program which goes into a machine. It is a systematic way of looking at learning. However we look at them, all of these systems approaches to the field of education and training have certain characteristics in common. The fundamental steps in developing a learning system are defined by Robert Hager:

> A learning system is a structured sequence of instructional events which has been tested and validated on a sample of the trainee population to accomplish a specified change in competence with optimum effectiveness and efficiency.

Specifically, the concept is delineated by the following boundaries:

1. A learning system emphasizes the importance of the individual learner. Instructional material is presented to him in accordance with his needs, starting at his current state of development and carrying him to the desired performance level.

2. The final criterion for the effectiveness of a learning system is the performance of the learner. Therefore, the system is tested, revised, and retested until it meets the desired specifications.

3. A learning system is based not upon loosely stated "objectives" but upon a specific and detailed description of what the learner is expected to do after training and of the conditions under which he is to perform.

4. In developing a learning system, the techniques and instructional media most suited to the training problem are selected. Economic as well as technical considerations are carefully weighed.

MOST PROMISING DEVELOPMENT

Since B. F. Skinner started people thinking about the teaching machine movement there have been many varied applications of the concept of programed instruction. It has been tried in numerous classrooms, in many military training situations, in many industrial training centers, in many homes, under many conditions, as homework, as a supplement to normal classroom procedures, without teachers, with teachers, with small steps and large steps, with overt responses and covert responses. The claims have been many, the subjects have been numerous; it has been tested, retested, and retested; retention studies have been carried out; concern has been given to the problems of administering the materials we call programs; the mass use of programs has been tried by television and kinescopes *ad infinitum.*

One can say without any qualification whatsoever that programed instruction today is not a fad; some of the machines may be, but the principle is not. Even though many battles still rage regarding its merits, it has a firm foothold in American education and training. It is today understood by thousands who understood literally nothing about it just a few years ago. The enthusiasts have had their day, and it is now being critically examined for the true potential it has to offer in the light of urgent current and future training needs.

THE ADVANTAGES OF A SYSTEMS APPROACH TO LEARNING

The increasing technical problems of training humans for what appear today to be superhuman tasks—exemplified most dramatically in our manned-spacecraft training programs—require us to look critically to the systems approach which has developed in American industry. It is essentially one which demands that we consider all the resources which can be brought together and interrelated specifically to produce a particular result. The outcome of applying the systems approach to training will be the design and development of an instructional "system" which will produce the desired performance by the trainee. Programed instruction technology provides the conceptual framework which will produce this integration.

The systems approach attempts to "maximize, in some sense, the expected value." [1] A system is a set of integrated elements designed to elicit demonstrated phenomena as efficiently and reliably as possible. It is a package whose every element has a specific function in producing the desired outcome. Programed instruction itself can be a system; it also may be part of an overall system which will include programed instructional materials as subelements. A systems approach is applied to the solution of a problem when its various elements can be defined, maintained, and manipulated toward the achievement of its objectives—in this case, solving the problem. Programed instruction provides parameters of an integrated education and training system. No other concept of instruction has done this.

---

[1] H. H. Goode and R. E. Machol, *Systems Engineering,* McGraw-Hill Book Co., Inc., New York, 1957, p. 313.

Lecturing, as attached to it as so many of us are, is probably the most ineffective teaching process we have. When we lecture, we rarely teach anyone anything. We are likely to do many other things instead. We may inspire and motivate some to look further into our subject; others we may entertain; still others we may bore; a very few we may instruct to a small degree. When as teachers we lecture, we are simply emitting auditory stimuli which are interpreted by each student in his own unique way, depending on his own idiosyncratic experience. In fact, it would be a most sobering and enlightening experience for all of us when we lecture if we could somehow (1) stop the mental process of each person in the room at a particular point, (2) by some device make a spontaneous record of his thoughts, and then (3) compare what we wanted to communicate with what the members of the audience "heard" while we talked.

Teachers are too often just stimulus machines; as such, they are not much more adequate than other such machines. In fact, some devices such as TV and radio sometimes get through to a mass audience much more effectively than most teachers. What is most notably missing from a lecture and other methods of communication is feedback.

EMPHASIS ON FEEDBACK

In order to instruct we have to communicate effectively. We have to know how effective or ineffective our communication has been before we know how to modify our efforts to communicate. Modification must be based on knowing where, how, and why we have failed in the first effort to communicate. In order to find this out we have to listen to feedback from the student. Until the loop is closed, instruction has not taken place. Very few students learn from teachers. Students acquire most of their knowledge from reading, studying, analyzing, and arguing. Teachers may inspire, motivate occasionally, and even illuminate an abstract or abstruse principle, but, it bears repeating, they rarely teach anyone anything, except in one specific kind of student-teacher relationship—the tutorial.

It is obviously impossible to effect a tutorial relationship with every student in every classroom in this nation. Some means must be found to mass-produce the elements of this relationship so that every student can have quality instruction at his own level. It would be wonderful indeed if we could package for millions of students the techniques and abilities of our master teachers (who are not very often our able scholars). We cannot depend on the present lock-step method of teaching for our spacecraft of tomorrow or in our missile sites of today. Programed instruction is the first step in an effort to develop an instructional process designed to meet the idiosyncratic needs of every student. It is an effort to package for all students the characteristics of the tutorial approach.

Now, what has all this to do with automated teaching machines and instructional systems? Teaching machines present teaching materials which have been developed, or programed as we now say, in a special way. A teaching machine is simply a device which presents stimuli and provides for active responses from the student. Teachers and lecturers serve as stimuli, as we have seen, but they cannot elicit active student response except in the tutorial relationship.

The manner in which the information that goes into the machine is prepared, the size of the increments of information, its sequence of presentation, and how the student responds to the materials throughout the program determine how effective the machines really are. We call this material and the manner in which it is prepared "the program," and for this reason the program is the heart of any teaching machine.

The student is led one step at a time along the learning path. He actively responds to a curriculum that has been so logically sequenced that his response always carries him a little closer to the ultimately desired learning. The student is required to respond to questions, solve problems, or complete exercises. Whenever he makes a response, he is immediately informed how correct his answer is and, when necessary, referred to a place where he is provided with additional information to correct his answer. It is this aspect of programed instruction which comes the closest to approximating the tutorial relationship.

The ideal program, according to Dr. Skinner, would be so constructed that every student would make no errors whatsoever in his responses. To accomplish this goal, the information is presented to the student in very small steps, and he is steadily cued or prompted in such a manner that he cannot help making the correct response. Learning becomes almost effortless but not thoughtless, and it is meant to be that way. Every response made by the student is an overt or a covert one—or both. It is the nature of the constructed response on the part of the student (filling in a blank, drawing a diagram, solving a problem, writing a word, and the like) which determines the extent to which he participates actively in learning. After he constructs his response, he immediately knows whether or not he is correct, and this knowledge or feedback is supposedly reinforcing. The burden is on the program, however, to lead the student to construct the correct response in such a manner that he learns by doing so.

THE FIRST AND BASIC STEP

All programed materials are crucially dependent on another prior step which experience has shown is probably the most important part of this technology. This is the "task" or "learning outcome analysis." The traditional statement of task or learning objective has been most inadequate. Such learning outcomes or job training standard elements as, "Be familiar with . . . ," "Understand the . . . ," "Operate the . . . ," and, "Repair the . . ." are not good enough. The analysis of learning outcomes, which initially guides the development of the programed instruction materials, must be intensive, extensive, and specific. This beginning step must define as completely as possible what performance the student is expected to demonstrate at the end of the program. This performance is called terminal behavior.

It is essential to programed instruction that the terminal behavior be stated concretely and explicitly. There should be no misinterpretation by anyone of what the desired learning outcomes are to be. In fact, this characteristic should hold for all educational and training programs. It is impossible, indeed, to develop an adequate programed instruction without proper definition of terminal behavior. Programed instruction forces the issue like no other technology we have developed.

Probably no greater spin-off benefit has accrued from programed instruction than the concern that has developed in education and training circles with the proper preparation of useful objectives in precise, measurable terms. Jerry Short has pointed out that

> One of the primary targets of the revolution called programed instruction was the moldy Bastille of educational objectives. Inside this prison under the old regime, courses were described in vague terms. Students were expected to understand, appreciate, and know things, and what this understanding, appreciation, and knowledge looked like was seldom considered and never elaborated.

> Since programming came directly from experimental laboratories concerned with the behavior of organisms, it is not surprising that its advocates viewed education as a process of behavioral change. A program was not designed to convey information. It was designed to produce a change in the behavior of the student. Its objectives were not to impart knowledge, but to alter the student's response to his environment. Thus, it was

argued, objectives of programmed instruction could best be described in terms of the stimulating environment and the student's behavior in its presence.[2]

In summary, then, the salient features of programed instruction are:

1. The program begins with a specific description in behavioral terms of desired learning outcomes.
2. The program is a carefully and logically arranged sequence of information designed to guarantee learning of specific material.
3. The student is required to be an active participant throughout the program by continuously interacting with the programed materials.
4. The program is arranged so that every student can proceed at his own pace.
5. The program provides the student with immediate knowledge of the correctness of his responses.

CHARACTERISTICS OF PROGRAMS

Programs are not just sentences and paragraphs with blanks and holes casually put in by the writer. The nature of the response the student is expected to make is a very crucial factor in their construction. The nature of the question the programer asks is equally significant. The fact that a student makes a correct response to a question may have little to do with whether he has learned much that is significant or relevant. In some cases when frames are poorly written or constructed, students may make the correct response without having had to pay any attention whatsoever to the stimuli. A student will utilize every bit of information in a well-constructed frame or in preceding frames to enable him to respond in a correct and relevant manner. Every time the student responds he should be learning.

This principle of *gradual progression* is illustrated in the following excerpts from a programed course prepared by David Klaus and William Deterline of the American Institutes for Research under a grant by the U.S. Office of Education. As the student starts the program, he is stimulated by a certain amount of information presented to him in what is called a "frame" to fill in each blank in it. He then turns the page and finds out immediately whether his answer is correct. The program aims to make the student correct as often as possible. These are the first two frames in the program:

---

[2] J. Short, "Useful Objectives," in Gabriel D. Ofiesh and Wesley Meierhenry (editors), *Trends in Programmed Instruction*, National Education Association, Washington, D.C., 1964, p. 162.

A-1	All substances are made up of atoms. Salt, for example, is made up of [ ]
a-1	atoms

A-2	Not only are solid substances like salt made up of [ ] but liquid substances like water or a gas like hydrogen are also [ ]
a-2	atoms made up of atoms

The student proceeds one step at a time. Each time he responds he is making a gradual progression toward mastery of the terminal behavior we desire to develop in him. There is no waste of experience to speak of. Behavior is rapidly being shaped or modified.

A little later in the program a frame which ordinarily would have been very complex and confusing to the student now makes sense. For example:

A-16	Hydrogen is the lightest element; its [ ] is 1. Uranium is the heaviest [ ] ; its atomic number is [ ]
a-16	atomic number element 92

An average high school senior student would be able to handle this frame after having participated about 30 minutes in the program.

A-53	An atom with excess electrons has a [ ] charge and thus is called a negative [ ] . An atom with too few electrons is called a [ ]
a-53	negative ion positive ion

Let's examine a frame in the second volume of this four-volume program which takes approximately 13 hours to complete. The double asterisk (**) indicates that the student should answer in his own words.

I-20 Positively charged particles shot through atoms are deflected because they are [＿＿＿＿＿＿＿] by the ** [＿＿＿＿＿＿＿]	
i-20 repelled positive charges in the nucleus (at the center of the atom)	

Although most programs are linear, other techniques of frame writing are constantly being developed. In some the students are called upon to give different types of responses from merely filling in blanks. They may be asked to draw diagrams, actually handle chemicals in a laboratory, work with hand tools on a workbench, solve problems, pronounce words, play musical instruments, or maybe just "think." In the following frames, from the American Management Association PRIME course, the student is asked to determine whether either of the answers to the question is correct, whether neither is correct, or whether both are correct. This is referred to as the NABB technique (neither, A, B, or both). Here again, however, the principle of "gradual progression" is operating. The student does not have to make any elaborate constructed response, but he does have to "think through" what he is doing.

55. Use the simplest, smallest motions possible. Which might be an example of this motion-economy rule?	using a device that requires body motions, rather than a device that requires finger and wrist motions only	sliding materials, rather than lifting and carrying them			
X	BOTH	A	B	NEITHER
56. Motions should be as simple as possible. The fewer the motions and the smaller they are, the less taxing and tiring the work will be. Which might illustrate this rule?	using a pushbutton operated by one finger rather than a lever that takes an arm movement	sliding materials rather than lifting and carrying them			
X	BOTH	A	B	NEITHER

					Use tools designed to reduce human effort.		Use the simplest, smallest motion possible.

57. Sliding materials, rather than lifting and carrying them, is an example of which motion-economy rule?

		X			BOTH	A	B	NEITHER

---

59. You know that the fewer the motions and the smaller they are, the less taxing and tiring they will be. Which of these motions is the easiest? Which is the hardest?
1) finger motions only
2) finger, wrist, and forearm motions
3) finger, wrist, forearm, and upper arm motions

1) easiest
3) hardest

---

60. Using a switch operated by a finger, instead of a lever that requires an arm movement, is the use of which rule of motion economy?

			Use the simplest, smallest motion possible.		Movements should follow a continuous curved path.

	X			BOTH	A	B	NEITHER

---

61. You know that motions can be ranked from easiest to hardest.
Rank these motions from easiest (1) to hardest (5).
a) finger, wrist, and forearm motions
b) finger, wrist, forearm, and upper arm motions
c) finger and wrist motions
d) finger, wrist, forearm, upper arm, and shoulder motions
e) finger motions only

			1)	3)	5)
			2)	4)	
1) e	3) a	5) d			
2) c)	4) b				

72. Employees are likely to regard any change as a threat to their security if previous conversions:	created uncertainty and confusion.	resulted in demotions or the displacement of some employees.

X				BOTH	A	B	NEITHER

73. Sometimes opposition to change arises from a misunderstanding of what the consequences of the change will be. For example, an employee will resist the adoption of a new machine if he:	realizes it will make part of his work easier and give him more time to devote to a more creative phase of his job.	thinks the machine will displace him.

		X		BOTH	A	B	NEITHER

74. Lack of information about the consequences of a change is the reason some workers try to delay the introduction of a new method. While waiting to learn what the consequences will be, they will probably:	play for time.	ask their supervisor about the change.

	X			BOTH	A	B	NEITHER

75. Playing for time is sometimes interpreted as resistance to change. Usually, however, it is an attempt to:	explore the change.	block the change.

	X			BOTH	A	B	NEITHER

76.	Once it becomes known that some kind of change is in prospect but no real information has been issued, employees will probably:	begin trying to estimate the impact of the change on them.	be willing to wait for the information and suspend judgment about the impact on them.			
	X		BOTH	A	B	NEITHER

86. Policemen need badges and military men need their insignia of rank. In business, the manager (does/does not) need to communicate his goals and how he wants his employees to reach them. He (must/must not) simply communicate position and rank.

does must not	

87. Which of the following would probably symbolize the top manager to his subordinates?
   1) his habit of circling his subordinates' typographical errors
   2) the way he dresses and talks
   3) the neatness or disorder of his office
   4) (none of these)
   5) (all of these)

5) (all of these)	

88.	The manner in which a top manager dresses, speaks, acts, and so on speaks volumes to the employees:	about the kind of person he is and how he is leading them.	about how, in a sense, he wants them to act.			
X			BOTH	A	B	NEITHER

89.	The manager as a symbol is the focus of leadership in his company. Therefore,			it is unlikely that anyone can substitute for him in bringing about a change in company morale.			his subordinates will seldom give him what he wants.
	X			BOTH	A	B	NEITHER

90.	If the manager is true to his purpose, so will his employees be, and:			if he is serious in his demands for quality in performance and product, they probably will not be.			if he treats people decently, they are likely to do so too.
		X		BOTH	A	B	NEITHER

CRAFTSMANSHIP

Programed instruction has brought to the preparation of training materials a badly needed concept of craftsmanship. Francis Cartier has lucidly pointed out:

> Programs sometimes teach better than books—better than live instructors using audiovisual materials—because there is one thing the programer does consistently and meticulously and religiously that others fail to do through laziness, ineptness, and willingness to settle for poor work: the programer follows a procedure through which he applies what he knows about learning. To every frame, every sentence, every phase of planning, writing, testing, revision, polishing, and final production, he carefully and consciously applies everything he knows about the teaching and learning process. For this one simple reason, he has given the world an enormous stride forward in education. For this one simple reason, he is to be celebrated, congratulated, and given a prominent place in the history of human learning. Let there be no doubt that he deserves all this. Consider the parallel between him and Henry Ford. Ford's automobile was a minor contribution compared to his concept of mass production.

Like Ford, the programer has given us a new concept of production of instructional materials—a far more important contribution than programing itself. He has made it an inescapable part of his programing procedure to apply everything he knows about learning, and we should be properly humble in the realization that with only a stone-age psychology, plus high standards and determination, he has put all of us to shame.[3]

Susan Meyer Markle in her recent contribution to the art of programing, *Good Frames and Bad,*[4] has more than demonstrated the skill and difficulty inherent in the development of effective programs and the construction of frames which teach. She explores the idea that if some programs are boring and tedious, they probably were written by boring and tedious writers.

A COMMITMENT

In the past when students did not learn and the available materials of learning were not easily understood, we rarely if ever blamed the teacher or the textbook writer. The student more often than not was to blame. Either he was too stupid or too dense to understand our "simple" explanation or— and this has been a recent rationalization in explaining away our failures as teachers—the student was improperly trained and educated by other teachers or schools. We have been prone to decline this responsibility for failure wherever we have had education or training. Programed instruction gives rise to an entirely new concept of responsibility. The burden of responsibility for the student's learning rests on the program and the instructional technology with which it is presented, not solely on the student. If the student does not learn, something is wrong with the program. It must be thrown out and a new one tried. Or it must be "debugged" *so that it will teach.* Or it must be revised; the material must be resequenced; or something else must be done to the program until it finally teaches; until, in fact, it is such an excellent program that it teaches practically everybody.

Some idealistic diehards are willing to say "teach *everybody.*" When we say *"practically* everybody," we are talking about 95 to 98 per cent of the target population. (The target population may be a more universal one, however, than we have previously considered it to be.) New vistas open up to the zealot of programed instruction. Students that other teachers and schools have given up on now become material ripe for cultivation.

---

[3] Francis A. Cartier, "After the Programing Fad Fades, Then What?" *A. V. Communication Review,* May–June 1963.

[4] Susan Meyer Markle, *Good Frames and Bad (A Grammar of Frame Writing),* John Wiley & Sons, Inc., New York, 1964.

Programed instruction is a commitment on the part of those who consider themselves teachers, instructors, and trainers to produce materials that will insure learning in as many persons as is humanly possible. It is the kind of commitment to learning that is made by any true professional to his mission's accomplishment regardless of what its nature may be. It is a commitment to quality.

Programed instruction and automated teaching, rather than dehumanizing man, will humanize him. Poor teaching and poor, dull, and boring instructors who have hidden behind routine and drill have led to much student failure and to the subsequent dehumanization of man. Programed instruction offers learning in the best Socratic and tutorial tradition of teaching, asking that we convince the difficult, stupid, unmotivated, gifted though neglected students—"tempest tossed" by other teachers—that the burden of learning is no longer solely on their shoulders but is now equally, if not more so, on the shoulders of him who would consider himself a true professional in the field of education and what may someday become the science of pedagogy.

Chapter 3

Programed Instruction and Industrial Training

Traditionally, management has not considered training an important area of concern. Too often it has considered even very crucial training problems casually, rarely appreciating the hidden costs of poor, inadequate, and inefficient programs. Too often have poor training procedures been hidden under the carpet of manufacturing costs. Clever bookkeeping and sleight-of-hand management conveniently obscure the necessity for tackling any training problem directly. When asked if his company should purchase a programed course to help solve a serious training problem, one executive said, "$15,000? Why, I'm getting that training done now, and my present training budget is practically zero."

Management has rarely appreciated the costly aspects of inadequate training. One reason has been an inability to identify the poor job performance which has directly resulted from inefficient and inadequate training. Industries rarely evaluate their effectiveness against a standard which is indicative of their ultimate potential. Since the competitors are often in the same boat, doing things in much the same way, industrial management has often been content to do things just a little bit better. The costly aspects of inefficient on-the-job training and supervision, the low morale and high employee turnover resulting from feelings of inadequacy due to lack of skills and competencies, the cost of inadequate products and rejects, the inability to respond rapidly to changing markets, and the lack of high reliability in productive capacity are factors rarely measured against the optimum work proficiency that could be achieved if workers were properly trained.

TRAINING IS IMPORTANT

We are witnessing a burgeoning management awareness of the importance of training. This awareness is necessary because of the increasing complexity of skills and industry's need for conversion due to its constant realignment of its mission and product.

Hidden costs of poor and casual programs can be found in the training of salesmen, customer representatives, and servicemen who project an image to customers. If lack of efficient training results in inadequate knowledge of the product, poor maintenance of the equipment, or an inability to deal effectively with people, the image of the company is decreased accordingly. Training is not a simple matter. Not only do poor and ineffective programs, or the lack of an appropriate philosophy on the part of management, have ramifications throughout the plant, but they may extend their impact to the industrial market and involve the entire corporate enterprise.

Customer engineers (salesmen) for a large corporation which markets computers represent a costly investment in manpower. The computers which they market, service, and maintain are even more costly. Achieving the best possible relationship between the customer engineers, the complex computers, and the customers is much too important to corporate objectives to be left to chance. Proper training, provided in a way which does not interfere radically with the customer engineers' costly time and which is guaranteed to increase their proficiency in interacting with the equipment, may ultimately be the most economical manner of increasing their output, even though a considerable investment may be required at first. This fact is being more and more recognized by companies such as International Business Machines and Sperry Rand Corporation in their philosophy of training as a capital investment rather than an expense.

In some cases inefficient training does not result from the procedures utilized in the training program but relates to the time when it is provided. Trainees may be entirely competent in a specific skill immediately following the completion of a formal course. However, certain aspects of this skill may not be required on the job until months and sometimes years later. The original training will be, in fact, a poor investment in such circumstances.

In some other cases a particular aspect of a job is so rarely performed that the most economical procedure is merely to provide the trainee with a guidance sheet or checklist when this part of his job becomes necessary or to provide some temporary on-the-job instruction directly by his supervisor. Inefficient training includes training at the wrong time, at the wrong place, and to the wrong person, and all of these faults contribute to hidden costs.

TRAINING BECOMES A PROFESSION

The crucial role that training must play in industrial growth and development raises many questions and forces many issues. The demand for a training technology will force us all to recognize the importance of training as a profession. Training programs will no longer be casually established on the basis of some vice president's whim. Nor will the training director be hidden in some office under the personnel director's wing. The day is rapidly approaching when the "vice president in charge of training" will have status on the corporate staff equal to that of other top management officers.

The task of finding highly skilled training personnel shares many of the aspects of the overall national teacher shortage. As we apply the emerging science of learning to industrial training, and as we develop the proper training technology, the demand for training skills will increase more rapidly than the supply. There is little likelihood that a sufficient number of people who are professionally qualified to handle the complex training problems of tomorrow's industry will be available—that is, if we continue training as we are now doing and have done in the past—for traditional and conventional methods will require many more instructors and trainers than can be found. Since no crash recruitment program can possibly solve the anticipated training personnel shortage, a new approach to training must be found. It is here. It is programed instruction.

Programed instruction, based on the laws of behavioral technology, promises much. It is difficult to find areas where it has not already demonstrated its contribution to effective training and education. The following representative list of courses indicates the wide scope of successful applications in industrial training situations:

Blueprint Reading
Basic Electricity
Industrial Safety
Assembly and Maintenance of Complex Equipment
Office Procedure
Key Punch Operation
Statistics
Management Decision Making
Product Knowledge
Fundamentals (of many different subjects)
Clerical Procedures
Sales Procedures
Bank Teller Training.

PROGRAMED INSTRUCTION RAISES SERIOUS QUESTIONS

The procedures for developing programed training systems so closely parallel those needed to solve the general question of "requirement for training" that often industry has only to ask whether it should develop a programed course for what it *thinks* is a training problem to achieve significant results. Often when the question, "Should we use programed instruction to solve a particular training problem?" is asked, a Pandora's box is opened. In the process of considering programed instruction as a method, new insights into the real requirement for training are often developed—although sometimes at a shocking cost.

The consideration of programed instruction therefore often results in a different perspective on the very nature of the training problem that was previously thought to exist. Thus, in some cases exploration of programed instruction has led to an awareness that there were *no* problems to begin with or that training had to be realigned or considered from a different point of view. Rarely in the past has industry made such an extensive analysis of training as it has been forced to make by the technology of programed instruction.

The first serious question raised by programed instruction technology has to do with the very *purposes* of training. Developing training objectives for programed materials has automatically meant a searching analysis of these materials' purposes. This, in turn, forces the training director and management to look carefully at the causes of inefficient and insufficient training. Since job and task analysis is crucial to the programing of effective instructional materials, the basic training objectives that have been previously thought desirable by management may now be seriously questioned or displaced. Not only does definition of the precise behavioral manner in which objectives must be stated become a difficult scientific endeavor in itself, but also the very origins of the objectives and of the training requirements become subjects for discussion, analysis, study, and concern.

The solution to the basic problem of fully utilizing its human resources which confronts industry today can be found in the answers to the following questions:

1. What kind of performance do we need?
2. Where do we need it?
3. When do we need it?
4. Can we get it by selection? How?
5. Can we get it by training? How?
6. Under what circumstances is it more efficient to proceed by 4 instead of 5, or 5 instead of 4, or to forget the problem completely?

Simple as these questions are, their answers require elaborate procedures. It is doubtful that satisfactory answers can be found without applying a systems technology to training.

THIS MATTER OF COSTS

There is only one reason for introducing a new technology. To be acceptable, it must be either cost reducing or cost avoiding. Certain procedures may be technically feasible but initially uneconomical and therefore undesirable. However, external forces which change or alter the marginal efficiency of the current training methods may make these procedures increasingly economical (for example, the introduction of very expensive equipment which makes human error more costly, an increase in labor cost, or the necessity simultaneously to increase productivity, lower the unit cost, and step up the volume). Top management must be told what can realistically be anticipated from programed instruction technology as it exists today, that it is growing in its scope and utility, and that ultimately it will have much more to offer. As it becomes more and more refined, it will, of course, decline in cost.

Changes are even now taking place in the technology which indicate that increasing attention will be given to the "maintenance" of programed materials and modules, making it possible to modify those subsystems more rapidly and more economically than is now the case. As the technology becomes more thoroughly scientific and as developmental procedures become more empirically validated, the cost of programed instruction will be reduced still further. Programed instruction is now in somewhat the same position as Thomas Edison when he had to try out more than 300 materials to find an acceptable filament for an incandescent bulb. More research into basic principles and concepts would have reduced his "trial and error" considerably. Management should be aware that as programed instruction develops, as it continues to ask the right questions, and as more is known about learning, it may indeed be possible to dispense with frequent testing and revision of programed materials.

Even in their present crude and primitive state programed materials have more than adequately demonstrated their superiority over conventional training procedures. The great cost of their preparation will be drastically reduced if industry provides the necessary research and engineering development support. Once we learn how to "talk to machines," it is entirely possible that they will be able to do their own programing. Then, programed instruction will produce its own economic advantage and not have to depend upon comparison with the hidden (though very real) costs of conventional training methods.

When industry is confronted with a training problem which is demonstrably concrete and overriding in its importance, it usually tries to find a solution at any reasonable cost. Very often, under these conditions, the cost of training is secondary to achieving performance goals. For example, an international airlines company sent two instructors thousands of miles to train a group of local employees in functions ranging from handling baggage to figuring out air freight charges. The 10 people who were trained were subsequently discharged (or quit) within a period of 30 days. The two instructors then had to return to train a new group. Even now, the repeated training requirement and the related cost continue to be a constant worry to the company, and it is compounded by an acute shortage of qualified instructors.

Another training problem confronting the same company stems from its necessity of developing highly reliable training programs for only 100 persons who are dispersed at far points throughout the world. These persons must be trained in the critical skill of computing the weight and balance of aircraft. An error—that is, incorrectly computing the revenue load to be carried—can be (and has in the past probably been) very costly. The cost of qualified instructors is prohibitive, and the number of people who need to be trained is small. Therefore, the company is now seriously considering the possibilities of programed instruction as a solution to its training problem. It is no longer a question of whether or not it should invest its resources in a new training technology. The problems are getting so acute that it has little choice.

WHAT MANAGEMENT MUST UNDERSTAND

In order for programed instruction to make a significant contribution to the solution of training problems, management must have a clear understanding of the technology—its present and future limitations, its present and future potential. Only a commitment based on such an understanding will produce the climate in which the technology can develop. Too often, those people who are intimately associated with programed instruction efforts in industry have found themselves working without support or resources because the requisite management insight is lacking. When the proper guidance of an informed management is absent, costly decisions are sometimes made which adversely affect the company's image and reputation. The lack of proper higher-echelon guidance in one case resulted in the initiation of a development effort long after the need for it had ceased.

Management must understand from the outset that programed instruction technology is concerned with developing training systems which are vastly different from conventional training literature and courses. This fact has been difficult for many training managers and writers of training literature to grasp. Programed training systems attempt to develop in the trainee *all* the necessary objectives which are specified or implied in the existing training literature plus additional objectives which management has determined are necessary if not in fact crucial.

Another basic point is that programed training systems are designed for use with a minimum of assistance from an instructor. Ideally, his assistance is not necessary at all. An efficient programed training system must be designed so that it will provide for continuous active involvement by the trainee as he performs guided practice on each of the detailed objectives of the course.

Unprogramed systems place the bulk of responsibility for learning squarely on the trainee. In conventional academic, military, and industrial instruction a student's success or failure is always imputed to him; rarely, however, is failure attributed to the instructional process itself. This assignment of responsibility is completely inappropriate since unsuccessful instruction is an expense that management can ill afford. Unlike the traditional lecture, film, or textbook, the programed system does itself assume the responsibility for achievement of effective training. It is not simply a vehicle for presenting information in a system by which the student must himself effect learning. Rather, it is supposed to structure the information in the most efficient manner for human learning—so that errors are rationally the fault of the program and not of the trainee.

Programed learning offers a unique advantage as an instructional technology. The effectiveness of every facet of the program can be tested. Unlike the traditional method, with its lesson plan and its teacher or lecturer, the program does not proceed by trial and error until success is achieved. Rather, it is thoroughly tested *before* it is incorporated into a training or academic course so that all ineffective content is revised and perfected and errors are minimized.

One major problem that has already frustrated many programers and training managers is eliminating areas of weakness in a program after they have been identified. Why isn't the program teaching? Where is it breaking down? Am I "underprograming" or "overprograming"? Is the program fully developed and ready for press? Can it be improved further? Is it worth the effort to make further improvements? How and where can improvements be made? These questions face many instructional programers all too frequently. If management is to provide enlightened leadership and guidance and make this effort pay off, it must understand these problems fully and quickly. Only then will the technology develop to the point where there are likely to be answers and good, quick solutions to these questions.

Programed training systems are predesigned for success because of the early investment in specification of required performance objectives, analysis of required content, and development of teaching strategy. When breakdowns in the system occur—when, that is, students do not learn—management must understand that it may be because the system did not permit an early measure of their performance against the desired performance level. Therefore, management must encourage the design of systems which will themselves diagnose why the trainees may fail to reach the desired terminal performance level. Simply stated, it must recognize that the present state of the art makes it difficult in some cases for the program designer to recognize and understand when he is off the track, on a tangent, or unaware of total system objectives. In addition, even when he is on the proper track, he may have no way of knowing when he has crossed the finish line.

The primary distinction between programed training systems and traditional systems such as correspondence courses, which have, in the past, been labeled auto-instructional because they require a minimum of instruction from a teacher, is this concept of prespecification, predesign, and pretesting. A program is typically different from the correspondence course in that it is developed through a process which assures a predesignated level of subject matter mastery by the particular student population. When programs fail to deliver this mastery level, it is sometimes taken by training managers as a reflection on programed learning rather than on the adequacy of the particular program or programer.

QUALITY CONTROL OF TRAINING

In programed instructional technology, management can have not only a system which is superior for the solution of training problems, but one which is also a means of controlling the quality of training itself. Let us assume that it is management's goal to develop a training system in which 90 per cent of the specified student population will achieve 90 per cent of *all* the specified learning objectives. If, during the development of the system, only 85 per cent of the test students achieve only 80 per cent of the specified objectives, management may ask what has gone wrong in those subareas where fewer than 90 per cent of the trainees achieve the predesignated objectives.

For example, if fewer than 90 per cent of the students answer criterion test item 32 correctly, then management can conclude that the system is failing to perform adequately on the particular performance specification which is represented by that item. At this point, questions should be asked whose purpose is to identify which element in the system is at fault. The problem may be stimulus control, subject matter sequencing, frame construction, inadequate illustration, insufficient animation, malfunctioning in display machines, or a number of other reasons. The problem may even be in the construction or validity of the particular test item. Management, for the first time, can focus sharply on training systems' weaknesses and correct them quickly.

MANAGEMENT'S TOOL

It is difficult to estimate the amount of investment made by American industry in training. Some experts have placed the annual expenditure as high as $30 billion. If so, then it is almost equal to the total cost of all public and private education in the United States. It is time for management to give serious thought to the compelling economics of industrial training and the importance of its relationship to corporate objectives.

The ideal learning situation, whether in industrial training or public education, has been described as a tutorial relationship with the educator "Mark Hopkins at one end of the log and the student on the other." This relationship is normally responsive to the needs and idiosyncrasies of the individual student. It truly represents an ideal model of education, one which it is impossible to duplicate precisely. Students and trainees are individuals; learning is most efficient when it treats them as such. Training technology must come to do so. Of course, people have always learned one way or another, successfully or inadequately. But there has been little effort to offer students valid individualized instruction.

One writer (with tongue in cheek) * summarized the manner in which the present school systems account for the individual differences between learners. He commented that the procedure, whatever it is, "*must* be successful, since it has not been abandoned after hundreds of years of use." He thought that "the process of putting dozens of different kinds of learners in the same environment and providing the same input to all seems to be an *economical* one and . . . very successful since it has been the choice of teachers for a long, long time." Then he likened it to what would happen if a dentist ran his

---

* My gratitude to Robert F. Mager for this "anonymous" contribution.

clinic like a school—if 40 patients arrived at the same hour in the morning and received the same treatment because experience had shown that most people needed that treatment. Certainly, he maintained, some patients would receive the treatment they required, but many would be left with holes in their teeth because they had not been given individual attention. Just so, many students are left with gaps in their education because they have been taught what is best for the average student, in a way the average student can best absorb the information. For the student who is not average, such education does not meet his need. And just *what,* can someone please tell us, is an "average student" anyway?

Further compounding the problem in our educational system is the increase in the number of students. As the total has grown, the proportion of properly trained teachers and instructors has gone down, and the amount of time that instructors can give to each individual student has kept decreasing. When a student has been unable to learn from or listen effectively to instructors, he has been considered just a poor student. We blame the student when we have failed to teach him properly. The dropout—perhaps we should say "pushout"—or failing student is not considered the victim of poor pedagogy; rather, the blame for his failure is placed on many other external forces in our society. Industry, however, cannot operate in this manner. Inefficient training and inadequate learning are costly. What phases of training have been least effective and therefore most costly have not been as obvious in the past as they will become in the future.

The typical description of the job of training director customarily includes a statement that he must keep informed about new methods and techniques for training. It is only when this is required that management will make the effort to find a training director who is not only informed but sophisticated in the application of new methods and techniques. Much has been said and written about teaching machines and programed learning. Some of it has been said with caution and some without. Numerous meetings of training specialists have been held, but it is ultimately top management that must endorse programed learning. Programed learning—in spite of the jargon, the cabalistic ritual, and the "expertism" which have accompanied it and in spite of the quack practitioners of the art—must be recognized as more than some new tool for the training director. It is a different, a systematic way of looking at industrial training. For top management it brings a completely new perspective to bear on its problem, not only in the field of training but possibly in the whole area of manpower management itself.

Chapter 4

Some Applications of Programed Instruction
In Industry and the U.S. Air Force

Probably no other approach to learning has been as systematically and rigorously studied as programed instruction. Certainly not in such a short period of time. The thousands of studies leave no doubt about one thing: Programed instruction teaches. Students do learn from it. In general it teaches much faster and more effectively than conventional teaching and training. Wilbur Schramm, in his succinct and lucid review of the research on programed instruction, states unequivocally that students learn from programs:

> They learn from linear programs, from branching programs built on the Skinnerian model, from scrambled books of the Crowder type, from Pressey review tests with immediate knowledge of results, from programs on machines or programs in texts. Many kinds of students learn—college, high school, secondary, primary, preschool, adult, professional, skilled labor, clerical employees, military, deaf, retarded, imprisoned— every kind of student that programs have been tried on. Using programs, these students are able to learn mathematics and science at different levels, foreign languages, English language correctness, the details of the U.S. Constitution, spelling, electronics, computer science, psychology, statistics, business skills, reading skills, instrument flying rules, and many other subjects. *The limits of the topics which can be studied efficiently by means of programs are not yet known.*[1]

Without at this point going into the question of whether programs teach better or worse than conventional methods, management can rest assured that there is every reason to believe trainees in industry can learn from and be trained by programed instruction.

[1] Wilbur Schramm, *The Research on Programed Instruction*, U.S. Department of Health, Education, and Welfare, Office of Education, OE-34034, Bulletin No. 35, 1964.

RESEARCH ON PROGRAMED INSTRUCTION IN INDUSTRY

Albert Hickey and William Laidlaw reported on a study involving 130 U.S. Navy Supply Officers using the adjunct type of program. The program was designed to train the officers in retail sales and ship's store management. The conventional instructor's lecture hours were reduced by 54 per cent. Student study time was reduced by 17 per cent, and the students' reactions were favorable.[2]

Hughes and McNamara reported what has since become a classic study. One hundred and ten employees (70 taking the program and 40 taking the course by conventional means) served as test subjects to evaluate the effectiveness of programed instruction in comparison with conventional training procedures in the use of the 7070 computer. Two classes were given the programed text and two classes were taught in a conventional classroom by a regular instructor. The average time for the programed instruction class was 8.8 hours; for the conventional class, 15 hours. The programed group scored higher than the conventionally taught class. Students who took the programed course were favorable in their attitude to this method of instruction.[3]

Howard O. Holt and C. G. Valentine constructed a programed text for basic electricity which was given to 34 telephone company technicians. Their test results were compared with those of 30 technicians who took the course by conventional means. Both groups took the same amount of time to finish the course, but two final examinations, one given immediately after training and the other six months later, indicated that the group taught by the program was superior in proficiency to that taught by conventional means.[4]

David S. Bushnell studied the effect of teaching machines in a voluntary education program for adults. The program, using a branching type of teaching machine, was electricity for journeymen. The three approaches that were studied were (1) self-instruction, (2) self-instruction plus live discussion, and (3) conventional instruction. Student attitudes and results favored the self-

[2] Albert E. Hickey and William J. Laidlaw, *Programed Instruction in Retail Sales* [Final Report to U.S. Navy Bureau of Supplies and Accounts, ONR Contract Nonr-3630(00)], ENTELEK Incorporated, Newburyport, Massachusetts, 1962.

[3] John L. Hughes and W. J. McNamara, "A Comparative Study of Programed and Conventional Instruction in Industry," *Journal of Applied Psychology*, Vol. 45, 1961, pp. 225–231.

[4] Howard O. Holt and C. G. Valentine, *An Exploratory Study of the Use of a Self-Instruction Program in Basic Electricity Instruction*, Report to Bell Telephone Laboratories, Murray Hill, New Jersey, 1961.

instruction plus live discussion. There was higher subsequent enrollment with this method than with the others.[5]

Albert E. Hickey and Jean Anywll studied the effectiveness of using programed instruction in the training of 120 package billing clerks for Spiegel, Inc. The 2,000-frame program resulted in a 34 per cent reduction in the average time needed to attain proficiency as it was measured by the criterion examination.[6]

To date research on the applications of programed instruction in industry and in education has consistently demonstrated that it increases learning proficiency or reduces training time, and it usually does both. On the other hand research concerning the various techniques of programing such as linear, branching, adjunctive, and others has not conclusively demonstrated the superiority of one over the other. Numerous studies of overt (out-in-the-open) versus covert (internal or thinking) responses also have not been conclusive. So many factors are operating and so little is yet known about the various elements of programing technology that one cannot expect more than the general finding at this time that programed instruction does work for at least a majority (probably 80 to 90 per cent) of industry's training problems. The value of the teaching machine has also been questioned by various studies. Here again most research studies have consistently demonstrated that machines do not have any superiority over the programed texts. This probably has been due to the primitive state of the art not only of programed instruction technology but also of teaching machine design and development.

MORE RESULTS

Although research efforts have been promising and undoubtedly will continue to be made, applications of programed instruction technology to industrial training problems have been steadily increasing in variety and scope. In October 1960 Eastman Kodak, International Business Machines, and the Foundation for Research on Human Behavior at Ann Arbor, Michigan, hosted a conference called "Programmed Learning: Evolving Principles and Industrial Applications." The conference was held to "examine the 'state of the art' in research on programmed learning *and the outlook for its applica-*

---

[5] David S. Bushnell, *Technological Change and the Journeyman Electrician: An Experimental Study in Continuing Education,* Stanford Research Institute, Menlo Park, California, 1963.
[6] Albert E. Hickey and Jean B. Anywll, *Programed Instruction of Package Billing Clerks,* Information Technology Laboratories (Itek), Lexington, Massachusetts, 1961.

tions in industry." [7] Speakers and discussion leaders included such prominent pioneers as B. F. Skinner, Arthur A. Lumsdaine, Robert Glaser, and John Hughes. Approximately 30 industries, including the large companies Procter & Gamble, The Detroit Edison Company, Union Carbide Corporation, Aluminum Company of America, Ford Motor Company, Radio Corporation of America, and Corning Glass Works, sent representatives. Both Eastman Kodak and IBM had pioneered a limited effort in the applications of programed instruction to their training needs. Their efforts were reported to the conferees along with discussions of the principles of programed learning, learning theory and future research, and known programs and programers.

It is significant to note that at the time the report on the conference was published (1961) the list of known programs and programers numbered no more than 50.[8] The day before the conference started (October 16, 1960) saw the publication of the first definitive text, *Teaching Machines and Programmed Learning,* edited by two of the conferees, Arthur A. Lumsdaine and Robert Glaser.[9] This book includes 47 basic papers and a 28-page bibliography plus a research abstract. Although there had been numerous provocative, overenthusiastic, and diatribelike articles published in newspapers and periodicals, the only other major publication of any merit which had been published prior to the Ann Arbor conference was Eugene Galanter's *Automatic Teaching: The State of the Art.*[10] The papers in this book were based on a symposium which was under the joint sponsorship of the United States Air Force Office of Scientific Research and the University of Pennsylvania.

Four and one-half years later the applications of programed learning to industrial training problems have certainly accelerated. During the 1960 conference Robert Glaser was asked, "Why hasn't industry used this programed instruction long before now?" He replied:

> It's interesting to point out in this regard that teaching machines have developed out of the psychology of learning. In a recent survey, I found out that in industry—and this is probably true in the colleges of education—most psychologists are employed to do other things than training. Training in industry is not carried out by people who have any experi-

[7] Jerome P. Lysaught (editor), *Programmed Learning: Evolving Principles and Industrial Applications,* Foundation for Research on Human Behavior, Ann Arbor, Michigan, 1961, pp. 155–159.

[8] *Ibid.*

[9] Arthur A. Lumsdaine and Robert Glaser (editors), *Teaching Machines and Programmed Learning: A Source Book,* National Education Association, Department of Audio-Visual Instruction, Washington, D. C., 1960.

[10] Eugene Galanter (editor), *Automatic Teaching: The State of the Art,* John Wiley & Sons, Inc., New York, 1959.

ence in experimental psychology of learning. Just now people who have had some work in experimental psychology are beginning to work at training in industry. But in the booklet that came out, "What's Being Done in Industry?" I noticed that there was selection, morale building, and things of this kind—training was omitted.[11]

RECENT APPLICATIONS

Irrespective of whether recent developments are due to the entrance of experimental psychologists on the industrial training scene, we remember that the characteristic elements and constant factors of programed instruction itself did emerge from the laboratories of learning psychologists, notably Drs. Pressey and Skinner. Whereas the Ann Arbor conference in 1960 relied on the one- and two-year experiences of IBM and Eastman Kodak, the applications today in American industry number in the hundreds, and literally thousands of people have been trained by programed instruction.

The National Foremen's Institute recently surveyed 350 large companies. Of 200 companies 20 per cent reported actual experience with programed instruction, a sizable increase in such a few years. The rest of the companies surveyed were exploring the subject and expected to use the technology eventually. It is also significant that the American Society of Training Directors found similar percentages in a survey which it conducted. Its study "showed that only 20% of the respondents were currently using PI but the overwhelming majority—98%—expressed keen interest in the field." [12]

Applications have been as varied as they have been numerous. Frank Fuchs and Leonard Silvern, using an aural-visual teaching machine (Hughes Videosonic), have taught fire-fighting recruits a 252-step lesson in "Fire Behavior." The course was given to 34 recruit firemen of the Los Angeles County Fire Department with positive results.

OTHER COMPANY USES OF PROGRAMED INSTRUCTION

Programed instruction has been used to provide teaching aids to first-line supervisors in job analysis and training evaluation. A similar program was developed for training first-line supervisors in interpreting various aspects of labor legislation. There are others for the same audience in cost control, discipline, communication, and other supervisory responsibilities.

---

[11] Lysaught, *op. cit.,* p. 75.

[12] "What You Should Know About Programmed Instruction," *Office Executive's Bulletin,* published by The Bureau of Business Practice, Inc., 24 Rope Ferry Road, Waterford, Connecticut, May 30, 1964. Copyright 1964, Bureau of Business Practice, Inc.

The Training Section of General Dynamics/Convair's Production Flight Department, in an effort to determine the effectiveness of programed instruction for use in ground school transition training for highly experienced flight crews, programed the Kollsman Integrated Flight Instrument System. The group receiving instruction by the program achieved as high an average as the group instructed by conventional teacher and methods. The group taught by programed instruction, however, spent 25 per cent less time finishing the course than those being taught by traditional classroom procedures in which the presence of a live instructor was needed.[13]

The following excerpts from the *Office Executive's Bulletin* report on programed instruction further show the variety of applications that industry is making in using programed instruction for its training problems:

Zenith Corporation (Chicago)—Uses P.I. to teach features of Zenith color TV to wholesale salesmen, and electronics to Quality Control Personnel. Plans to use P.I. to teach the union contract.

Merck and Co. (Rahway, N.J.)—Uses P.I. to teach union contract changes. Plans to use P.I. to teach Benefits Administration, Supervisory Practices, Wage and Salary Administration.

I.T.T. Labs (Nutley, N.J.)—Uses P.I. to teach math, electronics, and the facts about transistors.

Arthur Wiesenberger and Co. (N.Y.C.)—Uses and sells P.I. to teach salesmen basics of investments. Plans to use P.I. in general area of sales training.

Raytheon Co.—Aero-Weapons Division (Bristol, Tenn.)—Uses P.I. to teach industrial security, resistor color codes. Plans to use P.I. to teach shop mathematics, blueprint reading, and schematic interpretation.

Maytag Corp. (Newton, Iowa)—Uses P.I. to teach electronics. Plans to use P.I. to teach job skills and trouble shooting.

Bausch and Lomb (Rochester, N.Y.)—Uses P.I. to teach statistics and supervisory development. Plans to use P.I. to teach new product sales and service, new employee orientation, and unemployment cost control.

Humble Oil Co. (Houston)—Uses P.I. experimentally to teach service station attendants basic job skills. Training involves a custom-designed machine. Humble, in turn, sells the program and machine below cost to its dealers.

Lever Bros. (N.Y.C.) has developed a course for new sales trainees which

---

[13] Peter H. Selby, "Programing Auto-Instructional Training Materials for Flight Crews," *Training Directors Journal*, October 1962, pp. 46, 48, 54.

covers most areas of the salesman's job except face-to-face sales techniques.

The American Radiator and Standard Sanitary Corp.—Plumbing and Heating Division (N.Y.C.) has given selected salesmen "The Six-Point Program for the Sale of Hydronic Heating."

A Chicago casket manufacturer has used a program designed to acquaint funeral directors with a new type of casket sealing device.[14]

One of the most novel and radical applications of programed instruction is training personnel to listen effectively. The program "Effective Listening," developed by Basic Systems Inc., is being used by the Diamond Alkali Company of Cleveland for the training of its salesmen. The company, like others, feels that its salesmen should do less talking and more listening to the potential customer. The course is an aural one presented to the trainee on audio-tape. Diamond Alkali adopted the program after running a comparative study. It found that five of the six trainees to whom the course was given for test purposes scored higher than the highest scorer of the nine trainees who were not given the programed course.

More than 10,000 persons have taken this program in two one and one-half hour sessions, allowing one-half hour for the tests. Companies such as American Telephone & Telegraph, Dow Chemical, General Motors, Upjohn, Caterpillar Tractor, United Air Lines, Du Pont, Armco Steel, and others have utilized the course in portions of their training programs. The results in Exhibit 1 indicate the performance acquired in studies carried out in four companies and a University of Michigan seminar under the supervision of Dr. Ralph Nichols, a nationally recognized authority.

Dr. Nichols writes as follows regarding the listening course:

> Frankly, I feel that the Basic Systems program does a very good job of what they claim it is supposed to do. I took the training myself out of curiosity, and felt that I had learned a great deal at the end of three hours. Certainly, it teaches one to separate facts from ideas, principles from supporting evidence, major points from minor points. The authors do not claim that the training does much in the areas of establishing and maintaining emotional control of yourself as you listen, or in capitalizing greatly upon the differential between thought speed and speech speed. However, their training also does a lot to teach one to overcome distracting noises and irrelevant materials, and to recognize that there may be worthwhile and practical ideas turning up even though they are surrounded by apparently very inconsequential content.[15]

---

[14] Excerpts from *Office Executive's Bulletin, op. cit.,* pp. 8–10.
[15] In a personal letter to the author, January 1, 1965.

EXHIBIT 1

PERFORMANCE DATA ON EFFECTIVE LISTENING COURSE

Job Description	General Motors Institute Office Mgrs.	Liberty Mutual Insurance Co. Dist. Sales Mgrs.	Southern N.E. Telephone Co. Foremen	Dow Chemical Salesmen	Dr. Ralph Nichols Univ. of Mich. seminar Training Mgrs.
Average Experience (yrs.)	8	8.6	7.8	14.5	16
Average Education (yrs.)	15	16	12	16	16
Average Age	36	35	42	40	41
Average Pre-Test Retention Score	31%	34%	36%	30%	32%
Average Final Test Retention Score	76%	91%	75%	80%	91%
Average Increase In Retention	145%	168%	108%	167%	184%

Training time: Group administration requires about 2 1/2 hours; slightly less time is required when a student takes the program individually.

Industrial management has little preconceived notion about the limitations of the application of programed instruction. It is being tried in a variety of areas with new efforts constantly being made to explore possibilities that other institutions have hesitated to consider. The crucial test is, will it work? The increase in the efforts that have been made during the last few years implies that in many cases it has been working—and to management's satisfaction. All of these efforts, however, have been localized in nature. A study has yet to be made by American industry to determine the extent to which programed instruction technology can be applied to a large-scale training system. An approach in this direction was the study begun in 1961 by the United States Air Force.

A CASE: HOW THE AIR FORCE STUDIED PROGRAMED INSTRUCTION

The results of the research studies of programed learning that had been going on in our universities and research institutions during the past decade had been noted by the Air Force with some gratification. In October 1961 an Air Staff Policy Letter expressed an Air-Force-wide interest in programed learning. The Air Force's position was that an orderly and discriminate transition of programed learning from the research and development stage into the stage of actual use should be effected as soon as possible. Phase I of the Air Force program was to consist in the experimental application of the system of programed learning to current education/training programs on a restricted and discriminate basis. Phase II would represent an expanded utilization of the system and would be entered into only if, and to the extent that, the results of Phase I warranted it.

The Air Training Command began this transition in November 1961 by indoctrinating key personnel in programed learning to monitor and encourage experimental programed instruction projects at ATC training activities. In November 1961 this group met to develop goals and recommend policy for the ATC "experiment" under Phase I. The following specific objectives were identified:

1. Familiarization of all instructors and training supervisors with the concepts, terms, principles, techniques, and procedures associated with programed learning and automated instruction.
2. Development of a limited "in-house" capability (instructional programers) at each base to produce effective programed learning materials (programs).
3. Development and formal evaluation of experimental programs of

the programed text or scrambled book for selected units or phases of instruction which appear to be most suitable for programing.

4. Determination of the feasibility of further expansion, exploitation, and sophistication of programed learning techniques and their application to the training course of the Air Training Command.

In addition, training specialists were encouraged to identify and use "off-the-shelf" programed instructional materials in their training courses and to recommend Extension Course Institute courses and on-the-job training packages for the programing.

The first specific objective was to familiarize all instructors and training supervisors in the Air Training Command with the concepts, terms, principles, techniques, and procedures associated with programed instruction. Orientation training has been conducted throughout all ATC training activities and instructor training courses. Formal and informal briefings have been held at all training activities. As a result more than 8,000 personnel now have some familiarity with programed instruction.

The paramount problem, however, that confronted the ATC was training personnel for the Air Force as instructional programers proficient in the skills and techniques of preparing materials in a programed instruction format. It has to date conducted a total of 17 special training courses in which it has trained 352 men for the Air Force as instructional programers. Of this number, 258 were assigned to the ATC. David Klaus of the American Institutes for Research estimated two years ago that the ATC courses in programed instruction would, in essence, double the number of trained instructional programers in the United States.

The units which were programed were selected on the basis of identifiable training objectives, estimated man-hours to develop the program, the stability of course content, student flow, and peculiarity of subject matter. A total of 107 programs was initiated throughout all the ATC's training activities. They ranged from one to 18 hours of conventional instruction. Some programs covered entire courses of instruction while others were designed as modules to "instruct" in small segments of existing courses. This effort of the ATC has been described by the editor of the *American Behavioral Scientist* as "the largest of all automated teaching programs."

Evaluations of programed instruction versus conventional training methods were conducted under operational training conditions. Procedures for conducting them were forwarded to supervisory personnel. Variations dictated by unusual training conditions, academic facilities, or an unusual student flow were reported and treated as another variable. Essentially, the design of each evaluation observed the following pattern: Students were randomly divided into control and experimental groups. Where the class's size prohibited obtaining an adequate sample for each group, two similar classes were chosen for evaluation. Students for specific courses were selected on "the basis of similar academic background and attitudinal characteristics." This procedure resulted in highly similar populations. Control groups were trained in the conventional manner and experimental groups worked with selected course materials in a programed instructional format. Comparable pretests covering course objectives were administered to both groups to establish the initial repertoire. Both groups adhered to the same training schedule, class lengths were constant, and post-tests were administered, whenever possible, at the same time.

The Air Training Command was attempting to determine whether a programed course in lieu of, or as a supplement to, conventional methods of training would substantially improve the quality of the graduates and materially decrease the costs of training. Its standards were of extremely high quality. Before a programed course was finally acceptable for general publication within the Air Training Command it had to become a 90/90 package; that is, 90 per cent of the students must score 90 per cent or better on a comprehensive test covering ALL of the course's objectives. It was proud of this standard, and the programers had a sense of achievement when they developed materials which obtained this level of proficiency in the students.

The Phase I results to date showed that the programers were on their way to reaching their 90/90 objective, with reductions in training time averaging 40 per cent. One of the programs had reduced the training time as much as 83 per cent. At Chanute Air Force Base, for example, the programers turned out a six-hour block of instruction in "Basic Hydraulic and Pneumatic Principle." The programed course took only one hour, on the average, for students to complete and, at the same time, resulted in a gain in performance of 20 per cent. At Keesler Air Force Base programing reduced the training time for an introductory AC&W radar course from 15 hours to five hours, with 95 per cent of the students scoring over 85 per cent on the criterion test.

A program developed at Amarillo Air Force Base on the use of hand tools raised the average level of achievement by 33 per cent with a 40 per cent reduction in training time. The test for this package was of job performance —the actual use of hand tools in a realistic job environment—not a paper-and-pencil exercise. At Sheppard Air Force Base a program on reading and interpreting electrical diagrams is turning out students who score 16 per cent higher than those taking conventional instruction and with an average saving of 36 per cent in training time.

A program at Lackland Air Force Base on the use of oscilloscopes (one of

EXHIBIT 2
AIR FORCE PIP RESULTS

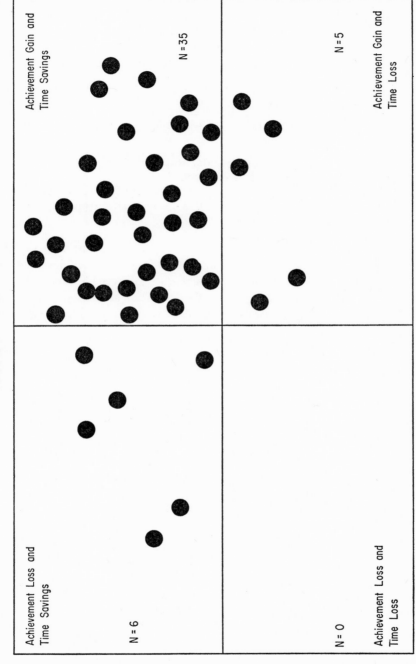

the first 90/90 packages) has reduced training time by 30 per cent and has increased achievement by 42 per cent. The students in the programed course average 98 per cent in contrast with those in the conventional course, who average 57 per cent.

A report made at the American Psychological Association in September 1963 stated that—

> Forty-six programs have been compared with conventional instructional techniques in the actual training situation. . . . The results are summarized as follows:
>
> In comparison with conventional instruction the programed packages indicate an average mean reduction of 33% in training time and a gain of 9% in achievement. The median reduction in training time was 40% and median gain was 11%. . . . This was accomplished with limited resources and experience.

A distribution of these results (see Exhibit 2) shows that in 35 of the cases the programed course had demonstrated an increase in achievement and a saving in time. In six of the 46 cases there was an achievement loss but a saving in time. In five of the cases there was an achievement gain accompanied by a time loss. In none of the cases were there both an achievement loss and time loss.

In an address before the National Society of Programmed Instruction in San Antonio, Texas, General James E. Briggs, the ATC Commander at that time, had the following to say with respect to the ATC study:

> Programed instruction? Breakthrough in Air Force training? I don't really know as yet. I do know this, however, that nothing has appeared on the horizon which has given us a more hopeful sign for such a breakthrough as has programed instruction.
>
> It was Ralph Waldo Emerson who said that the reward of a thing well done is to have done it. I am not saying that we have already done it. We are convinced that we have conclusively demonstrated that it can be done. I do not feel that we can confidently erase the question marks which follow the words "programed instruction" and "breakthrough" until we can look around us throughout the Air Training Command and find it a common sight to see students going through a variety of programed materials—each proceeding at his own optimum pace—each achieving the maximum quality performance he possibly could in the shortest possible period of time with the minimum assistance needed from a master instructor at a minimum cost. Even when this is a common sight, we must still continue to be alert to new ways, new methods, new ideas.

Chapter 5

A Systems Approach to Effective Performance

By Joseph A. Tucker, Jr.

TODAY, INCREASING RECOGNITION IS BEING GIVEN TO THE FACT THAT
the greatest asset of an enterprise is people. Recent advances in educational
science and technology now offer business a vastly improved means of upgrading the quality and effectiveness of its personnel. There is no magic.
Rather, this technology is based on a few simple but powerful ideas underlying the systems approach to improving performance.

WHAT A SYSTEMS APPROACH IS NOT

Let us suppose that a large milk delivery company in the Philadelphia
area has many salesmen delivering milk every day. These men must keep
records of their transactions as they do their work. When they return from
making their deliveries, they must complete several forms, requiring a
number of calculations, before they can leave for home.

The treasurer of the company, who is responsible for billing the customers, has found that he is seriously handicapped in his work, since only 30
per cent of the records turned in by the salesmen each day are made out
correctly. His staff therefore has to correct 70 per cent of the completed forms
before they can be used for accounting and billing purposes.

Once the treasurer recognized this problem, he decided to do something
about it. He began by looking at the tasks that he asked the salesmen to do
in completing the forms and decided that the procedures were awkward and

This chapter was originally delivered, in a somewhat different version, as a talk to the
Philadelphia Chapter of the American Society of Training Directors by Dr. Joseph A.
Tucker, Jr., then Senior Associate, Training Services, Cresap, McCormick and Paget, and
now General Manager—Training Systems Information and Training Services, F. W. Dodge
Company Division, McGraw-Hill Company, in New York.

confusing. He had his staff develop new procedures and forms which were much simpler to use. He put these into operation with the hope that his problem would be greatly alleviated. After several months of using the new forms, he discovered that only 30 per cent of *these* forms were being filled out correctly. He had new forms and the old problem.

At this point, the firm's top management decided it should take a look at the situation. An obvious conclusion was that there must be something wrong with the training of the men. The training director was consulted. He said that the men needed more training in simple accounting procedure and that only one hour was given to this topic in the present 40-hour "basic" training course. Since the marketing department had recently decided that it did not want its sales training done during the initial training period, the training director now had available eight more hours of "class" time that could be used for additional training in accounting procedures. He proposed that he develop materials on accounting procedures that would require five hours of this time.

At this point the company president stepped in. He called a meeting of all his top staff who were in any way involved in the management of the milk salesmen in order to review the problem thoroughly. The subsequent discussion was most revealing. The marketing manager pointed out that those men who were most meticulous about completing the forms did not turn out to be good route salesmen. They were not adept at obtaining new customers or even in protecting the accounts they were serving.

The personnel director indicated that hiring procedures were set to select men who liked working at outside jobs and who were neutral, at best, about paperwork. Next, it was revealed that the regional managers—who were extremely sales oriented—did not evaluate the performance of a milk salesman in terms of how well he completed his accounting tasks. The regional managers in fact had little sympathy for the treasurer's problem.

Further, no one had established what level of performance would be satisfactory to the accounting department. Since 100 per cent accuracy was obviously out of the question, would proper completion of 70 per cent of the forms be an acceptable standard? And if this were satisfactory, would the remaining 30 per cent still necessitate hiring a few clerks to correct the errors?

By this time, it was obvious that adding five hours of accounting procedures to the training course was unlikely to solve the problem. Finally, no one could say specifically what difficulties the men were encountering in completing the forms. No detailed analysis of the situation from the point of view of the milk salesmen had yet been made.

The president realized that, so far as this question was concerned, his organization had no clear-cut performance goal, no evaluation of the feasibility of various alternate solutions, no clear understanding of just why the milk salesmen were making the errors, no evidence of cooperation between the accounting division and the operating division, and—worst of all —no systematic procedure for tackling the basic problem.

What was revealed in this situation was exactly the opposite of systems thinking. The treasurer assumed that, because the symptom of the problem was detected in his department and was related to tasks for which he was directly responsible, he should take the initiative in solving it. This was certainly reasonable. However, he proceeded toward the solution without specifying clearly what objective he hoped to attain or what alternatives were available to him and without knowing—and this was most significant —what the real source of the problem was.

The training director was even more provincial in his outlook. The treasurer, after all, was a busy man with many other problems to be concerned about. The training director simply assumed that the treasurer (and after him, the top management) was right in thinking that the difficulty was procedural. It did not occur to him that he should be riding the trucks with the men to find out what their problems were. Nor did it occur to him that the amount of training required in procedures, if any, should be based on a study of job requirements and that the methods to be used in training should be determined in the same way.

With this true, but not atypical, story in mind, let us turn now to discussion of the rationale of the systems approach to effective performance.

THE BASIC CONCEPT OF A SYSTEMS APPROACH

The schematic drawing shown as Exhibit 1 serves as a background for our discussion of a systems approach to performance.* Top management's responsibility is to plan, to organize, to direct, and to review performance and make appropriate new plans. Planning sets the overall objectives of the various divisions of the enterprise and, consequently, standards of individual performance as well. Management organizes its enterprise so that it can direct its functional divisions in making their proper contribution to organization objectives. As a result, the organization performs to meet

---

* The conceptual model on which the following discussion is based is the work of Edward O. Malott, Director of Divisions and Director of the Management Course and Executive Action Course for the American Management Association.

overall objectives, and individuals perform to meet individual standards.

In planning, organizing, and directing the enterprise, management constantly reviews actual performance against objectives and standards to see whether the plans that were made are being carried through.

EXHIBIT 1

A SYSTEMS APPROACH TO EFFECTIVE PERFORMANCE

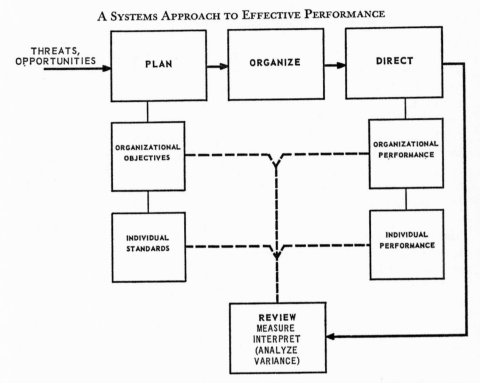

If management detects a variance between objectives or standards on the one hand and performance on the other, it seeks the cause. One possibility is that planning may be inadequate. On the other hand, significant variations between objectives and performance may result from improper personnel selection, inappropriate organization, awkward job structure, or similar factors.

Finally, difficulties may arise not from inadequate planning or organization but from the way the people are prepared to accomplish their assigned duties. Developing and maintaining their job skills and knowledge are the responsibility of the training subsystem shown in Exhibit 2.

The training subsystem operates in essentially the same way as the "parent" enterprise shown in Exhibit 1. Once management has discovered that a performance problem is quite likely to be solved through training, the training subsystem is brought into play. Training, like any other major responsibility of the enterprise, includes the functions of planning, organ-

EXHIBIT 2

THE TRAINING SUBSYSTEM

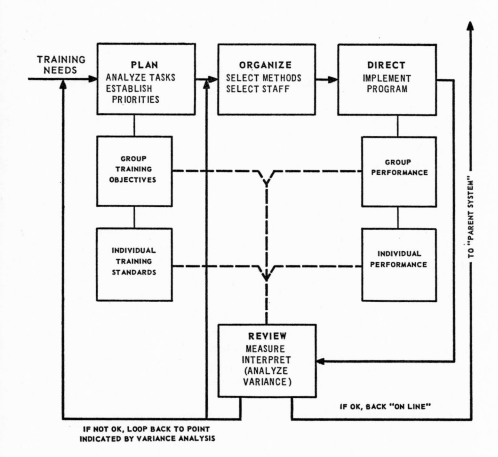

izing, directing, and reviewing. Modern training planning is based on task analysis and similar techniques rather than on the subjective impressions of training people. Training is organized to use the most appropriate methods of meeting the objectives established during the planning stage. The required training is then developed with the objective of teaching a person to meet performance standards. If a relatively large number of trainees fail to meet performance standards, the accuracy of the original statement of training needs or the appropriateness of the training methods comes into question. At this point, an analysis of the cause of variance is again indicated. Thus the training subsystem, viewed as a part of the overall enterprise, is a continuous and systematic process that is self-correcting.

You will note that the training subsystem has not been referred to as a training "department," for, when viewed in the systems context, the subsystem is often difficult to distinguish from the normal operation of the enterprise. Training, in fact, involves everyone and is basically a line responsibility.

KEY ELEMENTS IN THE SYSTEMS APPROACH

In the systems approach to training, four key elements should be considered:
1. Objective setting.
2. Planning.
3. Quality control.
4. Efficiency.

A systems approach to performance makes provision for all four of these key elements and, in so doing, avoids the parochial viewpoint and limited achievements which have characterized less comprehensive approaches in the past.

1. Objective setting. The value of training lies in its contribution to individual and group job performance and thus to the objectives of the enterprise. Viewed in this way, there are no "training" objectives as such; rather, there are operating objectives, some of which can be accomplished in whole or in part through training. Furthermore, this approach helps to establish priorities. It may be better to devote attention to crude training efforts of crucial importance to the enterprise than to polished efforts of marginal value.

Certain key decisions must be made if the most profitable training goals are to be met:

• The selection of the functions and positions to be given training attention.
• The selection of the best means of building or maintaining the competence of people.
• The determination of levels of proficiency to be attained.

- The determination of the relative emphasis to be given to each of four major training tasks:
  a. Initial training to bring new employees up to a desired level of competence.
  b. Corrective training to eliminate deficiencies in the performance of employees.
  c. Training to prepare people for higher-level jobs.
  d. Career development to consider both the individual's and the organization's long-term desires and needs.

Furthermore, the well-developed and well-stated training objective will—

- Describe in behavioral terms the kinds of performance which will be accepted as evidence that the learner has achieved the objective.
- Stipulate the conditions under which the performance will be demonstrated.
- Specify the criteria or required levels of acceptable performance.

2. Planning. After training objectives are established, programs must be planned and developed to accomplish them. Some considerations governing the design of these programs are as follows:

- Verification that the objective-setting phase has been properly carried out.
- Desirability of using available materials where appropriate.
- Importance of specialized programs for individuals or small groups.
- Provision for evaluating and controlling the training program.

3. Quality control. If anything characterizes "modern" training, it is the emphasis on improved quality control of human performance—the maintenance of people's performance and ability at established standards. The military services have long realized the importance of maintaining proficiency; they probably spend at least as much time, money, and effort in maintaining the skills of personnel as in developing these skills initially. Basically, the only ways in which this kind of control can be obtained are through the *prevention* and the *correction* of variance from standard (which, of course, presupposes the existence of a standard).

In the prevention of variance, we must ask ourselves:

- Are we accurately identifying the skills which may be forgotten or may deteriorate?
- Having done so, are we taking appropriate steps to maintain these skills?

In the correction of variance, we must ask ourselves:

- Is our system designed to draw attention to substandard performance?

- Does the system provide data which permit analysis of variances in order to determine their true cause?

4. Efficiency. Our final area of concern is whether our approach to performance improvement not only provides for objective setting, planning, and quality control, but also insures that these functions are performed efficiently—that is, with the least effort and at the least cost. The approach is efficient to the extent that it—

- Uses the available skills of the organization, without either ignoring or duplicating them.
- Recognizes that expenditure for maintaining or improving performance is an investment and should be treated as such in decision making.

METHODS AND TECHNIQUES

To implement these principles, we must have practical methods and techniques; otherwise, training becomes mere wishful thinking. Fortunately, since World War II many new training techniques, and greatly improved old ones, have been developed and demonstrated. But how do we use them? How do we know when to use them? How do we avoid overdependence on one technique? The best answer to questions like these lies in the concept of the training system. The word "system," when used to describe a training program, implies that (1) it is organized to accomplish well-defined objectives in the most practical and economical manner, and (2) it is based on an analysis that defines the role to be played by various tools such as instructional aids, programed instruction, and selection procedures.

THE NEED TO DEFINE THE PROBLEM

My thesis, then, is this: The key element in any management problem-solving activity is accurate definition of the problem. To those of us deeply concerned with training, there is far too much training being done on problems inaccurately diagnosed as being "trainable" when in fact their roots lie in selection, in organization structure or procedures, in evaluation, or elsewhere. We must constantly ask ourselves, therefore:

- What kind of problem is this?
- What are *all* its possible causes?
- To what extent does each cause contribute to the problem?
- What are possible solutions for each of the causes?

- What are the criteria of an "ideal" solution?
- What, also, are the criteria of a workable solution?
- To what extent must the "ideal" solution yield to the practical realities of organization life?
- What are the possible secondary effects of alternative solutions? In other words, what are the possibilities of getting extra mileage out of a given alternative—or, conversely, of creating new problems now or at a later date?

When we look at problems in this broad and systematic fashion, we have gone far toward clarifying the role that training can and should play. We are then in a position to undertake—and to measure—training in terms of objective setting, planning, quality control, and efficiency. On this basis, training can make contributions to an organization at a level previously undreamed of.

Chapter 6

How to Get Started

IN THE PREVIOUS CHAPTERS WE HAVE TRIED TO SHOW HOW PRO-
gramed instruction can meet the national need for education and training
technology; why programed instruction is more than just a technique or
a procedure for solving training problems; how programed instruction
brings a systems approach and craftsmanship to the solution of these problems; the unexpected benefits that accrue from the effort to apply programed
instruction to training; and the impact of programed instruction on other
aspects of training problems and on the very nature of the training profession itself. As programed instruction leads to the "systems approach," training reaches a high stage of development. Training effectiveness always has
been intimately related to cost in the past and will become increasingly so in
the future. Soon company audits will include searching audits of training
programs.

The professionalization of training should proceed from top management down. Programed instruction will not only assist in this effort; it will,
where properly applied, force the issue. All executives in the organization
will gain familiarity with the concepts of training technology. This will
enable them to initiate, support, and evaluate the training capability they
need in their operating units. Many executives realize that, even though the
original costs of initiating programed instruction efforts—exploratory or
otherwise—may be exorbitant, such efforts may nevertheless be necessary.
These managers are willing to commit their companies to high initial costs
because they have a grasp of the hidden costs of inefficient training and the
foresight to manage the technology in such a way that they can anticipate
eventual payoff. Keeping their eyes on performance, they are able to visualize
potential relationships between programed instruction systems technology
and conventional training procedures.

While the original cost of conventional training is less than that of programed instruction technology, subsequently the latter establishes a basis for

a much lower cost. If we plot costs against aggregate training hours, we will get a curve something like the following:

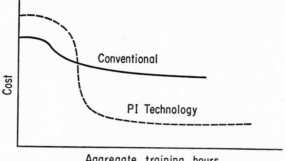

Though they know that programed instruction is a relatively new and young, even immature, technology, informed managers also recognize that it has demonstrated its ability to improve learning and therefore perform-ance. This technology will develop rapidly largely because it has achieved results. Certainly desired training results are being achieved for a larger percentage of trainees than has been possible in the past. Programed instruc-tion materials, even in their present primitive and crude format, have often made terminal and master performance possible for 90 per cent of the train-ees, in contrast with customary courses which have achieved less demanding results for only 60 to 70 per cent of the trainees after some have dropped out of them. In general, customary courses have not been quantitatively meas-ured by training directors. And rarely have they been measured by criterion-referenced tests. The major method of measurement seems to be an opinion poll of the trainees after they have completed the course; this is a qualita-tive measure, most certainly not a quantitative one.

An informed management recognizes not only that the quality of training has been substantially improved but that training time itself has been drastically reduced—sometimes by 80 or 90 per cent, frequently by 25 or 30 per cent. Not only these cost reduction factors but others too are important: the reduced demand on the time of the instructor; the decreased need for travel on the part of the supervisor; the decreased need for travel and daily expenses on the part of the students; and costly morale factors associated with company schools and their customary classroom training methods.

Such a management will find that when it uses programed instruction, it can predict training results, analyze costs more accurately and specifically, and, for the first time consider training expenditures as investments rather than expenses. Management has customarily thought in these terms—but not with respect to training. Programed instruction enables it to do so now. Having been so convinced, it can now ask the significant questions: "How do we get started?" and beyond this, "How do we do it?"

WHAT IS THE PERFORMANCE REQUIREMENT?

Even though the full impact of programed instruction in industry is still years away, it is time for the first step. Enough pioneering has been done and enough results have been demonstrated to inspire even small companies to begin on their own.

The first question that must be asked is, "What is our training problem?" In asking this question, management must forget completely, for the moment, how training has been approached in the past. Before a training system can be developed, a decision must be made about what its purpose is. Certainly programed instruction does save time. And a well-organized, validated, programed instruction based training system will probably save time but not necessarily cost less.

Effective training management encompasses not only training procedures and the quality and design of the training system; it is equally concerned with whether the training is necessary to begin with. Perhaps it is unnecessary. Programed instruction of itself does not determine that training is needed. Intelligent management, however, recognizing its high cost, now is seeking to determine that need, a thing it has rarely done in the past.

An analysis of the necessity for training is essential even when conventional training programs have already been established. Entirely too often a conventional course has been started because it was relatively easy to do so, there was little requirement for craftsmanship, and some executive's whim was easily satisfied thereby.

Even effective training is not necessarily efficient; in fact, it may be very inefficient. In far too many instances, although training is meeting performance requirements, the need could have been met with fewer instructors, less training equipment, cheaper but better simulators, fewer facilities, and—in some cases—with no training whatsoever. Performance needs can sometimes be attained by simply providing clear instructions; for example, a sound-slide may be located right at the work station on the job, and not off in a classroom somewhere, showing the trainee how to perform in specific detail even complex tasks. Many examples of "overtraining" have been found where expensive training was raising performance beyond what was required on the job. The question, "What is the training problem?" is related to the training question, "What type of performance is required that is not now available or will not otherwise be available in the future?"

When management invests in training, it is not investing in classrooms or in teachers or in course materials or in audiovisual devices or in training films. Rather, it is investing in a program which will produce performance of a particular type when there is no more economical means of obtaining it. Often, when a company buys a training package to train its salesmen, for example, it is not purchasing successful salesmanship skills, and therefore not performance, as much as printed materials or lectures or classroom exercises or checklists. Since the aim of programed instruction technology is to modify behavior, the ultimate measure of training is the performance of the student. Therefore, management must focus on performance initially and decide what type is desired prior to considering the feasibility of establishing a training program to develop the knowledge, skills, attitudes, and values necessary to achieve the desired behavior.

A specific description of "proper" behavior is necessary whether a bank wants its tellers to learn to speak "properly" to customers or an airline requires that its ticket clerks fill out reservation forms and use computer-based machinery accurately or at least with little tolerance for error. The performance requirement may be to design a PERT chart for a specific production problem or to solve an algebraic equation or to draw an electric circuit. The main thing that distinguishes programed instruction performance standards from those of traditional learning objectives is that the desired behavior can be described in such a way as to be measureable. This does not mean precise measurement so much as any measurement which will note a change in behavior or a gain in performance skill and achieve agreement among observers that modifications in behavior have actually taken place. Murphy and Goldberg define performance, as differentiated from "work" behavior, in the following way:

1. It consists of skills, capacities, and knowledge which top management wants employees to have so that specific organizational goals can be better achieved.

2. It consists of measurable changes in behavior.

3. It is not abstract.[1]

In the development of some programs, however, while there are measurable changes in knowledge, it is not always possible to determine or to measure the changes in behavior that are desired. For example, programed

---

[1] J. R. Murphy and I. Goldberg, "Strategies for Using Programed Instruction," *Harvard Business Review*, May–June 1964, p. 118.

materials which have been developed for Pfizer sales training are primarily on knowledge of diseases or conditions for the treatment of which Pfizer produces drugs. The purpose of the course may be thought of as increasing sales. A realistic appraisal of what can presently be accomplished with programed learning convinced Pfizer training management that the direct purpose of the programed course would be to give the salesmen more confidence in talking to physicians by giving them more knowledge. An explanation of performance needs will provide a description of the circumstances in which the performance will take place.

Therefore, before we can design a training system to meet our performance needs we have to decide what those needs are and determine that the only desirable and economical way of satisfying them is through training. Further, we must be careful that they are not overstated, for if they are, the cost may be excessive. Any number of performance patterns may relate to what we consider our training need to be; any one of these patterns can be selected as the specification for the training program. Each pattern may require a different type of program with different cost figures and different potential returns. But before an intelligent decision can be made, it is necessary to make a feasibility study of the training needs.

IS TRAINING NEEDED?

Before serious consideration can be given to training, whether it is program based or not, a feasibility study should determine whether training is necessary. The feasibility study is an analysis of the performance requirement followed by a further analysis of the most economical procedure necessary to acquire this performance. It may be selection. It may be training. It may be performance aids. From this point of view the feasibility study made at this point is one of top management's primary tools in decision making. If the decision is "no-go," management can realign its concern. If the decision is "go," management must determine through further studies and analysis how much training is necessary and what level and quality of performance are desired. Once these are determined, attention can be given to instructional strategies and to the design and development of the training system. If a feasibility study is well done, it will prevent unnecessary training or explain why the excessive cost of training is not justified by the requirement.

Any new training program should be established to correct a deficiency in performance. This deficiency may be present or anticipated because of future industrial commitments. The deficiency in training may be more apparent than real. A typist may make errors not because she is unable to perform accurately but because she has personal problems which prevent her from performing as required. She may need counseling, not training. She may need better supervision, not training. The feasibility study should determine where training is needed and where it is not. Therefore, management should be concerned with the reason for a performance deficiency.

Management may believe it knows the cause of a performance deficiency when in fact the real reason may not be apparent. For example, a man may not know how to fill out the proper forms. He may not *want* to fill out the proper forms. It may not even make any difference whether proper forms are filled out or not. What, then, *is* the problem?

Often training programs are established to increase performance capability when the real culprit is poor supervision or poor administrative procedures. If these are the reasons for poor performance, then training—even if it is programed and carefully designed—is not the answer and would be costly and inefficient. Before a training requirement can be adequately determined, we must be convinced that a defect in training is the problem itself, not other aspects of administrative organization and practice. When trainees do not know certain fundamental subject matter, when they are unable to perform a variety of necessary skills, when the performance deficiency that has to be corrected is actually traced to sheer inability to behave in a specific manner—when these, and not administrative practices, are the reasons for performance deficiency, then we can say that we do have a training problem. And where we do in fact have a problem, a training program must be established. But before this can be done, another significant analysis must be made of the nature of the performance deficiency itself.

Leonard C. Silvern succinctly summarizes the alternatives to human performance difficulties when he points out that management may: (1) eliminate the job, (2) re-engineer the job, (3) eliminate (fire) the man, or (4) re-engineer (train) the man. We must keep in mind that there are other ways, as Silvern points out, to re-engineer or change the man besides training.[2]

OBJECTIVES CAREFULLY DETERMINED

Through a careful analysis of the performance deficiency (PD), we arrive at this crucial step of determining our objectives for the training system. Most fruitful in this respect have been the stimulating and provocative ideas of Thomas Gilbert. He talks of the master (M) and the individual (I). The

---

[2] Leonard D. Silvern, *Fundamentals of Teaching Machines and Programmed Learning Systems*, Educational Training Consultants, Los Angeles, California, 1964.

master is the expert performer; therefore, (M) can also stand for *mastery*. And (I) stands not only for individual (trainee, target population, or student) but also for initial repertoire. Repertoire is referred to by some as entry behavior; that is, the behavior which represents the student's knowledge, skills, attitudes, and values when he enters a training program or system. Therefore, if it is decided on the basis of the feasibility study that training is a problem, we must determine what aspects of the problem we must solve. This necessitates determining the specific area for which we need training. How much training do we really need? Must we teach specific items of knowledge, develop the ability to solve certain types of problems, or develop certain specific behaviorally defined attitudes? What kind of performance does the trainee lack? How would we describe the deficiency in performance?

According to Gilbert, the basic question that we must ask at this point is described by the following formula:

$$PD = M - I$$

In this formula *M* stands for mastery, *I* stands for initial repertoire or entry behavior, and *PD* stands for performance deficiency. Once we have determined in behavioral terms the nature of *PD*, we have in essence charted our area of immediate concern. The determination of *PD* tells us essentially the area in which we must train the individual. When we use this formula, we do something that we have rarely done with any precision in training—or in education, for that matter. We ask ourselves: What does the individual student already know? What can he already do? What are his present attitudes and values and motives? What is the minimal entry level requirement that he must meet? Does he have the entry behavior necessary to complete the instruction? Does he have more than the minimum? Can he enter the training system at a more advanced point? Would this make training much more efficient than it would be if he entered along with students who have only the minimum requirement? Does he need the training system? Can he proceed without it? Gilbert would maintain, and properly so, that we frequently do a great deal of unnecessary training in areas where the student is already proficient. This may lead to administrative convenience but is often extremely costly. The solution to this formula is part of the strategy study which should follow the feasibility study.

MORE FEASIBILITY FACTORS

Before conducting the strategy study which will outline in broad terms how we ought to proceed, other considerations should be evaluated. It is necessary to know as much as possible about the mastery or terminal performance desired. It is likewise necessary to be familiar with all the available texts and other materials such as films, film strips, and audiovisual devices which have been prepared to provide training.

New information must also be obtained from management regarding future planning and policy considerations which may have a direct bearing on the feasibility study decision. Since the preparation of programed instruction based training systems is a long, elaborate, painstaking, and expensive procedure, an intelligently prepared feasibility study should consider time constraints. It would be folly to prepare a PIBTS that has an estimated time of completion long after the performance requirement has ceased to exist. Another issue is the stability of the system's content. If it is subject to constant change and erratic company policies, a training system may not be practical or feasible unless consideration is given to procedures which can upgrade the PIBTS rapidly and economically.

Another factor that should be considered in the feasibility study is the difficulty in acquiring complex conceptual learning and performance skills. People with these skills may be unavailable or unobtainable. Conventional training programs in the past have not produced sufficient numbers of proficient trainees. It is difficult for industry to hold on to proficient people. The turnover rate in this group is usually high. Just because something *can* be programed, in other words, it is not necessarily worthwhile to do so.

Conventional training programs have had problems with subjects which are imprecise, complex, or ambiguous. For example, it has been easier to apply programed instruction technology to mathematics than to principles of supervision, salesmanship, and other abstract or seemingly illogical activities. So the subject and the degree of proficiency that must be developed should be matters of serious concern. Can the subject be readily programed? This requires consideration not only of the logical organization of the skill or subject matter content but also of the potential programer's abilities and the state of the art. Attention should also be given to: (1) the complexity of the subject matter and its logical structure, (2) the availability of adequate programer talent, and (3) the development of instructional programing procedures. Plainly, programed instruction has developed in some areas more rapidly than in others. It is a mistake to assume that this has been due solely to the nature of the subject matter, for it has been equally due to overemphasis on small-step linear techniques. In the early years of programed instruction, those subjects were programed which were logical, discrete, and quantitative. Lately, however, a sincere effort is being made to apply the concept and principles underlying programed instruction to more complex areas of performance and knowledge and to a wider variety of media and formal training situations.

The functions and availability of conventional instructors deserve some consideration. One of the advantages of automated and programed instruction that has been widely touted is its capability to relieve the instructor of many routine functions. Even though routine drill is boring to both student and instructor, it is frequently quite important. The use of an automated training system will contribute to the relief of the boredom and at the same time introduce reliability and quality control. Psychologically, it is ideal to introduce automated training procedures because the training establishment is more likely to offer assistance.

Conventional teaching functions seem to fail and students do not learn effectively when the learning task is too complex. Instructors welcome the introduction of programed training assistance. When the skills are difficult to master through conventional training procedures and few master instructors are available, programed instruction systems should be considered even though the number of students or trainees needed is extremely small.

G. A. Eckstrand and his associates have considered this problem with respect to the use of the teaching machine in the modern military training complex.

> If it can be truly said that much military training involves the routine acquisition of knowledge and concepts, it is just as true that much military training involves the mastery of highly complex, extremely sophisticated skills both on the part of individuals and teams. Humans must be trained to monitor and control highly complicated machinery such as supersonic aircraft and aerospace systems. People must be trained to assimilate large amounts of information from diverse sources and make rapid decisions, as in missile count-downs. Teams of individuals must be trained to perform in an integrated manner in large data processing systems such as the USAF SAGE system. The skills involved in such operations are difficult to master and typically require long periods of intensive training involving such practice in realistic job environments. Historically, such practice was acquired in realistic job environment itself with an instructor present both for tutorial and safety purposes. Recent military systems, however, have been far too demanding on human skill to permit this approach completely; therefore, complex ground simulators have come into vogue to aid in providing both transition and maintenance-of-proficiency training. As weapon systems have increased in complexity, so too have the training simulators, and these modern devices now have complex instructor-operator stations and require teams of instructors and trainer operators in order to provide realistic training

sessions. Even so, the requirements for coordinating, controlling, and scheduling rapidly changing inputs, monitoring the complex response outputs of students, and providing for realistic interaction between the two are rapidly outstripping the capabilities of human instructors. Likewise, the requirements for rapid recording and analysis of complex, multivariate events is increasing, and it is upon this function that providing knowledge of results to the trainees and programing future instructional exercises is dependent.[3]

In other words, as our human skill requirements become increasingly complex the number and capacity of proficient master instructors decrease. In these circumstances the traditional instructor must be supplemented if not replaced by automated training systems.

When no instructor is available or when it is entirely too costly to provide instructors for a very few students even though the training is crucial, a self-instructional programed system provides an ideal solution. The more internationally based our industries become, the greater will be the requirements for packaging and sending to remote parts of the world instructional systems which use the language of the trainee and which meet training requirements thousands of miles from corporate headquarters. Also, through the development of packaged self-instructional systems the upgrading of training and the maintenance of skill proficiency can be controlled from one focal point in the industry complex.

ON-THE-JOB TRAINING

A common tendency in both military and industrial organizations to meet the problems of complex proficiency requirements, high turnover, and lack of effective master instructors is to shift the training responsibility to the manager and the supervisor. Witness, for example, the training of life insurance agents, casualty insurance brokers, real estate salesmen, and mutual fund brokers. Retraining requirements in American industry are increasing in scope and complexity. Automation is broadening the retraining base. As automation increases, industry is increasing its correlative responsibility for the retraining of displaced workers. This, in turn, is increasing the requirement for apprenticeship programs and management-supervised, on-the-job training programs. Many demands are made on the manager and supervisor

[3] G. A. Eckstrand, M. R. Rockway, F. F. Kopstein, and R. L. Morgan, "Teaching Machines in the Modern Military Organization," in *Applied Programed Instruction*, Stuart Margulies and Lewis D. Eigen (editors), John Wiley & Sons, Inc., New York, 1962, p. 95.

besides those of training. When the demands on the supervisor for on-the-job training become excessive, the training itself will suffer rather than the other commitments for which the supervisor has accountability.

Programed instruction systems provide the supervisor with a training tool which he can depend upon to produce the proficiency he requires. The greatest value of using the self-instructional systems and modules, however, is that the worker is away from his job for a minimum time, since, as has been adequately demonstrated, programed instruction reduces learning time by one-third of that devoted to conventional methods of instruction.

Management must face the fact that learning under any method, regardless of how efficient it may be, will require trainee time. This training time away from the job will never fall completely to zero. Programed instruction will probably reduce it to the lowest possible point without sacrificing the quality of the outcome.

Another advantage accrues to the supervisor of on-the-job training programs. Since this responsibility is only one of many he carries, he often has little time to devote to a rigorous examination of how effective his procedure is. A complete PIBTS, however, provides not only a well-sequenced and validated group of learning experiences for the student but also a group of criterion examinations which reveal the extent to which he improves in skill mastery and comprehension. The system enables the supervisor to measure the results of his training program with an accuracy and a precision that he has never had heretofore. (In all fairness it should be pointed out that this precise measurement could be had with conventional training systems, too, but most companies have not bothered.) It enables him to determine exactly whether the lack of proficiency on the part of his workers is due to inadequate training or inadequate supervision. This is significant because the supervisor now has accountability for both. Inasmuch as this type of management of human resources has to do with cost effectiveness, these issues deserve to be considered in an adequate and comprehensive feasibility study.

DOES IT PAY?

If the development of a programed training system will neither reduce cost nor increase the quality of training proficiency, management has no reason to embark on it. The primary purpose of a feasibility study is cost effectiveness. Providing learning experiences for students is costly. If management is to look upon such an effort as an investment rather than as an unnecessary expense, then it should be made as economically as possible, if at all. Training cost should therefore be computed with respect to not only how many students need the training and how much effort is needed to develop the training system but also how much value the desired performance has to the company and what the possibilities are of acquiring that performance by means other than in-house training.

Technology may easily solve some of the training problems to which it has given rise. Every day, industry is developing new black boxes to correct —automatically and instantaneously—malfunctions in old black boxes. A feasibility study should consider the possibility of investing company resources in an R&D effort with a high degree of probability for a payoff in the form of a black box which may make the training requirement unnecessary. In the interim, consideration may be given to a temporary, inadequate training system which will do a partial job until the hardware emerges which will correct the performance deficiency. Both training development and black-box research and development should be evaluated by relating the cost of each to productive work time. The feasibility study, which should be conducted by a staff organization independent of the training system development staff, proceeds in a manner similar to that of product planning and control. The only purpose of an industrial training program is to develop the specific performance required for various tasks and jobs. Any system, whether it is hardware or software oriented, which produces such highly reliable performance in the most cost-effective manner should be developed.

Before programed training systems were developed, industry rarely if ever made the kind of cost effectiveness study which is now a requisite to programed instruction. Owing to the costly engineering aspects of designing and developing such systems, old and conventional training procedures are today being appraised critically.

No formula now available provides the ideal manner for conducting a feasibility study. Every industry has different constraints operating. One industry, for example, may not have an adequate in-house staff capable of developing the programed training system even though all other factors indicate a "go" for the system. Outside programing assistance may not be available even though the proposed system is likely to produce an average proficiency performance grade of 95 per cent in contrast to 70 per cent for the conventional system. The cost of the proposed program may be $65,000 for 2,000 students for the first two years of operation, whereas the cost for conventional instruction (taking into account per diem and travel expenses) may be higher, say $84,000. Over the next two years, assuming that the training requirement still exists, the cost for the conventional program may be reduced slightly whereas the cost of the new system may be reduced drastically. In spite of this prediction, however, those making the feasibility study must keep in mind the availability of qualified programed instruction and training technologists. Since the quality of the training produced by the system is a factor in determining cost effectiveness, the availability of personnel to produce the quality must be a factor. Too often a feasibility study makes assumptions about quality without considering whether technicians to design the system are available. The resulting system produces such low-quality performance that the training by means of the new system may be as costly as was the conventional program.

Few feasibility studies have been produced which are acceptable models for industry to follow. There are definite trends, however, which suggest that in the years to come more consideration will be given to the development of more elaborate and comprehensive studies.

Conducting a feasibility study is in itself a costly process. Even when a "no-go" decision is made, however, it has not been money down the drain. Often an improvement in the conventional training program may result, or a training need which has previously gone undetected may be highlighted. Studies have led to the development of guidance packages to replace training programs; to a revamping of administrative procedures; to a reformulation of learning objectives in more specific and precise terms. These fallout benefits have accrued to conventional training practices even with inadequate and limited feasibility studies.

Frequently management asks for a simple answer to a complex question stated in simple terms: "What is the cost of programing course X? Or subject matter Y? Or hour of instruction Z?" When management asks this type of question, it may be given an equally misleading answer. Some programing companies estimate that they can program one hour of conventional instruction for $500. Others estimate as much as $3,000 per hour. The feasibility study asks a much more complex question, and, if properly done, provides a much more significant and pertinent set of answers.

Ultimately, management's decision to get started or not must be based on whether the performance that will be acquired through the program training system is worth the cost. Cost effectiveness is the crucial issue. The feasibility study is management's best tool in making an intelligent decision in this regard.

The study will not be too costly provided it is well conducted. Small projects call for small feasibility studies, and large projects call for fairly extensive studies. A feasibility study is excessive in cost, however, when inefficient personnel are carrying it out. Since the study will raise and seek the answers to some of management's most important questions, it is very important that the best men on the management training staff be put to work on it since they will help to establish the scope of the total system. Too often, feasibility studies have been performed by the "second team," and the "first team" is held in reserve for the so-called "real job." Good men may then have to follow a plan set for them by clods. If management considers the feasibility study one of the most important steps it can take, then it should put its best talent to the task. If this talent is not available, then, rather than delegate the task to an inefficient group, it should hire a group of consultants who know their job.

Chapter 7

The First Stage: System Design

THE IDEAL FEASIBILITY STUDY, WHOSE IMPORTANCE WAS DISCUSSED in the preceding chapter, results in one of two possible decisions. If it is "go," management can proceed to develop a programed instruction based training system (PIBTS), using the guidelines which are provided in this chapter. If the decision is "no-go," well, then, it's just "no-go."

Management, of course, always retains the prerogative of ignoring, in whole or in part, the recommendation made in the feasibility study. It may decide to "go" when the recommendation is "no-go" or not to "go" when the recommendation is "go." The inclination to go against the recommendation may depend to a great extent on the quality of the study itself. We know of no feasibility study conducted in government, industry, or the educational community which has combined the approach, quality, and parameters described in the previous chapter.

There is little doubt, however, that as programed instruction materials more closely approximate complete systems, studies will be made in detail. And as future studies become more and more comprehensive, management will be able to look to them for extensive guidance through accurate cost analysis.

Embarking on the development of a PIBTS is no romantic venture. If the feasibility decision recommending such a system is intelligent, training will close the gap between company objectives and the performance level of its current employees and of those about to be hired. The development of an automated, self-instructional system which minimizes the need for the human instructor should be pursued only when it is justified by economic considerations.

STRATEGY STUDY

Once a "go" decision is reached, it is necessary to begin a *strategy study,* the key to which is an analysis of the gap between trainee performance and that of the master or expert. The guidance of Thomas F. Gilbert has been exceptionally valuable in this connection. Except for his work, the concept of *performance deficiency* itself—although occasionally mentioned by others —has not been seriously pursued by any significant groups in the fields of instructional technology and conventional training.

In a brilliant discourse Gilbert has discussed the confusion between "acquirement" and "accomplishment." [1] He points out two ways in which the entry level behavior of trainees will differ: First, we may note that an individual lacks certain skills or other performance characteristics; second, we may focus our attention only on inadequacies in terminal behavior rather than noting the discrepancy between entry behavior and terminal performance. Any evaluation of entry behavior that does not take into consideration these factors (entry, terminal, and discrepancy) is seriously deficient. We have all seen frequent reference to the use of diagnostic tests in determining entry level characteristics of students. However, a diagnostic test which measures only accomplishment may not show that two different individuals with identical scores have two entirely different sets of acquirements (entry level skills) and two individuals with apparently radically different accomplishment scores may have identical entering-level characteristics. Only a diagnostic test which can also measure *acquirement* can reveal valid training analysis data. What is important is that regardless of the student's acquirement (which may be relatively high because he possesses a high percentage of the skills necessary), unless he "accomplishes" the terminal behavior his "acquirement" may have little or no value. Gilbert elaborates on this point as follows:

> Let us examine . . . the confusion between acquirement and accomplishment. You say that you know nothing about bank tellering; but this is not true. If you examine all the operations a bank teller uses to balance his books, you will find that you have already acquired most of them. Nevertheless, the few operations you have not acquired prevent you from accomplishing the objectives of the teller's job. In terms of what the teller and you know about his job, there is very little difference between you; in terms of the value of what you know, you are worlds apart. I say I know nothing of marksmanship, but examine my behavior when I attempt to imitate a sharpshooter: So small are the differences between my actions and those of the master that I can fool you until I fire the gun, and even then I don't miss very far. But a miss is as good as a mile, and

---

[1] T. F. Gilbert, "A Dialogue Between Teaching and Testing," in Gabriel D. Ofiesh and Wesley C. Meierhenry (editors), *Trends in Programmed Instruction*, National Education Association, Washington, D.C., 1964, p. 25.

the value of my repertory is miles apart from that of the sharp-shooter's.[2]

An analysis of the problem may well indicate that minimal training is necessary to bring about a small change in acquirement, which may in turn produce a great change in accomplishment. If teaching only a few important skills can double and possibly triple the effectiveness and value of an individual's performance capability, then to package this training and make it available in a manner suitable and adaptive to each individual's performance deficiency is the ideal of the training system. If an analysis of the target population—that is, the potential trainees—indicates that the great majority are comparable in acquirement and individual differences are not so striking as they appeared to be at first, then a self-instructional system has a marked economic advantage. The amount of training to be accomplished in this instance is less than was originally anticipated. The implications are obvious. The first step, then, is to determine the difference between present performance and desired performance. This is a difficult task, but no other starting point will determine the most economical procedure.

CONVENTIONAL STRATEGY

A "system" has been defined as a group of components organized to accomplish a given purpose, as we learned in the chapter contributed by Dr. Tucker. Conventional systems have been designed rather haphazardly to meet ambiguous performance standards. Those who would design and develop PIBTS cannot afford such luxury. The purpose of a programed system is to fill the gap of performance deficiency. Software (trainees and instructors) and hardware (media, text, teaching machines) components are organized and employed in accordance with specified procedures to turn out a product—correct and worthwhile performance. To do this a strong departure must be made from conventional training program strategy.

The practice of traditional programs has been to make an extensive analysis of conventional training materials—course syllabi, lesson plans, texts, and so on—that have been prepared by instructors or by technical writers. The strategy built upon this analysis has often been poor. Descriptions of mastery behavior have usually been arbitrarily arrived at by a course writer or subject matter expert, and review of the materials by non-

---

[2] *Ibid.*, p. 26.

behavioral technologists and managers too often focuses on the literary quality of the materials, not on an examination of their relevance.

Task and job analysis procedures have been extensively documented. Much concern has centered on what constitutes an adequate task description and on the extent of its psychological value. But a description of displays, activities, and procedures may not be very useful from a human engineering systems design point of view in making a training analysis. Whether this analysis is the function of the task or job analyst or of the training system designer is not the point. *What is significant and relevant is the extent to which the training program designer perceives the potential contributions of the mastery behavior description to the training task.*

Job and task requirements must provide as complete and accurate a description of mastery behavior as possible before they can be considered in terms of economical training procedures that will lead to their attainment. Specialists in industrial and human factor psychology have developed many procedures which provide guidance on how to arrive at adequate job and task descriptions. The methods of the Gilbreths and Frederick W. Taylor are well known, as is J. C. Flanagan's critical incident technique.[3]

Even though research and study in job and task analysis and description have been extensive, their direct application to training and to the development of training materials has been relatively minor and sporadic. A notable exception is the ideas of Leonard Silvern as he enunciates them in a definitive and monumental effort, a programed course entitled *Fundamentals of Teaching Machines and Programmed Learning Systems.*[4] Silvern, practicing what he is preaching since he has programed his ideas, begins with the concept of basic analysis and its principles and method, then moves to object, action, and information analysis and their combinations. Finally he derives forms in job analysis for combined analysis (object, action, information) for recording job performance so that a course outline to the teaching point can be developed for the preparation of the system.

Even interviewing subject matter experts or skilled "masters" and determining what knowledge, skills, attitudes, and values they think are relevant performance and job characteristics has not been done as extensively or meaningfully as many have claimed. The main difficulty has been the inability of many experts to verbalize the relevant aspects of their own job performance. The "expert" is often the person least able to strip his own

---

[3] J. C. Flanagan, "The Critical Incident Technique," *Psychological Bulletin,* 1954, pp. 327–358.

[4] Education and Training Consultants, Los Angeles, California, 1964. Refer to Units 3 and 4, pp. 88–134.

job or performance down to its essential requirements and characteristics. To do so often conflicts with his own requirement for self-esteem. The tendency —quite a natural and understandable one—is to make many tasks seem more complex and difficult than they really are.

To a great extent efforts in job and task analysis have concentrated on the superficial rather than the substantive features as they relate to the development of training materials. Robert B. Miller pointed out that in the early 1950's the Air Force recognized the need for training "to parallel the latest stages of development of equipment" in order to reduce the time lapse between the availability of equipment and the training of personnel qualified to operate and maintain it. Formal procedures were established to gather data about operating equipment before the equipment was even produced. He wrote:

> Considerable controversy has been expended on formats and symbols for entering behavioral information. *But . . . relatively little creative energy has been directed toward the more fundamental problems of what can and what cannot be expected of task information, or how to meet the problems of training design with those of behavioral description and analysis,* or of the inherent logical problems of any classification structure and operational validity. It seems fair to state that in task analysis the format has largely been confused with the concept. . . . A moment's reflection should show that task analysis is useful as a means of aiding the training designer, that the structure and terms used in communicating the analysis are most useful when they are compatible with whatever mode of conceptualization and decision is (or should be) used in training design.[5]

Irrespective of these issues, however, those who have looked to past procedures for guides to developing descriptions of terminal performance which are adequate for training design have found them inadequate for PIBTS.

OBSERVING MASTERY

Apparently the best—and most painstaking—way to make an adequate analysis of mastery behavior which will lead to a proper description of performance deficiency is to observe a group of experts who perform according to terminal behavior specifications. From this direct observation an analysis is made of critical skills. In theory, this will result in a complete description

---

[5] R. B. Miller, "Analysis and Specification of Behavior for Training," in Robert Glaser (editor), *Training Research and Education,* University of Pittsburgh Press, Pittsburgh, Pennsylvania, 1962, pp. 33, 34. (Italics supplied.)

of what the "master" has to do to produce the results management requires. Often, however, the task as required by management and the task as performed by the master may not be identical. Even the best master performance available at a particular time may not be the most efficient or desirable guide to the development of a training system. Instead, the system designer should direct his efforts to the level of performance required by management— assuming, that is, that the requirement is carefully defined and arrived at. Therefore, once a complete description of mastery behavior is available from direct observation, a critical study must be made to assess whether *everything* the master does in fact contributes to the required level of performance.

Let us assume that the required level of performance is designated by the letters X, Y, Z. The master, in producing X, Y, Z, employs skills which can be labeled k, m, n, s, t, x, y, and z. By manipulating these skills, however, we find that we can produce X, Y, Z by employing only skills k, n, t, x, y, and z; skills m and s are unnecessary. The designer must evolve a system which will produce performance skills k, n, t, x, y, and z only! He may very well be concerned with the relationship of these skills to each other and with their integration, but this is another matter.

It should also be emphasized, however, that it is not always desirable to eliminate m and s even when they are not required. An issue which is widespread in education and is becoming so in industry is that m and s, although not relevant to X, Y, Z, should be taught because they have the most "transfer" value in the long run. "Problem solving" or "creativity" or "discovery learning" is valueless as long as X, Y, Z is clear and immutable —as it is likely to become following this type of analysis. If performance is produced through rote training, however, we may be throwing out the baby with the bath water. The decision will be a matter of judgment. If m and s are pure ritual and consequently of no value, we should have no question that they should be discarded. If they are not, then the possibility of including them should be argued in light of their potential contribution to those aspects of performance with transfer value as well as to those aspects that are important but still difficult to describe and measure.

Whatever information is gathered with respect to job performance is useful only if it will assist a designer in making decisions which affect his system's development. If this information is properly gathered and collated, the description of desired performance should also provide some guidance to the priorities of various items in the design.

A further analysis must be made of entering behavior. Irrespective of such factors as IQ, motivation, and attitude, what elementary skills must the trainee possess in order to interact successfully with the training system so that he can learn to perform k, n, t, x, y, and z? The answer should set the base or the minimal level at which trainees may enter the system—they must possess these elementary skills which we can label k_1, k_2, n_1, n_2, n_3, and so on. In order to teach the performance of k the system can handle only trainees who have prerequisite skills k_1 and k_2. If a diagnostic evaluation of a potential trainee indicates that he cannot perform k_1 and k_2, then management must decide either to provide him with remedial training or to seek his replacement. Management is of course free to lower the base for the entry level, and the system can be designed accordingly, if economic feasibility warrants it. Some experts, in fact, maintain that theoretically there would be no limit to the point at which students could enter a training system provided it were designed accordingly.

Let us assume that we want to design a system to teach students how to extract the square root of four-digit numbers. Let us further assume we have determined that the entry level requirement is the ability to add and subtract. Nothing else. We have four potential students: A, B, C, and D. A can add, subtract, multiply, and divide, and he recognizes a square root symbol. The system should be so designed that he may enter it late and learn square root in a short time. B has the entry level requirement; further, the diagnostic pretest indicates that he already knows how to extract the square root of four-digit numbers. He skips the system completely. C can neither add nor subtract. He is not qualified to enter the system; his efforts to interact with it would be completely futile. D can only add and subtract; he therefore possesses the minimal prerequisite skills and enters the system at the initial point. All the men differ in performance. The ideal training system is designed to make up for the performance deficiency in the greatest number of available and needed trainees.

Susan Markle's program *Words* is one of the few "systems" to include a programed text and diagnostic test which are designed to handle A, B, and D—but not C. The teacher, along with the text and the tests, is part of the system. The following excerpts from the *Teacher's Manual* illustrate this point:

> The first half of the program (Chapters 1–8) is considerably easier than the second (Chapters 9–14). Average students who have mastered the first half can do the second half, but above-average students need less help in mastering the fundamental principles in the first half. Consequently the fast track makes it possible for them to skip well over a third of the items in Chapters 1–8.[6]

---

[6] Susan M. Markle, *Words: A Programed Course in Vocabulary Development,* Science Research Associates, Inc., Chicago, Illinois. *Teacher's Manual,* revised 1963.

The section in the *Teacher's Manual* called "Individualizing the Program" provides instructions on assigning students to the fast or the slow track. The following passage is illustrative:

> An example of a branch relating to a deficiency in previous training will be found in Chapter 4, Frame 6, dealing with prepositions. This item can be answered correctly only by those who already know what a preposition is. For those who need further instruction, an inserted sequence is provided. . . .

> A few [students] welcome the chance to skip items despite need for further instruction as shown by their inability to answer the criterion item. Teachers should be on the lookout for these overconfident students who constantly skip ahead and fail. They can be spotted easily by inspection of their answers on the branching sequences.[7]

The *Teacher's Manual* even provides suggestions for "a possible third track" for retarded students.

OBSERVING ENVIRONMENT

A training analysis leading to the design of an effective PIBTS will not only include a description of the significant tasks but will also provide some explanation of the environmental conditions which may influence the manner in which the tasks are performed. It must also consider other circumstances besides those of the physical environment. In what conditions will certain things go wrong? What supervisory actions and policies may affect the quality of job performance? When in the total job requirement will the described action occur? How frequently will it occur? What will happen to final job performance if a particular task is not performed at top quality? What are the critical areas for human error? The answers to these and other questions shed a great deal of light on the way the system can best be constituted.

PERFORMANCE REQUIREMENT ADEQUACY

If the performance requirement is comprehensively and carefully described, it will provide guides to what is to be taught and indicate how the requirement can be considerably reduced.

---

[7] *Ibid.*, p. 6.

Perhaps a change in the design of equipment will eliminate the requirement for a certain part of the current training. Or perhaps guidance and job aids are needed. A job aid is provided following the completion of training if job performance without the aid would be cumbersome and uneconomical.[8] A trainee may be asked, for example, to utilize a complicated formula to solve a problem. The need for the formula is not likely to occur until he has been on the job for about six months; even then it will occur rather rarely—and hardly ever without the supervisor's knowledge. To train him to make a computation long before it will be needed on the job, when he is likely to have forgotten how to do it anyway, is to waste both the student's and the instructor's time as well as management's money. It is advantageous to have an adequate analysis determine the proper sequence in the development of the system because such unnecessary training can be eliminated in the design stage.

FACTORS IN DECIDING TO DEVELOP A SYSTEM

Once a feasibility study has (1) established that a training problem exists, (2) described the performance needed to solve the problem, (3) analyzed the target population and the skills and knowledge of the entering student, and (4) determined in general terms the deficiency of current training practices, management then can confidently give the "go" signal to design a validated system to produce the required performance.

Prior to taking the first step, management should have asked the following questions:

1. Is the problem truly one of training?
2. To what extent has a training task analysis based on performance proficiency provided a description of the entry level skills required by the trainees?
3. What evaluation, if any, has been made of the potential trainee population, including a description of the skills, knowledge, attitudes, and values the trainees will bring to the program?
4. How adequate and comprehensive is the description of the performance needed? What skills, knowledge, attitudes, and values must the trainee have when he completes the course?
5. What is the nature of the discrepancy between questions 3 and 4?

Only after having reviewed the answers to these five questions can manage-

---

[8] If the reader cares to pursue this point further, he is referred again to L. C. Silvern, *op. cit.*, pp. 19–36.

ment decide whether or not it will further develop the training system. Merely to look at the objectives of the training system even if they are described in precise behavioral terminology is not sufficient for an intelligent commitment. The pivotal point for management in making its decision is the determination of training objectives. They must be studied, however, in the context of the other factors implied in the five questions posed above.

CRITERION TESTS

The training objectives are, in essence, the specifications for the system that will be developed. Before management can intelligently decide on the objectives, they must be translated into measurable terms. The first task, then, is to translate the objectives into a criterion-referenced examination. The criterion test tells management what the performance will be when the proposed training is given to a certain type of population. Management's review of the criterion tests can be one of the most crucial points in its commitment to programed instruction.

It may be unrealistic in many cases to expect managers to review and evaluate the criterion test in minute detail, particularly if the systems engineer is extremely knowledgeable and sophisticated. Candidly speaking, very few managers know much about what a job entails or about test construction. Such is not their province. Someone knowledgeable in these areas must analyze work and construct tests on their behalf. But once they decide on the criterion test, either directly or through their designated expert, they have in essence established and formally approved the specifications for the system and have started to develop a system which will require significant contributions in terms of human, financial, and physical resources.

One airline, for example, tried for more than two years to teach its personnel a complex mileage system of surcharges, fictitious destination, break points, and other highly technical considerations. The system (devised by the legal advisers of a group of airlines) is used for overseas fare construction when the passenger elects to deviate from standard routings. It is condensed to 28 rules, each of which has several exceptions. To develop an adequate criterion test for this program, the head of the instructional programing agency [9] took a crash course in how to be a passenger agent. He discovered that many problems in conventional training were being hidden under the ambiguity of course objectives. Even after much soul-searching, trial and

---

[9] National Marketing Limited, Montreal, Canada. Personal communication to the author dated December 26, 1964.

error, questioning of the sequence of subject matter, and reappraising the traditional pattern and formula for teaching the subject, the training problem itself was not truly pinned down *until an effort was made to establish an adequate criterion test.* If feasibility and strategy studies had been carried out first, the criterion test would not have presented such difficulty. Often, however, the demand for an adequate set of specifications for the criterion test forces a belated concern about the five questions mentioned earlier. The criterion tests for the airlines consist of four typical fare construction problems which are designed to examine the ability of the trainee to put regulations into normal practice, utilizing the knowledge he has learned through the training system.

A look at the frame of the program originally designed to solve this problem provides little information about the program's adequacy. A common tendency of training directors and even some programers in evaluating programed materials is to leaf through them, make a cursory examination of frame construction and the like, and offer a judgment about the quality of the program. Yet we just do not know enough about the process to be able to be so casual in our evaluations. The most dependable means at present for evaluating any programed material or system is to study the criterion test and the data which indicate its capability, when properly administered, to produce the necessary performance in a given type of student. The performance is described by the examination. The examination, however, is quite different from the customary pencil-and-paper tests common to conventional education. It is more akin to the technical and comprehensive on-the-job and apprentice performance examinations. Let us look, for example, at one of the frames originally used in the program designed to train the airline passenger agent in the problem cited earlier. It is reproduced on the next page. A manager reviewing this frame would find little in it about the purposes of the training program and the ability of the programed material to produce the skills—although he might get the impression that he was learning a great deal about the complexity of the training problem.

The criterion test for this program, on the other hand, is much more specific and precise and offers the manager realistic information about the performance objectives. Here is an example of one of the four problems:

Mr. Kaplan, an executive in Winnipeg, hasn't had a vacation in three years, and has decided to take off early in August for Europe and just kick around London and Paris a bit before going on down to Milan and then over to Switzerland. Then he plans to live it up a bit in Paris before coming home. However, he made the mistake of talking about it around

FRAME FROM AN AIRLINE PASSENGER AGENT TRAINING COURSE

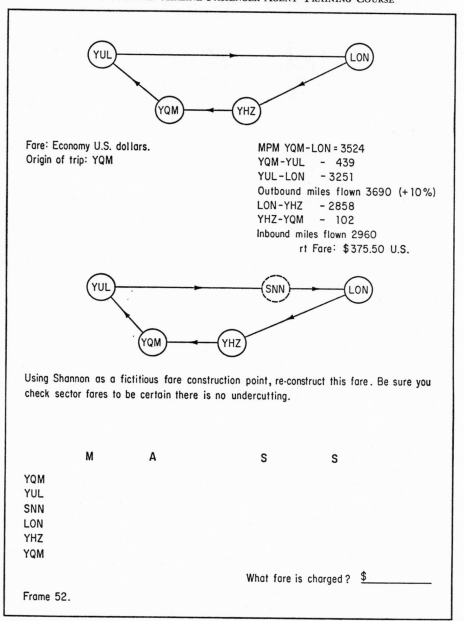

Fare: Economy U.S. dollars.
Origin of trip: YQM

MPM YQM-LON = 3524
YQM-YUL   - 439
YUL-LON   - 3251
Outbound miles flown 3690 (+10%)
LON-YHZ   - 2858
YHZ-YQM   - 102
Inbound miles flown 2960
                    rt Fare: $375.50 U.S.

Using Shannon as a fictitious fare construction point, re-construct this fare. Be sure you check sector fares to be certain there is no undercutting.

	M	A	S	S
YQM				
YUL				
SNN				
LON				
YHZ				
YQM				

What fare is charged? $_____

Frame 52.

the office, and the boss firmly suggested that, while good old Kaplan was over there anyway, he might as well look up some of their customers in Germany and do a little business on the side. Here is how poor Mr. Kaplan's itinerary finally worked out: YWG (AUG 8) LON (AUG 10) PAR (AUG 11) DUS (AUG 14) BER (AUG 17) PRG (AUG 20) FRA (AUG 23) SZG (AUG 26) MIL (AUG 29) GVA (SEP 1) DUS (SEP 4) PAR (SEP 7) LON (SEP 10) YYZ (SEP 15) YWG (Economy class).

Fare: $_____

Developing the ability to solve the *types* of problems represented in the criterion test determines the total specification for the training system. The buy-off on the criterion test is increasingly important when management contracts for the development of a PIBTS by an outside agency.

We can, of course, raise a host of questions and issues. For example, if the four fare construction problems mentioned above were invariable and had been thoroughly covered in the program, the criterion test, no matter how fine it looks, would be only a test of rote learning. If, however, the criterion test items were drawn, as is the case, from actual situations which arose in company operations and at the time of the test had never before been encountered by the students, the criterion test is in fact a useful means of evaluating the kind and amount of information that has been imparted. Other problems arise when the behavior is so complex and variable that it is impossible to test all of its manifestations. We have much to learn about criterion-referenced testing, too. But these are not insurmountable difficulties, and the intention of this discussion is simply to outline the general types of considerations which will confront management.

HIGH STANDARDS

The programing agency National Marketing Limited guarantees to produce for its clients the terminal behavior specifications which are represented by the criterion tests. Its guarantee is stated as follows:

> The NML guarantee is based upon the terminal behavior specifications, which define what the program is designed to accomplish.
>
> It is important that the client understand [that] a "course outline" is not a specification of terminal behavior.
>
> Terminal behavior is specified by, in effect, writing the final examination or the performance test. In this way, both the client and the programmer clearly understand what the trainee must learn—what he must know and be able to do at the end of the program.

The final capability must be developed to an acceptable performance criterion—and on NML programs this criterion is 90 percent or better.

[The] "interface chart" [shows] the step-by-step development of an NML program vis-à-vis the client.

If you agree to follow this charted plan, National Marketing Ltd. guarantees that on the final examination of the field test group of typical trainees from the target population, *90 per cent of the trainees will score 90 per cent or better.*

It is even more significant when we recall that the criterion-referenced test is rarely, if ever, a multiple-choice or true-false paper-and-pencil test; rather, it may often be a performance or problem-solving type of examination which comprehensively covers *all* the objectives. The implications for management are clear-cut. Here is the first hint that reliable training can be guaranteed to produce results in the same manner that other purchased products are guaranteed and that management will get what it pays for. More important, it can know what it is purchasing and easily test the quality of the product.

The president of a company may well ask, "Why only 90/90? Why not 100/100? Why not sell me training which will allow 100 per cent of my students to do 100 per cent on the criterion examination?" Good questions. Our answers are that the art of programing and the technology of education and training just aren't that good as yet. Furthermore, the cost to produce a reliable 100/100 PIBTS is quite possibly prohibitive; 90/90 is more economical and less elaborate to develop. Management may nonetheless find that certain performances are so crucial that in its specifications for the criterion examination these particular performances must be designated 100/100, although others are tolerable at a lower standard, say 90/90 or even 80/80.

The 90/90 standard of acceptability for programed material was first established by the Air Training Command of the United States Air Force. It was an arbitrary standard, difficult but not impossible to achieve, that established a high quality control point for in-house programs. It gave the programers a standard to shoot at and forced them to revise their materials until they achieved the highest level of craftsmanship. This high standard makes the system designer understand his commitment and responsibility so that he can be held accountable for a quality product.

One exception is made. For example, National Marketing Limited does not offer its guarantee if it cannot control the revision and validity testing of the program or if the training objectives are not measurable. In such cases it is not possible to develop an adequate criterion instrument.

One client, a railroad, had sharply increased its passenger traffic, but had been hampered by poor "out front service" of porters, waiters, and so on. As a stop-gap measure, a group of men was hastily assembled to ride the trains. These men were not trained in supervisory skills, and they soon took on a Gestapolike image in the minds of employees. Morale and service dropped to an all-time low. In this instance, the out-front employees needed training in customer relations, not in such service skills as setting tables, carrying luggage, serving drinks, or making beds. The criterion-referenced examination that was developed to provide the necessary training calls for role-playing in situations simulating on-the-job experience, such as dealing with tough customers, coping with unreasonable demands, and the like. Therefore, the programing company does not feel that it can guarantee criterion behavior. It is unfortunate that programed courses which claim to train individuals to be successful sales persons are not always designed in the light of this legitimate limitation.

The criterion examination is the crucial point at which the design of a system is completed and the development of a training package is begun. But it is useful only to the extent that it is carefully studied and reviewed and its inherent specifications for training are fully understood. The criterion examination representing management's total performance requirement is the most important instrument of quality control of the PIBTS.

Chapter 8

Developing the PIBTS

W<small>HEN</small> <small>MANAGEMENT</small> <small>HAS</small> <small>SUCCESSFULLY</small> <small>IDENTIFIED</small> <small>A</small> <small>SPECIFIC</small> training need, its customary practice has been to develop a training program to satisfy it. Measuring the effectiveness of the program has always been desirable; this measurement, however, has been dependent upon the ability of management to describe the specific purposes the training should fulfill. In some cases this has been done haphazardly. In other cases the needs have been so vague and indeterminate that the training programs themselves have been ill conceived, and their effectiveness has been difficult to measure. The need for a programed instruction based training system must be determined in a clear-cut and precise manner, and criterion tests must establish the basis for the program and provide an adequate measure of success. When management approves the specifications, or criterion examination, it is signifying that

- A training problem exists.
- A PIBTS will be developed to solve the problem.
- An adequate measure is available to evaluate the effectiveness of the PIBTS.

The development of a PIBTS is the third step in a five-phase cycle of events designed to provide specific training for the solution of training problems. In summary, these steps are: (1) determining the training needs (feasibility study), (2) developing criterion measures for specific needs, (3) designing the PIBTS, (4) presenting the training materials to the trainees, (5) evaluating the training given in terms of the curricular objective. At this point, the cycle begins again in the determination of additional training needs.

For many training programs, the phases of this cycle have often been performed haphazardly and out of sequence, as we have seen. In most cases one or more of the phases are weak links in the training system and result in failure. Failure in most cases is due to the fact that training needs have been so vaguely and so inadequately defined that the programs themselves have of

necessity been ill conceived, because they are derived from inadequate foun-
dations and their effectiveness cannot be measured.

As Joseph M. Madden points out, "The determination of training needs
may be broken down into two distinctly different types of activity. The first
is describing the work activity that is to be done by the individual to be
trained, and the second is inferring the training needs from this description." [1] In other words, the feasibility study becomes an inventory, catalogue,
or list of the tasks to be done on the job. After training needs have been inferred from the task inventory, criterion-referenced tests *must be devised for
each and every task on which training is to take place.* Management will primarily be interested in accomplishment testing, and according to what testing
determines, it will approve or disapprove. The PIBTS designers, however,
will be very much interested in the acquirement phase of criterion testing.

A PIBTS should ultimately consist of all training programs for a given
organization. Each training program should consist of a number of courses
which group together common tasks that are part of any job. The courses,
then, will consist of units of instruction or simply units which are organized
around each of the criterion test items. Finally, the PIBTS units will be
broken down into lesson units of varying lengths on different phases of the
task for which criterion test items have been developed.

For each unit an analysis is made of the "subordinate learning sets for a
given class of tasks." This approach is suggested by Gagné and his collabora-
tors on the basis of some of the most significant research which has been done
on the sequencing of instructional content. This research is summarized by
Wilbur Schramm as follows:

> Subordinate learning sets for a given class of tasks are defined as the
> answer to the question, If he were given instructions only, what would
> the individual have to know how to do in order to be able to perform
> this (new) task? Beginning with the final task, the question is applied
> successively to each subordinate learning set, and thus it is possible to
> identify a hierarchy of learning sets which grow increasingly simple and
> general the further they are from the final task. Gagne has tested this
> kind of analysis with encouraging success. It seems to provide a learning-
> based "logic" for designing programs, and also to make it possible for
> any student to begin "where he is," because his *mastery of any level of
> learning set can quickly be tested.*[2]

---

[1] Joseph M. Madden, "Determining Training Needs," in Gabriel D. Ofiesh and Wesley C.
Meierhenry (editors), *Trends in Programed Instruction,* National Education Association,
Washington, D. C., 1964, p. 124.

[2] Wilbur Schramm, *The Research on Programed Instruction,* U.S. Department of Health,
Education, and Welfare, Office of Education, OE-34034, Bulletin 1964, No. 35, p. 6. (Italics
supplied.)

Finally, the strategy is developed for each subordinate learning set to insure that students or trainees learn the required material. These strategies must take into consideration the nature of the learning environment, whether it is a classroom, laboratory, or on-the-job work station. Where a work environment is called for, the learning aids will also take on the characteristics of performance aids.

WHO WILL DO IT?

Several major functions can be identified in the preparation and development of a PIBTS: (1) task analysis, (2) criterion test developments, (3) instructional analysis and strategy, (4) media strategy, (5) frame or item preparation, (6) editing, (7) testing materials, (8) revising materials, (9) field testing, (10) revising, and (11) packaging. For very short modular courses or programs all or most of these functions can often be performed by one or two individuals. For long, complex training programs which need elaborate instructional systems, management must decide who should develop the PIBTS. The management of both small and large companies must ask whether any part or all of the PIBTS should be contracted to an outside agency or be given to an in-house developmental team. To what extent should management develop an in-house capability consisting of its own instructional programers, editors, illustrators, media specialists, and others? These questions require careful study and analysis. If an in-house capability for the preparation of the PIBTS is decided on, management must carefully consider which functions should be performed in-house or contracted for and which should be combined into functions performed by single individuals.

The Air Training Command, probably the largest training establishment in the world, has found it necessary to do all of these things itself. After having trained more than 300 instructional programers for the U.S. Air Force in contract schools, the Air Training Command had only a little more than 100 programers within its own organization. To use this limited but highly trained talent as efficiently as possible, it decided to have the programers develop comprehensive self-instructional training systems—lengthy courses rather than simple programed texts for a few hours of instruction. Consequently, it organized its program writers into instructional systems development teams of 10 to 20 people each. These teams, referred to as instructional systems development teams (ISDT), are headed by team chiefs reporting to the director of the Instructional Systems Division (ISD), who has a small staff to supervise the development of the training systems. A typical team organization is shown on the next page.

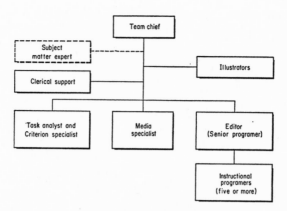

This organizational chart shows which functions are combined and which are separately performed by individuals in the preparation of PIBTS. The team chief is responsible for synthesizing and putting all materials into the training program. He is responsible directly to the chief of ISD. He is also responsible for insuring that subject matter experts are available for team members so that the content of the course may be translated through instructional technology into the most effective and efficient PIBTS. This is often necessary since under the team concept individual members are seldom experts or even familiar with the subject of the content of the course prior to the preparation of the PIBTS. The team chief is the person responsible and ultimately accountable for the development of the PIBTS. He may or may not have participated in the development of specifications for the system (criterion tests). In any case, however, he is responsible for meeting the specifications. It is obviously desirable that the team chief be a participant in the development of the feasibility study so that continuity from its development through the strategy study will be assured.

Since the criterion test is directly derived from the elements of the task analysis, it is often desirable to combine these functions and have them performed by a single individual, thus insuring continuity since the task analysis is developed directly from the job environment.

These "model" teams, stationed at eight technical training centers and training bases, are preparing comprehensive programed instruction systems for lengthy courses which have large numbers of students. Each team has assigned to it a subject matter expert in a temporary duty status to assist in maintaining technical accuracy.

The important point is that the team contains individuals who can perform specific functions. *What* functions the team can perform is more important than *who* performs them. There can be many answers to the question of who in a team will perform a specific function. Emphasis should be placed, however, on assigning the function to the member of the team who can best perform it. In some teams task analysis and criterion test development may be the work of one individual. In another team they may be assigned to two different individuals. Various patterns of team structure are possible. As yet no ideal team model has been developed, though the one discussed here works quite well.

Whether an industrial organization should develop its own team is a question that has to do largely with the amount of in-house training it has and whether the need for the team will be a continuing one.

However, even when a company does not acquire its own in-house programing staff, someone in the company must be knowledgeable and sophisticated in the state of the art of programed instruction technology so that liaison with contracting services can work to the company's advantage. Such an expert should have a firm grasp of principles, should keep abreast of developments, and should be capable of making a proper feasibility study and of advising management on the "sign off" of a criterion-referenced set of specifications.

If the company decides that it is not practical to maintain its own in-house team or teams, and if it decides instead to contract with an outside agency for the development of its training system, it should make certain that the outside agency has the capabilities of the model team illustrated earlier.

In some cases the team's criterion specialist or task analyst may initially prepare the behavioral analysis and criterion examination and may participate in the original design, gather and analyze data on the entering student, and determine the performance deficiencies which the system will be designed to solve. The criterion specialist may also at a later stage create diagnostic instruments to evaluate trainee progress and designate the point at which trainees may go from one part of the system to another. The task analyst assists the team chief in determining the ideal sequence of material. In analyzing student responses he provides guidance to frame writers and instructional programers on the form that subsequent frames should take. He works closely with the media specialist to design test items in nonverbal format. He assists in writing "criterion frames" which will indicate when a student has mastered a specific element in the instructional sequence or a particular part of the total sequence.

There is no question that the writing of diagnostic and evaluation items for programed instruction technology is becoming a highly specialized field and that training in such writing is valuable to the team manager. The criterion test specialist has to work closely with the editor, the media specialist, and, above all, the subject matter expert who represents mastery behavior. The criterion specialist must not be wedded to the traditional practice of aptitude and achievement test construction. He must be receptive to developments in performance testing procedures.

EDITING THE SYSTEM

After analyzing the information given him by the team chief and the criterion specialist, the editor or senior programer determines the sequence and strategy for the overall system. His primary source of data is the training task analysis, which should provide details of the knowledge, skills, values, and attitudes applicable to a given job, task, or training standard represented by the criterion test items. This includes descriptions of performance necessary for mastery; it does not include behavior which is not directly observable. Behavior which is inferred—for example, attitudes and motivational patterns—must be related to and based upon behavior which is directly observable.

The editor analyzes the entry level of the students and suggests the sequences his writers should follow in preparing the materials. And, in consultation with the criterion specialist, he produces a description of observations and measurements that are to be made of subterminal and terminal behaviors —perhaps in the form of instructions to the trainee to draw, solve a problem, write, manipulate, define, test, select, or differentiate.

STRATEGY

Once we know the mastery and terminal behavior and can define the characteristics of entry behavior, we can start thinking and talking about the experiences which will probably take the students or trainees efficiently to the level of mastery performance. The strategy now is to outline, in rather broad terms, the nature of the experiences we are going to structure and the kind of information (input) we are going to provide which will guide the students on the road to mastery. The editor should work closely with the media specialist and the subject matter expert to design the content of the instructional materials to fill the gap in performance deficiency. The sequence of information, the stimuli, and the nature of the stimuli are discussed and analyzed. We are now involved in what can be called "instructional analysis," whose basic question is, "How is the student going to reach the interim goals on the way to attaining the final objective of criterion-level performance?"

Another strategy decision is that of matching the content and sequence of materials with the most appropriate media, such as programed texts, kinescopes, live classroom demonstrations, film strips, audio tapes, and single concept films. Although much basic experimentation and empirical study are needed to validate our present best guesses, the media specialist should possess the latest knowledge that is available so that he can give the best advice.

TACTICS AND FRAME SIZE

After the criterion tests are developed, diagnostic items written, entry level and pretests prepared, appropriate media tentatively selected, sequencing *tentatively* determined, and an assessment made of the techniques that will be used in developing the frames, the team can begin producing the elements of the system. In tactics we consider not only frame construction but also the type of stimulus configurations which we are going to present to the student. We consider not only "small" steps but even "large" steps. The use of the word "small" in this context has in fact been an unfortunate one. We really don't mean small steps, although there was a time when some early disciples of programing would not accept a frame that totaled more than 25 words. The motto for programed instruction has been and remains even today, "One step at a time"—that is, one *optimal* step at a time. The optimal step, however, may differ for each level and each student.

No one has emphasized this point as well and forcefully as Susan Markle. In *Good Frames and Bad,* one of the most definitive programs written for programers themselves and for other instructional technology practitioners, she defines a frame (or item) as follows:

> A segment of material which the student handles at one time. An item may vary in size from a single incomplete sentence, question, or instruction to perform some response, *up to a sizable paragraph.* In almost all programing methods, it will require at least one response and will provide for knowledge of results before the student proceeds to the next item.[3]

Schramm has pointed out that "size of step has never been quite satisfactorily defined." He explains:

_____
[3] Susan Meyer Markle, *Good Frames and Bad (A Grammar of Frame Writing),* John Wiley & Sons, Inc., New York, 1964, p. 247. (Italics supplied.)

In some cases it has been expressed as the reciprocal of the number of steps used to cover a given body of material, but a program with fewer steps does not necessarily require longer leaps; it may merely have less practice or fewer examples.[4]

He refers to one series of efforts to measure step size by using training films. The experimenters varied the length of films presented to the student before they permitted him to respond. "They found that more learning came from gradually *increasing* the step size than from maintaining either very short or very long steps."

It should also be emphasized that the frame is not restricted to verbal content. It may consist of an illustration, a series of animations, a demonstration, or even a five-minute single-concept film! The size of a frame is determined largely by the point again emphasized by Markle when she states:

An *active response* to the total frame is obtained from a student when he is required to process *all* the information in a frame in order to respond. That which he does not have to use he may not notice and also may not learn.[5]

In other words, size is not so important a factor as efficiency.

The process of actually preparing frames represents the *steps* by which trainees have their performance "shaped" for each teaching point. Some, like L. C. Silvern, prefer the term "step," others say "item," but most programers use the term "frame," which is derived from the 35mm. frames of film on which initial programs were prepared for teaching machines.

One of the major points at which PIBTS differs from conventional lesson planning and writing of conventional training literature is the attempted use of the scientific method at the frame or step level in developing instructional content for trainees. The attempt to apply the scientific method is made as follows. (1) The programer assumes that if specific stimulus configurations are presented to the student in the form of frames, then a specific response will be elicited from him. This assumption is hypothesis at this point. (2) The specific stimulus content is then designed and prepared in a "high fidelity" simulation of a method that will be presented in the final PIBTS. (3) These stimulus materials (now frames) are presented to the trainee or student. (4) He responds. (5) An analysis is made of his response. If the response is incorrect, then the stimulus materials are revised until

---

[4] Schramm, *op. cit.*, p. 7.
[5] Markle, *op. cit.*, p. 6.

eventually the proper one, which actually elicits the desired response, has been empirically developed.

The illustrator must work very closely with the frame writer and the media specialist in designing the stimulus configuration of the frame. Illustrations should come first—not words. Rather than believing that if you can't say it in words, you should say it in pictures, the programer should believe that if you can't say it in pictures, then you should say it in words. Only after the illustrations are prepared should the printed words be chosen to supplement the illustrations, and not vice versa.

Many programs that try to reach all students, including the lowest level, have made their steps very small, which has proved dull and boring for those who could take their information in larger doses. Eventually, computer-based systems will be able to analyze a student's responses and determine the best sequence and the optimal size and quality of information he can handle.

Traditionally, frame writing has been the most difficult and painstaking part of programing. Rarely has it followed all the steps suggested in our model; yet if these steps were taken, this aspect of programing would not be so difficult as it has been in the past. To many people, including highly capable programers, programed instruction *is* frame writing; they consider it the be-all and end-all of programed instruction. To many others—and their number is increasing—it is only one significant stage in the tactics of developing a program. It is becoming evident that if proper criterion frames have been written and if the system has been carefully designed, frame writing can certainly proceed much more rapidly and efficiently and need not be as time consuming and costly a procedure as it has been in the past.

Frame writing is an art—just like such other presentation techniques as film making. The writer must determine the optimum amount of information to put in each frame. He must analyze and determine the type of response that must be elicited from the student. He must work closely with the illustrator and with the media specialist to put the stimuli in the most effective, attractive, and efficient form.

Originally, the use of various media in strategy decisions is approached from a logistic and economic point of view. Media are looked upon as hardware, and cost factors weigh heavily, as do maintenance factors. Now, following this strategy decision with respect to hardware, tactical considerations are given to media content. In consultation with the media specialist, the editor and his writers—or tacticians—should ask, "At what point in the sequence should audio stimuli be used? At what point should still illustrations be introduced? How realistic should the illustrations be? When should animation be used? Under what circumstances will animation be more effective than still pictures or words? When is a combination of media more important? How should a student respond to a particular segment or sequence?"

TESTING THE SYSTEM

An ideal system possesses maximum flexibility in the way that a hypothetical perfect tutor would be flexible. The system is capable of presenting material to the student in several media and it allows the student to respond in several ways. A system should use a variety of media and response modes so that the interaction of media and mode will produce the desired performance most effectively and efficiently. To do this requires that every element of the system be thoroughly tested.

Elements of the system are given limited tryouts to determine their general, content, and media effectiveness. Finally, a prototype package is presented in the desired order. Concurrently, the technical expert provides continuing technical review of the materials and ascertains the tolerance requirements and technical accuracy of the equipment. The technical review considers not what subject matter should be taught or how it is to be taught but rather how accurate and how clearly presented the material is.

Although it is not necessary for the program writer to be a subject matter or job expert, someone who knows the subject or job should review all copy to insure its technical accuracy. Therefore, if the team writing a particular program has no technical expert, one *must* be temporarily assigned. The subject matter expert not only provides detailed information about content and technical accuracy, he may also assist in identifying the initial capabilities and skills of the target population.

A word of caution is in order. The subject matter expert *may* know the characteristics of the student population, but it is equally likely that he does not. An expert in mathematics, physics, or bookkeeping may know little or nothing about seventh-graders, adults who have a seventh-grade education, General Motors' trainees, or Army privates!

Irrespective of their source, the team has to collect and assemble data on basic motivation, reading levels, speed of learning, aptitudes, reward systems, perseverance, and skill level of potential trainees. In some cases entry level tests are used to gather data, identify the target population as homogeneous or heterogeneous, and determine the span of individual differences —if this has not already been accomplished in the design.

The one need common to all PIBT systems is for constant testing and verification. Yet the usual practice is to do too little testing of the system. One difficulty is finding students who are representative of the target population. But if they are available, then even small parts of a program can be tested as they are written to assure that the material is suitable. In fact, one of the great values of programed instruction—and this has been empirically demonstrated—is that the whole program or small portions of it may be tested initially with only one or two students and finally validated on only 10 or 12 students. This limited number of testees has been successful when the student sample has been carefully selected. But the main danger in not testing the program frequently with representatives of the target population lies in the tendency for the teacher who has been trained in conventional teaching methods, and even for programers, to get further and further away from the students' world. An ideal program, in essence, is written by the student. Student feedback is invaluable, and programers must listen to students carefully if they are to develop a successful program. It is therefore important to get all material to the students as soon as possible. Actually, this practice is useful only to the extent to which the frame design is adequate. If it is inadequate, the programers may not find what they are seeking to learn during these preliminary steps. *The students' performance is the best clue to how effective a program is.*

The individual student tryout, which is the first "test flight" of the multimedia package, should stress the communicative aspects of the draft. Until the package communicates and elicits the required responses, this tryout should be given only to single students. Feedback from tests helps identify segments or units of the package that do not produce the desired behavior changes, and the package should be revised accordingly.

Following this series of revisions, the materials are presented to small groups of about 10 trainees and refined still further until 95 per cent of them reach a proficiency level of 95 per cent on the criterion test. At least 95 per cent proficiency must be attained in a small group tryout if the aim is to produce a program which will be validated at the 90/90 level in the field, since a loss of 5 per cent can be expected in going from individuals and small groups to a group tryout and field test of the system.

GROUP TRYOUT

When the program has been tried on several individuals and small groups and successively revised till it reaches a high level of performance, it is then ready for a group tryout. Even though these early tryouts are economical and useful in the initial stages, some contamination does creep into the results. When the programing team administers the program, a motivational influence is placed on the tryout students which does not exist in the field. The students are aware, for example, that their efforts are being carefully observed. Further, the atmosphere differs radically in a tryout situation and when a student is working with a program by himself or in a normal training situation.

These pressures create an environment in which the student does do his best. However, most programs are administered to groups of individuals when no programer is present. It is therefore necessary to determine how well the program functions independently of its author and to find out how group administration contaminates the results. The purpose, then, of a large group tryout is to determine the nature of the administrative problems that can be corrected by revising the program.

The designer of the training system must carefully study the conditions under which the program might best be used and make allowance in the design for those environmental conditions that would be ideal for the administration of the system. A manual detailing these conditions for the administrator of the program—whether training director, teacher, or supervisor—will help immeasurably and should be considered a significant part of the system. Administrative procedures for managing the PIBTS themselves constitute a subsystem in the design of a complete system. Supervisors who do their own on-the-job training will welcome a modular self-instructional subsystem that trains them in the proper procedures of administering the PIBTS, especially if the procedures are complicated and involved and if proper administration is essential for their successful utilization.

FIELD TEST

Once the large group tryout is completed and the system has been revised accordingly, the materials receive their most important and thorough evaluation. The package is tested in the field where it is expected to fly solo. Whether it flies successfully depends to a great extent on its engineering and development and on the accuracy with which contaminative factors were anticipated and corrected beforehand. If feedback from the operational field test indicates a need for extensive revision, it can probably be attributed to poor design and faulty developmental testing. The most extensive revision that should be expected following the field test is in the instructor's or supervisor's administrative manual or guide. Anything else can become quite costly.

Finally, the system is ready to be packaged. All written materials are in camera-ready manuscript. Where necessary, lesson plans are refined to force the live instructor to "program" his delivery. Requests are submitted for the mass production of subsystems such as kinescopes, audio tapes, laboratory equipment, simulators, 35mm. slides, single-concept films, sound slide audio-visual devices, and other items of hardware. Included finally in the package are all the presentation devices, along with a detailed instructor's or supervisor's handbook or training system designed to assist him in managing the materials.

Although the package seems complete, one detail remains. Provision must be made for continuing feedback so that the system can be refined if it is economically feasible to do so. As the system is used in the regular classroom or training environment, its adequacy can be determined from the user's point of view. The system designers can make changes and modifications. Further, provisions should be made for system modification in the field as changes in technology make subsystems obsolete.

It probably is apparent by now that there is no clear line of demarcation between the activities described in this chapter and those described in the preceding two. Almost half the effort described in this chapter is necessary —in one form or another—in order to determine the nature of the training problem and to make a feasibility study.

Firm guidance and direction will be available only when complete and valid PIBTS have been developed and when the models available are much more common than they are today. Until that time when we will be able to learn from many experiences, the fullest application of the scientific methods of systems engineering to the development of learning systems will remain something that looks good only on paper.

Chapter 9

Acquiring Programs

As we have already indicated, and as a review of the cases in Part II of this book will further support, industry to date has not adopted a unified comprehensive approach to the design and development of a complete programed instruction based training system which will solve a company's entire training problem. Until it does, programed instruction technology in industrial training will continue to be localized in the company which is trying to evolve a system. In consequence, many of the problems remain of concern to management and should be highlighted.

Liberty Mutual Insurance Company, for example, has the following perspective on the potential of programed instruction: The training population is widely dispersed—its 12,000 employees are scattered throughout 10 divisions and 160 branches. Geographical considerations have made training very expensive; further, a lack of uniformity has been noted both in subject matter and in the quality of instruction. Liberty Mutual considers programed instruction a solution because it provides uniformity of training and simultaneously reduces live-instructor requirements, thereby reducing costs by making possible more efficient use of instructor time.

This company uses programs prepared in-house principally for technical and company-oriented training and performance and off-the-shelf programs for noninsurance subjects. The programed materials are administered by the training staffs of various departments. The materials are prepared or selected directly by, or under the close supervision of, professional training people in accordance with plans formulated by a committee of training directors in the several operating departments. This company has not applied programed instruction extensively to the problems of customer education. The Loss Prevention Department, however, is making a pilot study of a safe driving program designed to teach drivers of large sales fleets.

The company has evolved a philosophy with respect to programing. "Concept programs" are considered as professional education while "task programs" are considered as training. Examples of concept programs used for professional education are Package Auto Coverage, Workmen's Compensation Experience Rating, and Loss Prevention Evaluation of Stairways. The training programs are basically clerical. Even though the general feeling is that tasks are easier to program than concepts, the company plans in the future to emphasize concept programs. Task procedures have at times changed overnight, thus affording the programer no opportunity to revise existing programs in advance of need. But concepts are less subject to sudden and radical change. Changes evolve slowly and infrequently, and when they do occur, the programer has plenty of advance notice. As a result updating should be rare and possible without pressure, and concept programs should be less expensive to maintain than task programs.

In the future this company will use programed instruction only for those phases of a job for which it is the most economical and best method. It plans to mix programed instruction with other training tools as seems desirable.

This "nonsystems" approach to training falls far short of the recommended specific and detailed feasibility and strategy studies and the design and development of complete PIBTS, even though the effort is considerably more comprehensive and systematic than is usually the case. It should be recognized that Liberty Mutual's concern and effort are typical of the best that is being done by single companies. A more complete case history is given in Part II.

OFF-THE-SHELF PROGRAMS

A company that decides to use programed instruction in training can do its own programing, embark on a joint venture with programing companies and consultants, contract for complete outside development of programs tailored to its needs, purchase already prepared off-the-shelf programs, or utilize a combination of these possibilities. Often the most suitable arrangement is not easily discerned. For an exclusive in-house effort, personnel in the company must be taught necessary elaborate and complex skills. And if, after being trained, they demonstrate exceptional talent, they may leave the company and go to work elsewhere at a more attractive salary.

There are many other considerations. By training its own personnel, a company can bring together in just a few people both subject matter expertise and programing capability. On the other hand it should be pointed out that training in-house programers is extremely difficult and often unsuccessful. A company should not expect to acquire very many programers in this manner. By purchasing off-the-shelf material programed for specific tasks and subject matter areas, the company can avoid the expense of developing its own program. Member banks of the American Bankers Association, for example, can purchase a validated seven-hour program on "Checks" that covers an Introduction to Checks, Parts of a Check, Endorsements, and Routing a Check Through the Banking System. The first copy of the program is costed out at $3, the second copy at $1.50, and subsequent copies at $.60 per student hour. The bank which buys this off-the-shelf program does not have to worry about developmental costs.

The Aerojet-General Corporation uses off-the-shelf materials extensively. Last year more than 12,000 hours of off-the-shelf programs cost less than $.50 per hour of instruction per trainee. In contrast, the cost of programs custom-prepared by outside programing companies has been variously estimated at $500 to $5,000 per training hour. In this light, the use of off-the-shelf materials appears attractive—sometimes deceptively so. Robert O. Brink points out that the telephone industry shares with other industries a common need for many skills—typing, filing, keypunch operation, and the like. However:

> The practices and procedures required in central office equipment maintenance, telephone operating, or preparation of customer service records are peculiarly our own. A minimum of the commercially available programs on the market meets our needs. The large bulk of published programs is on academic subject matter. While these provide a rich source of material for upgrading telephone employees in such areas as mathematics, electricity, and electronic theory, they do not provide the specific subject matter which is the backbone of our day-to-day training.[1]

EVALUATING OFF-THE-SHELF PROGRAMS

Though an off-the-shelf program is effective and inexpensive, it may contribute nothing to a trainee's performance on the job. Some companies will purchase such programs and make them available to their employees as a fringe benefit, although this does not help management to solve its training problem. Therefore, a company that relies heavily on off-the-shelf materials must be able to evaluate them critically for their potential value. *This is perhaps the most valuable role that a small in-house programing staff can perform.*

Though no adequate technique for evaluating programs by frames or in-

---

[1] Robert O. Brink, "Problems in Developing a Programming Capability," *NSPI Journal*, October 1963, p. 12.

ternal factors has yet been developed, a number of checklists or series of criteria have been composed for evaluating programed materials.[2] None of the checklists is adequate for all of management's needs. Nevertheless certain questions on these lists are fundamental and should be raised when consideration is being given to a large-scale adoption of off-the-shelf programs. These questions are applicable to the evaluation of custom-prepared and in-house programs as well.

Often programs contain some statement or list of objectives. The first question concerns these objectives and the form in which they are provided. The statement or list of objectives is far too often inadequate. But whether inadequate or precise and explicit, the publisher should be asked for the criterion-referenced examination, which should comprehensively represent *all* the objectives. *This is the clearest way for the publisher to provide the customer with an understanding of what the program purports to teach.* By carefully reviewing this type of examination, management can determine the performance that is supposed to be produced with certain types of trainees. If this information is unavailable or if the examination is a poor one—as most of them are—then management must design its own criterion examination and test the program against its objectives to determine the program's adequacy. In some rare cases this has been done successfully.

In selecting off-the-shelf materials management must determine the extent to which a program is suitable for its own trainees and whether it has been validated on a similar test group. Only a few published programs today provide an entry level test or clearly stated prerequisites that enable management to determine whether its trainees have the necessary qualifications to handle the program. The number of programs that are including this test, however, is increasing.

If a program has objectives similar to the company's and has been tested on students who are representative of the skills and accomplishments of these trainees, the next consideration is the teaching effectiveness of the program. What were the pre- and post-test gains? What was the average performance of 90 per cent of the students? To what extent was the program validated against an acceptable standardized examination?

---

[2] See "Checklist for Selecting Programs," *NSPI Journal*, July 1963, p. 4; "Programed Learning," Department of the Air Force Manual 50-1, July 30, 1964, pp. 6-1, 6-2; "Criteria for Assessing Programed Instructional Materials," *Audiovisual Instruction*, National Education Association, February 1963. A joint committee on programed instruction and teaching machines of the American Educational Research Association, the American Psychological Association, and the National Education Association's Department of Audiovisual Instruction has also inquired into the evaluation of programs.

The questions below comprise the National Society for Programmed Instruction checklist for selecting programs. It contains five general questions plus subquestions that management should try to answer before selecting an off-the-shelf program. Not all of these may be relevant to a given program. Management may wish others to be added to this list:

1. Does the programed course fit some part(s) of your curriculum or training plan?

    a. Does the publisher provide a clear statement, in measurable terms, of what the program teaches?
    b. Will the program require a change from the methods used in your teaching; for example, classical versus audio-lingual instruction in foreign languages, phonics versus whole word method in reading?
    c. Will the program content fit into your current curriculum or add to it in a way that justifies any necessary changes?
    d. Can your students finish the program in the time you have allowed for the subject matter?

2. Is the programed course designed for the students or trainees in your course?

    a. Are the skill and knowledge prerequisites for entry into the program clearly stated?
    b. Is there a test provided to tell you whether students meet the prerequisites?
    c. Do your students meet them?
    d. Does successful use of the program depend on any unusual requirements such as manual dexterity, visual acuity, mathematical aptitude, native fluency to English, etc.?
    e. Is there a provision for a well-prepared student to enter the program at some place other than the beginning?

3. Are the purchase, use, and maintenance of the programed course within the economic means of your school or training program?

    a. Is the total cost for materials, equipment, and upkeep within your means?
    b. Can the materials be used more than once to reduce the cost per student?
    c. If a machine or any other hardware is necessary, is it within your means?
    d. If hardware is necessary, are there any other programs you plan to use available for it?
    e. Can you make arrangements for the maintenance of the machine?

4. How effectively does the program teach?

   a. Do you know how other students, similar to yours, scored on a current standardized test of your objectives after using the program?
   b. Does the company provide a satisfactory achievement test for the program, and do you know how students similar to yours score on it?
   c. Do published post-test scores represent a satisfactory gain from a pretest?
   d. Do you know how and where program testing was carried out?
   e. Were the conditions for the program testing similar enough to your teaching situation to allow you to make a generalization?
   f. Is the material learned from the program retained long enough to be a base for further teaching?

5. Miscellaneous questions.

   a. If the program has been available for some time, can you visit a class in your area and see it being used, or correspond with an experienced user?
   b. Does the publisher provide a teacher's manual containing suggestions for enrichment activities to follow the program?
   c. Does the publisher provide a set of progress tests with suggestions for remedial teaching? [3]

There are other considerations in evaluating an off-the-shelf program. What is the average time required to complete it? To what extent does it need the administrative guidance of an instructor? How readily can it be upgraded? Is it accompanied by an administrative guide manual for the program director or supervisor? Is there any way to determine how well the material has been retained? To what extent does it need to be supplemented by other exercises and instructions? Can it be used by several students? The answers to all these questions will help management to evaluate critically the adequacy of programed materials that are not custom-tailored to a specific training need and are not produced by an in-house effort.

These questions are much more pertinent and useful than are questions about whether the program uses linear, intrinsic, mathetic, or other programing techniques; whether the reading or readability index is appropriate; whether the program is overcued or uses too much prompting; whether the trainee is required to make overt or covert responses; the frequency of responses and the extent of repetition and confirmation; and how frequently reviews are provided. These internal factors have little direct bearing on

---

[3] *NSPI Journal*, July 1963, p. 4.

management's problems. The main concern should be not literary or "programing" quality but how well a program produces the required performance. This should not preclude management from experiencing some concern with the motivational quality of the program. Even when it does produce the desired performance, management may still feel that it falls short of intrinsically motivating trainees to go through it. Editorial review of the program and careful refinement of it to make it appealing to trainees may be a legitimate endeavor. This concern with motivational quality, however, should not be allowed to contaminate the instructional features of the program.

There seems to be little relationship between the ability to inspect a program by its content and to predict its instructional effectiveness by simply looking at it. In one study Ernst Rothkopf, after determining the actual effectiveness of seven different programs which were designed to teach relationships between pairs of nouns in fictional anthropological subject matter, gave the materials to 12 high school teachers and principals and found that there was in fact a negative correlation between the actual effectiveness of the program and the ability of the educators to predict its effectiveness by inspecting it. The correlation was —.75.[4] The educators, by the way, were trained in programing.

HELP FOR SMALL COMPANIES

Because of the high cost of in-house and contract programing, various associations and trade organizations such as The American Bankers Association construct programs to meet the common training needs of their members. These organizations can not only develop custom-designed, functionally reliable programs for small companies with a common product and purpose but can also provide the technical assistance which will enable them to conduct feasibility and strategy studies, and, further, can assist them in upgrading off-the-shelf materials which fall short of specific needs.

Other trade associations are acting as clearinghouses for information about titles and general content of programs which may be available in certain functional areas. J. R. Murphy and I. Goldberg have compiled a list of typical functions for which off-the-shelf courses are available:

---

[4] Wilbur Schramm, *The Research on Programmed Instruction: An Annotated Bibliography*, U.S. Department of Health, Education, and Welfare, Office of Education Bulletin OE34034, 1964, No. 35, pp. 91 to 92.

Plant Maintenance and Operation
   Reading engineering drawings
   Sheet-metal layout
   Positive displacement pumps
   Pressure and its measurement
   Measurement for construction skills
   Pipefitting
   Shop mathematics

Sales Techniques and Product Knowledge
   Effective listening (an audio-lingual course)
   Needs—benefits selling
   Probing, shaping, and persuasion
   Interviewing skills

Data Processing and Systems Management
   COBOL (computer terms and concepts)
   Binary arithmetic
   PERT
   Inventory control
   Introduction to transistors
   Computer fundamentals
   Matrix analysis

Financial Analysis
   Reading and evaluation of financial reports
   Introductory bookkeeping and accounting
   Securities exchange and brokerage houses
   Business mathematics
   Introduction to securities trading methods
   The over-the-counter market
   Reading stock quotations [5]

When an executive reviews published information about available off-the-shelf programs, he may find that a program falls short of his standards in certain respects. He may decide, however, that it is economically feasible to buy it and turn it over to his in-house staff for refinement and upgrading. Under these circumstances the company should first test the program with a sample of its own potential trainee group to determine empirically where and how the program should be upgraded. Or the program can be tested by using it in a conventional classroom to augment conventional instructional procedures. The instructor can then provide guidance on refining the program since he will be using it as a guide and as an aid in his own teaching.

---

[5] J. R. Murphy and I. Goldberg, "Strategies for Using Programed Instruction," *Harvard Business Review,* May–June 1964, p. 118.

USING CONSULTANTS

No company, large or small, should settle for exclusive dependence on off-the-shelf materials. If management is firmly committed to fully exploiting instructional programing as a training technology, then it should seriously consider developing a limited in-house capability at a minimum and establishing some liaison with programing companies. In dealing with a programing company someone has to talk with its people in language they will understand and at the same time state the company's requirements fully and clearly.

In-house expertise may, in companies with a limited programed instruction effort, be possessed by only one or two people. These experts may do little if any programing; they may devote the major portion of their efforts to feasibility and cost studies and to developing program specifications or to upgrading off-the-shelf and custom-designed programs. If this is the case, consultants may be hired to assist as subject matter experts. This arrangement has several advantages. Since consultants are employed only when they are needed, the high cost of professional overhead is reduced drastically. Consultants can help find programing companies that specialize in certain areas and strategies, or they can do a feasibility or strategy study. A company may choose to form a consulting relationship with a programing firm to develop a program jointly with its own limited in-house effort. If this is done, company personnel will receive a form of on-the-job training while they work with the programing company.

Some programing firms work closely in a consulting relationship to assist an in-house staff in refining their programs and raising their level of effectiveness. Teaching Machines Incorporated, for example, has outlined just such a procedure. It asks the company doing its own programing to send it the following:

1. A list of behavioral objectives and/or a pre- and post-test for each unit of your program.
2. A specification of characteristics of your proposed target audience (for example, age, educational background, entering behavior, intelligence, and so forth).
3. A rough draft of your program.

The company is then offered a fixed-price proposal for performing the following services:

1. Your program will receive thorough *copy editing* to remove typo-

graphical and grammatical errors and technical inconsistencies (incorrect answers, misnumbered frames, and so on).

2. Your program will then be retyped, if necessary, in any format which you specify.

3. Your program will then be tested on six students who are representative of the target audience with the characteristics you have specified. Pre- and post-test scores, time, and *attitude* will be measured. (Retention measures can be gathered at your option.)

4. Your program will then receive thorough, frame-by-frame *behavioral editing* by a senior TMI staff member. The detailed results of this editing, with suggestions for improvement, will be provided to you....

5. Finally, you will be provided a *production plan* for your program. In this plan you will receive specific suggestions for:
   a. Format.
   b. Art requirements (and how to save money on art work).
   c. Scheduling further testing and revision (if necessary).
   d. Selection of a realistic completion date.
   e. Reproduction options....
   f. Methods of increasing the *publishability* of your program.
   g. Methods of increasing the *marketability* of your program.[6]

This kind of arrangement with a firm that has a proved and demonstrated capability allows some companies to have their cake and eat it. With a limited in-house effort, they can form a constructive working team of instructional programers, editors, and writers who can bring all their skills to developing a more valid system than would have been possible were the outside agency to supply the complete package. This arrangement also avoids one of the significant limitations in contracting for the complete job: When the program is completed by an outside agency, eventually the company usually has to return to the same agency for any updating or revisions. In addition, the limited in-house staff receives simultaneous training while the program is being developed. Such training will enable the staff to revise the program when this becomes necessary rather than depend on the outside agency to do this. Thus, the combined effort makes the professional services of a top-level programing company available at minimum cost; and, as the in-house staff acquires experience and sophistication, it can begin cautiously to expand into a self-sufficient and independent group if the company requirements justify an internal capability. A word of caution, however, from

---

[6] James L. Evans, "Dear Programmer," Teaching Machines Incorporated, Albuquerque, New Mexico, May 1964.

a company which pioneered programed instruction through its own in-house efforts:

> It should be recognized that it is very costly to develop a good programed instruction course. Therefore, the first consideration should be the purchase of available commercial courses to meet the training requirement. In some cases, the training requirement may necessitate the development of a custom course. Even here, it will likely be economical to have the course developed by one of the competent companies in this field. Only as a last resort should a company consider development of its own programed instruction courses.[7]

------

[7] Address to the National Plant Engineering and Maintenance Conference, Cleveland, Ohio, January 28, 1964.

Chapter 10

Programed Learning for Professional Education: Self-Instruction in Medicine

By Jerome P. Lysaught, Ed.D.

LIKE ENGINEERING, LAW, DENTISTRY, AND ADMINISTRATION, THE profession of medicine is faced with growing problems in curriculum and instruction. Advances in technology and breakthroughs in research have combined to accumulate knowledge at an almost geometric rate. The medical college recognizes that more is "known" about man, his afflictions, and their treatments than can possibly be taught in a four-year period. For example, it has been estimated that a first-year medical student must learn some 50,000 to 60,000 new words in his first two semesters of instruction—a larger vocabulary than is required for competency in a foreign language. The direction is clear, however; such complexities will increase both in sheer magnitude and in scope.

The first problem of the medical school (or of any other professional institution), then, is to select out of the vast accumulation of learning those items, fields, and areas that represent the core, or minimum knowledge, that all students must possess. Second, there must be a concerted effort to provide specialized training for those students who wish to follow individual paths beyond the core. In all this, time is at a terrible premium. Teaching must be extremely efficient; learning must be highly effective.

In its operation as a professional school, the medical college is not divorced from societal pressures. There is a recognized need to provide more physicians both by increasing the number of students in each medical class and by enlarging the number of institutions preparing physicians. At the same time, both new and established medical colleges face perennial short-

Jerome P. Lysaught is Assistant Professor of Education and Research Associate in Medical Education at the University of Rochester, Rochester, New York.

ages of faculty members to staff the schools and to instruct the students. The precious time of the instructor must be conserved, under these circumstances, and used to the best possible advantage.

Medical schools have responded to these pressures for change and innovation. It is significant that many of the measures developed to meet professional needs have revolved on the fulcrum of individualized teaching and self-instruction. At Western Reserve, for example, the competing pressures of the need for greater knowledge and the unavailability of greater time have led to the abandonment of the didactic lecture in favor of carefully developed materials and case problems for use by the student in self-education.[1] At Rochester, a new curriculum is designed to permit greater periods of free time plus elective subjects in order to allow the student flexibility in pursuing learnings beyond the core.[2] Many other activities could be cited, but the implications seem to be clear.

In order to accomplish as much as possible in four years, medical schools must waste no time in needless review and reteaching; it must be ascertained, however, that medical students are learning effectively both in the general and in the specialized areas. Because not all areas can be taught in the available time, students must become responsible learners who will continue their education well beyond the walls of the professional institution. To maximize the possibilities of attaining such objectives, the school must look at the individual students in a new light.

Much of the traditional approach to instruction in all professional schools is based on an implicit assumption that the students are homogeneous and that all of them should go through basic experiences in much the same way. Introductory and prerequisite courses are often required of all first-year students. Yet, if we know anything at all of measurement and learning, we know that the students are anything but homogeneous. For example, on most normal curves of intelligence, schooling, achievement, and so forth, medical students place well above the average. The normal curve, however, inherently tells us that the farther we get from the average, the greater the amount of difference between any two points on the curve. While we may want all medical students to know specific, basic facts, we can be certain that some will enter medical school knowing many of the facts already; some will enter knowing few, or even none, of these facts. Some will show a marked ability to learn quickly; others will learn quite effectively but re-

[1] J. R. Ginther, "Cooperative Research in Medical Education: Example from Hematology," *Journal of Medical Education*, September 1963, pp. 718–724.

[2] H. Jason, J. C. Donovan, and C. E. Tobin, "Assessing the Impact of a New Medical Curriculum," *Journal of Medical Education*, September 1964, pp. 880–881 (abstract).

quire far more time. And each of these differences will be of greater magnitude than we would find in an average grade school, for example, simply because our student population is displaced to the upper end of the normal distribution curve. Individual differences will be greater than normal. The resulting possibilities of dealing with these individual differences can make a great advance in solving problems of curriculum and instruction within the professional school.

THEORETICAL CONTRIBUTIONS OF PROGRAMED INSTRUCTION

No other development in self-instruction has caused so universal a reaction, or received so universal an acceptance, as programed instruction. In large part, this results from the fact that programed learning proceeds, like scientific advances in medical knowledge, from the laboratory analysis of behavior. Hypotheses are generated; experimental trials are formulated to test the hypotheses; only those generalizations that survive testing are confirmed. The reinforcement theory of learning and its implications for medical education have been discussed elsewhere.[3] It is not necessary to duplicate this information, but it is essential that we examine the theoretical contributions of the process of programing for professional learning.

Between the learning theory and the completed program there lies an essential process of development of the material. In this process, we attack many of the problems that are at the heart of professional instruction. The accompanying exhibit shows a schematic diagram of the steps to be followed in constructing a learning program. By examining a few of these steps in terms of the medical school, we may be able to cast light on the experimental results which have already been attained.

For example, in selecting a unit for programing, we must grapple with the problem of the core curriculum and with individual differences in specialization. Christensen[4] selected the area of pH and dissociation for programing on the basis that approximately 50 per cent of the first-year students in medical school came to class knowing the general formulations. It was impossible, however, to proceed with the more dynamic aspects of

[3] J. P. Lysaught, "Programmed Instruction: A New Departure in Medical Education," *New Physician*, April 1964, pp. 101–107.

[4] H. N. Christensen, "The Identification of Special Topics for Teaching by Short 'Plug-In' Programs," *Proceedings of the Rochester Conference on Programmed Instruction in Medical Education*, University of Rochester, Rochester, New York, 1964. See also H. N. Christensen, *pH and Dissociation*, W. B. Saunders Co., Philadelphia, Pennsylvania, 1963.

the subject matter until all the students were aware of the basic material. Traditionally, there had been a period of wasted time for the prepared students while others were brought up to a starting level. By selecting this particular unit for programing, the medical schools are able to give students a short programed sequence prior to their arrival on campus. Those who can pass a pretest need not take the program; those who cannot will find the program teaching them fundamental understandings in the area. By the beginning of formal course instruction, all students are prepared to go into the implications of the information without wasting time on the rudiments of the subject.

SCHEMATIC DIAGRAM OF THE AUTO-INSTRUCTIONAL PROGRAMING PROCESS
[Reproduced by permission from Lysaught and Williams, *A Guide to Programmed Instruction*, John Wiley & Sons, Inc., New York, 1963.]

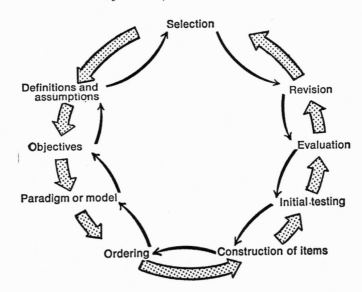

In defining the learners for an instructional program, the medical school can take a forward step in analyzing the utility and implications of the curriculum. Sherman and his associates [5] point out, for instance, that a program on breast cancer was subjected to analysis in terms of the learners, and that one immediate result was the realization that a student who was

---

[5] C. D. Sherman, Jr., J. P. Lysaught, and C. M. Williams, "Problems in Developing Concepts and Goals in Programmed Instruction," *Proceedings of the Rochester Conference on Programmed Instruction in Medical Education*, University of Rochester, Rochester, New York, 1964.

to become a pediatrician would never encounter a case of breast cancer among his patients, while an internist would need to know only certain aspects of diagnosis. In contrast, a surgeon would be required to have detailed knowledge about staging, treatment, and follow-up. While such differentiations are not exposed solely through the programing process, it is vital to the development of effective self-instructional materials that these considerations be taken into account. A good lecturer may possibly consider the individual needs of his students; a good programer cannot fail to do so if he uses the developmental process emerging from the theory.

As a final illustration of the theoretical implications for medical education of self-instructional programing, the development of behavioral objectives aids greatly in focusing instructional efforts and time apportionment. By stating in detailed fashion what it is that the medical student will *do* as a result of instruction to demonstrate that he has learned effectively a given body of knowledge, we not only conserve the energy involved in instruction, but we greatly simplify later testing and evaluation on these points. Wilds [6] has demonstrated that one can teach even a complex skill such as diagnosis when behavioral objectives have been written according to the process required for self-instructional materials. This has the further benefit of affording easy transfer to life situations, since the objectives include the behaviors that are required in actual clinical handling of patients.

RESEARCH ON PROGRAMS IN MEDICAL EDUCATION

It was in 1958, with college students at Harvard, that Skinner and Holland used the first programed instructional unit developed according to the reinforcement theory of learning. This was followed by a succession of experimental programs, many of which were geared for collegiate instruction. The first known attempts to develop medical programs emanated from the Dartmouth Medical School project in self-instruction which began in 1961.

In 1962, Green, Weiss, and Nice [7] published the results of a controlled study of learning in parasitology using a linear program developed at Dartmouth. They found that students using the self-instructional material at-

---

[6] P. L. Wilds, "Programmed Instruction as a Method of Teaching Clinical Problem Solving," *Proceedings of the Rochester Conference on Programmed Instruction in Medical Education,* University of Rochester, Rochester, New York, 1964.

[7] E. J. Green, R. J. Weiss, and P. O. Nice, "Experimental Use of a Programmed Text in a Medical School Course," *Journal of Medical Education,* August 1962, pp. 767–775.

tained significantly higher post-test scores over the course material than did students taught by conventional means, most particularly the lecture method. In addition, the efficiency of learning was greatly increased. More productive students were able to learn the material with less study time than would ordinarily have been expected. Less productive students experienced some time savings, but found their greatest reward in achieving higher on the post-test than would have been predicted. It is important to recognize that each one of these findings—high achievement, high efficiency, more individual freedom—follows the predicted pattern of results derived from learning theory.

To give balance to these results, Moore [8] has reported on later work in pharmacology at Dartmouth. Although he found that achievement is still high and that students do ask for and commend the program, he points out that there are redundancies in the material that could profitably be eliminated, and that no discernible difference could be found among those students who had responded overtly to each item in the program and those who had simply read through a modified version of the material with all blanks filled. While this latter point is one that requires further research, it is perhaps indicative that the programing process can contribute to effective learning primarily through its organization and presentation of material rather than from incidental modes of student response. In other words, it might be true that, given a good program, a student can approach it in a variety of ways and still learn effectively from it.

In another large-scale project in programed instruction, at the College of Medicine of the University of Illinois, the decision was made to explore branching programs in contrast to the linear materials being studied at Dartmouth. Miller [9] has discussed the results of a comparative study at three medical schools using a branching program in body fluid metabolism. Each school divided its students into three subgroups: a conventionally instructed group; one using a programed text; and one using the program in a teaching machine. On a comparison of achievement alone, the programed instruction groups excelled, but not significantly. When the factor of efficiency—as represented by hours of study time—was added to the analysis, however, striking and significant differences appeared in favor of self-

---

[8] K. E. Moore, "Program on the Autonomic Nervous System," *Report of the Department of Pharmacology and Toxicology*, Dartmouth Medical School, Hanover, New Hampshire, 1964. See case report in Part II of this volume.

[9] G. E. Miller, "Report to the Faculty, 1963–64," Office of Research in Medical Education, University of Illinois College of Medicine, Urbana, Illinois, 1964, pp. 77–80. See also case report in Part II of this volume.

instruction. In essence, the program students learned as much, and even a little more, in a much shorter period of time than did their comparison groups.

Again, not all results and reactions were overwhelmingly favorable. Some of the students expressed satisfaction with the conventional means of instruction and preferred them even though the program might provide greater learning efficiency. It is worth noting that this same phenomenon was observed [10] among adult learners who had characteristically been highly successful in using conventional methods for learning. Those whose success was more mixed were most receptive to trying new means for learning. In a later portion of the Illinois project, Bernstein and his associates [11] reported a finding not unlike that of Moore at Dartmouth. They discovered that, once material was programed, it could then be turned into a discursive text and still maintain its teaching effectiveness. Again, this seems to underline the importance of the programing process in the total effectiveness of self-learning; it may also provide substantial help for those who are more comfortable using conventional textbooks. The discursive programed textbook more closely resembles a medical text than does the linear or branching program with its requirement for some overt response at each sequential step. Again, more study is needed to warrant generalizations about the best utilization to be made of such materials.

A third project at the Western Reserve University School of Medicine has reported on the development of self-instructional materials in hematology which are prepared in much the same way as programed sequences, but which are more discursive than the linear or branching program. On the basis of its studies, the Western Reserve group [12] suggests that the students using self-instructional processes learned at least as much as the students taught by lecture and demonstration, and, in addition, assumed much more responsibility for their own achievement. This latter finding substantiates another of the hypotheses that arise out of our theoretical formulation concerning student reaction to a learning program.

In recent months, the spread of experimentation on programed instruc-

---

[10] T. B. Dolmatch, E. Marting, and R. E. Finley (editors), *Revolution in Training: Programed Instruction in Industry*, American Management Association, Inc., New York, 1962, pp. 30–31.

[11] L. M. Bernstein, J. Allender, and G. E. Miller, "Teaching Fundamental Concepts of Renal Physiology Using Programmed Materials," *Proceedings of the Rochester Conference on Programmed Instruction in Medical Education*, University of Rochester, Rochester, New York, 1964.

[12] J. W. Harris, D. L. Horrigan, J. R. Ginther, and T. H. Ham, "Pilot Study in Teaching Hematology with Emphasis on Self-Education by the Students," *Journal of Medical Education*, August 1962, pp. 719–736.

tion in medical education has been phenomenal. By the spring of 1964, one survey [13] disclosed that 17 per cent of the medical schools in the country were using learning programs as an integral part of their curricular structure, while almost 40 per cent of the institutions were actively engaged in research projects designed to learn more of the implications of self-instruction for professional training. These more restricted research projects have been similarly arresting in their argument for the effectiveness of programed teaching. They also shed some light on the limitations of this approach.

At the Tulane University School of Medicine, for example, two experiments were carried out to test the effectiveness of a linear program in radiation protection. Elder and his associates [14] report that the examination of achievement scores by appropriate statistical treatment confirmed that advanced medical students demonstrated comparable learning on the program when contrasted with those taught by means of a lecture. It was further noted, however, that when the program was used with students not possessing all the prerequisites assumed by the programers, the effectiveness of the material was sharply reduced. This, certainly, confirms the theoretical model for the programing process although it argues against the possibility of broad application for all programs throughout the profession.

There is evidence, however, that a medical program can be an effective learning device for certain limited purposes even if there is a wide difference in learner background. Brooke [15] has reported that the Communicable Disease Center program on amebiasis has been quite effective for both physicians and laboratory technicians, with both groups posting median achievement scores of 100 per cent on a post-test. In this case, however, the operational objectives were very closely defined and the subject matter was confined within a definite parameter.

Not all the benefits of programed instruction in medical education are confined to the student learners. Pierce and his associates [16] have discussed the traumatic, but educational, experience of a group of psychologists and

---

[13] J. P. Lysaught, C. D. Sherman, Jr., and C. M. Williams, "Utilization of Programmed Instruction in Medical Education," *Journal of Medical Education,* September 1964, pp. 769–773.

[14] S. T. Elder, G. R. Meckstroth, C. M. Nice, and P. H. Meyers, "Comparison of a Linear Program in Radiation Protection with a Traditional Lecture Presentation," *Journal of Medical Education,* December 1964, pp. 1078–1082.

[15] M. M. Brooke, "Preliminary Evaluation of a Program: Amebiasis—Laboratory Diagnosis," *Proceedings of the Rochester Conference on Programmed Instruction in Medical Education,* University of Rochester, Rochester, New York, 1964.

[16] C. M. Pierce, V. Pishkin, and J. L. Mathis, "Some Problems in Developing a Psychiatric Program," *Proceedings of the Rochester Conference on Programmed Instruction in Medical Education,* University of Rochester, Rochester, New York, 1964.

psychiatrists at the University of Oklahoma Medical Center who embarked on a project to program basic vocabulary for residents in psychiatry. The greatest stumbling block to their attempt—only recognized after many weeks of work—was that there was no consensus among the "experts" involved in the task on the majority of terms used in everyday clinical communication. When the attempt was made to make objectives of instruction and definitions of terms explicit, hidden obscurities of language were exposed. Only then were these professional workers able to deal with the fundamental problem that had hindered more conventional instruction for a long period of time. This is one more finding that suggests the utility of the programing process in improving instruction, even aside from the use of the instructional sequence itself.

Finally, Rondell [17] and others have reported on the efficiency with which the learning program permits the medical instructor to evaluate and revise an instructional sequence on the basis of an objective analysis of learner outcomes. This facilitates the constant improvement of instructional quality and eliminates much of the guesswork attendant on less overt forms of learner response.

ASPECTS OF RELATED RESEARCH

While research findings on experimentation within the professional medical school are remarkably positive, there are also activities within the related disciplines and paramedical fields that have great implications for the future of medical education.

For example, one demand on the practicing physician is that he educate his patient in diseases, their care and their treatment. This can often be both time-consuming and relatively ineffective. Nickerson [18] has reported a beginning study on the use of a self-instructional program for diabetic patients with a wide range of intellectual and social backgrounds. While much of the work was of a preliminary nature and the program is to be revised in the light of the experience, most of the patients did learn from the program, and all of them recommended it for other patients suffering from the malady. In an unreported study at the University of Rochester,

---

[17] P. A. Rondell, "A Program on 'Diffusion and Osmosis'—an Evaluation," *Proceedings of the Rochester Conference on Programmed Instruction in Medical Education,* University of Rochester, Rochester, New York, 1964.

[18] H. H. Nickerson, "A Teaching Machine for Diabetic Patients: A Study Report," *The Journal of the Maine Medical Association,* November 1963.

motor skills have been taught through the means of a program designed to help patients learn one-handed dressing. Still other experimental programs are aimed at helping alcoholics and drug addicts in the control of their problems. Each such program, as it is refined and made more effective, becomes an educational tool to be used by the professional man in the better direction of his own time and efforts.

The professional aid that the physician receives from nurses and technicians is also affected by the educational pattern that these people experience. We have already mentioned that certain medical programs are likewise effective for medical technicians, and we could add nurses and therapists as possible students for many sequences. One study at the University of Rochester [19] not only suggests that a learning program is quite effective for nurses but also promises that programing can redefine still another task of the physician. Specialists previously had been used as lecturers for a course on cancer nursing. The material was programed and tested in a controlled study. The students learned basic material more effectively from the program than from the lecture. This permits the physician to divest himself of the lecture entirely or, more hopefully, permits him to use his own time to greater advantage in taking the nursing students beyond the fundamental aspects of the subject matter—which they can acquire from the program—into the realm of doctor-nurse relationships in the care and recuperation of the patient. In any event, more efficient use of the professional man is made possible.

Perhaps the full extent of the impact of programed instruction on the future of the health profession can be seen in the successful attempt by Carter and her associates [20] to use self-instructional methods for the education of nonprofessional, unskilled workers in the food service departments of hospitals. While it is seldom discussed in meetings of medical educators, no one would dispute the fact that the most highly trained practitioner is from time to time forced to rely on the training of far less skilled employees in the medical center and hospital. There is now some evidence to indicate that the characteristics of programed instruction, including individualized rate of learning, active responding, and immediate feedback, can effectively overcome many of the natural handicaps involved in teaching the nonprofessional medical employee.

---

[19] J. K. Craytor and J. P. Lysaught, "Programmed Instruction in Nursing Education: A Trial Use," *Nursing Research,* Fall 1964, pp. 323–326.

[20] E. J. Carter, A. N. Moore, and C. L. Gregory, "Can Teaching Machines Help in Training Employees?" *Journal of the American Dietetic Association,* April 1964, pp. 271–276.

PERSPECTIVE AND PROSPECTIVE

Much has been accomplished in the little more than three years since research was launched on programed instruction in medical education. Yet
we are already beyond the point of asking whether the self-instructional
process will be effective in achieving high degrees of professional learning.
The next research parameters to be studied are those factors having to do
with the internal variables of programing that will enhance its effectiveness for the special class of learners involved in medical education. For
example, there is speculation that the high intelligence and strong motivation of the medical student will permit, and even demand, a more dialec-
tical kind of program model than is customarily used among collegiate
learners. There is also the need to explore the more extensive use of programed materials in clinical as well as preclinical teaching. Further, there
is the need to develop programing models that will effectively present
the unknowns of borderline research as well as the knowns of verified
practice.

So promising have the results been, however, in terms of both achievement and learner reception, that the pace of activity is noticeably quicken-
ing. More and more foreign medical schools are reacting to the American
experiment with projects designed to improve the instruction of their own
nationals through programed sequences. A greater number of professional
medical organizations are exploring the development of highly specific programs designed to meet the needs of specialized, continuing education for
the practicing physician and surgeon. In the midst of all this activity, little
of the bandwagon is apparent. Perhaps this is because programed instruction bears its own seeds of the experimental mind. The process is implicitly
self-questioning and self-critical. The very mechanism which commends itself to the professional mind militates against unprofessional use of the
process.

Much, of course, remains to be done. There is a shortage of readily available programed sequences despite the fact that their number is growing.
There is a pronounced need for the setting of evaluative standards against
which to judge the commercial programs which are beginning to make their
appearance. But there is the promise that programs can be objectively tested
and judged for their ability to produce learning among their users.

Both the proven gains and the potential contributions of programed
instruction to medical education are equally applicable to other professional

institutions. Schools of dentistry and law, for example, will find their problems varying more in degree than in kind from those of the medical college. Each profession will find it beneficial to explore those areas of curriculum and teaching in which self-instruction can lend new possibilities for achievement and motivation in student learning. And each profession will find that it must carve its own way to a great extent in order to ascertain the best methods by which it can bend this new teaching tool to fit its unique purposes.

Chapter 11

Special Problems and Uses

THE REVOLUTIONARY ELEMENT INHERENT IN THE CONCEPT OF programed instruction is the development of a different perspective entirely from what we have been accustomed to about the whole nature and scope of instruction in American industry and education. The resources of this new technology of teaching have not begun to be fully tapped. A review of the cases in Part II of this book reveals that many problems and applications of programed instruction technology have emerged which were not even contemplated five years ago. This chapter is intended to mention and highlight only a few of these problems and uses and to illustrate them by company application. These special problems and unique applications of programed instruction are (1) the training of detailmen, customer representatives, and salesmen, (2) validating programs, (3) rapid company growth and management support, (4) collateral employee training, (5) proceeding from off-the-shelf programs to in-house development, (6) customer education, (7) company in-house programs, (8) training appliance servicemen, and (9) comparing programed instruction techniques to conventional methods.

TRAINING DETAILMEN, CUSTOMER REPRESENTATIVES, AND SALESMEN

The most extensive use of programed instruction to train detailmen, company representatives, and salesmen has been accomplished by the pharmaceutical industry. Winthrop Laboratories' decision to use programed instruction stemmed from its need to train its field staff, consisting of approximately 500 representatives, to sell a new pharmaceutical product, which was an antibacterial agent of unique character. This product was its first venture into the field of antibacterials; consequently, its representatives had little previous experience and knowledge of the market. This situation made it possible to evaluate programed instruction as a training method without the drawback of some of the staff's having had previous training in the same subject matter.

The program Winthrop had developed consisted of an introductory section on microbiology and antibiotics and a second section on urinary tract infections, the area of use for which the drug was being marketed. The program was planned to consist of approximately 12 hours of study time.

The results obtained with it and the reaction of the men who studied it were greatly favorable, and the company was entirely satisfied with the new-gained level of knowledge. Many of the field staff told the company that they felt more confident discussing this product with physicians than any other product in the line. They also expressed a desire for more programing. Winthrop plans to use programed instruction again whenever feasible and when it definitely determines where and how this new method fits into the overall training schedule.

Many potential areas for training which have ordinarily gone unnoticed because of the many factors which prevented bringing the trainee and the program together have become possible through programed instruction. Ortho Pharmaceutical Corporation has used programed medical courses to train its detailmen concerning the features, effects, and proper use of its oral contraceptive Ortho-Novum. Ortho Pharmaceutical has also used programed courses to help its detailmen learn about the female reproductive system and sex hormones. This additional training would not have been possible without programed instruction.

George Dukes, Director of Training, Ortho Pharmaceutical, has pointed out that

> The PI approach to training permits management to set training objectives, and to insure the attainment of these objectives. They are able to do this by developing a set of terminal knowledge specifications which are then built into the program.

> The program is a tool for instilling the desired knowledge, and the final examination (which accompanies each program) is a tool for insuring that the desired knowledge has in fact been instilled. By this approach to training, a high quality program permits the kind of control managers dream about. At Ortho, we used Basic Systems programed medical courses to train our sales force when we launched Ortho-Novum. After 10 hours of study in the field, the sales force had a thorough understanding of the complex subject of female endocrinology. Enthusiasm was uniformly high.[1]

---

[1] Kirby B. Westheimer, "Strategies for Using Programmed Instruction in the Pharmaceutical Industry," Basic Systems, Inc., New York.

Ernest W. Johnson, Sales Training Director for Ortho Pharmaceutical, has stated that management has found the program solves one of the major problems in industry, ". . . that is, factual, correct knowledge being rapidly transferred to our salesmen. This was the only objective we had in mind when Basic Systems helped prepare our program. The management of the program increased its effectiveness. It could have just as well made it ineffective." [2]

The Sales Training Area of Merck Sharp & Dohme also has had some experience with the use of programed instruction. By the end of 1964 approximately 100 trainees and 300 experienced professional service representatives had been exposed to a program on diuretics and antihypertensive agents. A portion of this group has also taken one or more "retention builders," which are a series of review questions based upon the programed education courses that the employees have previously taken. These reviews are given approximately one month, three months, six months, and one year after the original course to bolster the men's knowledge and to insure that the material is retained. The time interval is dictated by the well-established theory that forgetting occurs most rapidly soon after a subject is learned and then levels off more slowly.

General Telephone Company of California has been using programed instruction for training customer representatives. This is the prime area in which the company is programing its training materials. The company has decentralized its training into three operating areas which have more than 13,000 employees. The fact that each area operates somewhat independently has intensified the training problems. Different training practices have evolved in each area, which is not desirable from an overall company point of view.

The independence of operations gave rise to training problems because of cross-training, transfer of employees, and other circumstances, all of which made the task of preparing training materials an extremely difficult one. The customer representative area was selected as a pilot project to determine the extent to which the instruction could be standardized on a companywide basis. In-house programers, who were selected from other areas, programed the master service record of the customer representatives. This is a form "on which is entered all entries, changes, and removals concerning telephone service and equipment of our customers in addition to many items concerning billing. It is the key tool used in our service offices." [3]

---

[2] Personal communication.

[3] Richard J. Morse, Instructional Programs Administrator, General Telephone Company of California, remarks before AMA's Special Conference and Exhibit—Programed Instruction—Hotel Astor, New York, August 27–29, 1962.

Another group of in-house programers was given the task of programing the instruction in telephone collection techniques. The relationship of this last area to the customer representative's job is explained as follows:

> [She] has to deal with the customer over the phone for the purpose of collecting delinquent monies. There are skills required to handle this activity by phone and also specific pieces of information that the customer representative uses in these telephone contacts. We doubted that we could teach these skills, as well as what we call tone of service, by means of a written program; however, we decided to give it a try. In addition, we were interested in measuring the amount of learning that took place through our program as well as retention. We were even more interested in seeing how well our students were able to relate what they learned to on-the-job performance.[4]

The programing of the master service record produced an analysis of training objectives in behavioral terms which was extremely rewarding. Robert O. Brink, the Instructional Program Supervisor, pointed out that "even had we decided to discard programing as a technique, for one or more of the training segments being studied, our expenditure in analysis would have been fully justified."[5] After the analysis was made, approval was sought for the objectives from senior management. Top management decided to use the program throughout the company. The spin-off benefits of the analysis were crucial and valuable. The programing staff made 15 or more suggestions for modifying the master service record, and it made additional suggestions to change the operating procedures as they related to the form. *Most of these suggestions were approved by management.* As Mr. Brink stated, management could now "look at training goals with a larger glass in order to define most precisely what behavioral characteristics we really want to train into a student. With these goals in mind, we could then return even to conventional instruction."

An unusual program which is being used more and more for the training of salesmen is the Basic Systems audio-lingual self-instructional program "Effective Listening." [6] Among many companies using this program is IBM.

Since listening is such an important skill to salesmen, obviously any procedure which will increase this capacity will be invaluable. There is no disagreement about the fundamental importance of listening to selling. In

---

[4] *Idem.*

[5] Robert O. Brink, "Programed Instruction—Industry Training Tool," *Telephony*, May 25, 1963, p. 20.

[6] Refer to the Liberty Mutual case history in Part II.

sales training courses, however, the customary procedure has been to lecture trainees on the importance of listening and urge them to do a better job in this respect. Even those conventional practices of trying to train people to listen through role-playing exercises do not provide a systematic procedure for teaching listening skills. The audio-lingual "Effective Listening" program, however, is a series of structured experiences for the student. The program is described as follows:

> The trainee is presented with a taped series of statements graded in length and complexity. The statements are narrated in many voices: male and female, high-pitched and low-pitched, rapid and laconic. They are alternately grammatical, ungrammatical, clipped, extensive, organized and disorganized. The program teaches the listener to capture the main content, cutting through emotion, background distraction, aversive content and long digressions.
>
> The trainee is instructed to respond, either orally or in writing, to the information presented in each statement. He is asked to answer pertinent questions or to summarize, and is provided the opportunity to evaluate his response by comparing it with the correct answer. As the program progresses, the taped information becomes increasingly more lengthy and complex and the required responses demand increasing skill.[7]

Judging by the performance data, the IBM trainees did acquire the new skill. One question which arose, however, was the extent to which a trainee would be able to transfer the newly acquired skill to the actual work situation and not be affected by the "halo effect" of the test situation. To answer this question, the group that took the program and another group that had no formal listening training were placed together in the same class in product and sales skills in the Electric Typewriter Division. Both groups were later convened in a class session dealing with sales techniques which used role playing. With no prior warning the instructors read a typical client's statement regarding the advantages and disadvantages of dictating equipment. They abruptly stopped the session and asked the trainees to summarize the statement. The 15 written statements were scored for content by someone who did not know which ones had received the training in listening. The trained group was able to grasp and organize 90 per cent of the informational content. The other group grasped and organized only 55 per cent. Only 12.5 per cent of the latter group organized a statement made by

---

[7] Technical Report, "Evaluation Use of Effective Listening," Basic Systems, Inc., New York.

the client into advantages and disadvantages, whereas 83.3 per cent of the trained group were able to do this.[8]

VALIDATING PROGRAMS

Some companies are introduced to programed instruction through being asked to validate programs for trade associations of which they are members. This is an ideal vehicle for them to develop guidelines which will help them find out what programed instruction is and what it can do for their training programs. It is a relatively inexpensive way of introducing programed instruction to management since frequently validation costs the companies very little. The American Management Association has had as many as four different companies evaluate and validate one of its PRIME programs.

RAPID COMPANY GROWTH

Companies which experience very rapid growth may turn to programed instruction to fill their lack of adequate training facilities and programs and to meet their suddenly skyrocketing training requirements. One such company is Interstate United Corporation.[9] This company initially investigated programed instruction at the request of its management, which realized that its rapid growth had created training needs of all kinds. The interest was further heightened by the fact that the vice president of corporate relations had come from a company which had developed its own in-house programing effort and had found it to be very successful. The importance of management support is well illustrated in this case. Since a top member of management was already completely sold on programed instruction technology, the Employee Development and Education staff was able to convince the rest of the company's senior management on its value.

The staff developed a highly professional slide presentation which spelled out the existing problems, the difficulty of correcting them by conventional training methods, and a demonstration of how programed instruction could

---

[8] *Ibid.*, Appendix C.

[9] Personal communications to the author from Jack Turner, Manager, Employee Development and Education Department, Interstate United Corporation, Lincolnwood, Illinois, September 23, 1964, and October 15, 1964.

train effectively in a shorter time and at lower cost in practically every area of the company.

A program on "Route Accountability" was chosen because the company was using a new accountability system and was having problems with the paperwork on which it all depends. The personnel who handle this particular paperwork are quite numerous and have a high turnover rate. This meant that the cost of developing the program and of training would be spread out over thousands of people and bring the unit training cost down over a few years to a low figure. A second program on "Employee Orientation" was selected in the hope that it would prove to be a good morale booster and because the company had expanded so greatly that comparatively few people really understood how it was organized and why it was organized the way it was. The management felt that the very least an employee is entitled to know is what kind of a company he is working for and that he is part of a large and very complex group incorporating every conceivable kind of skill.

COLLATERAL TRAINING

Increasingly American industry is assuming a responsibility not only for providing effective training which is directly applicable to an employee's job but also for providing education and training experiences which expand an employee's capabilities and contribute to his personal growth and development. Because this type of training already strains the customary educational facilities which a company may possess, many companies are starting to provide programed materials to their employees to help them to overcome technological obsolescence and what some have called technological illiteracy.

In this respect, Canadian National Telecommunications has made an extensive effort to make available to its employees programed materials in a growing range of basic subjects.[10]

Thanks to the cooperation of the Royal Canadian Air Force and the U.S. Army Signal Corps, experimental programs in mathematics, electricity, and electronics were made available to test their application in an industrial training setting. Even though these programs were only in a developmental stage, they were effective and did result in significant learning. The reaction

---

[10] Personal communication from J. R. White, General Manager, Canadian National Telecommunications, Toronto, Ontario, December 1, 1964.

to these courses by more than 300 of the company's employees was most encouraging.

The company did not engage in exhaustive tests of the relative merits of PI versus conventional instruction because it was convinced that PI was a valid concept. It did conduct careful checks to find errors and weak spots in the PI courses that it used. At the same time it gained a lot of useful experience on methods of handling and controlling PI courses.

The company is attempting to move very cautiously, and its supply of specific commercially available courses is being increased only when a definite level of demand is apparent and when it feels that the courses are effective. So far, it has not attempted to develop PI material on actual systems or operations peculiar to its business. However, key instructors are being given a solid grounding in PI concepts and techniques through continuing reading assignments, attendance at workshop seminars, and personal involvement with the testing and revision of actual programs. Based on information received from the Royal Canadian Air Force regarding recent developments with adjunct programing, an experimental adjunct-type program on a "Basic Introduction to Semiconductor Devices and the Z7OU Trigger Tube" is being developed. W. H. Cumberland, Training Officer, feels that the adjunct-type program offers distinct advantages for advanced training over either linear or branching programs. He is convinced that less development time and less paper are required to produce an adjunct program which will result in learning equal to that obtained by an equivalent linear or branching program.

Instructions in the form of a System Training Memorandum have been published by the Training Officer which lays down the procedure to be followed by employees when obtaining programed courses. The memorandum lists the courses which are available through the library for employee self-development. Any employee can make application for a course by completing a set of forms which are used both for control by the Training Officer and for routing of the course by the Librarian. Upon completion of the course the student is asked for his comments regarding its effectiveness.

For certain courses which require careful evaluation, employees are requested to complete a pretest, a frame response booklet, and a post-test to provide information regarding course effectiveness and problem areas. Test results do not appear on the employees' personnel records.

When a course consists of several volumes, a procedure is set up to permit more than one employee to be involved with a complete course at one time. Furthermore, a definite time limit is established for the completion of any course. For reasons of economics, maximum use is made of all available courses, and additional quantities are purchased only when the demand exceeds the current supply.

This company essentially has planted the seeds of continuing self-development for its employees, and the employee organization representatives, recognizing the training problem, have given support and encouragement. It is firmly believed that programed instruction applications will play a major role in future training and development of all classes and levels of employees.

OFF-THE-SHELF TO IN-HOUSE PROGRAMS

A safe and inexpensive way for most companies to investigate the feasibility of using programed instruction training materials in their training programs is acquiring off-the-shelf materials. If they prove inadequate, then the companies may give consideration to developing their own in-house effort or having programs custom designed by a programing agency to meet their peculiar training needs. A case in point is that of The Timken Roller Bearing Company.[11]

The company's first efforts and studies in the use of teaching machines and programed instruction were in the area of related training for apprentices. The off-the-shelf program used was TMI/Grolier's Fundamentals of Algebra, Parts I and II. The initial effort showed enough value that Timken decided to purchase more copies and several MIN/MAX II machines. The experience has been favorable.

After trying out the TMI/Grolier algebra program, the company decided that the available off-the-shelf materials were necessarily of a general nature and not specifically designed to meet its needs. It then determined to develop some in-house experience in the development of its own programs.

It sent one of its instructors to the American Management Association's seminar on teaching machines and programed instruction. This step it followed up later by sending another instructor to the programed instruction seminar at the University of Michigan. These two instructors then provided enough information to train and assist other instructors to begin to develop their own programs. As of August 1964, the company has developed through its own increased efforts experimental courses in slide rule techniques, lubrication, and safety training for supervisors.

---

11 Information submitted by John Neuman, Manager, Industrial Education, The Timken Roller Bearing Co., Canton, Ohio.

In the lubrication course programed instruction supplements conventional teaching procedures. In the regular classes lectures, slides, and other conventional methods of instruction are employed. When the course is concluded, a review is provided through the programed instruction materials. After a year and one-half of using the programed instruction techniques, the company is continuously evaluating their worth. Their greatest advantage is allowing the student to progress at his own speed, commensurate with his ability and his previous experience. Rather than eliminate the instructor, Timken has felt that it has freed him to devote more time to the slower learners and to the development of new courses. The company is still in the process of evaluating the experimental courses which it has developed in-house.

CUSTOMER EDUCATION

An area that offers one of the greatest promises for the application of programed instruction in American industry is that of customer education. This aspect of programed instruction has already been explored rather extensively by pharmaceutical firms. Programed courses teach content and the emotional message that usually accompanies them, but not enough attention has been paid to their "attention getting" value. Customers like them. Pharmaceutical firms have found that medical men are not the only group that responds to programed materials. Patients, pharmacists, salesmen, medical students, and some laymen find the courses interesting, even compelling. The allergy and hypersensitivity course developed by Pfizer Laboratories is a case in point.[12]

Since programed instruction is the packaging of the tutorial approach for the student and since the technology is not restricted to a programed text format, it has many uses in practically every medium of customer education. Program materials, according to one description, "can easily be distributed through direct mail; film strips can be programed as can exhibits at conventions; program materials have been offered in magazines, newspapers, tapes, and records; brochures; through teaching machines (some of them very small, portable and relatively inexpensive)." The possibilities for packaging programed learning experiences for customers are almost infinite.

Because of our mass media of communication and the mobility of our society, the buying habits of Americans are very erratic. People's lives are

---

[12] See the Pfizer *Spectrum* case history in Part II.

ordered differently today from what they were only 20 years ago. Audiences and customers are far more critical and sophisticated today than they were in the past. It is the retailer rather than the buyer who must beware. In an age in which knowledge is accumulating so rapidly, communication gains priority, and the retailer has to be where his customer is, if not in body at least with his message.

Programed instruction for customer education is one of the primary undertakings of the Educational Development Department of IBM's Data Processing Division. The major objectives of IBM's customer education programs are to enable customers to identify and properly use those IBM products (data-processing systems, system features, programing systems, and associated supplies) which best fit their data-handling needs.

Education Development writes curricula and produces programed courses. When new products or changes to existing products are announced, major changes in curricula and emphasis are frequently necessary. Considerable effort is expended to train instructors in the changes to existing courses as well as in new courses fast enough to meet the demand. The 1401 DPS Basic Programing-SPS had a high volume of customer training requirement. The Educational Development Department wrote frames for about half the course and tested them on a few volunteer customer students. The results were not entirely satisfactory, and so the department made revisions and scheduled another, more ambitious test. The program was administered to four customer classes under the supervision of the experienced instructors. The plan was to teach some of the topics by program for one week and by instructors during the second week.

The customers liked it. The instructors found that they had to help more during the first week than they expected, since the program was represented as "self-instructional." Also, they found that the sequence of topics included some that they ordinarily would not present during the first week of a conventional class but omitted some topics they would have presented. Their criticisms led to developing an elaborate plan for administering courses and to completely revising the 1401 course.

The department programers put more effort into the specification of objectives for the topics included in the new version. They wrote relatively small sections and tested and revised them as they went along. The new course consisted of approximately 1,300 frames and some "case study" problems for the students to work when they completed the programed sections. The program was tested on approximately 50 students, some of them customers and the rest IBM employees, under the supervision of "advisors."

In general, the students' reactions were favorable, but their achievement test scores and ability to work the case study problems were not so good as the advisors could have wished. There still appeared to be subject matter areas in which unforeseen difficulties arose. The objectives of the program were more subject matter oriented than task oriented, and a redefinition of goals was required.

The programers began reworking the course, dropping some topics entirely and changing their views on the relative importance and difficulty of other topics. For example, they added "enrichment material" and wrote new frames to increase the emphasis on certain topics. Multiple-choice tests replaced other testing procedures, making the advisors' task somewhat easier. The criticisms of the advisors who were continuing to administer the second version of the course aided the programers in this effort. They printed a "final" version which is currently in use. This has proved to be much more acceptable to the advisors and is warmly accepted by customers, some of whom have reported that it trains their employees better than conventional methods do.[13]

Another application by IBM was developing customer education programs for punched-card data-processing principles. These courses, whose curricula were well defined, were occupying much of the time of instructors who were actually qualified to teach newer, more advanced, data-processing courses. A detailed comparison of the curricula with the customers' needs revealed a discrepancy: No matter which course any customer student attended, he was almost certain to spend part of his time learning about machines he didn't have and mechanical functions he would not be employing. Accordingly, the programers designed the course to allow each student to learn about the individual functions and machines that he wished, to the extent that he wished, and in an order that he felt was most appropriate.

More than 3,000 behavioral objectives were specified for this course, and high performance criteria were established. The course was so designed to instruct any student who chose to learn mechanical operations that he would take no more than 20 minutes of actual machine time to reach the required level of proficiency. A classification system was devised whereby any objective for one machine that was behaviorally analogous to an objective for another machine was put in the same category. This procedure highlighted specific objectives, mostly in the area of mechanical operation.

The programers wrote frames and composed, tested, and revised notebook entries until they established that the techniques would teach the particular

---

[13] Information submitted by N. S. Schulte, DP Education Development, IBM Corp., Endicott, New York.

machines' operations, as specified. They also wrote, tested, and revised other series of frames, for objectives relating to one machine but analogous to other machines, until the objectives were met. When this developmental phase was complete, frames, objectives, tested sample artwork, and subject matter expertise were available for a vendor, who completed the large amount of writing and small amount of developmental testing necessary.

The final program is more than 15,000 frames in length; it consists of an introductory course and 11 others, each of which is an independent machine course. Field tests were held with customer classes under the supervision of members of the Education Development Department. The customer reaction was overwhelmingly favorable and, more important, the course met the behavioral objectives and was in fact essentially self-administering.

In the field of customer education IBM currently offers 16 programed courses in punched-card data-processing principles and machines, one course in computer fundamentals, and three courses in specific programing system languages and techniques. Courses are designed for different types of students. For example, the Fortran course is designed for scientists, engineers, mathematicians, and programers who need to communicate with the computer to solve mathematical problems. Another course is designed for persons who will operate an IBM 082 sorter in a punched-card data-processing installation.

Every programed course designed for customers has a clear statement of objectives so that anyone taking the course will know exactly what he is expected to learn. Whenever a customer enrolls for a course, he is not exclusively dependent on the programed materials. After enrollment a student is assigned an advisor who is a subject matter expert. The advisor orients him to the course, assists him in setting up a progress schedule, and aids him in other matters intermittently throughout the course. Upon its completion, the advisor administers a final examination, collects the course materials, and presents the student with a certificate indicating that he has satisfactorily accomplished the course's objectives.

COMPANY IN-HOUSE PROGRAMS

A company may produce its own in-house programs for a variety of purposes. The RCA Service Company, for example, produces programed courses for in-house training, stock sales, and custom use by other firms. This last category accounts for the bulk of the output. Although programing is not centralized in the company and various departments have undertaken to do their own programing, the majority of programing is done by "RCA Educational Programs."

For its own use the company has prepared programs on the following topics: (1) computer programing, (2) symbolic logic, (3) basic electronics, (4) transistors, (5) data processing equipment, and (6) sales.

The emphasis in programs developed for external use has been on sales training including product information. Two stock programs are available from RCA: (1) "Basic Symbolic Logic" and (2) "A Programed Guide to Writing Autoinstructional Programs." Seminars in the writing of autoinstructional programs are also conducted periodically.

One of the major projects completed by RCA Educational Programs is "Introduction to Electronics," a 16-lesson course developed for RCA Institutes and used by them in their correspondence courses. A study was made comparing this program with the conventional course used up to that time. Three hundred students comprised both the experimental and control groups. The experimental group using the autoinstructional materials generally scored higher than those using the conventional materials. Although both groups produced test scores of 90 per cent or better for well over 90 per cent of the test students, comments from the students generally favored the autoinstructional materials. RCA has, therefore, considered the discontinuance of the conventional materials.

In spite of this company's variety of in-house efforts and although it is seriously considering the programing of other courses, management does not find a clear economical advantage in using programed instruction in all its training activities. What will possibly happen is that the company will gradually program certain courses as they become due for revision. Management also feels that public acceptance is a factor that will have a significant influence on the extent of its further programing.

The General Telephone Company of California has been developing in-house programs since 1960. These have demonstrated the value of programed instruction to the company in improving its training program and in saving some training dollars. The programers have emphasized information operator and customer representative training. One of the most significant benefits that has accrued from its efforts is the concern and attention that have been paid to training objectives because programed instruction technology imposes a precise behavioral definition and analysis of learning outcomes. Even in subjects which were too costly to program the analysis of objectives has increased the efficiency of conventional training. In the programed courses training time has been reduced by an average of 40 per cent, and students have achieved higher performance results on criterion tests. In addition to these advantages programing has helped give rise to standardized training practices. Also, the programed materials which have been validated are available for refresher training, and they have minimized the number of additional instructors required and alleviated scheduling problems. The instructor can utilize her time more effectively and can "now devote her best efforts to each trainee's development, guiding and evaluating individual progress toward the established performance objectives. In many cases the instructor is also able to overlap other administrative duties while supervising the training room." [14]

A final spin-off benefit is the data which have been collected for the use of the company's Personnel Testing Coordinator. These precise data have contributed "to a definitive, meaningful battery of tests for both new hires and intracompany transfers." [15]

The company has not restricted its efforts to in-house programs. It has purchased an off-the-shelf program and used it in training keypunch machine operators. It was necessary, however, to revise the program to fit the needs of its Revenue Accounting Department operation. Training time in this course has been reduced 50 per cent with no loss in proficiency. The company had four trained programers on its staff at that time.

TRAINING APPLIANCE SERVICEMEN

The potential inherent in the self-study aspect of programed instruction training systems is extending the possibilities for training in many areas that had not been considered feasible for management conducted training programs. Until the advent of PI, training in these areas has been rather haphazard on the job. For example, a major industry in the United States is the servicing and repair of consumer products. Americans spend more than $16 billion annually for services; this amount is expected to double by 1975. The number of servicemen alone has doubled since 1945. The latest census comprises well over 2 million. The training problem is put into sharp focus when it is realized that in the home appliance industry more people service appliances than produce them. This makes the training and upgrading of appliance servicemen a key factor in the industry.[16]

---

[14] Robert O. Brink, "Programmed Instruction—Industry Training Tool," *Telephony*, May 25, 1963, p. 20.

[15] *Idem.*

[16] Paper read by Robert A. Isackman, RCA Service Company, at the 1964 National Convention of the National Society for Programmed Instruction.

The training of the field serviceman is a much more complex problem than that of training the factory production worker, which is often rather simple and usually done in a controlled or formal classroom environment. An instructor is readily available. Training materials have been carefully prepared. The appliance serviceman, however, has to be trained to operate effectively on relatively complex equipment in a rather unusual environment. Often an instructor is not present and the training takes place rather haphazardly in the laundry or kitchen of an anxious, complaining, or irate housewife.

A consideration of objectives in the training of the appliance serviceman should emphasize the basic training he must receive and the special training which must exist under a variety of environmental constraints. Neither programed instruction nor any other recent innovation in training technology is developed enough to claim to train a serviceman in handling his problems while contending with interruptions, distractions, and often disturbing pressures. Robert Isackman comments that "all of the complex factors that can make a serviceman effective, or defeat him, must be considered in the overall training objectives." The RCA Service Company, in considering this training problem, has given some thought to the nature of the target population for which programed instructional materials may be developed.

Its experience indicates that recruits can be assumed to have little or no knowledge of basic electricity and at least one-third have no previous appliance repair experience. The average educational background generally includes high school attendance. Many recruits are expert "tinkerers," and generally they have a good mechanical aptitude which attracts them to this type of work. The basic training task is twofold. The course must cover both the fundamentals of mechanics (hydraulics, gears, etc.) and basic electricity (electrical circuits, thermoelectricity, etc.). Beyond this basic training there still remains the problem of training the novice servicemen to be troubleshooters and to work effectively in the field situation.

The lack of standardized methodology of training; the fact that instructors are generally experienced servicemen who have rarely had any training as instructors and lack effective pedagogical skills; and the fact that each manufacturer and independent service organization creates its own training materials and devises its own methods—all these have led the RCA Service Company to consider programed instruction as a vehicle for providing the basic knowledge and standardized quality training which will increase the ability of the servicemen to handle more complex electrical circuits in modern-day appliances.

RCA Educational Programs has just completed a 400-frame program for the American Gas Association which will serve as an introduction to electrical circuits in gas appliances. This program is now being used to implement training of servicemen in a number of utility companies. The RCA Whirlpool Service Training Department has an autoinstructional program covering wiring diagram symbols. The Appliance Service Training Department of RCA Service Company is developing a training course that will teach the fundamentals of troubleshooting. It intends to use test panels to simulate realistic circuits and allow self-instructional practice in circuit analysis.

To assist in the self-instructional materials, the wiring diagrams which are used are very carefully and simply prepared so that the novice technician can easily read and follow them. These diagrams are tested on new servicemen to eliminate any possible confusion which may exist. Test points are prominently displayed. Wires do not cross each other. Procedures to be followed are detailed in a simple manner.

RCA Service Company feels there is a continuous need for upgrading appliance servicemen to enable them to troubleshoot new types of electrical circuits as they are introduced in new products. Utilizing PI for the presentation of such material seems like a natural solution to this type of training need since it has the obvious advantage of providing the economy and proven effectiveness made possible by using a self-instructional methodology.

COMPARING PROGRAMED INSTRUCTION TECHNIQUES

There have been enough comparisons made of the applications of programed instruction and conventional teaching methods to training and education problems in industry, government, and private and public education. The superiority of programed instruction over conventional textbooks has been more than adequately demonstrated. American industry is no longer making these comparisons in such large numbers. It is convinced. Furthermore, as Stanley Levine has pointed out—

> Developing a program is quite different than writing a text-book. Comparison of the two reveals fallacious thinking because the objective of each is different. Text-books are basically reference books organized with a logic that is not necessarily motivated by learning. They *present* information which the instructor must integrate with his own methodology of instruction. Programed instruction is actually a course involving both content and method. It is not written as such, but is developed and molded by means of student feedback into a functioning course.

Both the text-book and the programed instruction course have contributions to make. As a reference source, the text-book is much more effective than a programed instruction course. However, in a learning situation PI is much superior. Your objective should determine your choice of types of materials used.[17]

Industrial training managers in general are becoming convinced that further comparisons between approaches which are essentially dichotomous are wasteful. Programed instruction based training systems, because they bring together both content and methodology and permit the student to administer and manage them, have a built-in superiority. Time and effort should now be concentrated on developing a system which will meet in as valid a manner as possible *the most stringent specifications that can be imposed upon it.*

The literature of programed instruction, both the research oriented and that concerned with applications, is replete with comparisons of the various techniques of programing, especially the techniques of frame writing. There has been an overconcern with such dichotomies as linear versus branching, constructed response versus multiple choice, small step versus large step, covert versus overt responses, and programed text versus teaching machines. These studies have not been conclusive in any respect except that teaching machines in the present state of the art have not demonstrated any inherent superiority over programed texts. There apparently is room in the art for all types of techniques of frame writing. There is little in the way of a theoretical base for any one procedure over the other. The designers of future programed instruction based training systems will undoubtedly use their own judgment and try anything that will work. It is apparent that concern will increase with developing a variety of techniques for accomplishing behavioral task analysis. The trend is to use a variety of techniques in one program, to increase the use of panels and illustrative materials, and to substitute the criterion test for the behaviorally defined objectives. As Levine has urged, everyone should "stop comparing—start using."

---

[17] Stanley L. Levine, "A Clarification of the Definition, Construction, and Evaluation of Programmed Texts," remarks presented at the Annual Convention of the National Society for Programmed Instruction, San Antonio, Texas, April 1964.

Part II

Case Histories of
Programed Instruction

Nothing will ever be attempted if all
possible objections must be first overcome.

Dr. Samuel Johnson
1709–1784

Aerojet-General Corporation *

Aerojet-General Corporation relies rather heavily on off-the-shelf materials for its application of programed instruction to its training programs.

Aerojet-general is using 27 programs, 3 u.s. industry auto-tutors, 17 MIN/MAX III Machines, and 8 textbooks.

Last year Aerojet's Sacramento plant provided more than 12,000 hours of training through programed instruction *at a cost of less than 50 cents per hour of instruction per trainee.* This included all direct costs—for example, labor and materials—but did not include the salaries of the participants.

A minimum of supervisory overhead was required. One girl was able to schedule, process, grade, evaluate, load, and perform all other tasks necessary for the operation of such an effort. The PI training office is centrally located in the 18,000-acre plant. Each trainee comes to the PI school from his work station in accordance with a prearranged schedule. The schedule is arranged to meet the needs of the company. At the end of the program the trainee is given the opportunity to evaluate the effectiveness of the program. These evaluations are filed by course name and are used to improve the entire activity.

The Personnel Development Department does not evaluate programs in accordance with any rigorous set of principles. It believes that the customers—the trainees themselves—are the only ones qualified to evaluate program effectiveness. If the trainees do not like the program and consider it unacceptable, then it is canceled. If a program meets their requirements, it is made a permanent part of their training activity.

Richard E. Johnson, administrator of the programed instruction project

---

* Information for this case submitted by Richard E. Johnson, Administrator, Programed Instruction, Personnel Development, Sacramento plant, Aerojet-General Corporation, Sacramento, California.

in the Personnel Development Department, points out that it is important for the man who is selling programed instruction to management to know what is going on in PI and to have the confidence of his management. Second, he must be prepared to compare the program which he is selecting or developing with similar programs. If no other program exists, he automatically has an advantage. This lies in the fact that he can say, "PI is available. You can have it now. We can do it now. These are the terminal results the program will bring. This is how much it will cost." PI courses are easier to sell because they are better identified, but they must be sold at the top initially. Senior managers will automatically sell them to all operations under their control. Mr. Johnson advises that the case for PI be presented to one group at a time and with only one program. This does several things. It provides all the people in the organization who are involved in the project with a mutual understanding of one block of information. They all receive the same information. This information then acts as a vehicle which has a side effect, which is the solution of unrelated problems within the organization structure itself. Johnson states this as follows, "Programed instruction, when presented to an individual organization as a group, becomes a communication vehicle by stimulating communication within the organization. This stimulated communication adds to the solution of any production, engineering, or manufacturing problems which may exist within that organization."

The criterion test, if it is available, is used as the main index of what the course contains. If no criterion test is available, Aerojet uses the outline of the course, supplements it with the previous students' notes, and shows these as guides to the new student. The new student is also provided with a brochure on programed instruction which tells him what programing is and what courses are available. An outline of the courses' contents is provided. He is also given a list of errors which have been found in the program and is encouraged to add to the list. There follows a description of one of the 27 courses which are described in the brochure and made available to all the 16,000 employees of 52 divisions who are encouraged to take advantage of these programed materials.

INTRODUCTORY DESCRIPTIVE STATISTICS

Duration: 50 hours

Course No. 03-117

General Objectives:

This Programed Instruction course is designed to acquaint the trainee with the rudiments of Statistics. Material covered in the program includes: definition, elementary theory of measurement, descriptive and inferential statistics, distributions, and correlation and regression.

Table of Contents

American Bankers Association *

In August 1962, as part of its research into programed instruction, a member of the Association staff attended an American Management Association seminar on the subject. In February 1963 he was sent to the seminar run by the Bureau of Industrial Relations at the University of Michigan. On the basis of the insights gained at these seminars and other research, the Association's Management Committee approved the request of the Personnel Administration and Management Development Committee to form a Subcommittee on Programed Instruction to determine how programed instruction could be utilized effectively in the banking industry. The results of the meeting of the Subcommittee in September 1963 were relayed to ABA members throughout the country. The subsequent efforts are described here.

IN JULY 1963 BANK PERSONNEL NEWS INFORMED THE MEMBERSHIP of The American Bankers Association that the Personnel Administration and Management Development Committee had initiated a programed instruction project. This report indicated that although PI had more than adequately demonstrated its effectiveness in employee training, the developmental costs of programed materials were so high as to "put them beyond the reach of the thousands of smaller and medium-sized banks." The project was initiated to bring PI to as many banks as possible at as low a cost as possible. The chairman appointed a subcommittee on programed instruction to "exercise overall supervision of the project, including selecting the consultant, designating specific jobs for programing, assuring general applicability of material to banks, etc." The membership of this subcommittee consisted of three training specialists from large banks that had already begun to

* Information for this case submitted by Robert C. Albright, Assistant Director, Personnel Administration and Management Development Committee, The American Bankers Association, New York; and Harold L. Moon, of McGraw-Hill Information and Training Services, New York, who was at Stevenson, Jordan & Harrison Management Consultants, Inc., when the described work was done.

use programed instruction, two personnel officers who were oriented toward training, and two representatives from small banks whose training needs differed from those of larger institutions.

In September 1963 the subcommittee decided to review existing programed instruction materials "and their adaptability to bank training situations" and to survey "commercial banks to determine what they had been doing in the field of programed instruction." The subcommittee's intent was to serve as a PI clearinghouse to the banking industry and to "develop specific programs for use by all banks." Since there was a great deal of variance in banking procedures, it was decided to determine which job functions that were common to several positions could be programed. Following this, the plan was to select a consultant who would "design, prepare, and test interchangeable training modules, or units of programed instruction, for multiple use in a number of similar job functions. For instance, a training module covering the various parts of a check could be inserted in the training programs of a teller, a bookkeeper, or a person responsible for opening new checking accounts." Other suggested subjects were check endorsement, customer service, loss protection, verification of signatures, basic check cashing considerations, and placing holds for uncollected funds or cashed checks.

It was felt that if a number of common job functions could be identified, 30 to 50 per cent of the training requirements for these positions could be programed. The hope of the subcommittee was that these flexible training modules could be made available to banks at a reasonable cost and that the income from the sale of these modules would be used to develop additional programs.

The consultants worked in cooperation with the subcommittee to: identify the training areas in banking in which programed materials could produce the greatest immediate benefits; determine the characteristics of the trainee population; identify the typical conditions under which programed materials would be used in bank training; specify the training objectives and the subject matter; and develop a suitable programed training unit. After the consultants met with the subcommittee, they conducted interviews with 40 persons in four New York City banks and in one large bank and four smaller banks outside the city. Those interviewed were training officers, tellers, clerks, and trainees.

The preliminary study identified the teller and his functions as a most important asset—or a serious liability—to the bank because of his contact with the public. The increasing demand for tellers and the automation of many clerical procedures have eliminated many positions in which potential tellers have formerly received on-the-job training in bank operations. Preliminary study also indicated that much of the knowledge that all tellers need is also applicable to a variety of other bank positions. In other words, tellers, clerks, and bookkeepers share a common need for similar knowledge. In view of this consideration, the first subject selected for programing was "checks." It was felt that since "a good knowledge of checks —what they are, the various restrictions on and requirements for their use, and how they are processed through the banking system—is basic to most teller, clerical, and bookkeeping positions, and much of this information is important to virtually all bank employees," this was an ideal initial project. An analysis of the trainee population indicated that the materials should be written at a "normal adult" reading level.

In July 1964 the newsletter of the Personnel Administration and Management Development Committee announced that the developmental work of the PI unit on checks had been completed and that the field test was under way. According to the newsletter, the banks that participated in the field test were asked to try out the program on the following four groups of new bank employees, who, research had indicated, constitute the bulk of new bank hires:

a. Young men who are high school graduates.
b. Young women who are high school graduates.
c. College trainees.
d. Mature women who have returned to the labor market after a period as homemakers.[1]

The field test was designed to determine (1) the effectiveness of the program, (2) the adequacy of the format, (3) the adequacy of instructions, and (4) the adequacy of administrative procedures. The banks selected to administer the field test were among those that responded to a letter inviting banks of various sizes throughout the country to participate in this study. The letter said, in part:

> These programs are designed to teach new bank employees essential facts they need to know about checks. They are called programs because they use programed instruction—a new method of teaching which requires the student to respond in writing as he learns.
>
> These programs have been prepared in consultation with bankers and have been tested on bank employees during the initial development stage. However, because we want to give the programs a wider test and

---

[1] *Bank Personnel News,* The American Bankers Association, New York, July 17, 1964, p. 1.

screening before they are distributed nationally, we are asking you, among other bankers, to participate in a final field test. The information obtained from this tryout will be used as a basis for a final revision.

The information in these booklets will be useful to many kinds of bank employee—tellers, proof clerks, transit and clearings personnel, bookkeepers, EDP personnel, college trainees, and anyone else who may handle checks.

Further, the instructions for field-testing the units on checks provided introductory information to the bank supervisors on programed instruction; specific, detailed instructions on orienting the student; and procedures for administering the experimental program. Even a suggested six-day study was provided; if the banks wanted to combine two days' work into one, they were told, "In this case we suggest that you have the student do one day's work in the morning and the other in the afternoon, rather than do two days' work at one sitting. We strongly suggest that you do not ask the student to do more than two days' work in one." Such complete instructions for the administration of a field test as were provided by the consultant firm are rare indeed.

Thirty-seven banks in 28 cities and 19 states participated in the field test. One hundred trainees (44 males and 56 females) completed all the program units and all the tests. Of these trainees, 96 per cent had graduated from high school; 16 per cent had had some college education; and 20 per cent had graduated from college. The trainee population included auditors, bookkeepers, business machine operators, clerks, management trainees, secretaries, tellers, messengers, pages, and three unassigned trainees. All trainees were given pretests to determine entry level knowledge for each unit. Some trainees in banks having deposits of more than $500 million did their study in four sessions in two days. Some of those in banks having deposits of $100 million to $500 million did not adhere to the recommended schedule but rather suited a schedule to their individual requirements. All the trainees in banks under $100 million followed the recommended study schedule.

Field test results are shown as Exhibit 1. Interestingly, even though the males scored higher than the females on pre- and post-tests, the females gained 247 per cent in knowledge whereas the males gained only 185 per cent. Even though this was not a 90/90 unit (74 per cent scored 90 per cent or higher), 92 per cent of the trainees did score 80 per cent or higher (92/80), which is significantly higher than has been customarily achieved with field tests. Statistics on time spent in study were received for only 26 per cent of the trainees, some of whom took as little as 3 hours and 40 minutes whereas others required 10 hours and 50 minutes. The average or mean time was 6 hours and 35 minutes. Although the females gained a higher percentage of knowledge than the males, the difference was not significant; and there were no significant differences in post-test performances due to sex, education, experience, size of bank, job classification, or study schedule.

EXHIBIT 1

MEAN SCORES BY LESSONS

Lessons	Sex	Pretests Per Cent	Post-tests Per Cent	Knowledge Gained Per Cent
Introduction	Males	53	96	83
to checks	Females	38	91	139
	Both	44	94	110
Inspecting	Males	46	89	93
the face of	Females	40	86	117
a check	Both	42	87	106
Endorsements	Males	41	95	120
	Females	35	92	152
	Both	37	93	137
Routing the	Males	19	96	407
check through	Females	13	90	612
the banking	Both	15	93	500
system				
All lessons	Males	33	94	185
	Females	26	90	247
	Both	29	92	216

Both trainees and supervisors were highly receptive to programed instruction as a training procedure. Following are some typical comments by trainees:

"I liked and enjoyed this program very much. It has taught me so much about checks in such a short time."

"I'm an older woman. I wish we had more programs like this one. I really enjoyed it."

"By studying and learning alone there is a certain element of self-satisfaction achieved. I was very impressed."

"Speaking as one who has not studied in years and who has never learned to 'scan,' I prefer this to textbook study. It took me considerable time on the pretests and programs, compared to the young people, but on the post-tests I finished ahead of them, or simultaneously, which speaks well for the effectiveness of this teaching method."

Representative supervisor comments are as follows:

"Having observed the employees while they were working on the program, and having listened to the various comments, my evaluation of the program would be high."

"Participants were very receptive. I took . . . the programed instruction myself. We all felt that we learned a great deal without the learning becoming burdensome."

"Based on this experience with our people, programed instruction will be used fully and enthusiastically at [this bank]."

"The operations officer who actually conducted this for us was quite impressed with the material presented and the method of instruction and has already recommended that we purchase the program when it is available."

Only a few of the trainees felt that the program was boring, there was too much repetition, or too much writing was required. These are frequent criticisms within the small group of trainees that are not strongly in favor of programed instruction. All supervisor comments were favorable. A few suggestions were made for minor revisions in the material.

Even though the results of the field test were satisfactory, it was felt that the unit could be improved by a final revision. The consultant firm therefore analyzed all test results, answer sheets, and trainee and supervisor comments to identify weak spots and those subunits which could be improved. The greatest amount of revision was done on the lesson on which the trainees scored lowest in the post-test. The overall program was lengthened approximately 10 per cent.

Even while the field test was being conducted, the subcommittee announced through its chairman, Alfred E. Langenbach, vice president of The First National Bank of Chicago, that it had "agreed to publish and distribute nationally the programed unit on 'securities' developed by training directors and trust officers of major New York City banks through the New York Chapter of A.I.B. with McGraw-Hill, Inc. as consultant." [2] This program consists of a unit on stocks and one on bonds, which, it was felt, could be useful in training bank employees who handle securities.

The subcommittee has asked other banks which have used off-the-shelf

---

[2] *Ibid.*

programs to share their experiences with the subcommittee and with the readers of *Bank Personnel News*. The first such review, published on October 17, 1964, was written by Sanford Kleiner, assistant vice president of Chemical Bank New York Trust Company, about a programed typing course.[3] In this respect, *Bank Personnel News* serves as a clearinghouse for reports on successful PI efforts. The following points, for example, were made in Mr. Kleiner's review:

> The system has been used successfully with nine-year-old youngsters and mature adults. In the first Navy tests (where Robins developed the process), 13 men mastered the basic keyboard with 97 per cent accuracy in 4½ hours. In one military test, the records accomplished as much in 11 hours as a control group achieved in 30 hours with standard classroom procedures.
>
> At Chemical New York, the secretarial training unit has used the living method course for beginning typists since 1960. Beginners in training courses use the records in a six-hour program and then proceed with drill books and other practice material for speed and accuracy development.
>
> In addition, over 150 clearance (note) teller trainees have taken a 10-hour course during the same period. The typing course for clearance tellers is an integral part of their training, and results in an average of 15 w/m touch typing. The introduction of this training makes it possible for clearance tellers to type all tickets prepared during their day's work. . . .
>
> The training center at Chemical New York has had its record player adapted to accommodate plug-in listening stations. This enables up to six students to hear the records either through individual head sets or directly from the phonograph speaker.[4]

In the September 1963 meeting at which the subcommittee outlined its future activities, it was recommended that a brief booklet in programed instruction format be prepared for distribution to top management at all banks describing this new training technology and its potential in creating savings through the more effective training of their personnel. This program was prepared by the consultant for the American Bankers Association. The program (1) defined programed instruction, (2) attempted to show how it could help management, (3) provided four examples of successful

---

[3] Lewis Robins and R. Harris, *The Living Method Typing Course*, Crown Publishers, Inc., New York.
[4] *Bank Personnel News*, *op. cit.*

results with it, and (4) presented an 18-frame unit on its advantages. The last criterion frame follows:

---

18. List six general advantages of programed instruction.

1. _____
2. _____
3. _____
4. _____
5. _____
6. _____

(Any order is acceptable.)
Trainees master the material.
Instruction is uniform.
Training time is reduced.
Instructor time is reduced.
Individuals can be trained.
Training can be decentralized.[5]

The panel and frames shown here as Exhibit 2 illustrate how this program was oriented toward senior management's perspective. In addition, this orientation program offers guidelines and suggestions on selecting and using programs best suited to training needs. Through *Banking—Journal of The American Bankers Association* and other media, members of the subcommittee and other senior management personnel are explaining programed instruction and its potential to their colleagues and others in the banking industry. Typical is a recent article written by Otis D. Brown, assistant vice president and training director of Bankers Trust Company in New York City. These are the main points of Brown's message:

> Perhaps the most important gain from a balance-sheet point of view is the marked savings in training time. These training-time reductions typically range from 20 per cent to 50 per cent depending on the kind of skill being taught and the quality of the program.
>
> A correlative benefit is that the teaching is more uniform and consistent. . . .
>
> Companies like PI because it is more flexible. You don't have to delay training a new person until a class starts or some key employee is free to begin teaching him. Along with this is the fact that the training can be decentralized. For branch banking systems this means the programs

---

[5] *Programed Instruction—Saves Time Makes Sense,* The American Bankers Association, New York, 1964, p. 13.

EXHIBIT 2

TYPICAL EXPERIENCES WITH PROGRAMED INSTRUCTION

	Results with Conventional Instruction	Results with Programed Instruction
First National City Bank Teller Training		
Average on final exam	82.9%	86.2%
Average student time	3 weeks	1 week
Du Pont Reading Engineering Drawings		
Average on final exam	81%	91%
Average student time	17 hours	12 hours
IBM Introduction to 7070 Computer		
Average on final exam	86.2%	95.1%
Average student time	15 hours	11 hours
Spiegel Package Billing		
Average on final exam	OK for line work	OK for line work
Average student time	40 hours	26 hours

THE ADVANTAGES OF PROGRAMED INSTRUCTION

1a. About one-third of the hundred largest banks in the U.S. are using programed instruction, and about the same proportion of the largest companies in other industries are also using this technique.

The facts in the table on the opposite side are typical of the results they have obtained. Compared with the conventional methods, programed instruction generally produces (higher/the same/lower) final examination scores. (Look at the data in the table.)

higher

1b. With programed instruction the trainees generally master the material in (more/the same/less) time. (Look at the table.)

less

EXHIBIT 2 (*continued*)

1C. When the companies in the table used programed instruction in place of their old methods, they found that their trainees learned_____in _____time.

---

more
less

---

5. Programed instruction can reduce the cost of training. For example, many banks give formal orientation training to all new clerical employees. A typical orientation session may last three days. One day will be devoted to introducing people and explaining the history and policies of the bank. The balance of the time will be spent teaching some facts about banking. Three days of full-time attention from an instructor are required to train the new employees.

From this description, two cost factors that might be reduced by using programed instruction are the time of the_____and the time of the _____.

---

trainees
instructor

---

12. Here is another typical bank training problem:
A bank must train twelve new employees per year as tellers. The employees are high-school graduates with no banking experience.

When an experienced bank teller gives on-the-job training, he quickly teaches the most common procedures. But he must carry on with many of his regular duties as well. Therefore, he does not always have time to teach the trainees all the facts they should know to do their jobs intelligently and well. Less pressing topics are delayed or even neglected until the trainee makes a mistake or an unusual situation arises.

The main problems in this case are:

1. inadequate mastery of subject-matter by the trainees, and
2. a shortage of instructor time.

Programed instruction offers these relevant advantages:

_____

_____

Trainees master the material.
Instructor time is reduced.

EXHIBIT 2 *(concluded)*

16. A bank has thirty small branches dispersed over a wide area. In a year, each branch must train three or four new employees in the fundamentals of banking. Management wants to assure uniform, high-quality training in all the branches, but the distance between branches makes it difficult to bring together in one place enough new employees to justify a formal training program.

Aside from reducing training costs, how can programed instruction help solve this problem? List all the relevant advantages.

Training can be decentralized.
Individuals can be trained.
Trainees master the material.
Instruction is uniform.

can be used on the spot where the man is. The people primarily concerned with training in the company have a continual check on how well the program is being administered because of the final examinations that go with every program. . . .

Another bonus is that where PI is used in on-the-job situations, it frees the supervisor or other senior person from the need to spoonfeed the learner. The supervisor can use the time for other work which he used to have to devote to teaching the ABC's of the job. . . .

Banks acquiring these units [programs developed by ABA] will have a tool for teaching some banking fundamentals. The program on checks will not only be as useful to the new clerk in check processing as it will be to the new teller, but also can be used in many situations. With these units as building blocks, some of the larger banks will want to develop tailored PI courses for teaching their own procedures.[6]

Programed instruction in the banking industry is picking up momentum. Few industries have committed themselves to programed instruction in solving their basic clerical training problems as rapidly and intensely as has this one. Since programed instruction costs were excessive, ABA recognized that this service could eliminate duplication of effort and reduce substantially the cost of programing those subjects that are fundamental and common to bank training. It recognized, however, that it needed the acceptance and approval of senior bank management and the assistance of expert consultants, and its efforts to enlist the cooperation of these two groups have had marked success.

---

[6] Otis D. Brown, *Banking—Journal of The American Bankers Association,* September 1964.

American Telephone and Telegraph Company *

The American Telephone and Telegraph Company conducted one of the earliest exploratory studies of PI made by a major American industry. Subsequent developments in the use of PI to train telephone operators and salesmen who sell wide area telephone service (WATS) also illustrate AT&T's continued exploration of the potential of PI in the solution of its training problems.

A

In 1959, the same year that Professor B. F. Skinner of Harvard began teaching a portion of his basic psychology course using a self-instructional program, the Bell Telephone Laboratories began an exploratory study of programed instruction.[1] The results of these first efforts produced a course in basic electricity consisting of 2,600 frames and requiring 3,500 responses. The program was written so that its content matched the content of a course in use in an operating telephone company. "In addition to the program, there is a panel book of 170 illustrations which supplements the program, a book of summary notes and tables, three sets of supplementary complex problems, check-out tests for each section, two final examinations, and other odds and ends." [2]

Like many early programs, this one initially was prepared on cards and tried out with clerks. After a number of revisions, it was printed in both teaching machine and text formats. The experimental study of this program by the Bell Telephone Laboratories occurred under highly controlled conditions in which aptitude, interest, and intelligence tests were administered to the trainees along with a knowledge pretest. Several classes of trainees

---

* Information for this study submitted by H. Oliver Holt, Director of Training Research, American Telephone and Telegraph Company, New York.

[1] H. O. Holt, "Development of Self-Instruction Programs for Telephone Company Training," *Telephony*, November 23, 1963. [A more complete report of the basic electricity study is to be found in J. L. Hughes (editor), *Programed Learning: A Critical Evaluation*, Educational Methods, Inc., Chicago, Illinois, 1963.]

[2] *Ibid.*

worked through the self-instruction program and were compared with another group of classes taught in the conventional lecture-discussion manner. Of the 64 trainees who participated in the study, 30 took the conventional course and 34 took the programed learning course. Proficiency of the two groups was assessed with two comprehension examinations given both immediately after training and six months later. "Scores on the two final examinations clearly favored the programed instruction group." [3]

The range of scores for the programed course was far more restricted than the range for the discussion group, and almost all students in the programed group scored at or above the mean of the lecture group immediately after training. The significant differences which were found between groups immediately after training were found persisting six months later.[4]

From this experience, a great deal was learned about the cost of preparing programs and the amount of careful, detailed work involved in the empirical development of programed packages.

After the experimental study was completed by the Bell Labs, the parent company of the Bell System, the American Telephone and Telegraph Company, decided to publish the program for use in the operating telephone companies. Eventually it will be replaced by a program which will be based upon an analysis of job requirements.

B

The next major development in the use of programed instruction by the Bell System involved the training of telephone operators, particularly long distance telephone operators—referred to in the industry as "outward" operators.

In April 1960 the American Institutes for Research (AIR) undertook a research and development contract with the American Telephone and Telegraph Company. The contract called for a complete task analysis of the actual requirements of the "outward operator" job. Five memorandum reports were prepared describing the steps and results in the activity during the developmental period prior to the major tryout. The contract with AIR was most significant for programed instruction in that specific training and performance criteria were developed in 11 areas which were made a part of the initial contract—before the task analysis was undertaken.

---

[3] *Ibid.*
[4] *Ibid.*

These criteria are listed here because they represent examples of the types of questions which must be answered by a comparison study.

Training Criteria:

Length of initial training	The experimental course should be 25 to 33 per cent shorter in student time than the pre-experimental course.
Cost of initial training	The experimental course should be 5 to 10 per cent less expensive.
Initial training coverage	The experimental course should include practice of more call conditions than at present.
Length of subsequent training	The "on job" training required after initial training should be shorter after the experimental course than after the present course.
Attitudes about training	Attitudes of students, supervisors, and central office management about the course should be at least as favorable as comparable studies about present courses.

Performance Criteria:

Outward toll service	The experimentally trained operators will be able to meet recommended service index objectives and be better in the "objectives" area than the pre-experimentally trained operators.
Call carrying efficiency	Operators trained experimentally should carry call "loads" immediately after training equal to 70 to 80 per cent of the five best operators in the office; this should increase to 90 to 95 per cent in three months and to 100 per cent in six months. These loads should be better than those for similar periods by pre-experimental operators.
Operator key pulsing ability	Key pulsing accuracy on commercial calls (100 attempts) will be comparable to that of the five best operators immediately after training, and greater than that of pre-experimental operators. Experimental operators will be able to key pulse 35 seven digit numbers in three minutes.

Operator tone of service	According to standard observations, the experimental operators will meet the appropriate objectives on tone of service, with more effective tone of service than the pre-experimental operators.
Operator retention of job skills	At three- and six-month intervals after training, experimental operators will be able to handle accurately more call conditions than pre-experimental operators.
Customer satisfaction	During the sixth months after training, experimental operators will receive more customer commendations and fewer customer criticisms than pre-experimental operators.[5]

The selection of outward operator training was fortunate because controlled comparisons could be made of the cost and the quality of training. The project, as pointed out previously, began with a detailed analysis of the performance requirements, which were identified through several sources including: "observation of operators; interviews with operators, supervisors, management, and training personnel; study of written job procedures, equipment, and management and administrative principles and guidelines presented in recommended 'circulars' and other written material." [6]

The results of the job analysis suggested that skills could be grouped into four general areas: perceptual, manual, communications, and intellectual—obviously with overlaps between them. Approximately 125 specific skills were identified and, within the intellectual area, literally hundreds of items of information were enumerated.[7] Based upon the job analysis, a programed training system was developed which consisted of seven phases for which seven diagnostic progress evaluations plus a final performance appraisal were developed. The experimental course consisted of 37 "learning guides" (programed texts), two tapes, and seven supervisor-conducted discussions. This material was designed to meet all the requirements of the training and performance criteria.

A note of contrast between the conventional course and the programed course is necessary to understand the comparative value of the programed course. In the conventional course, a supervisor trained two operators at a

---

[5] Richard O. Peterson and Ronald P. Yuzuk, "Final Report: Experimental Comparisons and Course Implementation," American Institutes for Research, Pittsburgh, Pennsylvania, August 1963, p. 2.

[6] *Ibid.*, p. 5.

[7] *Idem.*

time in lock-step and spent 100 per cent of her time with the trainees. In the programed course, a supervisor taught only on a one-to-one ratio but spent, on the average, only 55 per cent of her time with the student and 5 per cent in preparation, thus potentially freeing her for other supervisory activities 40 per cent of the time. In spite of this, or because of this, training costs were still reduced. While the experimental course was still in development, the Bell System changed its procedures of training from conventional instruction to a one-to-one ratio; therefore, the 40 per cent time free from training activities represented even more significant savings in supervisor time.

Ten offices in the Bell System were included in the study. The "pre-experimental phase" of training using conventional instruction began in June 1961 and continued through the fall; training by the experimental course began in December 1961 and ended in May 1962. Actually, however, since three- and six-month retention tests were included to compare post-training retention, the total experiment extended over a year and a half. These are some of the results of the experiment.

Training time was reduced 27.3 per cent, or within the 25 to 33 per cent criterion. The results of reduced training are summarized as follows:

	Average Hours	*Average Days*	*Range in Days*
Pre-experimental	107.9	13.5	10.5 to 17.5
Experimental	78.3	9.8	7.5 to 15.0
Difference	29.6	3.7	
Per cent savings	27.3		

It should be noted that the fastest student completed the course in 60 hours while the slowest student took 120 hours, or twice the time. This ratio of one to two for the slower student is common with programed instructional materials.

Contract specifications called for the experimental training to be 5 to 10 per cent less expensive than the existing conventional training. A summary of training costs comparing the pre-experimental controlled course with the experimental programed course is shown on the following page.

It is interesting to note that almost half of the estimated dollar saving comes from student wage costs and a quarter of the reduced training costs comes from the reduction in the use of controlled practice operators. Thus the average savings of 29.4 per cent on student cost were well beyond the proposed 5 to 10 per cent savings through the use of programed instruction.

Contract specifications indicated that the programed group should receive practice on more call conditions than did the conventional training group. The conventional training provided practice covering 144 call conditions. For the programed course, an average of 160 call conditions was covered, or 11 per cent more conditions than the original course.

	Cost Per Student	Supervisory Cost Per Student*	CPO Cost Per Student	Total Per Student Cost
Pre-experimental	$154.19	$116.74	$37.96	$308.89
Experimental	112.35	93.00	12.61	217.96
Difference	$ 41.84	$ 23.74	$25.35	$ 90.93
Per cent of total per student savings	13.5	7.7	8.2	29.4

* Based on use of supervisor time on training activities.

Contract specifications stated that subsequent training should be shorter for the programed course than for the pre-experimental conventional course. The subsequent training was of three types: *continuation training,* which was a series of planned lessons away from the board; *day-to-day training,* which usually consisted of questions asked by the supervisors; and *progress training,* in which supervisors analyzed the performance to ascertain additional training needs. An analysis of the records of the two groups showed that 21 per cent fewer questions were asked by the operators who received the experimental programed course. For continuation training the conventional operators needed nine hours covering 19 additional call conditions, whereas the experimental course operators needed only seven and a half hours covering about 17 conditions, an average saving of one and a half hours, or 16 per cent.

Initial contract specifications called for a favorable attitude on the course by students, supervisors, and central office management. Three attitude inventories were developed for use by these groups. Results indicated that the students of both the conventional and self-paced programed course were satisfied with their training. However, the conventionally trained students wanted more flexible pacing, while the experimental program students were overwhelmingly in favor of their self-pacing and individualized review and practice. Both supervisors and central office management were highly in favor of the programed course; however, they suggested that additional review be incorporated in it.

The initial contract called for improved performance in six specific areas. The performance of the programed experimental group was superior to the conventionally trained students in four of the six areas, almost identical in one, and inferior in only one: speed. The program-trained operators also compared favorably with the five best operators (in the ten trial offices) on some tasks.

It should be noted that the original programed course was designed to minimize error, not to maximize speed. Based on the results of the experiment, the course was revised, and, among other things, efforts were made to increase the speed emphasis without sacrificing accuracy. This revision took several months to complete, since a number of major and minor changes were made. An extensive administrative guide was prepared for use by central office management personnel and training staffs. The training guide for supervisors was revised and reorganized to give further programed structure to the supervisor-conducted instructional units. In the revision, the number of learning guides for the operators was reduced from 37 to 34 and the number of supervisor discussions was increased. Three practice tapes were added to the existing number available for student use. Five study guides were prepared to train supervisors to give the course. Five evaluation forms—four interim and one final—were developed so supervisors could make a series of 11 progress evaluations during training. Key pulsing evaluation forms were used to record 100 observations on key pulsing in actual calls. Control sheets for practice calls and their details were also developed. Finally, equipment identification labels were developed for use early in the equipment orientation.

It can be seen from this case study that the meticulous planning in the use of the course produced substantial dividends for the Bell System. This revised programed training course has now been introduced in all companies of the System.

Furthermore, the techniques have been refined and extended to other types of central office training, including one programed training course which utilizes a sophisticated programed simulator for learning, practice, and evaluation.

C

An additional significant use of programed instructional materials by companies of the Bell System is reported by the American Telephone and Telegraph Company in the training of salesmen in a new service offering—wide area telephone service, or "WATS," as it is called. The results of this use of a programed text are significant because the trainees were older employees who averaged 11.4 years of total service, including 6.4 years of sales experience, while 55 per cent had some prior experience in selling WATS.

The WATS programed text was introduced by AT&T to the operating telephone companies of the Bell System in late 1962 and early 1963. As with the other two programs, evaluation instruments were developed concurrently with the programed text. They consisted of two parts which were designed to measure mastery of information about WATS as such, as well as transfer or application of knowledge to solve new problems. In a follow-up study, information was obtained from more than 1,000 salesmen who were trained and tested. Comments and suggestions about the program were tabulated from about 1,500 salesmen and supervisors. More than 70 per cent of the salesmen availed themselves of the opportunity of making spontaneous comments about the program. Salesman satisfaction with the course is indicated by the fact that the ratio of comments was six to one in favor of the programed course. The test results showed that an average appraisal score of 78 per cent (173 of a possible 223) was achieved. Part I, designed to measure factual knowledge, showed that an 83.5 per cent average appraisal score was achieved, while on Part II the average appraisal score on knowledge transfer was 71.2 per cent. Conventional instruction was not available for comparison purposes.

The conditions under which the programed text was taken provided a basis for worthwhile recommendations for the use of future programed materials. Only 49.2 per cent of the salesmen took the course during working hours, and 79 per cent of these took it on a scheduled basis. Of the 50.8 per cent who took the programed course outside working hours, 86.5 per cent took it away from the normal working location. Interestingly enough, neither length of time for completion nor achievement scores seemed to vary significantly with these factors or conditions. This finding suggests that programed materials can be effective when used as part of a home study program. Nevertheless, AT&T concluded that "to gain assurance that trainees will complete this or other programs within a minimum elapsed number of days, and within a minimum number of working days, indications are that the work should be done on a scheduled basis." [8]

The three training programs, *Basic Electricity, Outward Operator,* and *WATS,* were all carefully introduced by AT&T to users in the operating telephone companies. These served to give supervisors and trainers experi-

---

[8] H. A. Shoemaker, "A Follow-up Study of WATS Programed Training," American Telephone and Telegraph Company, 1964.

ence in the use of programed materials in three major departments of the Bell System and, by and large, received generally enthusiastic acceptance. The initial success and acceptance of PI have led to additional effort, and as of this writing AT&T has completed four additional programed courses which are in use in the system and has several more under development.

The Atlantic Refining Company *

The Atlantic Refining Company has experimented with programed instruction for several years. It had been using techniques remotely similar to programed instruction before becoming aware of machine teaching technology. Since that time, it has embarked on a so-called extrinsic-intrinsic-mathetic route on a very limited scale and has concluded that the best method is one that teaches regardless of the "rules."

THE ATLANTIC REFINING COMPANY'S FIRST EFFORT AT PROGRAMED instruction was a 35-frame experimental program on logic circuitry prepared in 1961. It was convincing. In spite of a number of both deliberate and accidental bad frames, it did teach 30 people who knew little about electricity how to draw a circuit for a very challenging problem.

Following this experiment, Robert Royce of the Training Division attempted to teach the training staff what little he knew about the art of programing. The most useful result of this effort was a tape-recorded program that taught employees to use the touch system on the ten-key adding machine. This was prepared by one of the members of the staff.

For the next 12 months, several members of the training staff continued to work on writing programs without completing one that was considered significant or put into widespread use. This is partly explained by the fact that the company's major training needs have to be met rather quickly regardless of the complexity of the material or course of instruction, and good programed materials simply cannot be prepared and validated as fast as other types of training.

Actually Atlantic is using very little programed instruction in its formal training—probably less than 1 per cent of its total effort. The company is not so much disenchanted with the concept as it is convinced that other

* Information drawn from correspondence with Robert Royce, Training Division, The Atlantic Refining Company, Philadelphia, Pennsylvania.

approaches can be more efficiently prepared for most of the training done in the company.

The largest use of the technique is in the Atlantic dealer training schools, where five short programs are used to teach basic product knowledge to service station dealers. These programs are called "Teach Yourself Texts."

The company is using very few stock off-the-shelf programs. The consensus is that many of those that have been reviewed are poorly done and, like canned training films, do not meet the company's training needs. Two of Du Pont's gasoline programs prepared by Basic Systems have been used with generally satisfactory results. Few employees, however, have used the off-the-shelf programs on file, partly because management has made no special effort to "sell" them. The primary purposes in obtaining these programs were to study the techniques of other programers, to evaluate the ability of programing firms in the event that the company should want to contract for a special job, and to explore the content for possible use in training. Atlantic did publish and circulate a list of these programs, but the response was slight because many of them were not job-related. Those that might have been useful were found to be too short, too long, too academic, too childish, too boring, too poorly taught, or simply inappropriate for employee needs. This is the rationale for not attempting a hard sell to either employees or supervisors.

So far the company has contracted for only two programs—"Red Ball" and "PCV," both prepared by RCA. They are now in use both in the dealer schools and in the service stations. It is doubtful that adequate evaluation results will be obtainable.

A program called "Answering the Telephone" has been prepared in-house and has been made available to all new office employees. Another in-house program on "How to Use the Slide Rule" is used by new members of the sales force preliminary to learning the analysis of sales statistics and ratios in the classroom. This program was prepared to help them deal with the kinds of figures they would actually have to work with—a task which available programs did not do. Although this program was never "polished," the results apparently satisfied the trainers, so further development efforts were discontinued.

Another in-house program was "Square Root." This is somewhat unusual in that its use is devious. It is used in a classroom session on "how to train" along with several other self-instructional texts. Its purpose is two-fold: to teach square root and to provide a subject for trainees to use in teaching others in a group situation.

Atlantic has not evaluated the results of any of its in-house programs.

The telephone program was used to introduce programed instruction to office management as an instructional technique, as well as to meet a specific training need. The programs were turned over to personnel people, who have put them into use, but no attempt has been made to validate them by on-the-job performance. The slide-rule program is tested only by the instructor's observations of performance in the classroom. Having satisfied himself that the trainees learn from the program, he now assigns it as week-end homework. Since slide rules are not required on the job, no formal on-job check is made. Those who use it are the ones who find it useful in analyzing financial statements. The company has evidence that the program has encouraged a few trainees to buy slide rules and use them on the job.

The management staff at Atlantic has never gotten into the practice of comparing programed instruction with conventional training largely because it is convinced that this kind of research would be a waste of time. In other words, it is convinced that programed instruction works and doesn't feel obliged to prove it. Robert Royce's personal opinion is that most of the research done in the field is wasted effort. He feels that instead of trying to prove programed instruction's value by comparing intrinsic with extrinsic or machine with text, and so on, programers should concentrate on how to use the wide variety of available teaching and training techniques in their programs, with or without hardware. He feels strongly that programed instruction has much more to offer than even the polished professional realizes. He also feels that programed instruction "rules" have unnecessarily prejudiced many against the use of hardware. He states his position as follows:

> We're not concerned with proving anything by before-and-after tests; we know it works if it's done and administered well. We also know that its limitations are similar to those of any kind of training and that actual job performance is highly influenced by factors (stimuli) other than those at work when the job is learned. (For example, one employee abandoned the touch technique learned on our ten-key adding machine after being subjected to criticism by fellow employees who were old-timers who had always used a hunt-peck system.) These remarks are not meant to imply that we never intend to measure results through at-work performance tests, for if we ever install a programed instruction lesson intended to teach fully a functional job segment (as some companies claim to have done), we would make such an evaluation.

As to developing a programed instruction course that will do the job more effectively, the training people feel a really good program of any length on a significant subject must have widespread value for a sizable number of employees. However, training needs often vary widely throughout the company and are shared in common by only a small number of people.

Sometimes the most interested member of management wants people to change their behavior but has no real concrete learning objectives. In one instance Mr. Royce drafted a preliminary linear program on a highly practical and worthwhile subject for dealers, only to have a sudden change in procedure negate the entire effort. In another, he was half finished with a mathetics program on a subject that had given trouble for years when the affected department decided to have computers do the work instead of people. So computer experts programed the procedure.

To alleviate the problem somewhat, Atlantic's programers have drafted a sample which they feel could be polished for inclusion in an industrial programer's basic training. It is attached to this case study as a supplement.

The experience of this company has led to these tentative conclusions: (1) Motivation to learn must exist and be relatively strong before a person will attempt to learn anything by any method, including programed instruction. Motivation through the exposure of a trainee's inadequacy can be built into the program itself, but this is sufficient only if the trainee knows he *has* to learn the information or skill involved. The employee's environment must be conducive to learning first. (2) Conditioning can be accomplished with human beings only in a limited way. The best program in the world will not change a person's on-the-job behavior unless the behavioral change is seen as desirable *by the trainee*. He reacts not just to the program itself but also to social pressures and other stimuli in his own world of reality. People tend to resist change until their current behavior is no longer appropriate or adequate for the situation. Once they feel a strong sense of inadequacy they will seek new forms of behavior, but only then will *any* kind of teaching have a strong effect in determining how people actually *do* what they've *learned about* doing. (3) Effective programed learning is easier to develop if it teaches people to *do* things instead of just teaching them *about* things. Learn-to-do programs also seem to be more effective because they appear more meaningful to the trainee and give him a greater sense of accomplishment. The programer must use judgment, however, so that he avoids programing what the trainee can do simply by following procedures or some other form of instructions. He must also be certain that what the trainee is expected to do is in fact teachable. For example, many supervisory skills cannot really be taught because the stimuli are so multitudinous and variable that a list of multiple discriminations might reach infinity. Then,

too, many subjects fall into the category of "no right answer." Here, of course,
the objectives must clearly identify whatever limitations are in effect.

Finally, Mr. Royce feels that—

> Programed instruction is a highly effective tool that we still haven't
> learned to make full use of. Most of what appears to be most practical
> for programing, outside of the tasks of lower-level employees, seems
> to be minutiae which are of relatively little significance in the total
> scheme of things. Good programed instruction of the future (not that
> done according to formula) will probably prove to be that done by
> machine or simulation (with or without the aid of computers) and will
> be highly job oriented. This means that bigger investments will have to
> be made in training and, therefore, that the management of a corpora-
> tion must first recognize the value of such investments.

Supplement

Program Planning

> A PI Lesson in planning for central-staff training personnel whose
> duties and responsibilities include identifying training needs, selling
> training, establishing objectives, planning and designing training for
> all departments of an integrated corporation, training trainers, and
> occasionally conducting special courses.

- Now that you've had an opportunity to experiment with intrinsic, extrinsic,
  mathetic, conversational chaining, mixed, and "modern" programing,
  it's time to consider how you're going to plan your activities so that you
  can effectively program lesson plans and also carry out your other training
  responsibilities. This lesson will help you do that. It is an example of
  another type of "modern" programing. It will provide no immediate
  confirmation, because it is designed to help you gain insight into problems
  like those which you must face alone and solve for yourself at work. To
  benefit from this lesson, you must study every item carefully and follow *all*
  instructions. When you have completed this lesson, you are to show your
  written responses to your supervisor and discuss them with him in detail.

*   *   *

- *Before you begin—*
  Make sure that you have the following materials:
  1. Writing pad
  2. Carbon paper
  3. Pencil(s)

*   *   *

- In this program, your responses are to be recorded on writing paper rather than in the program itself. You are to record each response on a separate sheet of paper and make a carbon copy for your supervisor's use during your discussion with him.

* * *

- On your first sheet of writing paper write the words "Planning Work-Sheet."

Subsequent work-sheets need not be titled, but to keep them in order you *should* number them. Please *remember to do this.*

* * *

- *Assume that the following statements are true:*
Yesterday you sold the idea of programing a one-hour basic course on the fundamentals of electronic data processing for foremen and supervisors whose jobs are likely to be affected by automation in the next year or two.* Knowing that you have the whole-hearted approval of your supervisor and the department that will be affected, but that you also have other commitments to meet, you set the following goals:
  1. Statement of objective(s) prepared and approved—one week from today.
  2. Task analysis and outline of course approved—three weeks from today.
  3. Test frames approved—four weeks from today.
  4. Program drafted for trial—seven weeks from today.
  5. Revised program ready for field test—10 weeks from today.
  6. Program published and installed—15 weeks from today.

Now be realistic.
Consider the information given and your own schedule of activities for the next three months, and determine whether these goals are realistic for you.
   a. If so, record on your planning work-sheet the date on which you expect to install the program. (If you feel you can better the goals listed above, use your planning work-sheet to revise them so that you have a practical working schedule to follow.)
   b. If not, revise the stated goals to fit your own situation. Record on your planning work-sheet the actual dates which you feel would be reasonable for each step in the process.
   c. In either case, record and circle the date on which you hope to install the program—the one you would tell the line manager to aim for.

* * *

- *On work-sheet No. 2 record today's date and assume the following information to be true:*

---

* The training director should substitute whatever PI assignments seem most appropriate.

Today you've found an unexpected opportunity to talk briefly with your subject-matter expert (the only person in your company qualified). During your conversation you scribble a statement of objectives (as you see them) on a piece of paper for his consideration. He tells you that he will need to give them additional thought but agrees to discuss them with you at a time you find convenient within the next two days. Will this affect your schedule in any way?

    a. If not, explain why on work-sheet No. 2.

    b. If so, revise your schedule as you see it on work-sheet No. 2.

*   *   *

• Since your initial discussion of objectives with the subject-matter expert you've encountered a wide difference of opinion as to the precise behavioral changes desired. Through extra effort on your part, you've finally engineered agreement on objectives and have full approval. However, two weeks have passed since you prepared your first planning work-sheet.

Consider how this information (along with your *real* job commitments) will affect your PI goals and use work-sheet No. 3 to revise them. (If no revision is necessary, explain why.)

*   *   *

• On work-sheet No. 4 jot down the date three weeks from today.

Assume that since the objectives have been established you've found time (at work or at home) to outline the course and develop test frames. Assume also that your subject-matter expert agrees to check them out in any way you wish and discuss them with you whenever you find it convenient— tomorrow (three weeks plus one day) if you say so.

Consider how this will affect your schedule. If you want to change it, do so on work-sheet No. 4. If not, explain why.

*   *   *

• On work-sheet No. 5 record the following date: five weeks from today.

Now assume the following facts are true:

1. On the date recorded on work-sheet No. 4 your subject-matter expert contracted an illness which has kept him away from work until today.

2. He has not had an opportunity to fully evaluate the material you submitted to him.

3. His backlog of work will prevent him from getting back to you for at least one week from the date written on work-sheet No. 5.

How will these facts affect your schedule? Make whatever revisions you feel necessary on work-sheet No. 5. (If you see no need for revision, explain why.)

*   *   *

- On work-sheet No. 6 record the date six weeks from today, and assume that the following facts are true:

Your task analysis has revealed a controversial practice, which is being discussed by the line organization. Today you learn that a committee is being formed to resolve the issue. It will meet two weeks from tomorrow and expects to announce a decision that same afternoon.

Make whatever revisions to your schedule you feel necessary on work-sheet No. 6. If you see no need for revision, explain why.

* * *

- On work-sheet No. 7 record this date: one week from the committee's decision. Assume the following facts to be true:

Despite a heavy work load of other assignments you've had to do, the committee's decision has made the programing task much simpler than you'd anticipated. As a result you've written a surprising number of frames (or exercises), tested them successfully on other staff members, and are almost half finished with your first draft.

At 11 o'clock today you are asked when you hope to have the program completed for a field test. Feeling optimistic, you give the following date:

_____.

(Record on work-sheet No. 7 the date you think you'd aim for.)

* * *

- Assume that the date is the same one recorded at the top of work-sheet No. 7. Write that date at the top of work-sheet No. 8.

On this date your supervisor is out of town. At 4 o'clock his boss calls you into his office and asks you to develop a special 40-hour course for foremen, teaching them their responsibilities and, to the extent possible, how to carry them out. The course is scheduled to begin one month from today. You are to submit a draft of your proposal three days from the date recorded on work-sheet No. 8.

Considering this assignment along with your other commitments, revise your PI goals accordingly. (If at this point you have any comments or questions you'd like to discuss with your supervisor, add them to work-sheet No. 8.)

* * *

- On work-sheet No. 9 record a date approximately one week after the scheduled starting date of the special course for foremen. Assume that the following statements are true:
  1. In the past 30 days you have completed your work on whichever non-PI job you have been giving the highest priority.

2. You have also agreed to revise a one-day session in the training program for your starting salesmen, edit a manual for mechanical workers, attend a three-day seminar in New York, draft a proposal for a major change in the company's basic supervisory training program, evaluate the new employee's induction program, conduct a 15-hour course in report writing, prepare individual management development recommendations for 10 supervisors, give a talk to a local professional association, answer a 12-page survey questionnaire, coach a newly appointed trainer, test an off-shelf PI text on 12 trainees, and sell the idea to nine division heads that they should appoint supervisors to attend a one-week course designed to prepare them to become trainers in the basic supervisory training program. These tasks must all be accomplished within the next eight weeks.

3. Various commitments, emergencies, and travel have prevented you from making any further progress on your schedule for the PI course since you last revised your schedule.

Considering these facts, use work-sheet No. 9 to plan more realistically for the PI course.

*   *   *

- Mark another sheet of paper (work-sheet) No. 10. Then:

  1. Reflect on the various exercises you have just completed.
  2. Revise your PI schedule more realistically. Include specific target dates.
  3. Determine how you are going to plan your work from this point on to make sure that you are able to include PI in your repertoire of training techniques. Write your conclusions on work-sheet No. 10 and discuss them with your supervisor.

Burroughs Corporation *

A

Computers come in many shapes and sizes, and new designs are being marketed all the time. The cost of adapting programs from one computer to another is considerable. To minimize this cost for business oriented programs, and to create greater flexibility, COBOL (COmmon Business Oriented Language) has been developed. The Burroughs Corporation established a programed learning course to familiarize its personnel with COBOL and enable them to write programs in this new computer language. A high level of proficiency was achieved as measured by criterion performance. Though Burroughs' aim of having at least 90 per cent of the trainees attain at least 90 per cent of the skills and information covered in the program was not quite achieved, management was satisfied that the study showed PI to be clearly superior to conventional procedures in teaching COBOL. The significant cost saving accruing from this course stems largely from the fact that it can be packaged and sent to field offices rather than paying to bring students to the home office to be trained.

THE BURROUGHS CORPORATION WANTED TO USE PROGRAMED TRAINing materials to teach its sales technical representatives to assist customers in translating business-oriented problems into the common computer language, COBOL.

The American Institutes for Research was the consulting organization responsible for preparing the materials, supervising the preliminary tryouts, and developing the subsequent revision; and Burroughs conducted the field trials and developed the criterion examination. Data on these efforts were analyzed by the company and further revisions were made by the programing staff. The company assigned a technical representative to assist the consulting staff in obtaining and interpreting the technical information.

* This case is based upon information contained in H. H. Shettel, Doris J. Clapp, Judi L. Northrup, and Ann P. Delatte, *Development of a Programmed Training Course in COBOL,* American Institutes for Research, Pittsburgh, Pennsylvania, December 1963; and upon information and data provided by Carl A. Powers, Manager, Programed Instruction, Sales and Technical Education, Burroughs Corporation, Detroit, Michigan.

Through the use of COBOL, programs written for one computer can be used for another computer if a COBOL compiler program is available for the second computer. The Burroughs B-5000 Information Processing System contains such a compiler and was selected as the system around which the instructional program would be built.

The overall objective for the programed materials was to teach the company's sales technical representatives to write programs in COBOL. Even though the representatives are required to help a customer analyze his problem, it was not the purpose of this project to develop training materials to assist in this analysis, nor was it intended to cover complex problems. Burroughs expected that these facets would be covered by on-the-job training and experience. The programs that the sales technical representatives were to be taught to write in COBOL were based on problems that had already been analyzed.

Since Burroughs was to develop the terminal performance examination, it agreed to prepare test items which would indicate the level of business problems the newly trained representatives should be able to program in COBOL. This test therefore provided the company's specifications for the material that the programing staff was to produce.

So that its representatives could discuss customer problems intelligently, Burroughs also decided that they should know the language and concepts of COBOL. In this respect, however, the amount of information that would be taught was critical. It could be overdone.

Before developing a prototype of the programed instructional package (PIP), AIR prepared an outline of the course covering elements which company experts felt would achieve the required objectives. The programing staff also used the criterion test developed by the company and analyzed the contents of the available COBOL source documents. Since the COBOL compiler program for the B-5000 system was being developed at the same time as the PIP, close liaison with the company's technical experts was necessary. Even after they had accomplished some frame writing and testing, revisions in the PIP were necessary because of this concurrent development and the lack of stability of the language itself.

Burroughs hoped that 90 per cent of the trainees would be able to achieve a minimum of 90 per cent proficiency on the criterion examination. In summary, it hoped that through the PIP the trainees would be able—

> . . . to define specific technical terms, to understand (that is, to generalize to new situations) the basic concepts and the structure of COBOL routines, and, when provided with an analysis of a moderately difficult business problem, to be able to write a COBOL computer program that

would solve this problem in an efficient manner. For example, the trainee was required not only to define "procedure branching verbs," but also to identify the need for these verbs in various situations, and to demonstrate his ability to use them in actually writing sample COBOL programs.[1]

The trainee population, as specified by Burroughs, was as follows: The majority of the trainees had four years of college, and the remainder had at least a high school education. The minimum IQ was 110. They had had past experience with the programing of computers and a familiarity with problem-oriented common languages such as Fortran and others, but none had received any formal training in COBOL. Since this population was considered to be homogeneous with respect to prior knowledge, it was not felt necessary to use any such instructional programing technique as branching which would make use of an individual's specific learning requirements. It was found during the field trial that some of the students displayed some knowledge of COBOL before taking the PIP and that, therefore, the use of a technique which could have taken advantage of their prior knowledge might have made the program more efficient.

Even though the trainees were required to learn approximately 400 terms and symbols as an integrated body of knowledge, the consultants pointed out that—

> The intricacy of the task is not indicated by the *number* of terms, but rather by the vast network of relationships and rules associated with them. . . . Thus, in a way, each COBOL concept may be thought of as a "tree," with numerous ramifications, or branches, which touch on other "trees." [2]

Other problems that were considered in programing strategy were the difficulty of using English words in a different context from what one had previously used, the requirement to develop a set of complex conceptual and verbal skills, and the facility to apply them. Programing problems included the size of steps, the nature of the sequencing, and whether to use overt or covert responses. All these considerations had implications for strategy designs. An analysis of the criterion examination, for example, indicated the requirement for constructed responses. Since the population was homogeneous, it was decided to use a linear rather than a branching sequence. The heavy dependence on technical terms emphasized the need for immediate reinforcement and confirmation, and the necessary strategy required

---

[1] H. H. Shettel *et al.*, p. 6.
[2] *Ibid.*, p. 9.

an analysis of the structure of the concepts. The relationship, for example, between the four divisions of a COBOL program—(1) identification, (2) environment, (3) data, and (4) procedure—implied a high degree of inter-action among them. The following example was noted:

> Suppose the programer has stated in the *Environment Division* that a particular file is assigned to the PRINTER. Since the PRINTER only records in alphanumeric, which is termed the NONSTANDARD RE-CORDING MODE, the recording mode clause for this file in the *Data Division* should be RECORDING MODE IS NONSTANDARD, or else the clause may be omitted since the compiler will assume that a file assigned to the PRINTER will be recorded in alphanumeric. This is to cite but one particular instance of the relations which exist among the four divisions.[3]

Therefore, it was impossible in the strategy and sequencing to cover each division in sequence, and a "spiral approach" was devised to organize the PIP. This approach was described as follows:

> Information on each of the divisions was recycled at two higher levels of complexity. The program developed for this course thus utilized three different levels: basic, intermediate, and detailed. At each level, informa-tion was taught within its own hierarchy, or division, and related as much as possible to information associated with other hierarchies. Spi-raling through each division three times also permitted the inclusion of review material on a systematic basis.[4]

The program consisted of approximately 4,554 frames covering 400 con-cepts along with the associations and rules relating to each. This number averaged about 11 frames per concept, but there were a number of excep-tions. The reference format alone required more than 200 frames, for in-stance. The program also utilized flow charts, models, illustrations, and 26 exhibits and job aids. It contained more than 900 external references to exhibits, or approximately one reference for every five frames.

A preliminary tryout was conducted by the programing staff with four subjects from the local Burroughs office. Only one of the four was able to complete the entire program. However, interaction between the four sub-jects and the consultant staff was intense and detailed. Every conceivable aspect of the program was discussed, which provided useful guidance for subsequent revision. These revisions were intended to improve the frames by reducing the number of prompts required and clarifying the wording.

The 24 sales technical representatives on whom the field test was con-

---

[3] *Ibid.*, p. 11.
[4] *Idem.*

ducted were given a pretest covering only the first unit of the program, which included introductory materials such as the meaning of COBOL and the general functions of the four divisions. The test consisted of 40 items, 34 of which were completion items while 6 required correcting minor errors in statements. The range of scores in the pretest was from 5 per cent to 77.5 per cent with a mean of 38 per cent. As noted, this group was not as "homogeneous" as it was thought to be, although it was pointed out that even a score of 77 per cent on this basic test was not an indication of sufficient knowledge to write a COBOL program.

The students worked on the PIP's in a classroom for an average of six hours a day. They were constantly monitored and were asked to make any comments or raise any questions they had regarding individual frames or portions of the PIP. Two hundred comments were received. Immediately upon completion of the PIP the trainees took the criterion examination, and following this they answered an attitude questionnaire. All field test activities were conducted by Burroughs.

The amount of time the individual trainee took to complete the PIP ranged from 52 hours to 94 hours, with an average of 70 hours. Even though these figures include the time spent in recording comments, they still indicate the variability of individually paced instruction. We can conclude, however, that the PIP would take less time than the 70-hour mean indicates. Interestingly, as the trainees progressed through the program, they completed fewer frames per minute because of the greater amount of activity required for responding to the later frames, some of which may have required 15 or 20 minutes to complete. The error rate per frame, however, *decreased* as the frames became more complex (average error rate was 2.2 per cent). This finding was in contrast to the increasing error rate in the preliminary tryout and was explained in the report as follows:

> This appears to indicate that the increasing rate in the preliminary tryout was due to the widely spaced learning sessions and that, in spite of increasing complexity, with more optimally spaced sessions the program builds increased proficiency in COBOL. This effect may also be due in part to the gradual adaptation of the trainee to the methodology of programed instruction; that is, the trainees gradually became skilled "program takers." This result also appears to indicate that the spiral approach was successful in integrating the more complex facts; otherwise, error rates would certainly have increased despite any adaptation to the method of instruction. Also, the revisions that were made in the program on the basis of the earlier individual tryouts of the program further reduced the error rate.[5]

---

[5] *Ibid.,* p. 31.

The criterion examination consisted of three parts. A trainee could score 72 points on Part One, 10 points on Part Two, and 1,005 on Part Three, which was the programing problem. The maximum score thus was 1,087. Only 22 of the 24 trainees completed the criterion test. The median scores on Parts One and Two were 74 per cent and 86.1 per cent respectively. The median score on Part Three, which was the most important and most heavily weighted part of the examination, was 91.5 per cent. The median score on the complete examination was 90.25 per cent. Of the field test group 91 per cent made a score of 80 per cent or higher on the examination, which indicates that at this point the program was a 91/80 PIP. The most significant finding, however, is the average on the programing section (Part Three), which was the best measure of performance. The consultant staff had no question that the trainees had acquired a high degree of proficiency in writing COBOL programs. Even though Burroughs did not make a comparison study with conventional teaching procedures, its own estimate was that training by conventional methodology would require five to six weeks to achieve the same level of proficiency.

As is customary, the trainees were asked to complete an attitude questionnaire on which they remained anonymous. Nine questionnaires were filled out. The trainees indicated that PI should be used often in future courses and that instruction through programed materials was acceptable, and even superior to conventional training.

The PIP was revised on the basis of what the programers learned from the nearly 200 comments which were made and from the error rates on the specific frames and the test. All frames on which three or more trainees made errors were revised. Revision consisted in adding or rewriting frames. In rewriting, however, care was taken not to lower the error rate by simply increasing the degree of prompting. When a change was questionable, the final basis for making a decision was the responses made on the criterion test items.

The company has prepared the revised PIP and distributed it to its field offices throughout the country. Acceptance has been highly favorable, and in many offices the PIP is replacing conventional instruction. Apparently the results were encouraging enough for Burroughs to decide to use the PIP for internal training in lieu of the conventional techniques and to make it available commercially for use by others.

B

This second history of Burroughs' effort in PI describes the development and use of a new format which was designed for the compact

COBOL text. It apparently is far more acceptable to the students than the original COBOL text. More important than this, however, the format has demonstrated to Burroughs management that an acceptable text can be written at a small cost and in a short time.*

The Burroughs Corporation figures its training costs as so much per man, including the costs of preparing the material, transportation, and subsistence allowance during the training period. Even though programed instruction has eliminated or reduced subsistence allowance and transportation costs, the cost of preparing the material has remained rather high. The only way to reduce this cost is to apply PI in a manner that will decrease the preparation and reproduction time and still maintain the PI concept.

In developing a new format, therefore, along with considering the cost, which was evaluated at $10 a frame to prepare a text which is generally 2,500 frames or more, there are other items of equal, perhaps greater, importance. These are the students' reactions to the format, the frame style, and the level of training achieved.

Even though the format is new, the technique is not. Burroughs' newest text consists of a series of study pages each one of which is followed by a series of linear frames. The concept is to provide the student with a series of points which are interrelated and appear in sequential order. (See the exhibit, which shows the responses and frames of three sets of Lesson 5.) A set of frames follows the study page; one applies to each point covered and is written in the same sequential order as the point appearing on the study page. Thus if there are seven points on the study page, there are seven frames. The responses are on the lefthand page, which is the back of the study page. After the student has completed the first set and checked his responses, he turns the page for a second set of frames on the same points. The same procedure is followed as with the first set, and the student then turns the page for a third set of frames. The variation in each set of frames is the amount of prompting provided. The first set of frames is highly prompted, the second set is less prompted, and the third set is not prompted. It was found advantageous to the students to underline for emphasis the key points on the study page.

The new format has reduced the cost of preparing the text by approximately $4 per frame. The preparation time was also greatly reduced. The current COBOL text took from three to three and one-half months to write and three weeks to reproduce. The original COBOL text required eight

---

* Information for this case submitted by Carl A. Powers, Manager, Programed Instruction, Sales & Technical Education, Burroughs Corporation, Detroit, Michigan.

months to write, another four months to lay out, and a final eight weeks to reproduce. Reducing the time has also, of course, reduced the cost.

Another advantage of the new format is its greatly reduced size. As in most linear texts a great deal of space was formerly wasted between frames. By using a study page more of the teaching is accomplished on one page with only reinforcement required. The new format is easily typed, and its layout is simple, which further reduced the cost. The new format eliminated much of the page turning required by the usual linear text in which the frame is generally on one page with the responses on the next. In those programed texts whose frames and responses are on the same page, usually some device is necessary to hide the answer, such as a mask. The first COBOL text required the student to turn a page for every frame, then return to the beginning when a portion of the frames was completed, and then finally to reverse the book in order to complete the frame on the reverse side. The new text requires turning only three pages per lesson and does not require checking the response as each frame is completed.

Students who have studied both formats feel the new one presents the material at a "higher level," even though it has essentially the same content. The students also feel that the new format is less tiring. Constructed responses are still required, but less frequently. The new format is like an ordinary text but still forces interaction with the materials. Further, the study page provides a source of reference for the students.

The new format is equally effective as a linear program. Therefore, it is considered a definite improvement over the old one because its additional advantages were not gained at the expense of any effectiveness in training.

Carl A. Powers, the Manager of Programed Instruction, presents the following rationale for having adopted this format in addition to the advantages of such factors as low cost, ease of reproduction, less preparation time, and equally effective training:

> Most individuals in industry are accustomed to learning from a manual or textbook. Study habits of this type, when going through a straight linear program, have caused some difficulty. Each individual tends to spend a great deal of time on a particular frame, thinking that the point will not be introduced again. As a result, the completion time for this type of text is longer than it should be. Through the study page concept, the method of training is more familiar to the individual, and as a result it is more acceptable. Also, the individuals we hire as salesmen are professionals who are accustomed to learning and thus should be able to grasp more than one point at a given time, particularly if all points are interrelated. Therefore, by introducing five to ten points per study page we are raising the level of our training to meet the ability

of the individual. This definitely has a psychological effect on the salesmen and has also made this type of format more acceptable.

The new programed text was validated on 25 individuals who took three examinations throughout the course. The results are as follows:

	NUMBER OF STUDENTS	RANGE
EXAMINATION 1	15	100–95
	5	94–90
	2	89–85
	2	84–80
	1	79–75
	—	
	25	

	NUMBER OF STUDENTS	RANGE
EXAMINATION 2	14	100–95
	5	94–90
	4	89–85
	0	84–80
	1	79–75
	0	74–70
	1	69–65
	—	
	25	

	NUMBER OF STUDENTS	RANGE
FINAL EXAMINATION	12	100–95
	10	94–90
	2	89–85
	0	84–80
	1	79–75
	—	
	25	

Since preparing a programed course in the new format is different from preparing one in either a linear or a scrambled-book format, Mr. Powers recommends the following method.

1. *Analysis.* Collect all material to be taught and divide it into logical segments. Each segment should be further divided into approximately five to ten points. These are the points that will constitute the frames for a particular study page.
2. *Examinations.* Write all examinations first. An estimate is approximately three examinations for a 75-lesson text. A study page and three sets of frames constitute a lesson. Of course, this can vary with the complexity of the material being taught and/or the audience for whom the text is intended.

3. *Study pages.* Write all study pages before writing any frames. Underlining or capitalization can be used for stress and emphasis.

4. *Frames.* Frames must be written with the least possible number of words while still stressing the point. An excellent method for writing frames is to write the set of three for one point before writing those for the second point. Write the third frame for the set first. This is the criterion frame and the student should respond to the entire point being taught. By labeling them 1c, 1a, 1b, and then 2c, 2a, 2b, and so on, the frames can easily be separated for sets 1, 2, and 3. When writing these frames it is best not to vary the wording too abruptly for the three frames on the same point. The student doesn't have many frames in which to conquer the point, and extensive rewording could cause confusion.

5. *First draft.* After all the frames are written for a lesson or after all the lessons are completed, then segregate 1a, 2a, 3a, and so on into a set of frames, and the same for 1b, 2b, 3b and 1c, 2c, 3c.

6. *Testing and revision.* The first testing should include approximately four or five individuals representing a cross-section of the audience for whom the text was written. Revision requires a careful analysis of the response each student gave to each frame. Two important points can be learned from this. First, if three out of five students gave the same wrong response to a frame, then the frame was too easily misinterpreted. Second, if three out of five students gave different responses to a frame, then either the frame is poorly worded or the build-up to the frame was not sufficient. In any case, the frame and possibly the study page must be changed.

An additional important feature in preparing a program in this manner is that the format provides both horizontal and vertical reinforcement. That is, each frame on a given point provides reinforcement, and since all points on a given study page are related, one frame can be used to reinforce a point covered in a previous frame in the same set.

The new format has proved itself highly effective for Burroughs' training managers. They do not yet know whether it would be equally effective in other areas and for other types of individuals. On the basis of their experience, however, they do suggest that it might be valuable for the following groups:

1. Sales and technical personnel in industry and selected skilled workers.
2. College students, especially junior and senior levels.
3. Above-average high school students in selected courses.
4. Adults being educated in selected groups.

Supplement

LESSON 5. USE OF MA 01–99 AND READ KEYBOARD

Like mechanical crossfooters, memory addresses 01 through 99 (MA 01–99) are considered to be *"non-destructive"* memory. The contents of "non-destructive" memory can be increased or decreased by *direct addition or subtraction.*

Like the Sensimatic, MA 01–99 are programed through the use of *three sections* (A, B, and C).

A	Add	Data listed on the keyboard may be *added, sub-*
B	Subtract	*tracted, or non-added* independently in the three
C	NA	sections.

A	Add	Unlike the basic Sensimatic, data listed on the
B	Add	keyboard requires a "Read Keyboard" pin con-
C	Add	trol, in the Other Controls area, to be *recognized.*
Other		
Controls	RK	

Keyboard			
Entry	5.00 ——	RK——	5.00 *Recognized*

A	NA	Unless "RK" (Read Keyboard) is programed,
B	NA	any data listed on the keyboard will be ignored.
C	NA	
Other		
Controls		

Keyboard	5.00 ——	no RK ——	5.00 *Ignored*
Entry			

When "RK" is programed, data listed on the keyboard may be *printed, and/ or added, subtracted, or non-added.* When "RK" is programed, keyboard data will add to any section *programed to add,* or subtract from any section *programed to subtract.*

Programing to cause addition or subtraction is accomplished by pin *control.* Unless a section is pin-controlled to "add" or "subtract," all data will *non-add in that section.*

The *basic function* in all three sections is to *"non-add"* all data.

RESPONSES—FIRST SET

1. accumulation
   data
   prior contents

2. three
   A, B, C

3. add
   subtract
   add

4. recognized
   processed
   Read Keyboard

5. keyboard
   ignored

6. added
   subtracted
   non-added

7. programed to subtract

8. pin-controlled
   add

9. non-add
   section
   not

Frames—First Set

1. Non-destructive memory can accumulate data since data can be introduced without destroying its prior contents. The non-destructive character of MA 01–99 enables the _____ of _____ without destroying their _____ _____.

2. Sensimatic accumulators are programed in three sections. The _____ _____ sections used in programing MA 01–99 are also identified as _____, _____, and _____.

3. Data may be added, subtracted, or non-added in any of the three sections, by programing each section, A, B, and C, to _____, _____, and non-_____.

4. A Read Keyboard pin is required to recognize and process data listed on the keyboard. Therefore, for a keyboard entry to be _____ and _____, programing must include a _____ _____ pin.

5. Keyboard entries will not be ignored if an RK (Read Keyboard) pin is programed. However, without an RK pin, a _____ entry will be _____.

6. When RK is programed, print and/or add, subtract, or non-add will occur. Therefore, RK permits keyboard entries to be printed and/or _____, _____, or _____-_____.

7. Keyboard data will add to any section programed to add, or subtract from any section _____ _____ _____.

8. Addition and subtraction are pin-controlled. If a section is not _____- _____ to add or subtract, all data will non-_____.

9. When a section is not programed, the E 2100 will non-add all data. The basic function of the E 2100 is to _____-_____ all data when a _____ is _____ programed.

RESPONSES—SECOND SET

1. accumulate data
   destroying
   prior contents

2. three
   A, B, C

3. added
   subtracted
   non-added

4. Read Keyboard
   recognize
   process
   keyboard

5. keyboard entry
   ignored

6. printed
   added
   subtracted
   non-added

7. a) programed
      add
   b) programed
      subtract

8. pin
   data
   non-add

9. non-add
   section
   programed

Frames—Second Set

1. The ability of non-destructive memory to accumulate data permits MA 01–99 to _____ _____ because it can be introduced without _____ their _____ _____.

2. The functions of MA 01–99 are programed in _____ sections which are identified as ___, ___, and ___.

3. Keyboard entries may be _____, _____, and _____-_____.

4. Whenever listed data is to be recognized and processed, programing must provide for a _____ _____ pin because this control is required to _____ and _____ any _____ entry.

5. Without an RK pin being programed, any _____ _____ is _____.

6. While some keyboard entries may be non-printed, the RK instruction permits keyboard entries to be _____ as well as _____, _____, or _____-_____.

7. Keyboard data will:
   a) Add to any section _____ to _____.
   b) Subtract from any section _____ to _____.

8. When it is not necessary to accumulate data, if a section is not _____-controlled to add or subtract, all _____ will _____-_____.

9. The E 2100, within any section, will perform the basic function of _____-_____ when the _____ is not _____.

Responses—Third Set

1. accumulate data
    without destroying their prior contents

2. three sections
    A, B, and C

3. A, B, and C
    add, subtract, and non-add

4. Read Keyboard
    recognize and process any keyboard entry

5. keyboard entry will be ignored

6. printed and/or added, subtracted, or non-added

7. a) add
        programed to add
    b) subtract
        programed to subtract

8. pin-controlled
    data will non-add

9. non-add
    section is not programed

Frames—Third Set

1. Non-destructive memory such as MA 01–99 can _____ because data can be introduced _____ _____.

2. Like the Sensimatic accumulators, MA 01-99 can be programed in _____ _____ which are identified as _____.

3. Keyboard entries may be programed in sections _____ to _____.

4. Programing of a _____ pin is required to _____.

5. If an RK pin is not programed, any _____ _____.

6. The programing of RK permits keyboard entries to be _____ _____.

7. Data read from the keyboard with an RK instruction will:
   a) _____ to any section _____.
   b) _____ from any section _____.

8. If a section is not _____ to add or subtract, all _____.

9. A section in the E 2100 will perform the basic function of _____ when the _____.

Chemical Bank New York Trust Company *

The Chemical Bank New York Trust Company is convinced of the value of programed instruction as a training technique. It finds PI to be extremely effective although it also recognizes that PI is *not* a panacea or cure-all for every one of its training problems, and, therefore, that it should not be used indiscriminately. However, when integrated with other techniques, it is far more productive than conventional procedures of a few years ago.

AMPLE EVIDENCE OF THE BANK'S SUPPORT OF PROGRAMED INSTRUCtion can be found in the number of times it has permitted publications such as *The American Banker, Banking Magazine, American Society of Training Directors Journal, Bank Personnel News,* and *American Institute of Banking Faculty Magazine* to report on its experiences. The bank has also permitted qualified spokesmen to give talks on the subject before such groups as The American Bankers Association, American Society of Training Directors, New York State Industrial Training Council, Office Executives' Association, and American Institute of Banking. The bank is an active member of the Programed Instruction Association, National Society for Programmed Instruction, and American Society of Training and Development, in which it further supports programed instruction.

The bank first became aware of programed instruction through the increasing number of articles on teaching machines and programed learning in the various technical and professional publications which were read by its managers. In 1960 bank personnel took part in the field testing of the preliminary tapes (an application of Lewis Robins' "reinforced learning system") of the IBM Proof Machine course. The results were highly favorable.

* Information for this case (1) was submitted by Sanford Kleiner, Assistant Vice President, Personnel Division, Chemical Bank New York Trust Company, New York, (2) was excerpted from notes on a talk presented May 7, 1963, at ASTD Conference, Chicago, by Donald R. Alversen, and (3) was derived from material provided by Dr. Albert Hickey, President, ENTELEK, Inc., Newburyport, Massachusetts.

When one vice president learned the 10-key portion of the course in 15 minutes, management support was assured.

After this another reinforced learning system course for beginning typists was tried out. The keyboard (touch typing) was learned in four hours by using phonograph records, and a skill level of 15-25 WPM was achieved in ten hours. The total cost to this point was $1,000 for IBM tapes, $400 for tape recorder and listening stations, and $10 for the typing course, for an expenditure of $1,410.

The preliminary knowledge and experience with programed instruction were presented in enthusiastic terms to the bank's Training Committee, a group of senior officers with policy and budget powers over bank training functions. This committee directed a full study which included attendance at conferences devoted to training innovations, such as the 1961 ASTD conference study of information gleaned from Skinner, Hughes of IBM, and others. After reviewing exhibits, learning of the various experiences of other companies, and reading books and articles devoted to related topics, the training staff programed a small section of the bank's teller course.

They selected the Paying and Receiving Teller Course for their initial effort for several reasons, among which were constant training load (200–250/yr) and many operating procedures. Six consultants placed bids, ranging from $5,000 to $15,000 and containing a variety of conditions, for developing a program. After all factors had been weighed, ENTELEK, Inc., of Newburyport, Massachusetts, was approved by the Training Committee in November 1961. One of the conditions of the contract was to establish an in-house capability to program future materials. Therefore, a number of trainers on the staff received full instructions and developed the requisite programing skills under the consultant's guidance. Later, the bank hired a full-time programer who spent two weeks with ENTELEK to undergo intensive training.

The consultant spent a week with the bank's subject matter experts and provided instruction and assistance in preparing outlines and setting objectives, agreeing on approach and methodology, teaching PI principles, teaching the delegation of writing assignments and work flow schedules, and later editing the materials prepared. In-house staff was responsible for outlines, objectives, criteria, frame writing, testing and rewriting, initial editing and revision, and statistical validation, which included test runs, item analysis, revision, and retesting.

The effort was not without its problems. One programer was lost; another was unsuccessful. There was a continued heavy training load. There were the usual problems accompanying any new training innovation and overcoming the usual stereotyped thinking and apprehension regarding programed instruction. The clerical problems inherent in the initial in-house production and reproduction of this work were many, but the personnel involved eventually gained a measure of sophistication in this area.

The linear program consisted of 1,600 frames, required 2,400 responses, and was bound in four program texts and three exhibit booklets. The program took eight months to prepare (it was utilized in full in August 1962) at a cost of approximately $18,000. The cost included consultant fees, materials, production, duplication, binding, and a "teaching machine" in the form of a National Blank Book binder with sliding mask.

The program was validated by the trainees' achieving an average of 93 per cent on the terminal tests. It took an average of 16½ hours (12 to 22 hour range) to administer the program. The program replaced from 17 to 20 hours of lecture. However, 20 per cent more basic material was added to the program during its construction.

In itself a significant and rarely accomplished measure of the effectiveness of programed instruction was the performance appraisal which was completed for each trainee by his supervisor after 60 days on the job. "Satisfactory" and "outstanding" ratings were received by 90 to 97 per cent of the trainees in the work categories evaluated, which included the handling of various types of transactions (deposit receiving, check cashing, and so on), money handling, proof sheet, and customer relations. In only one area—the ability to find their own errors when not in proof—were fewer than 90 per cent of the trainees rated satisfactory. This fact indicates a possible need for programing a new section on error finding.

Student attitudes revealed a positive reaction toward programed instruction from 70 per cent of the trainees, 20 per cent were neutral in their reaction, and a negative reaction was given by 10 per cent. The survey was concerned with such factors as speed and quality of learning, concentration, need for thinking, interest, and preparation for practice (simulated role playing), as contrasted with traditional forms of instruction. Only 3 per cent of the trainees had used programed instruction frequently, 3 per cent occasionally, 19 per cent one to three times, and 75 per cent not at all.

The bank's capacity to write its own programs is quite beneficial. For one thing, it can revise the teller course as necessary whenever procedural changes take effect, which happens much more often than was originally anticipated. It also can program new subjects much less expensively, although it did take the precaution of having its consultant edit much of the early effort.

The bank's Training Center, which handles the skills training of all new employees, has established a Programed Instruction Unit to develop new courses as applicable, to up-date current programed material as required, and to introduce "off the shelf" materials pertinent to its needs. Centering the function at the Training Center does not limit it to clerical applications, however, for it also has been applied to other job categories ranging from machine trainees to management development seminars.

The bank management can look back to a number of solid achievements, including a complete revision of the teller course when its procedures were radically changed after the installation of the computer system; a coupon clerk program for temporary office help; and a savings teller course. The company now is studying requests for other programs, and there are also at least six projects that it would like to initiate itself.

The coupon clerk program merits elaboration since it is unique. Every quarter, as bond coupons become due, the bank has to hire a large number of temporary clerks to process them. This means training a new crew each quarter since the likelihood of getting the same temporary workers is slim. After testing the programed material, making the necessary revisions, and retesting, the bank worked out an arrangement with the agency supplying the help whereby the agency gives the program at its office on its time, and only those who pass the course are referred for work. Thus, the bank is able to save training time, to eliminate unqualified employees and those who decide they wouldn't like the work, and to obtain a better-trained group of workers.

The training function in the bank is the responsibility of an assistant vice president, Personnel Division. He points out that the bank sees no bounds to the use of PI as long as it recognizes PI's limitations and does not try to make it the answer to every training problem. The bank is only beginning to utilize fully the potential of PI; retraining personnel for new skills has been more successful because of programed materials now available commercially (IBM equipment, typewriters, adding machines, and so on). However, subjects not yet fully programed for use in business and industry—attentive listening, customer relations, and the entire area of culture—need development.

Managers at CBNYTC feel that programed instruction does work and that it is a useful teaching tool. They plan to use not only their own in-house developed programs but also off-the-shelf and customized programs where appropriate and feasible. They have cooperated with American Bankers Association to help cut down the cost of programing and to prevent duplication. Although they have not used teaching machines, they do not exclude the possibility of their future use. The Bank Training Staff sees the heaviest future use of programed instruction as being in the area of on-the-job training.

Dartmouth Medical School *

This is a brief report of a programed course on the autonomic
nervous system which was offered to students in the Department of
Pharmacology at Dartmouth Medical School. Several years ago it
became evident to members of the Department of Pharmacology and
Toxicology that they were confronted with students who were deficient in their knowledge of the autonomic nervous system. This
knowledge was essential since without it the students could not adequately comprehend the action of the "autonomic drugs." Ways
were sought to correct this deficiency.

IN 1961 DRS. E. J. GREEN, R. E. GOSSELIN, AND K. E. MOORE WROTE A
linear programed instruction manual which was designed to review and
to introduce new information on the anatomy and physiology of the autonomic nervous system. They have used and slightly modified the program
for the past three and one-half years. The course consists of 231 frames and
three rather detailed panels.

During the first year of its introduction the Medical School class was divided into two groups which were matched in terms of prior class standings.
Half the class was issued the programed textbook, and the other half was
assigned conventional reading matter which covered the same topics as those
in the program. The students were told they would be examined on the
material and they might review it as much as they liked. Those students
using the programed text were instructed not to do any outside reading,
and those assigned conventional reading were not to examine the programed
text. All students were instructed to keep a record of the amount of time
they spent preparing for the quiz. At the end of the week the same objective
examination was given to everyone.

To analyze the results of this experiment, an index of study efficiency

* Information for this case submitted by Kenneth E. Moore, Ph.D., Assistant Professor of
Pharmacology, Dartmouth Medical School, Department of Pharmacology and Toxicology,
Hanover, New Hampshire.

was defined as the ratio of the percentage of correct responses made by each student on the quiz divided by the number of minutes he spent studying. On the basis of this index, the program group performed significantly more efficiently than did the nonprogram group. Two elements contributed to this better performance: somewhat higher scores by the slower students in the program group than by the comparable students in the nonprogram group, and shorter preparation time by all students using the program. The better students in the two groups did equally well on the quiz, but those using the program spent less time preparing for it. These results were distinctly favorable to the programed instruction.

The next year the class was divided into three carefully matched groups. Each group was issued the same material but in a different format. The members of one group received the programed textbook. Members of the second group received the same material on a tape for sequential viewing in a simple commercial teaching machine. The third group received the material as a straight text; that is, as a series of consecutive statements in which the blanks had been properly filled in. Under supervision the students were allowed to go through the program once. Immediately after, they were all given the same examination. Another, unannounced, examination was given one week later.

The Medical School had hoped to demonstrate that the students who were required to fill in the blanks would read more carefully and retain more information than those students who were not required to respond actively to the study material. Upon analyzing the data, however, the instructors found that for both tests the three groups had scores that were not significantly different from one another. Furthermore, it took longer for groups 1 and 2—that is, those who were required to fill in blanks—to go through the program. Thus it appeared that the concept that the overt responses required in teaching programs make for better understanding and retention was not borne out by the experiment.

Even though the results of the experiments were less than hoped for, the program has been continued in use for several reasons. The department is convinced that the program offers a good review and background for the lectures on autonomic drugs. More important than this, the program was received very favorably by the students. This is not due to novelty or "halo," because the students have PI in other courses. Advanced students also have consistently advised first-year students to use the program when they are studying the autonomic nervous system in anatomy. Also, some students have requested a chance to use the program when they are studying for the National Board Examinations.

The major complaint of students is that the program is too redundant. Drs. Gosselin and Moore have attempted to correct this problem by increasing the program's density. The program is given during the first week of the course, when a four-hour period is set aside for the students to go through it.

Elmhurst National Bank *

The case history of the Elmhurst National Bank of Elmhurst, Illinois, illustrates the application of an off-the-shelf programed instruction course developed for teller training.

THE ELMHURST NATIONAL BANK AT ELMHURST, ILLINOIS, EMPLOYS some 100 people, 25 of whom are tellers. This 25 per cent of the staff is a most important part in terms of continued bank growth since it comprises the people who are most closely associated with the customers and prospective customers. Since the public judges a bank according to the interest, capability, and cordiality of its tellers, a lack of any of these qualities induces an immediate negative reaction.

Instruction of the tellers was previously limited to on-the-job training coupled with the American Institute of Banking courses, but there was no adequate manner of measuring its efficiency. It was extremely difficult to know just how thorough a job each teller was doing with each customer. An earnest teller, willing to work and listen, was successful, while others sometimes failed. A constant problem was time. Training a man takes time, and to train a man ineffectively represents a costly waste of time. What was needed was a relatively fast means of educating the entire teller force in a majority of the situations with which it could expect to be confronted.

When the commercial training firms began to program bank duties for instructional purposes, Elmhurst National Bank became interested in the results. Contacts with banks using programed learning convinced the management of its potential.

The bank investigated the *Essentials of the Bank Teller's Job* program which was commercially offered by the publisher, Educational Methods, Inc., of Chicago. It bought the program after satisfying itself as to the com-

---

* Information for this case submitted by Arthur E. Oriel, Educational Methods, Inc., Chicago, Illinois, and excerpted from an article by Lester Madsen, Assistant Cashier, Elmhurst National Bank, which appeared in the October 1964 issue of *Auditgram*.

prehensiveness of its teaching materials. The bank felt that the course was so comprehensive that a student would have difficulty with the final examination if he did not first review the text.

Essentials of the Bank Teller's Job is a course which has six manuals:

a. *Rudiments of Negotiable Instrument Law* (BT 101). This defines a negotiable instrument and gives the seven characteristics which a document must possess to qualify as a negotiable instrument. It deals with those aspects of the law which the teller *must know* to perform his job efficiently.

b. *Types of Checks* (BT 102). This manual teaches the teller the nine most common types of checks and money orders. Adequate provision is made in this lesson for the teller to have a complete set of the checks used in his own bank. He can then compare each with the general types of checks encountered in this lesson.

c. *Types of Endorsements* (BT 103). It teaches the teller the most common types of endorsements and the rules and regulations which govern each. Through examples and practice exercises the trainee is taught to recognize different types of endorsements and to be alert to the requirements of each.

d. *Check-Cashing Procedures and Identification of Customers* (BT 104). Here the trainee is taught the commonly required procedures for identifying customers and the basic safeguards used in cashing checks. A complete checklist of check-cashing procedures is provided at the end of the program. Ample provision is made for a list of identification and check-cashing procedures which are specific to any bank.

e. *Types of Accounts* (BT 105). This manual covers the major types of accounts encountered in the teller's job. It provides space for the trainee to record the color (or other) code used in his bank for signature cards and the fees charged by the bank for different accounts. The instructor should supply the trainee with a complete set of the signature cards used in the bank, a fact sheet on fees for different types of accounts, and other materials specific to the bank.

f. *Detecting Counterfeit Money and Handling Mutilated Currency* (BT 106). It shows the way our money is manufactured and specific procedures for identifying and withdrawing from circulation both counterfeit and mutilated currency. It provides the trainee with actual practice in identifying bills and detecting counterfeits by careful examination of their features. It gives specific instructions on how to handle both counterfeit and mutilated currency.

The program comes with a complete instruction booklet for the supervisor. The total cost of the program is $19.95 for one copy, two to five copies are $19.30 each, and six to ten copies are $18.50 each. This cost includes all six booklets, the binder, and a manual for the supervisor. The criterion test usually is given at eight-week intervals between the pretest and the post-test. The publisher is developing an alternate form of this test. According to the latest figures which the publisher has received, this course has been bought by nearly 2,000 banks and savings and loan associations across the country and in several foreign countries. Nearly 200 banks have used the course for training purposes. It is difficult to know exactly how many courses are used in training because often the publisher has nothing to go on except the fact that a bank has ordered multiple copies. Banks have ordered anywhere from two to a hundred sets.

Some banks use the program in group study sessions (about 25 per cent); the other 75 per cent use it as individualized self-instruction. In about 95 per cent of the banks, tellers or teller trainees are required to take the course. In the remainder it is voluntary. More than half the banks using the course require *all* tellers to go through it; the rest use it only with trainees. The average grade on the pretest for trainees and tellers with less than one year of experience is 45 per cent. The average pretest score for experienced tellers (from 1 to 25 years of experience) is 51 per cent. Review or refresher courses for experienced personnel seem indicated, which perhaps explains why more than half the banks require the entire staff to finish the course.

The publisher is compiling norms on the test. It now has data on about 300 cases and expects to have another 500 cases soon and then will have reasonably adequate norms from the pretest. The banks tend to implement the post-test slowly, so the publisher will probably have to wait a bit longer for adequate norms on it. The average pretest grade for all tellers, regardless of their length of experience, so far received is 49 per cent. The average post-test score for about 100 cases is 87 per cent. So far there have been no retention studies. Banks often are not in a position to do research (except the giants), and since the course is used by many small and medium-size banks across the country, the publisher usually has little control over how the course is administered or what data will be collected.

Banks are adopting the course at an increasing rate. In a recent survey of banks using the course, all that responded said that the course has resulted in increased teller efficiency, understanding, and accuracy. Surprisingly, a third of the banks also indicated that tellers show more interest in their work after taking the course. Most also indicated that the course gives new tellers increased confidence in their ability to handle the job. The course was tested in six banks before publication, and revisions were made on the basis of data gained. The publishers are planning to revise the present course on the basis of knowledge gained from banks now using the course. It is likely that new lessons will be added and the method of programing used will be updated.

The publisher helped the Elmhurst Bank management with the introduction of the course in March 1964. The bank gave all teller members of the staff a quiz on "Essentials of the Bank Teller's Job." *This was a multiple-choice answer pretest, and it proved to those being examined that there were a great number of general banking questions they could not answer.* Test results were conclusive. The average score was 45 per cent, and oddly enough the teller with ten years of experience did little better than the one hired six months previously. The average length of service was three and one-half years. This surprising showing on the pretest results led the bank's management to accept the PI course as a challenge. It was convinced that the learning process could be helped by an atmosphere of relaxation, so it staged the classes in the comfort of the employee lounge and served coffee and rolls at each session. Classes were held one afternoon each week over a six-week period with one session devoted to each of the six course subjects which we examined earlier. Management felt it was necessary to de-emphasize the academic aspect by assuring all tellers that their individual results would be held in strict confidence.

The bank managers found the course to be both interesting and challenging to their employees. Their interest developed a proper attitude toward the course and toward their role in the bank. The course reduced training time while increasing training effectiveness. It reduced instructor and supervisory time, and it produced uniform teller training throughout the bank. The class average of 45 per cent in the pretest jumped to 90 per cent in the final examination. The review test given at the eighth session was just as conclusive regarding the course's success as the pretest had been in pinpointing the lack of teller knowledge. Management feels that the course gave the tellers an awareness and an understanding of many problems which they once solved helterskelter or by guesswork and luck. The tellers now seem to be surer of themselves. They seem to know when to process, when not to process, when to refer, and when to ask for help. They are more alert, more interested in their jobs. Even the customers have commented on the courteous, intelligent treatment given by the tellers.

Class response was best summed up, according to Lester Madsen, assistant cashier, with the comments of a teller who found that the class was fun! "I worked for three years as a teller, and I'll tell you frankly I didn't know half of what I learned in just those eight short sessions. I've got my texts at home, and I've gone back to them several times—once to review the whole course and other times to look up answers to questions that had come up on the job."

Management feels that since the course is designed to be used at home, in the bank, in the training classroom, or on the job, it will be useful to train new tellers as they join the staff. The only shortcoming in the course is its general treatment of all teller transactions, but the bank feels that it can easily tailor specific parts of the instruction to its own needs by bringing these points out in classroom sessions.

First National City Bank of New York *

The First National City Bank of New York made one of the earliest applications of programed instruction technology when it utilized programed tapes for teaching techniques on the IBM proof machine. Since that time the bank has developed one of the most extensive applications of the mathetics approach to programed instruction in industry.

THE FIRST NATIONAL CITY BANK OF NEW YORK BEGAN USING PROgramed instruction tapes for teaching techniques on the IBM proof machine in September 1960. This was one of the earliest applications of programed instruction. Two years later, the bank added a training unit to the staff of its centralized training center.

Because tape-recorded instruction was particularly effective for training in machine techniques, First National City Bank implemented a similar course as early as May 1961 to teach Friden Flexowriter operators.

No written material is involved in teaching the operation of Friden Flexowriters. Instead, the program is made up as a tape-recorded presentation. The Basic Operator Training Course, which had previously been taught by people from the Friden Company in approximately five weeks, was reduced to about two weeks in length. This intradepartmental program was used by the Stock Transfer Department but is not used extensively now as the course is needed only to train newcomers to the department. Significantly, the Friden Company instructors have not been called on for the past two years by the Stock Transfer Department, and it is not anticipated that there will be any need for them to train bank personnel in the future in this area.

As a result of their experience with the Flexowriter course, training personnel realized that more application could be made of the mathetics ap-

* Information for this case provided by Gordon M. Rhodes, Assistant Cashier and Director of Training, First National City Bank, New York.

proach of simulated exercise for the majority of subjects that were being taught at the centralized training center. A long-range and extensive PI project was therefore established, beginning with a program for teller trainees. By October 1962 the experiments had been so successful that a programing capability of four people was incorporated into the centralized training center. This in-house capability is now the guiding force for the further utilization of programed instruction and the application of mathetics in the training program. First National City now appears to be the principal user within industry of the mathetics technique, and it is also one of the primary banking institutions using programed instruction in its training ventures.

The following excerpts from an address which Gordon M. Rhodes made to a conference of the Savings Banks Association of New York State highlight the rationale of the bank's effort in programed instruction and its emphasis on the mathetics technique:

> We first experimented by utilizing an off-the-shelf tape-recorded instructional program designed for IBM proof machine operators. To our amazement, training for the basic operation of the proof machine which took three weeks or more under on-the-job training techniques required only about two and one-half to three days to accomplish using this self-pacing audio presented programed course. . . . We added training of typists to operate the Friden Flexowriter . . . with equally outstanding results. These results divulged that the trainees learned fast, retained information better, and reached maximum trainee output at much earlier stages. . . .

> Our experience under conventional instructional methods in a centralized training facility proved to us that retention of instructional material under verbal instruction in classroom style ranges from about a 40 to 45 per cent level and that under the most desirous role-playing concept there is a great difficulty in a transferral of knowledge of this verbal instruction to the role-playing technique. The knowledge that this difficulty existed in the past caused us to be extremely critical in our further investigation of programed instruction in order that we might choose a methodology which when introduced could increase behavioral attitude of the student population, as the instruction program progresses.

> Unlike other techniques of programed training, mathetics does not require constant written responses in the programed text by the student, nor does it require that instructional information be furnished to the student only in small-step progression. This approach rather perceives that information closely allied to other information should be presented to the student in larger segments. (In some instances the segment can be as much as one to one and a half pages of material.) Coupled with the

theory is an additional stimulation resulting from an inclusion, in most instances, of a simulated exercise augmenting the written responses which may be required. It is this physical reinforcement contained in the simulated exercise which acts as an extremely strong reward of learning which other methods of programed instruction do not normally include. It is also this physical reinforcement that in our application of programed instruction creates a smooth transfer of knowledge when the student moves from programed instruction to actual role-playing technique in our centralized training facilities.

The application of this technique for tellers (and ultimately for many other clerical tasks for which the training center bears responsibilities) utilizes a programed text which requires certain written responses, tests the individual on a self-checking basis, and is coupled with a desk-top style simulator to provide students with the physical reinforcement previously mentioned. This program is provided on a self-pacing basis in order that the slower students do not hold back the faster students and so the faster students do not force the slower students to proceed at a pace superior to their capabilities. Programed text, properly prepared during the initial stages and ultimately completed with the aid of copy editing, should provide complete self-instructional capabilities with little or no need for questions on the part of students other than for clarifying purposes, since the complete program presents to the student a sequence of stimulus, response, and reinforcement situations.

First National City's study was therefore more concerned with reducing training costs and developing superior capability than it was with statistics about test results. Nevertheless, statistical data were accumulated by means of a final written examination which had been used for nine years for all teller trainees who had finished the conventional course.

In February and March of 1963, teller trainees were divided into a control group (taught by conventional methods) and an experimental group (taught by PI methods). Educational levels were not considered in separating the trainees into the two groups, lest the validity of the test be affected. But it was found, nevertheless, that the various levels of education were about equally divided between the two groups. After the 25 trainees in the control group received the pretest, they were given the four-week conventional course consisting of three weeks (48 hours) of verbal instructions combined with role playing and one week of role playing. The 39 trainees in the programed course were given one week of programed materials and two weeks of role playing.

The post-test was administered to the conventional group at the end of the third week of the four-week course and to the programed instruction group at the end of the first week. The mean score for the conventional group was 82.86, and for the experimental group it was 86.18. Further, the programed course allowed the faster students to go into role-playing activity sooner. Moreover, programed instruction allowed the management to insure a uniformity of training procedures that was not likely to be attained in conventional classes. Also the programed course relieved the instructors of responsibility for 48 hours of lecturing and teaching procedures and permitted them to concentrate on individual problems in the role-playing sessions. Under the conventional procedures, students had difficulty in transferring knowledge gained in the verbalized exercise to the role-playing phase. PI virtually eliminated this hurdle. And finally, students were enthusiastic about the methodology of programed instruction. All these advantages were much more significant to training management than were the statistically favorable results.

First National City is giving the greatest emphasis to programed instruction in those courses which have the largest student population in order to reduce training time and provide better instruction, so that more students can receive the course in a single year. It is anticipated that over a long period the need for basic training courses will diminish and the bank will be able to branch out into subject areas which are not now taught in its centralized training facility. Some research has already been done on the feasibility of applying the in-house programers' efforts to subjects outside of the merely clerical areas and capitalizing on the advantages of in-house training to benefit both the bank and its people.

Senior management is aware that in most instances programed instruction reduces training time and costs and at the same time provides better retention for the students. This is of considerable interest to the bank's managers, and they have never resisted the use of programed instruction as long as the needs have been properly analyzed and the results have been worthwhile.

Programed instruction is not used arbitrarily. Instead, a member of the training staff makes continual surveys of all possible applications of PI so that it can be used to the best advantage.

Long-range plans extend beyond three to four years. It is hoped that these plans will provide the bank with program materials not only for clerical training but ultimately for some phases of lower management training.

First Pennsylvania Banking and Trust Company*

Since May 1963, 88 trainees of The First Pennsylvania Banking and Trust Company have successfully participated in its teller training course. Programed instruction provided the basic information necessary for the tellers to perform various functions and make certain decisions. The management of the company has been impressed with the uses to which PI has been applied to date, with the uniformity and standardization of information which can be transmitted to the trainee through PI, and with curtailed training costs.

THE PROGRAMED INSTRUCTION COURSE FOR TELLER TRAINING CONSISTS of four volumes of 323 pages containing 1,686 frames and exhibits. The exhibits, which each trainee must process, are actual items of a teller's work. The source is an adaptation of the Chemical Bank New York Trust Company's program, which was developed by ENTELEK, Inc., in conjunction with Chemical's personnel.

The First Pennsylvania Banking and Trust Company has sponsored formalized classroom training for four years and has trained from 60 to 75 tellers a year. The adaptability of PI to packaged economic instruction is illustrated by the fact that as few as three and as many as nine students have studied at one time in a classroom which is ordinarily set up to accommodate only five students. The trainees have ranged in age from 19 to 48; have had varying degrees of education, ranging from high school to college graduate work; and have ranged from none to 20 years' experience in bank work. The majority train only for teller work but some take other types of bank training programs.

The size of the training program would not permit a comparison study with two groups of students, half being taught conventionally and half by

---

* Information for this case was provided by Albert E. Hickey, President, ENTELEK, Inc.; William J. Boland, Vice President, The First Pennsylvania Banking and Trust Co., Philadelphia, Pa.; and Kathryn C. McDermott, Assistant Vice President in Charge of Training.

programed instruction, or alternating classes between conventional and programed instruction courses.

Classroom schedules are flexible. Conventionally, the instructor followed an outline which was always subject to change in order to take students on visits to the Transit and Proof unit, the Bookkeeping section, the Money Department, and the Federal Reserve Bank or to show them films and hold discussions on customer relations. The programed instruction course also follows an outline and has the same interruptions.

Both the instructor who taught the conventional classes in 1961–62 by lecture and the PI instructor provided an estimate of the approximate number of hours they devoted to the various subjects. The answers are below.

SUBJECTS	HOURS PI	HOURS LECTURE	DIFFERENCE
Receiving Deposits	9:00	13:35	− 4:35
Cashing Checks	10:15	12:50	− 2:35
Club A/C's	1:30	:45	+ :45
Retail Banking Payments	2:00	1:00	+ 1:00
Bonds and Coupons	1:45	1:00	+ :45
TOTAL	24:30	29:10	− 4:40

The following incidents underline the value of programed instruction:

    a. One trainee was sick three days during the course. Her grandmother picked up her programed instruction lessons, which the trainee did at home. On returning to work, she was up to the class and in her next test on this subject had a mark of 90.

    b. One trainee came to the class two days after it had started. She took the lessons home at night and caught up to the class.

The first PI instructor, who had previously taught the conventional course and had helped to develop the PI course, was asked his opinion of the PI course. He remarked:

    1. It forces the slower students to work, but they became enthusiastic about it.

    2. Bright trainees become bored quickly.

    3. The average students' response was in between the bright and slow students; that is, they became bored, but not as quickly, and were less enthusiastic than the slow students.

He pointed out, with respect to his comment regarding bright trainees, that the course was designed for high school graduates of average intelligence who had no banking experience.

The conventional course consisted of three weeks of instruction at the tellers' school followed by two weeks of guidance by a senior teller in a branch office. The time saved through PI was spent by the trainee in counting money, proving deposits, accepting loan and club payments, redeeming "E" bonds, and gaining more general information and background about his duties.

The only scoring data available relate to 37 trainees:

    a. Trainee scores after conventional courses ranged from 65 to 100.

    b. Trainees having partial PI courses ranged from 78 to 100 (nine cases).

    c. Trainees having full PI courses ranged from 80 to 100 (37 cases).

PI technology also made possible a uniform presentation of training materials, which led to reliable instruction and quality control. The bank had discovered that it could keep capable operating personnel as instructors about a year before they became bored. It has had four different instructors in the four years the tellers' school has been in existence. The human factor of dwelling too long on what the instructors like and not enough on what they dislike had resulted in a lack of uniformity in teaching the trainees. The bank has always had "emergencies" when it has had to rely on the trainees to get other kinds of work accomplished on time. These shifts in duties interrupt and decrease the tellers' training time, which contributes further to lack of uniformity. PI covers the same material in the same way for all trainees.

Another advantage of PI is lower training costs. The bank has been able to cut down some of the salary expense of "waiting for a class to begin." Trainees employed a day or so after the class has started and trainees absent a day or so because of illness can now catch up with their classmates by studying after hours or at home. Trainees can start to work as soon as they are hired and do not have to wait for classes to commence. It is hoped that this fact will eliminate "waiting expense" entirely. For the four-year period 1960 to 1963 this cost has averaged $1,774, as we can see in the figures below.

1960	$2,155.00
1961	2,172.50
1962	1,802.00
1963	966.00
	$7,095.50

PI training was interspersed with visits to various financial institutions, lectures, practice periods, and actual performance of work required by the exhibits contained in the material to alleviate the monotony of answering questions in frames. Quite a few trainees (about 25 per cent) asked to take the lessons home. Seven trainees out of a group of eleven suggested that the PI course be read at home and the day be spent in more practice and actual work.

The company is now determining what other areas of training can be improved with PI. Six classes have been instructed with programed materials, but the company believes that further studies are necessary in the average time the trainee spends reading and solving the PI materials. The bank will continue to study the possibilities of eliminating formal classes and training people as they are hired. It also plans to experiment with eliminating the classroom and training students in the branch offices instead. Answer sheets will be sent in at designated times, tests will be administered by the instructor, and the trainees will return to their appropriate branches to continue their training. The present tellers, especially the weak ones, will be given PI materials to read and the answer sheets to fill out by way of refresher training. The bank anticipates that it will be able to cut the cost of the training program considerably through these efforts.

The $5,000 spent in developing programed materials can be regained in from two to three years by reducing the pretraining costs. If the company can successfully train tellers in the branch offices, considerable additional savings will accrue.

Even though management admits that it might be difficult to prove, it is convinced that the programed course saves time, has more depth, gives more information and background, provides more uniformity, and costs less than the previous conventional course. The company now has material that the tellers can review periodically either in whole or in part.

Starting with the November 1963 class, "attitude toward PI" questionnaires have been given to 22 trainees, with the following results:

- Sixteen said they learned more by PI than lectures; five learned the same amount from both; and one said he learned less by PI.
- Thirteen said PI taught faster than lectures, eight said the two methods took the same amount of time, and one said PI was slower.
- Twelve said PI held their concentration better than lectures, six said the two methods were the same in this respect, and four said that they concentrated less during PI.
- Seventeen said they would like to see PI used in more training programs, four said in only some others, and one said in no other.
- Eleven said PI made them think more than the lecture method, four said there was no difference, and seven said that PI challenged them less.
- Thirteen felt that PI was interesting, and nine did not agree.

- When contrasted with lectures, however, 12 said PI was more interesting, two said they could see no difference, and eight said PI was less interesting.
- Seventeen felt that PI prepared them for the practice sessions, three said it prepared them only somewhat, and two said it did not.
- Four had had previous experience with PI, and 18 had had none.

Management concluded that adapting another company's (Chemical Bank New York Trust Company's) course was much less costly and took much less time than would have been necessary if it had started from the beginning and had developed its own totally new program.

The following comment is typical of the management point of view:

> Even if the blessings of programed instruction, that is, time and cost savings and better instruction and retention, are proven to be invalid, it was worth the time and effort. We now have a "textbook," so to speak, for our Teller Training Course. This insures us that at least we will always cover the full course of instruction, which is particularly advantageous in a company of our size where we always have rush assignments that interrupt the trainees' instruction. This, also, could mean that training programs should be pulled away from operating units.

General Electric Company *

(Re-entry Systems Department)

The Personnel Development Division of General Electric's Re-entry Systems Department has made programed instruction an integral part of its employee development education program. The auto-instructional aspects of programed learning seem to lend themselves ideally to this self-development program.

THE RE-ENTRY SYSTEMS DEPARTMENT OF GENERAL ELECTRIC HAS 4,500 employees: 2,600 professionals and 1,900 clerical workers, draftsmen, machinists, and other preprofessional people.

General Electric's business is one of changing requirements. New jobs are created, old ones eliminated. The employees must be able to respond to these changes, and the employee relations philosophy is that it must be ready to help them make these adjustments. With this in mind it developed an educational program which it believes to be the finest, most progressive, most effective industrial education step yet taken.

The approach is called simply a self-development program. It is aimed at hourly and nonexempt salaried employees—preprofessional people. The program offers each of them an opportunity, over a period of months or years, to work out an individual career development plan to prepare themselves for better jobs. Also, it enables them to keep current on changing technologies which could make their present jobs obsolete. It is part of the industry's solution to the problems of undertrained employees.

The perspective regarding undertrained employees is that they are not incapable of performing on their current jobs. But they would be confronted with serious economic problems should these jobs disappear, because many

* Information for this case submitted by Mary S. Pratt, Specialist, Personnel Development, Re-entry Systems Department, Missile and Space Division, General Electric Company, Philadelphia, Pennsylvania.

have no other significant skills. The company position is that personnel development is its concern, but—

> You can't herd people into a classroom, lecture them, and feel you've met their individual training needs. We treat each individual's development on an *individual* basis—and most important, that *individual* determines the career route he wishes to follow. Thus: self-development.

General Electric's approach is one which allows each individual the freedom to pursue those activities he feels will best expand his basic abilities. It also establishes his freedom not to participate. No one is forcing him. The program is simply spelled out to him. He determines—with advice and counsel, if he chooses—how actively he wants to participate in his future development. Employee relations personnel merely supply the map which he may use to route his adventure in advancement. His steps are two practical ones. First, he is given his own self-development workbook and action plan. In his workbook, he answers a series of questions about himself, which enables him to analyze his assets regarding education, experience, and effective performance. This analysis helps spotlight his abilities and objectives. He begins to consider where he wants to be next month, next year, next decade. The second step is longer: He develops his own action plan. What will it take to accomplish these new objectives?

Employees are free to map this second step themselves, but most choose to consult with their managers and with Personnel Development people. From these consultations may well come the specific plans of action that they will take. In many cases, their development may be programed over an extended period of time—even up to four years. An action plan may consist of (1) enrollment in special night courses at a nearby college, (2) assignment to a rotating series of jobs, (3) special depth reading, (4) participation in special seminars, (5) company courses, (6) a series of informational discussions with managers about each individual's chosen field, and (7) individualized programed learning courses.

Programed instruction has proved to be immensely valuable and popular. These courses cover such subjects as basic mathematics, algebra, trigonometry, calculus, electricity, electronics, transistors, and written communication. Each student operates on his own. He receives a programed textbook structured for self-study. There are no formal classes and no instructors. Average study time ranges from 10 to 20 weeks per course, and constant contact is maintained between students and those Personnel Development people who offer guidance and encouragement. When necessary, personal consultation with specialists is arranged. Frequent tests are conducted to measure progress. Upon satisfactory completion of a course a certificate of achievement is given to the employee and a notice goes into his personnel folder to call attention to his increased skills.

Many General Electric employees have been unable to take advantage of training opportunities in the past; shift work, heavy overtime schedules, out-of-town assignments, and other personal matters have precluded regular attendance at conventional classes. Programed textbooks, which could be used on a student's own time and at his own pace, seemed to provide a solution. The first two or three courses the company used on a trial basis were well accepted. In September 1964 it offered 19 courses; these are listed on the next page. To date nearly 600 employees have enrolled; approximately 200 have completed one or more courses. There have been about 100 drop-outs—some left the company, some decided to take outside courses, but the majority indicated they could not complete the courses at the time because of work pressures or heavy overtime schedules and that they wanted to start again later.

The Re-entry Systems Department uses only off-the-shelf programs; it has never constructed an in-house course. So far its need has been for basic theory and it sees no reason for competing against authorities in the field by programing its own—at least until it has had more experience with the technique. At present no PI is used in its conventional instructor-taught courses. PI has previously been used in four courses; two were very successful, two left much to be desired. In the opinion of Mary S. Pratt of Personnel Development the success of PI in conventionally taught courses depends entirely on the instructor's attitude. Those instructors who like the method have inspired the students to achieve, those who do not like it have passed this attitude along to the students, and results have been less than satisfactory.

The department has had no problems of management acceptance, but it has had administrative problems. Training management strongly believes an educational program utilizing PI must be administered by someone who knows the field and understands what it cannot do as well as what it can do. There has to be a good deal of personal contact with the students to motivate them. Courses cannot be taken at their face value—that is, it is not enough to rely entirely on what the publisher says they will do. Nor should only the publisher's self-tests be used. Others should be prepared by company subject specialists or instructors. Counselors should be available to help students. Not only should self-tests be scored and returned to the student, but each wrong answer should be explained so the student knows where he went wrong.

The greatest concern of the Personnel Development office is to insure that the student takes only the course he needs, not what he thinks he needs. Mrs.

Pratt puts it this way: "A student enrolls for basic math. You know he is a high school graduate and should understand this subject. Give him a comprehensive test first. If he does well, talk with him—you'll probably find that what he wants is algebra, but he was uncertain about his knowledge of arithmetic."

The employees have made many comments regarding the PI part of the self-development program. The following are some typical comments.

A secretary in Employee and Community Relations was the first of the

PROGRAMED TEXTBOOKS USED BY
GENERAL ELECTRIC COMPANY, RE-ENTRY SYSTEMS DEPARTMENT *

McGraw-Hill

Basic Electricity, by New York Institute of Technology
Basic Electronics, by New York Institute of Technology
Basic Transistors, by New York Institute of Technology
Logical Electronic Troubleshooting, by Donald H. Schuster
Programed Blueprint Reading, by Coover & Heisel

Doubleday and Company, Tutor Texts

Basic Computer Programing, by Theodore G. Scott
Programing Techniques, by Theodore G. Scott

Encyclopaedia Britannica, Temac Texts

Basic Math, by Daniel G. Bobrow
Algebra I, by Daniel P. Murphy
Language of Algebra, by F. William Lawvere
Introductory Calculus, Part I, by Daniel G. Bobrow
Introductory Calculus, Part II, by Daniel G. Bobrow
Introductory Descriptive Statistics, by John E. Milholland
Trigonometry, by Daniel L. Luckham

Lord Products

Improving Your Written Communications
The Secretary, Jill of All Trades
Cutting Office Costs Through Work Simplification
Methods Improvement and Work Controls

Harcourt, Brace and World, Inc.

English 3200 (Grammar and Usage), by Joseph C. Blumenthal

---

* Teachers' manuals and suggested tests are available for many of these courses. Others have integrated self-tests with answers. General Electric has devised its own progress tests for most courses.

RSD employees to enroll. Although thoroughly skilled in the mechanics of secretarial work, she felt that she needed to improve in written communications. She comments, "The Written Communications course has not only helped me increase my effectiveness in writing, it has given me a new self-confidence in what I write." Like so many other employees, she appreciates the program's lack of regimentation. She enjoys studying at her own leisure.

A foreman in the Building Services function is one of the seven foremen now enrolled in the self-development program. He was attracted to it, he says, "because there were no classroom sessions to attend" and because, as a foreman, he felt the need to improve his ability to communicate. He too is enrolled in the Written Communications course. He speaks for many second-shift people when he states, "The program has brought 'equal opportunity in education' to the night-shift employees."

Upon completion of the programed course each student is asked to fill out a questionnaire. What follows is a questionnaire as it was filled out by one of the students.

> Do you like this method of teaching? *Yes.*
> What did you like best about the course? *It permitted me to move at my own pace.*
> What did you like least? ...
> Would you recommend that we offer it to other employees? *Yes.*
> Other comments: *The subject matter was clearly and concisely presented with many examples and illustrations. It is the first time I have taken a course organized in this form and would heartily recommend it to others.*

The self-development employee program has been quite successful. This success has obviously not been due solely to programing, but PI has played an integral part in it.

What success has the program enjoyed? When it was announced in the fall of 1963 through internal news media, discussions at employee meetings, and word of mouth, the course enrollment snowballed immediately. Of 1,900 employees, 1,500 signed up for plan books in the first 60 days. Two months later, 300 employees had completed their self-appraisals, undergone counseling, developed action plans, and begun courses of study. Especially attracted were second- and third-shift people, who normally felt left out of the development picture.

Three other points are of great interest. Surprisingly few drop out. The very climate in which the program operates limits the dropout problem. By the time an individual has progressed as far as laying out an action plan, he has already demonstrated the kind of self-motivation which will steer him through to successful completion of his plan. The cost is far more economical than regular courses, since there are no instructors to pay and no classrooms to maintain. The program has received enthusiastic support from managerial people up and down the line. Many supervisory personnel have themselves quietly requested special individual training.

Training managers are convinced that the program is without question the most rewarding answer they have found to the need to offer each individual an opportunity to develop his own future. Every preprofessional employee now has the opportunity to grow in skill and performance.

Because it benefits everyone—the individual, the company, the customer; because its flexibility allows the employee to proceed at his own pace toward the objectives he wishes to attain; because the responsibility for development is put on the man most concerned—himself; and because the program has met with enormous employee success and requests for its description have come from all over the nation, this program is felt to be the most promising step forward in industrial education. It treats industrial education not as a remedy but as a forward-looking, useful activity geared to meet the performance needs of the business.

The following excerpt from a brochure given to potential students is illustrative of the information and guidance which are provided:

Self-study is the keynote for the following courses:

Interest in self-development is the ingredient that will arm students with the determination and perseverance to complete the course selected. All are done at home; the student progresses at his own speed. Progress tests are required. Subject experts are available for personal consultation. All completion times are approximate. Students may start courses at any time—dependent only upon availability of textbooks.

Enrollment cards—Form No. 7-9663—are available in the stock room or in the Personnel Development Office, Room 5211. If you have any questions call Extension 2993.

*   *   *

BASIC MATHEMATICS

Review of arithmetic and its application. Especially for students who desire to continue with the study of math, but equally suitable for shop personnel who need math to qualify for promotional opportunities.

Prerequisites: Supervisory approval.

Duration: 20 weeks.

ALGEBRA I

First year algebra. The traditional high school algebra has been enriched to include additional basic concepts useful in a further study of math. This course also includes applications of algebra in some basic work in plane geometry and numerical trigonometry. Additional concepts such as fractional and negative exponents are discussed to complete the logical development of certain topics.

Prerequisites: Completion of a course in basic mathematics or equivalent, plus supervisory approval.

Duration: Approximately six hours per week—20 weeks.

The Headquarters Air Force Control System (473L) *

This programed instructional subsystem for teaching a man-computer query language uses a two-phase approach. The first phase consists of a linear programed text; the second consists of an adaptive, computer-directed instructional program. This instructional subsystem is designed as an on-the-job training vehicle to produce high levels of skill in the man-computer communication process as well as knowledge concerning the principles upon which that process is based. The significance of this project lies in the design of interacting programed text and computer-directed instruction. This design appears to hold promise for producing efficient man-computer communication in the education and training information systems of tomorrow.

THE HEADQUARTERS AIR FORCE CONTROL SYSTEM IS A HIGH-SPEED data processing computer with data storage and display capabilities which make it the terminal link in a chain of information processing and transmitting subsystems valuable in optimizing the decision-making process on a global basis. Developed for use by the Air Force Command Post at Headquarters, USAF, it is currently being integrated with other automatic command and control systems of the Air Force. This integrated automatic facility enables the Air Force to manage its resources with speed and efficiency, and provides staff personnel with a complete, up-to-date picture of the status of its forces and facilities throughout the world as well as with current planning information.

Since any member of the Command Post should be able to operate this information system when the need arises, and since the system has no special-

---

* Information for this case drawn from Doris J. Clapp, David P. Yens, Harris H. Shettel, and Sylvia R. Mayer, "Development and Evaluation of a Self-Instructional Course in the Operational Training Capability Query Language for System 473L, U.S. Air Force Headquarters," Tech. Doc. Report No. ESD-TDR-64-662, Air Force Electronic Systems Division, Decision Sciences Laboratory, L. G. Hanscom Field, Bedford, Massachusetts, 1964.

ized computer communication console operators as such, the training requirement existed to design a general-purpose query language training course suitable for command and staff personnel with different levels of responsibility. The training problem that was isolated for this study concerned only information retrieval. Specifically, it involved developing a technique to train the military user to "talk" with the system in query language about the contents of the data files. The course is addressed to that portion of the Command Post task which is essentially a translation problem (English to query language and vice versa).

In an ideal training situation, a course of instruction is conducted as part of the actual job situation and is integrated or interfaced with the job. The job would be so designed that it would "teach itself." Even though this approach is not often feasible in practice it may be entirely the thing to do where jobs are already highly automated since *the operational equipment itself can be used to control training procedures and such conditions as pacing, content, feedback, and sequencing.* Training in such automated systems could be tailored to the idiosyncratic needs of each trainee.

Since the automated system that was being used for data retrieval could be programed to provide training and had the appropriate input and output facilities, initial equipment cost did not have to be a consideration. Of course, it may not always be wise or advantageous or economical to utilize the system itself as a training device. As the report pointed out, "If training requirements are uniform for all trainees, there would be little training advantage in a flexible approach, regardless of how easy it would be to implement." From this point of view, other training procedures and media may need to be considered.

The feasibility of using a computer-directed training program in this system relates to the nature of query language as well as to the availability of the computer. Query language is a pseudo-English language with a fixed format, special punctuation, and specific abbreviations. It is sufficiently rigid to make it well suited to detailed analysis by computer methods, and to design a program that detects the flaws in an incorrect statement and codes each flaw under a classification system was comparatively easy. With such an approach, a trainee can write specific query language statements and submit them to the computer for judgment. The computer analyzes these inputs and selects proper corrective material that aids the trainee to recognize and correct his errors. In this way, the computer is used not simply to determine whether an answer is correct or not but as a truly analytical and adaptive training device.

Use of the computer in the training subsystem determined the design of a training overlay for one of the console message composers. This overlay provided the trainee with direct access to control of the computer-directed training functions. The two random access disc storage units permitted rapid location and retrieval of information. From an instructional point of view this prevented a long delay between input and output.

If training could be given directly on the operational equipment which is to be used on the job, then optimum transfer of the training would accrue. A further advantage of using on-the-job equipment is the capability of the computer portion of the operational equipment to provide for the greatest adaptability to the individual requirements of all the trainees.

None of the students had had any previous training in query language; all were equal in their initial repertoire of system skills and there was little if any difference in their knowledge of the query language. Therefore, it was decided that the adaptive qualities of the computer would not be required during the initial training period; instead programed texts were used, with simple exercises (not computer-directed) conducted at the system console occasionally for motivational purposes.

The programed texts, which covered the fundamental aspects of the subject matter, produced differences in knowledge and skill. In the initial phase of programed-textual instructions individuals were able to bring to bear their different learning skills and aptitudes. A group that had the same level of knowledge initially had varying degrees of knowledge and skill later in the training. Since the delay between the initial and final phases tended to increase this variance, it was in the final phase that the computer-directed system could be expected to make a greater contribution in the training.

In the field test of the textual programed phase, the average completion time for all 15 trainees was 29.1 hours. The range was 20.1 to 37.9 hours. It should be pointed out that complex problems were not covered by programed materials; these were to be covered by the computer-directed phase.[1] The programed text did, however, teach the trainees to write relatively simple statements that would retrieve the desired information about moderately difficult problems. Other objectives which were achieved in phase one included developing familiarity with the 473L system, the organization of information in computer storage, and the operation and capabilities of the computer-retrieval programs. The average performance of the 15 trainees was 86.1 per cent (range 63 to 98 per cent), and eight of the 15 trainees scored 92 per cent or above. The field tryout results supported the original assumption that the trainees' level of knowledge would vary upon completion of

---

[1] The computer-directed portion is still in development.

phase one. This finding also justified the use of the adaptive computer-directed program in phase two.

The trainees were requested to complete two questionnaires: a background questionnaire, which was used to assess prior experience and general knowledge; and a questionnaire on programed instruction (given after completing phase one) to evaluate the trainees' attitude toward various aspects of the programed course. All the trainees considered PI an acceptable method of instruction—neither easy nor hard, neither boring nor interesting. Interestingly, the massed group that devoted about seven hours per day to studying the programed materials felt too much time was given to this type of instruction, whereas the spaced group (about two hours study per day) felt that more time per day should have been devoted to the programed materials. Generally, the trainees believed that the best schedule for a PI course was about four hours per day, with the massed group favoring more time per day than the spaced group. Trainees also agreed that the material was covered at about the right speed. The spaced group liked the amount of writing they had to do but the massed group would have preferred a little less writing. When trainees were asked to make a general evaluation of programed instruction, they indicated that it approached excellence as a method of instruction.

Trainees tended to slightly underestimate the degree of favorability in the attitudes of the others who took the course. Thus, most trainees guessed that the others considered programed instruction a "good" way to learn as against the "better than good" evaluation they themselves made. This same phenomenon was found in another study in which the same questions were asked of 62 military personnel who had just completed one or more programs.[2] It is difficult to know how to interpret this finding, since it could mean either that the trainee projects his real feelings to his fellow trainees, or that his perception of the others' attitudes is colored by what he hears them say in informal sessions. The responses on the other items in the questionnaire tend to support the latter conclusion, since no reluctance to note negative feelings was apparent. In comparison with conventional training methods, the trainees felt that programed instruction was better and requires less time.

On a general level, trainees indicated that for future courses of this type programed textual materials should be used frequently. They felt it would be valuable in learning to read and write a foreign language. The attitudes

---

[2] H. H. Shettel, H. R. Sand, Judi L. Northrup, and J. W. Staman, *Development of Programed Instructional Materials for Selected Subject Matter in the Ordnance Guided Missile School*, U.S. Army Ordnance Guided Missile School, Redstone Arsenal, Alabama, 1964.

on these two items were practically identical, indicating reliability of response. For those training courses in which the use of programed materials would be appropriate, the trainees in the massed group recommended their use for a large part of the course, while the trainees in the spaced group recommended that they be used for about half the time. This may be compared with the difference in the daily schedule recommended by the two groups. In both cases, those who had more concentrated training favored a higher PI concentration, in relation to other activities, than did those who had less concentrated training. On the final item relating to the specific value of the course on query language, all trainees felt it would be a valuable training method. Trainees in the massed group were slightly more favorable than were those in the spaced group. Both service rank and educational level were positively correlated with final proficiency obtained by completing the course.

The adaptability of the computer as a teaching device may be greatly increased by building into it a self-organizing feature for operating directly upon the *internal* organization of the instructional material. (This technique has been successfully implemented on a limited scale in an Air Force study on training in speed reading.)[3] At first, this might take the form of changing performance parameters on the basis of experience with trainees. For example, the computer could check the time scores of prescribed numbers of trainees, compare these against existing criteria, and make changes in the criteria if necessary. Other parameters that could be internally modified include factors for determining the trainees' overall performance and the number of errors required before some action is taken—such as displaying a text reference after a review set. This updating program could make accessible a statistical program to determine the significance of the differences obtained. The advantage of such a system is that it can continually revise program criteria on the basis of interactions with the trainee and thus provide the sequencing and choice of sequences best suited for each trainee. This would result eventually in an "optimum" training program for each individual. While these notions are not within the scope of the present effort, they are considered to be logical extensions of the training strategy described here and may well lead to a computer-based rationale for training that is clearly superior to those possible with other formats and media of presentation.

---
* T. R. Strollo, *A Generalized Teaching Machine Decision Structure with Applications to Speed Reading*, Tech. Doc. Report No. ESD TDR-64-523, Electronic Systems Division, Decision Sciences Laboratory, L. G. Hanscom Field, Bedford, Massachusetts, 1964.

International Business Machines Corporation *

A

IBM has five field engineering education schools which are responsible for all the training of customer engineers in some 200 branch offices across the United States. Each customer engineer is responsible for the maintenance of IBM machines and programs in his own territory. Each has to be trained on a wide variety of equipment and programs so that he will be able to provide immediate and efficient service for the customer. After encouraging results from an early effort with PI in 1960, action was taken to program a significant portion of the existing training effort. The schools have produced 81 programs representing more than 1,000 hours of instruction. The use of PI to train customer engineers is described in this case.

THE TRAINING THE CUSTOMER ENGINEER RECEIVES IS IN TWO general categories: basic training and advanced training. The basic training is given each year to new customer engineers. In educational background, these men range from high school graduates with two years of experience or trade school training to graduate engineers with EE or ME degrees. Following a routine orientation in the branch office, the employees participate in a nine-week training program which is designed to equip them with the necessary skills and information to service the basic line of punched-card accounting machines. The course consists of a detailed study of organization and data flow for eight machines. The trainee receives four hours of lecture and four hours of lab each day. The laboratory periods provide training in removing and adjusting mechanical units, diagnosing machine malfunctions, and repairing mechanical, electrical, and electronic circuits. Following his basic training, the trainee returns to his branch office and is assigned to a small territory where he puts into practice the skills he has just learned. Territorial assignments are increased as proficiency grows. Following a six-month

---

* Information for this case submitted by L. T. Deabler, formerly Manager of Education Processes, IBM, Armonk, New York, and W. R. Munns, Manager, Education Planning, Field Engineering Division, IBM, Rochester, Minnesota.

to one-year period, the customer engineer, now having proved himself capable of handling additional and more complex machines, is given advanced training in either a company education center or his own branch office, depending upon the machine that he is to study. At the education center he is trained on large complex systems and on new products. These courses range from three days to six months. Other advanced training courses are conducted in the local branch offices by qualified instructors. These courses last from one day to three weeks.

The customer engineer spends a good part of his time in training. Additional courses not only represent added responsibility but take the trainee away from his home and family and allow less time to practice the training he has already received. With the amount of necessary training and the demand for higher quality increasing in each new course, new and more efficient methods of training were necessary in order to reduce the customer engineer's time spent in training. Programed instruction appeared to offer at least a partial solution to this problem. As early as 1960, planning groups from the schools released a program for field testing. The results were encouraging. After several more experiments to gain the necessary skills and develop workable techniques, a group of 20 people in the Rochester, Minnesota, school was commissioned to program a major portion of the existing basic program. Since this initial effort, Rochester and the four other schools have produced 81 programs representing more than 1,000 hours of instruction. Additional programs are currently being developed.

Originally, in developing the PI materials, every man worked independently. Each was assigned one program and did all the work on that program, which included outlining the subject material, writing the frames, editing, drawing illustrations, and testing the program. It became obvious early that this approach left much to be desired; it was impractical to expect each person to become expert in all these facets of programing technology. Subsequently, the department was organized with five new positions, each requiring extensive training and, where possible, experience. The five positions were: (1) writer, (2) technical editor, (3) program editor, (4) illustrator, and (5) audio technician.

A writer assumes complete responsibility for a training package. The department feels that three to six months of in-house training on the principles of PI and good writing techniques are required to produce acceptable writers. Experienced classroom instructors are selected because they are already subject matter experts and have demonstrated themselves to be excellent instructors. The technical editor is primarily responsible for the technical accuracy of the written material and also acts as adviser to the writer. Since he must have the same qualifications as the writer, these positions are often rotated to relieve the boredom of frame writing. The program editor not only corrects all grammatical errors but also insures good format and adherence to the company's publishing standards. This position requires an English major with a working knowledge of the technical language used by the company. The illustrator is not only responsible for accurate illustrations that supplement the text, but he must also understand the problems of illustrating mechanical and electrical devices for teaching and publishing. The audio technician is the unique member of the team, because the company feels that very often audio training tapes are necessary. Many programs are released in the form of student workbooks with instructions on tape rather than just in straight text. The audio technician must therefore have not only a good speaking voice and a knowledge of sound recording equipment but also the ability to edit scripts to prevent stilted speech on tapes.

In order to mass produce programed instruction courses without any adverse effect on quality, it is necessary to establish sound workable routines with checkpoints at critical stages of program development. The routines are divided into three sections: design, production, and publication (see Exhibit 1). The design section develops the training package. The writer and the technical editor write their detailed statements of terminal behavior based on job requirements, skills, and knowledge. The first checkpoint occurs here. When the statements have been approved, the criteria tests are developed, tested, and inserted in the existing training program. Again, approval is necessary to continue. Approval is contingent on the result of the testing and the subjective opinions of subject matter experts. The design phase takes approximately half the total time required to complete the training package. At this point, the production phase begins. The writer and the technical expert outline the material and determine the best sequence in which to teach the various parts of the subject. When the outline is complete, the illustrators and program editor assist the writer in developing the format of the package. Again, approval is necessary to continue. The writer now begins developing frames, and each section in turn is approved by the technical editor and the program editor. The illustrators develop the necessary drawings, graphs, and charts. The illustrations, first-draft typing, and preliminary audio tapes (when required) are merged to start the process of testing. The program is first tested, outside the programed instruction group, by instructors who have been previously trained in the subject matter. Revisions are made when necessary. The program testing is then continued by instructors who are not familiar with the subject, by single or small groups of students in the school, and, finally, by complete classes of 12 to 18 men. After each testing, changes are made as determined by the comments of test subjects and the results of the criteria tests and average time factors. When all concerned are satisfied with the program, approval to publish is granted. An estimate is made of the number of students who require training during the next six months, and the first edition is printed and distributed. During the first six months a thorough record is kept of each student's performance and his opinion of the new program. The student evaluations and errors in the material are reviewed, changes are incorporated into the first revision, and the program is reprinted. All programs are then monitored periodically and revised when necessary.

There is no standard format for the PI materials. Each training program for customer engineering education is analyzed to determine the most efficient format and techniques. Because of their length and complexity, some programs are more efficient with standard classroom and laboratory techniques; others adapt quite readily to standard PI formats; still others appear to be more efficient when PI and classroom training are combined.

Those courses or subjects that require up to 40 hours of student time and a great number of student enrollments are often quite economical in PI format. Programed learning courses produced by the programing group for this type of subject incorporate a variety of formats, including constructed response text (Skinner); multiple choice responses with branching (Crowder); or combinations using audio training tapes, outside panels, visual aids, and diagnostic exercises. In some programs, not only the material but even the students' time and activities in theoretical learning and machine practice are "programed" in order to reduce the fatigue resulting from prolonged activity of one type. All information and practice behaviors are reduced to small steps, each step requiring a specific response from the student. Courses are sent to the student in his own branch office, where he undertakes a voluntary course of study. One person in each branch office is responsible for gathering materials, administering the test, and reporting the results of the program and qualifications of the student to the group that originated the program.

Many courses which exceed 40 hours of training or which have a high degree of complexity and require formal classroom and laboratory training in a plant training center have some terminology and fundamental principles that can economically be programed and given to the student in the branch office before he attends the school. This builds up the initial repertoire of the student and enables him to handle classroom-laboratory training more efficiently. These programs rarely exceed 30 hours in duration and are de-

EXHIBIT 1

PROGRAMED INSTRUCTION FLOW CHART

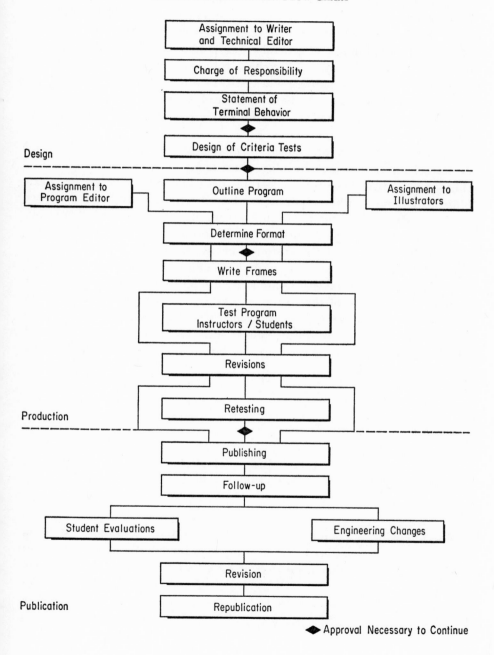

signed to account for a wide variety of individual differences in the student. For example, management feels that a class of 16 to 20 students from various parts of the country and with various training backgrounds can be shaped into homogeneous groups ready to start a highly concentrated training program. Since they arrive at the plant school knowing the machine's language, principles of operation, and general organization, they can make maximum use of their formal training. Preschool training courses also simplify the instructor's job by eliminating the necessity of presenting introductory material to new students, some of whom may already be familiar with the subject, while others may have had little or no previous exposure to the new technology.

Another advantage to programed instruction is referred to by the company as post-school or "feature" training. Since many of the more complex machines and systems have special features designed to provide greater flexibility to customers who require special applications, only those customer engineers who must service the special features need to be trained. By placing the training of these special features in PI format, total time at the school location is reduced and the customer engineers are trained only on the equipment they will be servicing. Another significant advantage of this type of program is that of review. Quite often a long period of time will elapse between the training of the customer engineer and the first time he is required to service a given feature on his machine. Because this information is available in PI form, the customer engineer can review the principles of the feature, maintain his proficiency, and bolster his confidence in his ability to meet an emergency.

B

Since early 1961 the Sales Training Department of IBM's Office Products Division has been writing, evaluating, and using programed instruction. The following is a summary of the effort to date.*

The following is a summary of the sales department's complete training program: All new men are hired on the first of the month, spend two weeks in branch offices, and then come to New York for a ten-day basic school. Soon

* Information for this case submitted by L. T. Deabler, formerly Manager of Education Processes, IBM, Armonk, New York, and Miss Phoeba Suica, Education Planning Representative, Office Products Division, IBM, New York, New York.

after they return to their branch offices, they are given a territory. After one to two months on quota, they return to New York for a ten-day sales school. The total training program consists of:

- Field training—two weeks
- Basic school—ten days
- Field training—three weeks
- Quota—one to two months
- Sales school—two weeks

The basic school is designed to review product knowledge and teach demonstrating and selling techniques. When the students return to New York for sales school, the instructors concentrate on teaching more sophisticated selling techniques, familiarizing the students with competitive products, and discussing problems which have occurred in the students' territories. The branch office manager is provided with a detailed outline for the five weeks of field training. At sales training, attention centers on the man's first two weeks with IBM—the two weeks prior to basic school. During this time he is supposed to learn the nomenclature, features, and benefits of the Model C Standard typewriter; Model C "Executive" * typewriter; "Selectric" * typewriter; IBM "Executary" * dictating equipment (dictator's unit, secretarial unit, and combination unit); and supplies (ribbons, carbon paper, typing elements, and IBM Executary supplies).

The feeling in the Sales Training Department was that if it was feasible to equip the men in the field with product knowledge, more classroom time could be devoted to "how to sell." This led to the investigation of PI. If PI proved successful, it should provide the following advantages:

- All the students would arrive at basic school with uniform product knowledge.
- Less time would have to be devoted to teaching product knowledge in the basic school.
- It would not be necessary to inconvenience the manager or a senior salesman in the branch office by requiring him to teach a newly hired man basic product knowledge.

At the present time, trainees are learning nomenclature on the following through PI: Model C Standard typewriter, Model C Executive typewriter, centering and justifying on the Executive typewriter, and Model C Standard with decimal tabulation.

The nomenclature of the Model C Standard with decimal tabulation is learned between basic and sales schools. Further programed instruction on

---

* Trademarks.

the Selectric typewriter has been written and evaluated and is now being printed for field distribution to new employees.

All are primarily short-frame, linear programs requiring short responses. For all the programs the student is required to have the piece of equipment in front of him and is constantly referring to it.

When the new men arrive at basic school, they are given a 96-item test which covers the topics they should have learned in their branch offices. Twenty-four of these questions deal with information which is taught by PI and 72 questions deal with topics which are taught by other means. This test has been given to 48 men. Their average on the material taught by programed instruction is 77 per cent, while the average on topics taught by conventional methods is 52 per cent. In both formal and informal interviews the students report that the programed instruction is the most valuable part of their training materials.

The following is a short description, with test results, of the specific programs.

Model C Standard Electric Typewriter. This program consists of 504 linear frames and takes four to six hours to complete. This was the first program written by the Sales Training Department, begun in April 1961 and completed a year later. The program teaches the functions and operations of the Model C Standard typewriter with partial coverage of the internal mechanisms which directly power the typebar, carriage, and platen movements. The program was given its first evaluation at the University of Kentucky in February 1962. The average time for completing the program was 4.26 hours. On a 30-item pretest, the students averaged 26.1 per cent. On a 130-item final examination, the average was 85 per cent. The range was 72.8 per cent to 94.1 per cent. Following a revision of the program, it was tested again in March 1962 on three IBM sales trainees in a test office. Their average on the 130-item final examination was 88.5 per cent. Three students did not take the program but learned the material in the conventional method. Their average on the same examination was 76.5 per cent. Following another revision, the program was again tested in September 1962. On the 100-item examination the PI group (16 trainees) scored 90 per cent and the conventional group (12 trainees) scored 80.3 per cent. Only 100 items were used on the examination rather than 130 because 30 questions were eliminated which were not covered by the conventional training course. Again in December 1962, 13 more sales trainees who took the program in their branch offices were tested upon arrival at basic school. Their average on the final examination was 88.1 per cent.

Model C Executive Electric Typewriter. (a) Work on the Executive typewriter was begun in September 1962, and the program was completed three months later. This is a 213-frame linear program which takes the student from 1½ to 2½ hours to complete. The program assumes a knowledge of the Model C Standard typewriter and teaches only the additional features and differences of the Executive typewriter.

(*b*) In October 1962 two sales trainees took the program. On a 48-item examination, which was given immediately after completing the program, they averaged 80 per cent. The program was revised and tested again in November 1962, this time on 14 sales trainees at the basic school. Their average on a 48-item examination was 85 per cent.

(*c*) The program was again revised and distributed to the field. The May 14 class, consisting of 10 sales trainees, was tested in New York. Their average was 81 per cent. The June 13 class, consisting of 16 sales trainees, had an average of 81 per cent when they were tested upon arrival at the basic school. In these last two experimental groups, the test took place approximately two weeks after completion of the program.

(*d*) The 48-item examination was also administered to students who had learned the material in the conventional method. These tests were run at four different times. The table below indicates the averages of these four groups.

Control Group	Average Per Cent
December 13, 1962	63.0
January 18, 1963	51.1
May 14, 1963	55.6
June 13, 1963	62.0

Standard Electric Typewriter with Decimal Tabulation. (*a*) This program was begun in November and completed in December 1962. The program assumes a knowledge of the Model C Standard typewriter. This is the first program to attempt to teach a selling demonstration. The program consists of two parts.

(*b*) Part I teaches the nine additional tab keys and how to use them. It also teaches the salesmen how to compute key strokes saved when using decimal tabulation rather than a standard typewriter with only one tab key. Part II is a selling demonstration containing 48 blanks. The student has learned the information which will correctly fill in these blanks in Part I.

(*c*) In January 1963 this program was tested on 18 sales trainees. Their average on a 10-item examination was 90 per cent. The range was 65 per cent to 100 per cent. Minor revisions were made on the program and it is now being used for field training.

IBM Selectric Electric Typewriter. (a) This program was begun in February 1963 and completed in November 1964. It teaches the functions and operations of the Selectric typewriter with partial coverage of the internal mechanisms of selection, tilt, and rotation. This is a 215-frame linear program which takes the student from 1½ to 2½ hours to complete.

(b) In January 1964 the program was given its first evaluation when it was administered to 18 sales trainees at the basic school. The average on the 50-item examination was 79.7 per cent. The range of scores was 66 per cent to 88 per cent. The men in this group did not have Selectric typewriters available when they took the program. The program was again tested on 24 sales trainees at the basic school in February 1964 when the typewriters were available. The average on the 15-item examination was 74 per cent and the range was 50 per cent to 92 per cent. In the same month the program was again revised and then sent to four new trainees who took the PI in their branch offices. Their average on the 50-item examination was 87 per cent. The final revision to the program was completed in October 1964. Frames were added to teach the automatic impression equalizer and the impression selector control. To date only one group has been given the course by conventional procedures. This was in December 1963, and 30 students in the basic school were involved. Their average on the 50-item examination was 71 per cent.

Centering on the Model C Executive Typewriter. The centering program was begun in January 1963 and finished in April 1964. It teaches centering on the Executive typewriter using the grommet method. It consists of 42 frames and takes the student an average of one hour to complete. As he takes the program, the student is constantly referred to the typewriter. The program was evaluated on 11 sales trainees. No test, as such, was given. After completion of the program, the student was required to center several titles. All students were successful.

Justifying on the Executive Electric Typewriter. The program on justifying was begun in January 1963 and completed in April 1964. It teaches the student how to justify the right margin on the Executive typewriter. The program consists of 63 linear frames and takes approximately 1½ hours to complete. This program, like the one on centering, requires the student to make constant use of his typewriter. The program has been evaluated on 12 sales trainees. No formal test, as such, was administered. At the completion of the program, the trainees were required to justify a short paragraph. All trainees were successful.

Magnetic Tape Selectric Typewriter. (*a*) A problem developed in May 1963 in training an effective sales force prior to announcing the Magnetic Tape Selectric typewriter scheduled for June 29, 1964. This was an entirely new concept for the men to learn. Training had to be accomplished without an adverse impact on present or future electric typewriter or dictation equipment sales. Moreover, training time and machines were limited. A further complication was that the typing ability of the salesmen varied widely.

(*b*) To solve these problems, about 80 people were trained in New York. Forty of these formed a nucleus to conduct training in the 10 districts throughout the United States. All field managers and quota salesmen were trained during the two weeks prior to announcement at their district locations. The managers then went back to their branch offices and trained their salesmen as the machines became available. Finally, a program was written on the hardware not only because test results show the superiority of PI over conventional methods, but because the quality of the classroom instruction would decrease further down the pyramid of instructors—not because of their inability to teach but because of their limited experience.

(*c*) Programed instruction in the Magnetic Tape Selectric typewriter (begun in June 1963 and completed by May 1964) is a short-frame linear program consisting of three sections, each followed by a practice session. Total completion time including practice periods is approximately nine hours. Section I (211 frames) teaches how to record and play back and how to make corrections on the document only without changing the material recorded on the tape. Section II (180 frames) teaches searching and all possible tape changes necessary for updating tapes. Section III (63 frames) teaches all features necessary to do automatic, unattended letter writing.

(*d*) There were many more problems in writing a program on an unannounced product than had been encountered in writing PI on products already in the line. Among others, constant machine improvements required rewriting the program. To help solve this problem, the frames were recorded on magnetic tape and the MT/ST was used for making revisions. There was also a lack of naive test subjects. Ten persons from the Sales Training Department participated. Eight were instructors; all were ex-salesmen or representative of the best salesmen in the division. As the men took the program, they made comments about frames which were unclear. Two-man teams were assigned to do the practice sessions at the completion of each section of frames. The information gained in watching the men go through the practice sessions was used in rewriting certain frames and the instructions to the practice sessions. There were several reasons why the men worked as two-man teams during the practice sessions. For one thing, because of the lack of training machines it would be necessary to pair the men during field training. For another, typing ability varied. A man who could "touch"-type was therefore paired with a man who couldn't type at all. One man did the initial recording, but both had sufficient time to do the remainder of the exercise (skipping, correcting tape, playing back, and so on). Even though the test subjects were not naive, they proved extremely helpful in determining unclear areas of the program. This was the first program to be taken by the entire sales force. The reception has been very favorable: "This is the best piece of training material I've ever received." "Why don't we have more programed instruction?" "If it hadn't been for the PI, I wouldn't have been able to learn the material."

C

This case highlights IBM's efforts to program the total student study activity throughout an eight-hour day rather than just program subject matter content. As such it illustrates one of the major contributions of programed instruction to educational technology.*

It was early in 1962 that IBM's management became aware of a shortcoming in the presentation of programed instruction courses. Many students indicated that the long tedious hours of reading one small frame after another were more than they could handle. There was no question about the quality of the material or about the students' ability, but it was obvious that they would not be able to take full advantage of the technique unless the material could be made more palatable. IBM decided to attempt to program the total student activity throughout an eight-hour day rather than just program material. Up to then, the students' endurance had been approximately two to three hours; a normal 40-hour program therefore required well over a month to complete. Management believed that by taking advantage of all programing techniques, with an acute awareness of the students' total activity, it would be able to increase student acceptance of programed instruction and at the same time decrease the total period it would take to train the student on any one course. Since this concept was new, it decided to choose a machine for which there was already a sufficient number of trained

---

* Information for this case submitted by L. T. Deabler, formerly Manager of Education Processes, IBM, Armonk, New York, and W. R. Munns, Manager, Education Planning, Field Engineering Division, IBM, Rochester, Minnesota.

students who could provide back-up in case of program failure, and a machine that would enable them to show a large dollar savings.

It chose the IBM 88 Collator, which is a high-speed card-filing machine that arranges punched cards in a sequence desired for subsequent operations. The operation of the IBM 88 Collator had been taught by conventional field training methods for approximately one year. The course consisted of approximately 16 hours of classroom lecture and 16 hours of laboratory work for hands-on experience. These classes continued during the development of the programed instruction package. When the terminal behaviors and criteria tests were developed, they were incorporated into the existing course in order to develop a set of norms against which to judge the effectiveness of the programed instruction.

The programed instruction course was developed completely in-house, using two trained staff instructor-writers and a publication staff consisting of an editor, typists, and illustrators. The course was divided into two major sections—mechanics and circuits—so that the mechanics section could be used in courses about other equipment that used the same mechanical base. The mechanics section consisted of an audio training tape, a study guide, and a machine part which served as a visual aid. The circuits section consisted of three audio training tapes, a study guide, and a component orientation lab project. The total course required approximately 23½ hours to complete. Most of the material was presented to the student in audio form while he looked at or wrote in a study guide. The student was exposed to pictures, diagrams, and written instructions. There were also a few sections of framed instruction inserted for variation and to allow for branching by students with more experience. When learning sequential items, the student looked at and responded to "growing" diagrams. At the beginning of the sequence, only one small portion of the diagram was readable and the other parts were heavily screened. As the sequence progressed, more and more of the diagram was exposed. The program did not provide hands-on or laboratory time until the training was complete. Wherever possible, the objectives of the laboratory portion of the original course were programed into pencil-and-paper exercises or exercises with simulators or visual aids. Also included were a number of self-tests and diagnostic exercises that allowed the student to determine his own proficiency.

At the completion of the course the student was required to fill out an evaluation sheet which reflected his opinions, the amount of time he spent taking the course, any errors, and suggestions for improvement. Each student was tested on the terminal behaviors with a comprehensive paper-and-pencil test.

The results were rather startling. Since programed instruction had already proved itself, no extra attempt was made to justify the effectiveness of the program. In general, examination scores obtained by the regular classes in process during the construction of the program were equal to or slightly below those obtained by the students who used programed instruction. These tests included regular paper-and-pencil tests as well as timed diagnostic tests on the machine. In addition, a questionnaire was sent to each student's manager three months after the student had completed the programed instruction, asking the manager to rate the student in five separate categories on the basis of performance in customers' offices. The results were tabulated in December 1963 and are reproduced in Exhibit 2. Two comparisons are particularly noteworthy.

EXHIBIT 2

	4 OUTSTANDING *Per Cent*	3 WELL FITTED *Per Cent*	2 SUITABLE *Per Cent*	1 NEEDS IMPROVEMENT *Per Cent*
Ability to diagnose trouble	4	64	32	0
Quality of corrective action	13	65	22	0
Capabilities on this machine (88 Collator)	4	60	36	0
Capabilities on other machines	7	64	29	0
Ability to work with minimum assistance	11	65	24	0

(*a*) The two categories "Capabilities on this machine" and "Capabilities on other machines" have a strong correlation, indicating that after the PI course and just three months' experience the students were as capable of servicing the IBM 88 Collator as they were with one to five years' experience servicing other machines, even though they did not receive any laboratory experience during the course.

(*b*) A comparison of the rankings of the student's ability to work with minimum assistance with accepted rankings for other courses indicated that the students who received programed instruction required about 50 per cent less assistance. This suggested that PI was successful in identifying the meaningful content of the laboratory portion of the conventional course and could be used as a substitute for hands-on experience.

Since the original intent of the study was to produce a program that would be favorably received by the students and one that would allow the students to pursue the training for a full eight hours a day, each student was asked to complete an evaluation form that could be compared with existing evaluations from previous PI courses. In addition, 12 students were interviewed after their evaluation sheets were received to confirm the validity of the evaluation questions and also to gather additional information. Even though the first 63 evaluations that were received did not indicate that the average time of the study periods had increased as had been expected, the comments in response to the question, "How well did you enjoy this type of training (audio tape)?" indicated that the students were very much in favor of it over the previous "all text" types. A separate survey revealed that old study habits and instructions from the students' managers were responsible for the short study periods rather than any defect in the material itself. An experiment was conducted with a limited number of students to determine the optimum time for a study period. The students in this group indicated that four hours each day was reasonable under field conditions, and with several short "coffee breaks" they would be able to study effectively for six to eight hours each day without undue fatigue. The results of this experiment coupled with comments from field management led to the conclusion that future programs should have four-hour study periods. This allows the student to complete the training in a reasonable time and gives the added advantage of having the student available to retain the responsibilities for his territory during training.

During the first six months of using programed instruction in the field course, evaluations indicated that several changes in the original program would be desirable. Since the students received no hands-on training, many of them were unaware of their capabilities to service the machine until they had actually done so in the customers' offices. In order to reduce any feeling that he would not be able to recognize the components of the machine on his first call, each student was supplied with five 16" x 20" photographs of the machine. From these photographs the student could locate and identify more components than he was originally required to do in the conventional training course. The photographs also gave a better understanding of the relationship of one part to another in location and size. A second change was also indicated by the course evaluations. Each student who completed the course took a final paper-and-pencil test, administered by his manager. Many of the questions on this test were diagnostic and therefore required a transfer of training from an understanding of proper machine operation to an understanding of improper operation and the diagnosis of malfunctioning components. The student's manager was often unable to explain the correct answer satisfactorily or to explain why an answer was incorrect. A complete set of explanations for each correct and incorrect answer was therefore supplied, along with the quiz. These changes were apparently successful in solving most of the problems. In a recent survey of 118 students responding to the question, "How well do you enjoy this type of training (audio tape)?" the percentage of "excellent/good" responses had increased from 74 per cent in the original survey to 88 per cent, while the percentage of "fair" responses had decreased from 18 per cent to 12 per cent and the percentage of "poor" responses had decreased from 8 per cent to less than 1 per cent.

Liberty Mutual Insurance Company *

The Liberty Mutual Insurance Company has 12,000 employees, approximately 2,500 in the home office and the rest scattered throughout the country in nine divisions and 160 branches. This case reports two applications of programed instruction technology. The first is the Basic Systems audio-lingual program, "Effective Listening." The second is Liberty Mutual's program prepared under the guidance of ENTELEK, Inc. It is a 40-hour course to teach Claims Representatives to handle reports and claims stemming from automobile accidents and other mishaps.

A

LIBERTY MUTUAL TESTED AND EVALUATED THE BASIC SYSTEMS AUDIO-lingual self-instructional "Effective Listening" program at a sales managers' seminar. The program was administered to a representative sample of ten sales managers to measure the acceptance, administrative characteristics, and appropriateness of this course.

Limited use of the course began in the fall of 1963, and it was installed throughout the company in the summer of 1964. Many departments have used the course, including Administrative Services, Sales, Loss Prevention, Business Policy Production, Underwriters, and Claims.

The rationale for investigating the possible use of this course was that communication skills are extremely important in selling and servicing policyholders. Listening is the foundation of good communication and has a direct bearing on satisfying the specific needs of both current and prospective policyholders. The use of this course has enabled Liberty Mutual to increase the listening efficiency of its sales managers by providing decentralized training at a relatively low cost.

* Information for this case submitted by Warren E. Marshall, Assistant Vice President and Manager of Personnel Development, Liberty Mutual Insurance Company, Boston, Massachusetts; Dr. Irving Goldberg, Director of Training Systems Division, Basic Systems, Inc.; and Dr. Albert Hickey, President, ENTELEK.

The ages, experience, and education of the sales managers who took this course in the field test were appropriate for it, and a pretest had demonstrated that they could benefit by it. The pretest average for the ten employees was 34 per cent; the range was 10 to 49 per cent; the average age, 35 years; the range, 26 to 47 years. The average experience on the job was nine years; the range, from three to 16 years; and the average formal education of the group was college level.

Test results suggested that Liberty can realize improvements in effective communication throughout the organization through the use of this program. The average final examination score was 91 per cent, with a range from 77 to 100 per cent. The improvement in listening skills as measured by the post-test score was 168 per cent. The results of using the "Effective Listening" course at Liberty and at other companies were similar. These results are compared in Exhibit 1 of Chapter Four (p. 65).

Trainees were enthusiastic, as shown by the following comments:

- "It made me realize the importance of getting to the pertinent points of a man's statement so as to quickly understand what he really means."
- "I believe it could be easily enough administered for us to take it to a salesman for a similar test."
- "Developed a greater consciousness of the importance of orderly conversation."
- "I think this method is useful in training salesmen in many aspects of their job."

There was also a positive reaction to using audio tapes in programed instruction; 90 per cent of the trainees preferred audio-programed instruction to the regular classroom method and felt that they "learn more than they would have from a teacher in the same amount of time." The results of the field test of the "Effective Listening" course are summarized in Exhibit 1.

Liberty Mutual has 1,258 salesmen in 38 district offices who can be trained in their own offices with this self-instructional program. The only equipment needed is a tape recorder, which every district office now has. Training specialists can visit the district offices and administer the program to as many as 15 or 20 trainees in three-hour periods. A further advantage is that 20 new employees can be given the course each month for an indefinite time. Moreover, the training can be extended to women office personnel—sales assistants, personal sales representatives, and customer service representatives—who deal with customers and prospects on the phone and who can be trained inexpensively in this critical listening skill.

Liberty's divisions have reported their experiences with the course. The following excerpts from one such report are typical.

EXHIBIT 1

SUMMARY OF FIELD EVALUATION RESULTS, "EFFECTIVE LISTENING" PROGRAM
LIBERTY MUTUAL INSURANCE COMPANY

TRAINEE	1	2	3	4	5	6	7	8	9	10
Age	38	30	30	31	37	26	44	33	37	47
Last Grade of School	BA	BA	BA	BS	BA	BS	BS	BA	BA	BA
Job Classification	District Sales Manager Charlotte	City Sales Manager New York	City Sales Manager Detroit	District Sales Manager Milwaukee	City Sales Manager Lakewood	City Sales Manager St. Louis	City Sales Manager East Orange	City Sales Manager Brooklyn	Division Training Director Atlanta	Training Director Brooklyn
Years of Experience	16	7	6	5	4	3	16	6	13	10
PRETEST SCORE	10%	36%	49%	49%	16%	42%	36%	29%	48%	29%
TOTAL STUDY TIME*	3 hr 15 min									
FINAL EXAM SCORE	94%	77%	94%	100%	85%	100%	94%	94%	94%	82%

* Includes Part I, Part II, Exam, and Questionnaire for Group Mode

Thirty-five participants and two guests at these seminars took both pre- and post-tests. The average pretest score was 34; the post-test, 82, for an average gain of 48 points.

Of the 37 who answered, 16 claimed that before taking the course they had been able to summarize spoken remarks adequately as the speaker proceeded. The other 21 admitted previous inability to summarize such remarks. All but one of the 37 felt they could do so after taking the course.

In answer to the question on how successful they thought audio-programed instruction was as a teaching method, 34 thought they learned more than they could have learned from a teacher; three thought they learned about the same.

Eleven participants specifically stated that there was nothing about pro-gramed instruction that they disliked. The dislikes of the others were scattered. Difficulty in understanding the speakers was mentioned by two men.

Two liked audio-programed instruction less than conventional classroom teaching, five liked it just as well, and 28 preferred it. Two did not answer.

The most-liked features of the listening program were its pace, its step-by-step progression, and the way it made the listener appreciate his progress and capabilities as he went through it.

LMI now uses "Effective Listening" as part of its training for all personnel who are in contact with policyholders or the public and for all personnel in supervisory management or staff positions. Its place in the individual's training schedule depends on his present and future work assignments.

B

"You," in the text of the frames reproduced in Exhibit 2, means one of 80 women hired each year by Liberty Mutual Insurance Company to be inside claims representatives. This sequence is the introduction to a 2,500-frame program developed by Liberty Mutual over a period of a year and a half.

The program is of interest on two counts. First, the claims representative's task is typical of many intermediate-level decision-making tasks. To meet this common training requirement, the program combines a computer block diagram with programed instruction to teach white-collar girls how to make fairly complex decisions. The diagram and a form book are used not only in training but later as guides to performance on the job—a "human engineering" feature which reduces from two months to two weeks the time required to bring a newly hired woman to full productivity on the job.

Also interesting are the administrative lessons learned in developing this program. At its inception, each operating department at Liberty Mutual administered its own programing requirements. There was no central staff to coordinate the administrative activities and apply combined experience to programing projects. Midway in the development of the program a personnel development staff was created. The Claims Department could easily utilize this staff to achieve optimum results in handling administrative concerns with budget, personnel, conduct of technical review, and use of consultants.

There are some 250 Claims Representative (CR) positions in 120 Liberty Mutual Claims Departments from coast to coast. The annual turnover in this position is about 35 per cent, so about 80 new women are hired or promoted to the position and trained each year. Although some of the women hired are college graduates, the majority who are promoted to the position have a high school education, which is the basic requirement.

The Claims Department recognized the requirement for a more efficient training regimen for this task and initiated the project. It hoped the program would—

1. Standardize the minimum training required.
2. Free local supervisors for supervision of case load.
3. Lead to job standards.
4. Bring CR trainees to full production faster.

Having selected an objective, the Claims Department assigned three people to attend a two-week in-house programing course: a branch office claims supervisor with a comprehensive knowledge of claims and the claims representative's task; a branch office claims representative; and a home office Claims Department staff writer.

After attending the course, the three were long on claims-handling knowledge but still short on programed instruction experience. Two graduates of the in-house programers' workshop, with a year of successful PI projects in their dossier, were assigned as advisers. The group met periodically with the consultant from ENTELEK, Inc., bringing the total project personnel to six. The group was responsible to the director of claims training.

Although the new programers were acquainted with the CR task, they had had no experience in reducing task information to task or training specifications. Conversely, at the outset the consultant and the experienced writers had only a superficial understanding of the task and its complexity. As with many intermediate-level decision-making tasks, the complexity of the process was not readily apparent. Furthermore, the claims procedures

EXHIBIT 2

FRAMES FROM LIBERTY MUTUAL'S CLAIMS REPRESENTATIVES COURSE

1. Look at Figure 1. It is clear that Mr. Able and Mr. Baker have been involved in an ***.

automobile accident

2. Both parties have suffered a financial loss in the accident, but it looks as though Mr. _____ is responsible.

Able

3. Both Mr. Able and Mr. Baker carry automobile insurance. In fact, Mr. Able is _____ by Liberty Mutual.

insured

4. Perhaps at one time or another you have been involved in an accident. Recall the procedure. After you inform the police (if that is necessary) you should inform your _____ company.

insurance

5. If, like Mr. Baker, you think you have suffered a loss, you will probably make a _____ against the other party.

claim

6. So it is in this case. Mr. Baker will probably make a _____ against our policyholder, Mr. Able.

claim

7. Fortunately for Mr. Able, he carries automobile liability insurance with Liberty Mutual. In fact, when Mr. Able and Mr. Baker exchanged information after the accident, Mr. Able told Mr. Baker that he is insured by ***.

Liberty Mutual

8. Consequently, Mr. Baker may make his _____, not to Mr. Able, but directly to Liberty Mutual.

claim

9. In that case, somebody in Liberty Mutual is going to hear from both *** as a result of this accident.

Mr. Able and Mr. Baker

10. In your new position as _____ _____ you may well be that person.

Claims Representative

FIGURE 1

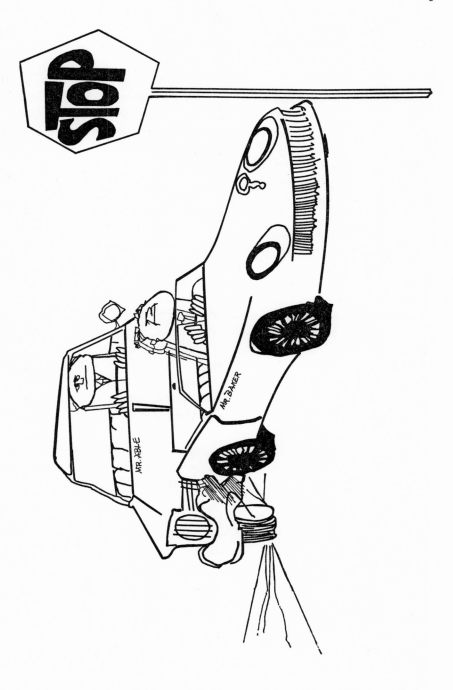

manual cited departmental standards for which the manager was responsible but did not state specifically how these ends were to be achieved. In other words, the departmental responsibilities were not broken down into separate tasks.

The project began with only an arbitrary standard for length: 2,500 frames. The project budget had not been predetermined. Standards can often be amended or added as the necessary data and cross-breeding of job knowledge and training methodology progress, but there is always the danger that they will be overlooked. Unfortunately, centralized and experienced company programed instruction project management was not available at the outset of the CR program. However, the Claims Department's utilization of the newly created personnel development staff as well as its own training staff underlined the need and advantages for centralized authority.

The 120 claims offices fulfilled the CR function in a wide variety of ways. To measure this variability and sort it into a manageable or logical number of categories, some 26 claims representatives were assembled at the home office for a fact-finding seminar with the project team. Armed with the resulting data, the project team drew a picture of the logical structure of the task; that is, the sequence of decisions required in classifying each case for subsequent processing.

Originally it was expected that the program would cover all three phases of the task. But, as the full scope of the project began to unfold, the original objective was modified. The program would cover only the *first* phase. The balance of the training requirement would be met by other, more conventional means. Although the coverage was cut by at least half, the estimate of 2,500 frames remained constant.

The principal product of the task analysis was outlined in a block diagram of the first phase. This was amplified by an outline of the successive steps, the conditions for assigning each case to the individual categories, and the associated clerical routines.

As the task routines were teased apart, a list of *behavioral* objectives was developed, and the complete task was divided along logical lines into four subtasks. Each writer took responsibility for at least one subtask. To this point the team members had performed successfully as a group. Now they began to function independently. One team member, who was most insightful in the logical analysis of the task, had the most difficulty in frame writing; her complex style tended to interfere with the stimulus response contingencies within the frame. With counseling this problem was in part remedied, and the consultant easily edited the frames.

And so the program grew frame by frame into a large and amorphous mass. This is often the case with the first draft. Problems of positive and negative transfer and of concept formation do not emerge or crystallize until virtually all the behavior has been framed. Although this is the *usual* procedure, it is not the necessary procedure.

At this point the program was a detailed, valid, sequentially ordered statement of the behaviors required in the task. At least 75 per cent of the frames specified appropriate job-related responses. The remaining responses were relevant, but not exclusively so.

The first objective in editing the program was to show the trainee the general configuration of the task—not its details but its major topographical features, its boundaries, and how it fitted into the general process of claims handling. In short, the objective was to give the novice a quick trip around the golf course, with perhaps a glimpse at the pleasures of the 19th hole, before returning him to the first tee.

The introductory tour of the CR task was accomplished in a 100-frame unit entitled "Once Over Lightly." The first 10 frames are the ones reproduced in Exhibit 2. By the time the trainee had completed the first 100 frames, she had handled in a cursory way the case of Able versus Baker. In the process she had used two on-the-job training aids also introduced at this stage. One aid was a "computer block diagram" or "decision map" that assisted her in making a chain of three to nine separate decisions in classifying each case. These chains were assembled from a total of 38 different decisions, some with two alternative outcomes, some with three, but each with its own set of criteria. In the decision map, shown here as Exhibit 3, the diamonds represent the decision points—the questions a claims representative must ask herself or her respondent in classifying each case. A case was classified when the girl reached a rectangle, which represented a form to be filled out. In all, there were 11 different forms, one of which could be filled out in as many as 13 different ways.

The decision map was a refinement of the block diagram developed originally in the task analysis. The refinement was the specification of the covert questions asked at each of the choice points.

The decision map is a remarkably comprehensive picture of the task. But two things are missing. First, the conditions for answering the successive questions are not listed. These conditions are sometimes black and white, such as "over $250" or "$250 and under." Other decisions require judgment with respect to liability or coverage. The conditions for each decision were taught to the *unaided recall* level by the programed instructions.

Also missing from the decision map are the detailed instructions for filling out the forms and routing the material. The 38 different procedures for

EXHIBIT 3

LIBERTY MUTUAL'S DECISION MAP

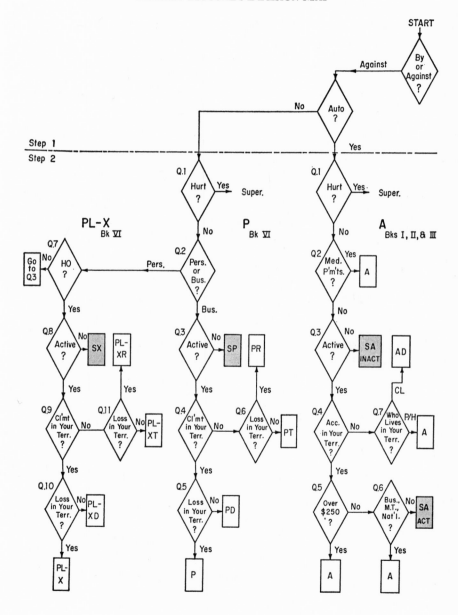

EXHIBIT 3 *(concluded)*

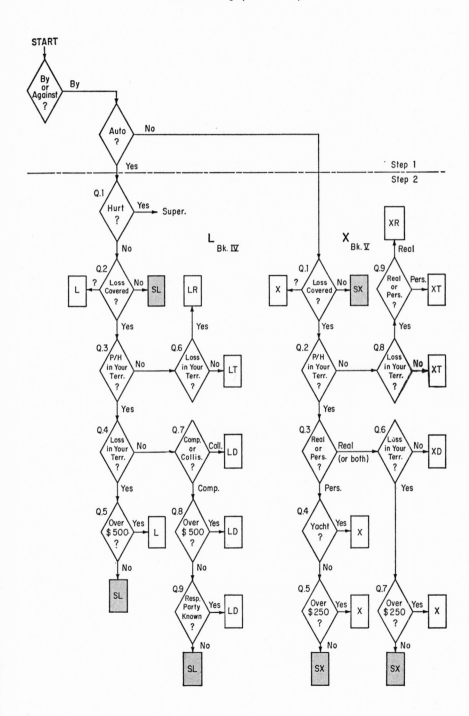

filling out the 11 different forms were taught to the level of aided recall. The aid to recall was a form book, the second on-the-job training aid, which contained examples of the several ways in which each of the forms was to be filled out. The examples did not contain data, but they indicated the spaces to be filled in and the criteria for answering the questions or the alternative responses, whichever were appropriate.

The addition of the training aids, particularly the form book, made it possible to remove many frames and many more illustrations, thus reducing the bulk of the program by perhaps 25 per cent. The program was bound in four units corresponding to the major categories of claims cases.

The draft program was tested on four girls who, by educational background and Life Office Management Association test criteria, were considered representative CR candidates. Three were high school graduates assigned to other tasks, and one was a newly hired college graduate already selected to be a branch office claims representative.

The average time to complete the program was 34 hours, with a range from 30 to 40 hours. The program, administered in four-hour sessions, required less than two weeks of part-time, on-the-job study to complete. The error rate was very low; the girls missed an average of only 13 of 2,500 response opportunities.

Some 50 criterion frames, requiring comprehensive classification or form completion behavior, were the primary targets for analysis. From information gathered during depth interviewing and on the basis of certain response latency, various parts of the program were amended to bolster learning of particular subroutines.

The girl who was currently assigned as a trainee reported to work as a Claims Representative each afternoon following the morning instruction period. She was thus able to utilize her accumulated learning to handle appropriate cases assigned to her. At the end of two weeks she was at the criterion level of production for an "acceptable" Claims Representative, a point not usually reached for some two to three months when a girl is trained by conventional "over the shoulder" methods.

Although Liberty Mutual had developed other programs this one will be the model for future intermediate-level decision-making programs. Such future programs will contain an introduction, a decision map where complex decision making is required, a form book, and programed instruction in decision conditions and response details.

The block diagram will be adapted for use as a training and on-the-job performance aid. This should also expedite program development, even when several people are working on a program simultaneously.

Liberty Mutual will continue to use a consultant for selection and advanced training of programers. Time in program editing could be saved in using a consultant for task analysis and final crystallization of the program around key concepts and behaviors. However, the problems of fact finding are likely to be overwhelming time consumers for any but experienced Liberty personnel. Thus, Liberty Mutual will continue to use consultants in a purely advisory capacity in the task analysis and crystallization process. Finally, the format developed for the CR program should act as an excellent guide in making the process of concept crystallization work faster.

Life Insurance Agency Management Association *

The Life Insurance Agency Management Association (LIAMA), recognizing the importance of a technically competent insurance agent force, felt it necessary not only to train the agents as well as possible but also to release managers from supervising training activities and allow them more time to do the job of sales training directly The ultimate objective of this PI effort was to save the managers' rather than the trainees' time while increasing the trainees' mastery of the subject matter.

EVEN THOUGH IT HAS BEEN DIFFICULT TO DEMONSTRATE A SIGNIFI- cant relationship between knowledge of life insurance on the part of agents and the ability to sell insurance, LIAMA "did show that agents who have more knowledge tend to have a higher persistency of business than those with less. But we have all recognized for a long time that men who know very little about our product can sell a lot of it and keep much of it on the books." [1] The importance of knowledge, however, has increased with the correlative increase in the complexity of the insurance field. Also, as S. Rains Wallace and P. W. Thayer have pointed out, "Whether it sells insurance or not, life insurance education is justified because it supports to some degree our pretensions to a professional relationship with our clients." [2] LIAMA noted in previous studies that there is great variety among agents in their level of accomplishment and sophistication in basic knowledge of insurance.

---

* This case is based upon information and data provided by Dr. David J. Klaus, Associate Director of the Training and Education Program of the American Institutes for Research, Pittsburgh, Pennsylvania; AIR Final Report "Development of Self-Instructional Materials on the Fundamentals of Life Insurance" by D. J. Klaus, H. H. Shettel, D. J. Clapp, and P. Welsh, dated October 1961; the *Proceedings* of the 46th Annual Meeting of the Life Insurance Agency Management Association, November 1963; and P. Welsh, J. A. Antoinetti, and P. W. Thayer, "An Industrywide Study of Programed Instruction," *Journal of Applied Psychology*, Vol. 49, 1965, pp. 61–73.
[1] Article in the *Proceedings* (*op. cit.*) titled "Steps into Life Insurance" by S. Rains Wallace and P. W. Thayer, p. 117.
[2] *Ibid.*, p. 118.

LIAMA felt that one of the factors contributing to this variety was the difference in the interest and training capabilities of the managers in the field. Previous studies by LIAMA indicated that some managers in fact know less about life insurance than the average agent. In spite of this, the managers are trainers.

At the 1962 Annual Meeting of LIAMA Mr. Wallace presented the results of a study of training and supervisory activities in 22 large urban agencies. He presented to the 1963 meeting some of the conclusions of that study.

> These general agents apparently believe that an agent in his first quarter can be adequately trained and supervised through the investment of approximately nine days of supervisory time. Never again does he need as much as five days per quarter, although they may give him two days of help with his prospects.
>
> The general agents apparently don't believe in field work. Two and one-half days of training and supervision and approximately one-half day of selling assistance in the field is about right for the first quarter. After that, less than two days per quarter needs to be spent in the field with a man for whatever purpose.
>
> To sum up:
>
> * Agents need life insurance knowledge.
> * Some get it—some don't, probably because a large proportion of our managers have neither the ability nor the desire to teach knowledge.
> * The amount of sales training, and particularly field training, given to our new agents today is woefully small. We are not making an adequate effort to protect the sizable investment we put into recruiting and financing our new agents.[3]

What was required, then, was a training methodology which would free the managers from an undesirable activity or from a task which they were not adequately trained to perform and at the same time improve the sophistication and knowledge of the agent in insurance. The search for this training technology was not due to any concern with saving the agent's time. In fact, as Wallace points out:

> All of our data would indicate that there is plenty of agent time available for education and training. In fact, I believe we could accomplish much in lowering our agent turnover if we would give more thought to filling the new agent's time with activities which he can perceive and accept as important to him.[4]

---

[3] *Ibid.*, pp. 119 and 120.
[4] *Ibid.*, p. 120.

Programed instruction appeared feasible and deserving of investigation because it would be self-instructional for the agent and would minimize the amount of supervision needed by the manager. The other characteristics of PI such as individualized instruction, self-pacing, standardized content, no contamination by unenthusiastic instructors, quality control of training, and the validation of the instructional materials all appeared desirable.

A logical question raised was that inasmuch as PI as a technology for training had more than proved its usefulness in numerous other areas, why was it necessary to determine its feasibility and value for life insurance training? Wallace answered this question as follows:

> We had to recognize that the training materials which our industry has produced through some 40 years of cooperation and study are generally recognized by experts as exceptionally well done. To replace any of them with a new gimmick, in the absence of evidence that it will do at least as good a job as what we already have, involves a very considerable risk.
>
> Second, all research on the self-instructional method has not obtained favorable results. . . .
>
> Third, as I have indicated, most of the supporting evidence comes from "captive" students such as those in schools and the armed forces. Our agents are something less than captive. . . .
>
> Fourth, much of the research has been done on relatively short programs. Ours is considerably more extensive.
>
> So, we had to ask ourselves whether this technique would work with the more mature, differently motivated, and more loosely supervised men we are recruiting into our business. For example, there is a simple and mundane question which we have sometimes failed to ask in the past, to our sorrow. Will they sit still for it? Will they actually use it? Will they finish it? . . .
>
> Finally . . . we had to think in terms of agents scattered across the North American continent, in large and small agencies, combination, ordinary, multiple-line, where remote control is the order of the day.[5]

LIAMA decided to develop a text program instead of a teaching machine program and to use a linear rather than a branching approach. This decision was based on the rationale provided by an analysis of the desired terminal behavior. This analysis indicated that the majority of the topics had to be learned to the point where the student could recall the answer rather than recognize the correct answer from among several alternatives. A contract was established with the American Institutes for Research (AIR) because of

---

[5] *Ibid.,* pp. 124 and 125.

its leadership in the research on and development of self-instructional materials. LIAMA provided AIR with the specifications for the program and made available Phil Welsh, an assistant program director, as a resident technical coordinator.

Even though four areas (job knowledge, attitude, selling skills, and work habits) were identified as important in the training of life insurance agents and capable of being developed through programed instruction, LIAMA decided to emphasize informational content since it would be the least difficult to prepare and the most susceptible to a field evaluation. This approach would also lay a foundation for subsequent development of other materials in a self-instructional format. LIAMA submitted to AIR a detailed description of typical life insurance trainees.

> At their time of employment, approximately one-third of the trainees are unemployed. Less than ten per cent of the remaining trainees are students still in school. As to age, approximately fifty per cent of the nonstudents are thirty or older; more than seventy-five per cent are over the age of twenty-six.

> Roughly two-thirds of the trainees have attended college and more than one-third of the total group have received college degrees. About ten per cent of the total group have completed high school. At the time of employment, approximately fifty per cent of the trainees have been out of school seven years or more.[6]

Since not all subject matter was to be learned to the same level of thoroughness, various teaching formats were used, especially for the construction of the criterion frames. Short constructed-response sequences and items or a few multiple-choice items were used for those concepts with which the agents need only be familiar. Completion items were used for those concepts which will later be reinforced on the job but in which new agents should receive initial training. Those principles which the agents must understand thoroughly and be able to state clearly were presented in a manner which required the trainees to reproduce the answer accurately. A fourth area of concepts is those which require integration of various pieces of information by agents so that they can answer and see the implication of questions asked by prospective clients; these concepts were tested by providing trainees with complex examples.

The following samples from the criterion test provide illustrations of some of the different types of items: [7]

---

[6] American Institutes for Research, *op. cit.,* p. 3.
[7] *Ibid.,* pp. 45, 46, 47, and 52.

SCORING KEY FOR THE CRITERION TEST

This scoring key was used to score the criterion test. Many of the questions on this test can be completely and adequately answered only by making more than one specific point. For example, a complete answer to Item 1 should contain a total of four statements, two to completely define a limited-payment policy and one each for two appropriate examples of such a policy. Credit was given for each acceptable portion of the response constructed by the trainee. Exact wording was not required and most trainees supplied more complete responses than the essentials given in this key. The order in which the points were made was not important, except where a specific order of responding is indicated by the nature of the question.

CRITERION TEST QUESTION	ACCEPTABLE RESPONSES	TOTAL POSSIBLE NO. OF POINTS
. . .		
2. A *convertible* term policy allows the policyholder to **＿＿＿＿＿.	exchange term policy for permanent protection policy (and) within a limited but specified time (and) no medical exam required (and) conversion effective at either original or attained age	4
. . .		
5. The *net amount at risk* on a policy is defined as **＿＿＿＿＿.	face amount minus policy reserve	1
. . .		
10. List five settlement options.	cash payment (and) fixed amount (and) fixed period (and) interest option (and) life income, period certain	5
. . .		

16. Compare an ordinary life policy and a limited-payment policy with respect to, (1) protection, (2) premiums, and (3) savings (cash surrender value).		ORDINARY LIFE	LIMITED PAYMENT	
	protection periods		equal	
	premiums	lower	higher	
	cash surrender value	lower	higher	3

. . .

66. Mr. F, age 30, borrowed
$25,000 from a bank to
start his store. He agreed
to pay it back over a
period of 20 years. If he
died before the loan was
fully paid, however, the
bank would foreclose on
his store and leave his
family with no source of
income. Therefore, he
wanted the right plan of
insurance to protect the
loan. He decided on a
*————————.   20-year term   1

Even though the previous examples did not contain any items using multiple-choice responses, such responses were called for at various points in the program. Frame 103 in Unit V-A, for instance, reads as follows: [8]

In the table below, use the words, "equal," "lower," and "higher" to compare the limited-payment policy and the ordinary life policy.

	LIMITED-PAYMENT POLICY	ORDINARY LIFE POLICY
Protection Periods	(equal)	
Annual Level Premiums	(higher)	(lower)
Cash Surrender Values	(higher)	(lower)

(The student was required to make the responses which appear in the parentheses.)

One feature was not noted in other programs, either in industry or in education, and that was the use of review sequences. These followed each section, and an overall review sequence constituted the last section of the program. "Each review sequence recapitulated the original teaching sequence, but involved larger steps and required less extensive building-up to reach criterion performance." It may take four or five frames to build up a particular concept; however, it will often require only one frame for the review. Consequently, this frame would contain the response for that particular unit in toto.

———————

[8] *Ibid.*, p. 8.

The first revision of the program was based upon the responses of two subjects. The program was subsequently revised three times, using each time the responses of four subjects to both programed frames and criterion test items. When a frame was missed by more than one subject, it was studied for possible revision. The frame was then revised, the frames prior to it were revised, frames were added, or the sequence was rearranged.

The following table shows what happened to the program after the third revision: [9]

TABLE 1

MEAN RUNNING TIME IN MINUTES FOR GROUPS OF FOUR SUBJECTS ON
EACH COMPLETE UNIT OF THE PROGRAM FOR THE LAST TWO REVISIONS

	UNIT I	UNIT II	UNIT III	UNIT IV	UNIT V	UNIT VI	UNIT VII	UNITS I–VII	FINAL REVIEW	CRITERION TEST
After the Second Revision	112	198	227	62	331	17	211	1158 (19.3 hrs)	223 (3.7 hrs)	116 (1.9 hrs)
After the Third Revision	98	188	178	52	298	16	177	1007 (16.8 hrs)	179 (3.0 hrs)	103 (1.7 hrs)

The table on the facing page shows the trend in the error rate following the revisions.[10]

In November 1963 Paul W. Thayer reported to the 46th Annual Meeting of the Life Insurance Agency Management Association that nine companies of different types and sizes had been involved in the study and that 1,070 students had used *Steps into Life Insurance.* Seven companies used the course under field or agency training conditions and two under classroom conditions. The former companies represented the debit side of three combination companies, three ordinary companies, and one all-lines company. Thayer maintained that this was "the biggest study ever conducted on programed instruction." [11]

Conventional training methods were administered to 517 students. Both groups took the same final examination. They were comparable with respect to age, education, and IQ. The conventionally trained group had considerably more life insurance education, averaging 94 hours, while the program-instructed group averaged 45 hours of previous education. In spite of this

[9] *Ibid.,* p. 20.
[10] *Ibid.,* p. 21.
[11] Wallace and Thayer, *op. cit.,* p. 126.

TABLE 2
MEAN PER CENT ERROR ON SUCCESSIVE STAGES OF PROGRAM REVISION
FOR SUBJECTS WITH AND WITHOUT THE FINAL REVIEW

		UNITS I–VII	FINAL REVIEW	CRITERION TEST
After the First Revision	No Final Review Group	3.2%	—	26.7%
	Final Review Group	0.9%	3.3%	12.5%
After the Second Revision	No Final Review Group	1.5%	—	10.6%
	Final Review Group	1.3%	1.1%	7.0%
After the Third Revision	No Final Review Group	0.5%	—	6.2%
	Final Review Group	0.5%	0.4%	4.1%

difference between the two groups, however, the average in every company was significantly better for the *Steps* group.

Even though questions were asked in the study which were research oriented and related to the theoretical problems of human learning, of more concern to management, however, were the practical questions such as: Will agents use the books? Will they learn as much as with conventional programs? What is the most efficient method of using the programed texts if they are chosen?

Obvious indication of the extent to which the nine companies cooperated with this study is illustrated by the degree of involvement on the part of the trainees.

Each trainee studying *Steps into Life Insurance* took a short life insurance quiz before he started studying, kept a record of the amount of time he studied, filled out a questionnaire dealing with his reactions to such books, and took a two and one-half hour final examination a few days after he finished. So we wouldn't favor the *Steps* trainees, scoring of the exams was adjusted where the conventional course didn't cover the same material as *Steps*. The trainer kept a time record, also completed a questionnaire dealing with his reactions to the books, and either kept records of the amount of time spent covering comparable materials when training conventionally or made an estimate of conventional training time. Home office personnel at John Hancock also took the final examination a second time, several weeks later, to see if the learning conditions which were the best when a person was tested immediately after studying were still the best in terms of long-term remembering.[12]

Twelve different groupings of students were made to study three major categories of learning conditions. Three theoretical questions that were asked were the necessity for the review book, the necessity for the trainee to write out his answer in each of the frames, and the necessity for the trainee to say the correct answer immediately after making his response. (This last question will be discussed presently.) If neither review nor writing was necessary, then obviously both time and costs would be saved. The review book added about one and one-half hours of study time and meant that an additional book was required. The result of this study indicated that those trainees who studied the review book did slightly better on the examination than those who only studied the programed books. The significant finding, however, is that this difference, although slight, was maintained over a longer period of time.

> Some of the home office personnel at John Hancock were tested a second time four weeks after they finished *Steps*. Others were tested the second time 16 weeks later. No additional education was given between the two testings. Although there was some forgetting, in each case the trainees who had the Review Book were still superior on the exam to those without it.[13]

Wallace and Thayer therefore concluded that the additional trainee and trainer time to administer the review book is worth the gain. Another question was whether the students should write their answers, say them aloud, or use their own judgment. To say the answers aloud meant that they could make their answers in considerably less time than writing them, and there was little difference in examination results. Another advantage to saying the answers aloud is that it makes it possible to reuse the books, an item of cost which should be considered. However, the manager then has no record with which to review the students' activities. In summary, Wallace recommended that if management wants to—

> . . . save as much as possible of the agent's time and your education money, use the "say" method. If you want to ensure that your managers can obtain accurate and quick information to protect against the possibility that agents will try to bypass or dead-head, use the "write"

---

[12] *Ibid.*, pp. 130–131.
[13] *Ibid.*, p. 135.

method, particularly if you are concerned, as I am, about the effect of familiarity upon the attitude toward the course.

In either case, if the managers are saved 10 hours of time on the average, as our study indicates they will be, and their time is worth even as little as $2 per hour, your ultimate saving should be great.[14]

When LIAMA got to the point of full-scale evaluation, four major criteria were utilized: (1) use, (2) achievement, (3) time, and (4) attitude. Achievement was measured by an examination consisting of 30 short-answer essay questions and 80 multiple-choice questions. The 30 essay items were based directly on the program and closely resembled the criterion frames in the program. The 80 multiple-choice items were borrowed from existing tests of fundamental life insurance knowledge and consisted of three parts: (1) 30 items covering material judged to have been covered by the program and written in language judged to be similar to the program language; (2) 25 items covering content judged to have been covered in the program but with no regard given to language or terminology; and (3) 25 questions covering material whose content was judged not to have been directly taught by the program and with no regard given to language or terminology. Success on this last group of items would be indicative of the transfer value of the program since the trainee would have to deduce the correct answer to these questions because of his mastery of the program materials.[15]

Another interesting finding was that it was not necessary for the trainees to see whether their answers were correct since the program had been designed so that they would make very few errors. Having or not having the answers does not make any difference as far as trainee time is concerned, but it does affect the trainees' attitude toward what they are learning. They prefer to have the answers. This being so, it was recommended that the books be printed with answers, especially since it would not cost anything in student time and was a plus factor in developing a favorable attitude toward PI.

Regarding the trainees' attitude, Mr. Wallace wrote:

More specifically, 94 per cent of the *Steps* trainees studying in the field stated that their over-all reactions were favorable or very favorable, two per cent were neutral, and four per cent were unfavorable or very unfavorable. Eighty-two per cent found it easier to concentrate on self-instructional texts, while six per cent found it harder. The bulk of the trainees also found that, compared to conventional textbooks, *Steps* was less boring, they could study longer, *Steps* highlighted important

[14] *Ibid.*, p. 144.
[15] Welsh, Antoinetti, and Thayer, *op. cit.*

material to be learned better, *Steps* was a better basis for preparing for an exam, and programed textbooks were preferable for further study. When given the opportunity to volunteer comments as to what they like about *Steps,* only two per cent listed nothing, while 30 per cent stated they liked the repetition and 36 per cent said the material was well prepared and gave good coverage. They also remarked upon ease of learning and remembering, being forced to concentrate, etc.[16]

Trainers also were enthusiastic about the programs. Ninety-six per cent were favorable or very favorable and 4 per cent unfavorable or very unfavorable. The most frequently mentioned complaint on the part of the trainers (19 per cent) was that they had no way of knowing whether the trainees were learning until tests were administered.

Since *Steps* was so effective in the classroom, the consultants recommended that it be considered as required training at the agency prior to an agent's entering the centralized school.

The study was conducted to determine not only whether programing would be effective for this particular course but also whether PI technology has any significant implication for the management association's educational problems. On the basis of LIAMA's study, we are justified in concluding that PI does hold promise for other areas of training. Probably one of its most significant values, however, is the spin-off benefit of increased ability to write other course materials.

---

[16] Wallace and Thayer, *op. cit.,* p. 138.

Martin Company, Denver Division *

Training through the application of programed instruction at the Denver Plant of the Martin Company is a well-planned exercise. Beginning with the development of programed training for the Titan familiarization course, positive results have led to a significant impact of this effort on other aspects of the training programs. The administrative problems which emerged with the requirement to send programed packages to remote training sites were studied for their implications for other automated instructional systems. Problems in training instructional programers and producing custom programs for company clients were also explored.

THE TECHNICAL TRAINING DEPARTMENT OF THE MARTIN COMPANY (Denver Division) performs technical training and training research functions. Executives in the Division have read widely about programed instruction to see to what extent they could adapt it to their training program. The staff were impressed with the effectiveness of PI technology and certain aspects of its economy, and they wanted to develop a program related to the firm's training needs.

The training staff members held a series of 30-minute orientation sessions for management, designed largely to gain its confidence, at which they pointed out the serious need for accelerated teaching procedures to keep up with the technological strides being made in the missile field.

The orientation sessions discussed briefly the history of PI, the educational and psychological principles upon which it is based, the advantages inherent in the technology, and some of the results which other industries had achieved through its use. Everyone who attended the sessions worked through a sample program developed by the training unit.

This session was followed by a question and answer period. The questions

---

* Information for this case submitted by R. W. Walker, Supervisor, Personnel Requirements & Evaluation Unit, Martin Company, Denver, Colorado.

which were raised are typical of those heard in such industrial training sessions:

- Why should our company use programed instruction?
- Does programed instruction teach as effectively as do traditional courses?
- What is the effect of losing the personal instructor-student relationship typical of classroom training?
- What type of student reacts favorably to PI?
- Will the more sophisticated individual become bored with the auto-instructional technique?
- What subject matter can be programed?
- Which is more effective—the branching, linear, mathetic, or adjunct program?
- Are teaching machines necessary?
- How do costs and savings compare with those of conventionally taught courses?
- What is the ratio of preparation to administration time?
- Does our company have the talent necessary to develop programs?
- Should our company buy off-the-shelf programs, use the services of consultants, or do its own programing?

The variables among industries, manufacturers, and training philosophies make it impossible to provide pat answers to these questions. Each question has to be weighed and answered in the light of each firm's circumstances.

Following these orientation sessions the training staff established parameters for immediate projects. A modest budget was suggested along with the recommendation that the initial efforts be concentrated on a single training area to provide an opportunity to evaluate the program writers, determine costs and savings, and evaluate the effectiveness of the PI techniques.

The selection of material for programing was based on the following criteria:

- Budget.
- Stability of subject matter.
- Number of potential students.
- Length of program.
- Complexity of material.
- Availability of knowledgeable human resources.

An analysis of these criteria led to the selection of a program for a priority course that would be used by a large number of students over a long period of time, that would be of "average" complexity and moderate length, and that could also be taught by the conventional method.

Martin found that the larger the student population, the less was the cost per student per training hour. No specific formula has been developed for determining the number of students needed in a program to make PI economically feasible, but by estimating PI cost per student-hour and then comparing it with projected costs of conventional training, a determination could be made about which training method would yield the most profitable results. For example, it cannot be stated flatly that it is impractical to develop a 1,000-frame program for 20 students. The product quality that depends upon the training received by these 20 people must be the determining factor. In some instances, a program of 1,000 or 5,000 frames would represent a small investment compared to its impact on the company's success.

The course selected for programing was "Titan II Weapon System Familiarization." In addition to meeting the criteria mentioned previously, there was a significant need for such a course at remote missile sites. Moreover, since the technical training instructors were already teaching the course conventionally, it provided an opportunity to compare costs, achievement, and student retention.

After the program was selected, a choice had to be made between using the services of a consulting agency and developing an in-house capability. Some consideration was given to the fact that professional programers could ultimately deliver a more sophisticated and possibly more effective program than company employees could produce. However, the amount of orientation, studying, and reviewing needed to familiarize consulting personnel with the subject was so great the company decided the programing job could be done in-house at a substantial saving. It was willing therefore to trade off a small amount of quality for a large amount of money.

Once the general subject had been isolated and the decision had been made to use the in-house effort, considerable thought was given to developing a PI unit. It was felt that the initial build-up of the programing organization should be executed with prudence, and that the first program should be produced by one individual who would devote full time to the effort. The person who was finally selected had a master's degree in psychology and experience in industrial training, curriculum development, statistics, psychological testing, and writing. Although he was not an expert in the subject matter, he had an extensive mechanical background.

After the staff had trained their capability, made a task analysis, and determined their objectives, they forecast program time requirements and approximate cost. The cost of developing a program is directly related to its length. Length, however, is not the sole criterion. Others are: complexity of the subject material; dynamics of the course material; experience and subject knowledge of the program writers; objectives; initial behavior repertoire; number of students; number of concepts or program elements; technique and format of program presentation; and extent of program validation and editing. The staff do not favor determining the cost of a program by the cost per frame. They point out that a 1963 survey of the literature revealed a cost-per-frame range of $2.50 to $40.

The 613-frame familiarization program took three and one-half man-months to produce, or a little less than one frame per hour. The program cost $5,600, including overhead but not reproduction costs. To reproduce 100 copies of a program cost $20 per copy, whereas 1,500 copies cost $2.50 per copy. By amortizing programing expenses for 1,500 students, the familiarization text cost the company approximately $5.25 per student, including reproduction costs. This cost-per-student figure has more validity, and more significance to management, than have the cost-per-frame figures.

Since the development of their first program, the Martin technical training staff have had to evaluate a number of proposals in terms of cost, number of frames, and date of delivery. Because some of these proposals have been based on a fixed price contract, extreme caution has been necessary in analyzing the work to be done. To obtain realistic estimates for program proposals, they broke down the development sequence into its smallest task components; then they estimated the time it would take to perform each of these tasks by using a 180-frame program of "average" difficulty as a base. For six months, they maintained an accurate record of their programing activities and plotted actual time against projected time from program conception through final production. The resultant estimate of the size and cost of a programing proposal was reasonably accurate.

The familiarization program was administered to students in the classroom in the presence of a monitor. When compared with the conventionally taught course, the familiarization course resulted in an increase of 9 per cent in test scores and a decrease of 34 per cent in time. Students were similar with respect to background and experience.

Criterion tests were administered 30 to 45 days after completion of the familiarization program. Tests revealed a 2 per cent loss of retention. Student reaction was overwhelmingly in favor of PI. Such comments as "the best I have ever had" were not uncommon. Negative reactions were centered primarily around the concentrated effort required. Though the students had periodic class breaks, they were exposed solely to the program for two consecutive days. After student reactions were summarized, the critique sheets were submitted to management and played an important role in assuring its continued interest and support.

The training staff were now concerned with the question, "How effective would PI be when self-administered in a noncontrolled environment?" (that is, without a monitor present). To find the answer to this question, 40 salaried employees completed the course at home and were also administered the criterion test. Their scores showed no significant difference from those of students who had completed their programs in a classroom during working hours. Although it was impossible for the home study group to keep accurate time records, interviews indicated it had spent approximately the same amount of time on the program as the classroom group.

A self-administered training program out of direct control of the training organization presents numerous administrative problems. How do we maintain control over the programed texts that are mailed to requesting departments? How sure can we be that a student will complete a program, once started? Can management impose time limits on students who work programs on their own time? What about completion diplomas and recognition of students who complete the programs? Although answers to all these questions are not now available, moderate success has been achieved in overcoming some of the administrative problems.

With each programed booklet the student receives a self-addressed, stamped postcard, asking him to fill in his name, address, job title, and the date he started his program. One month later, another self-addressed card is sent asking if he has completed the program, taken his test, and received his diploma. If he has not completed the program, a follow-up card is sent after one month. If he has completed the program, he is advised where he can take his examination. If he has taken the examination and the test administrator has certified a passing score, a diploma is issued and a record is sent to the personnel office for the student's file.

When programs are shipped to remote missile locations, they go directly to the site's training coordinator, who keeps a list of all people who receive the program and forwards a copy to the Denver training organization. The names on the list are checked against the self-addressed postcards to determine which students have failed to return their cards. A second card is sent to them, requesting that they return the information. Thus, a relatively complete record is maintained giving the whereabouts and progress of each program recipient.

Training coordinators at the sites give proficiency tests and, periodically, notify the Denver training staff of the students' scores. These coordinators also notify managers and supervisors of the receipt and distribution of programs in answer to requests.

Programs are publicized through management channels by internal correspondence or by presentations at staff meetings. A record is kept of all requests for programs. The procedures at Martin-Denver's home facility are the same as those used at the remote sites. No program completion time limits are imposed on employees who take courses voluntarily. Even though no pressure is exerted on the individual, a record is kept of his progress. The prevailing opinion is that a program will be completed only if it is sufficiently interesting or challenging to make the man want to do so. The program writers continually try to meet these requirements.

If a supervisor wishes his employees to complete the program in a specified time, he is advised of recommended time limits and allowed to set his own deadlines. Experience has shown that students tend to procrastinate if they are not given a required completion date. Therefore, supervisors are urged to set time limits.

Traditionally, employees are given a series of training courses taught by PI or other training methods. After completion of these required courses, they are given on-the-job training under the guidance of experienced supervisors. Here the value of theoretical training comes under close scrutiny. If previous training has been sufficiently effective, the employee will make a smooth transition between classroom and job. If his training has been below par, he may never make a satisfactory transition.

The company has trained observer/evaluators who watch and evaluate performance of certain employees on the job. They also interview employees and their supervisors for training feedback, submitting reports periodically to their training department. All pertinent training deficiencies are reported to the program writer or course administrator. These reports constitute a running testimonial to the value of PI.

Martin has made PI courses available as part of its voluntary evening school program for employees, who may take TEMAC courses on basic math, algebra I, algebra II, geometry, and introductory calculus. From the McGraw-Hill series they may take courses in basic electricity, basic electronics, basic transistors, sets, relations (a modern math presentation), groups and fields, and advanced modern math and introduction to probability. This program was begun with basic math and algebra I series in the spring of 1964. The other courses were added at later dates.

Since the company's first effort, its training staff has cross-trained a dozen program writers, all of whom had previous industrial training experience. The qualities of the most successful programers include an above-average intelligence, perseverance, detail-consciousness, ability to emphasize, creativity, flexibility, and management identification. The company looks for good communicators and successful organizers who are knowledgeable in the subject matter. The company has had greater success in teaching subject matter experts to write programs than in teaching competent writers to become subject matter authorities. It feels, however, that this problem applies only in programing technical subject matter.

When an individual has been brought into the PI unit, he is given a position description, a general orientation to PI, and an individual training plan which contains the short- and long-range training requirements. After he has proved himself, he is required to attend and participate in a recognized workshop for program writers. With as little as two weeks of conscientious in-house training, a writer can begin to develop his first program. Even though such a program may be short and lacking in sophistication, it does enable the appraiser to predict the writer's potential.

Since the stringent requirements of programed instruction may demand an abrupt departure from usual behavior, Mager's book, *Preparing Objectives for Programed Instruction,* is used to train the neophyte to come to grips with the problem of identifying objectives. It is up to the beginning writer's supervisor to see that the writer transfers Mager's principles to the real-life situation. Poorly defined objectives often lead to the necessity for rewriting, which is costly and time consuming. Therefore, a programer is not allowed to write a single frame until the terminal behavior has been clearly defined.

Another potential that is carefully observed in training a would-be writer is the ability to prepare a task analysis, since this requires substantial integration between the program writer and subject matter experts. A submissive programer is greatly handicapped in performing a skills analysis. To gain information for programing requires repeated interviewing, questioning, "brainpicking," and clarification. The task analyst must determine his sources of data—whether they be operating procedures, engineering drawings, design releases, specifications, basic data, test procedures, professional journals, texts, articles, or other means. A sound bit of advice is: Be wary of hiring a program writer who is not an aggressive self-starter. If the writer cannot research the necessary information, unaided, from the existing sources of material, the supervisor may find himself with a spoon-feeding problem.

The ability to write frames is another characteristic that is carefully observed. The creative individual who has a flair for stimulating and grammatically correct writing is an asset to the program; the field has need of more such writers. Two source books used to train frame writers are Markle's *A Programed Primer on Programing* and Brethower's *Programmed Instruction and Programming Techniques.* Most effective in teaching the technique of frame writing have been the extensive program critiques of the psychologist, from which the writer gains first-hand knowledge of the subtleties of effective frame writing.

Although the Titan familiarization program had no customer-imposed deadline for completion, many of the program packages developed since then have had a firm date commitment. Sometimes the requirements for delivery are unrealistic. For example, a 3,000-frame program was required for one customer in two months. How can this be done by a unit manned by three writers and one secretary? First, they asked for the obvious—more time. The customer gave two more weeks. Then they eliminated classroom validation, relying entirely upon naive student validation. This, of course, lowered the validity of the program, but it reduced development time by about 10 per cent. To reduce production time still further, the customer was required to provide the necessary documents and research data from which the program was developed. This eliminated the need to gather data from a variety of sources. Yet another time-saving device was the reproduction of prelined multilith masters. Previously, all masters were individually lined—a time-consuming task.

Recently one more shortcut in the program development sequence was taken. At first, the program draft was typed on 3″ x 5″ index cards and circulated from one subject matter expert to another, then from one naive student to another, and finally returned to the staff for revision. This process consumed two weeks. Now, the original draft is reproduced by the ditto process and distributed to subject matter experts and naive students simultaneously. As a result, programs are being returned to the staff in two or three days, technically correct and student validated.

Michigan Bell Telephone Company *

Programed instruction for electronic technicians at Michigan Bell Telephone Company, Detroit Plant School, shows the application of PI technology to presenting both verbal content and laboratory learning experience.

THE MICHIGAN BELL GENERAL ELECTRONICS COURSE WHICH WAS developed in accordance with the principles of programed instruction covers the subject matter areas of elementary static electricity and moves through DC and AC theory relays, transformers, electron tube circuits, semiconductor and transistor circuits, and transmission fundamentals.

The average time to complete this training course is 144 hours, the range being from 72 hours to 240 hours. The trainees are technicians, and most of them are high school graduates. Their IQ's range from 90 to 130, with the majority falling well above 100. The students range in age from 20 to the early 50's. They are selected for this training by their field supervisors.

On the average four to six students start the course each week. The starting times are staggered always, one or two men starting on Monday, another one or two on Tuesday, and finally one or two on Wednesday. However, students may enter the program on any day of the week and at any hour of the day between 8 AM and 5 PM.

The classroom has booths where the trainees can complete the linear programs and make constructed written responses. The classroom also contains an area which is used for testing. There are usually two instructors in the classroom; one is there largely to monitor the testing booths and has the main control over student activities; the other assists students in the laboratory sessions.

When a student enters the classroom on his first day, he is provided with a set of four pretests in arithmetic. If he passes these pretests, he begins the

---

* Information for this case submitted by C. G. Valentine, Michigan Bell Telephone Company, Detroit, Michigan.

course with the first set of programed materials. If a student fails any of the four arithmetic pretests, he is given remedial programs covering the areas of his weakness. After finishing the remedial programs, he again takes the tests in those areas he previously failed. If he still cannot meet the minimum scores in arithmetic tests, he returns to his work without attempting to take the program, unless further remedial instruction seems justifiable.

The booths are so shaped as to give maximum work space in a relatively open area. They are acoustically treated to minimize sound reflection. Background music is fed to each booth so as to raise the ambient sound level and to minimize distractions from other sounds in the room. If the trainee needs help during this portion of the course, he signals the instructor by pressing a button on the left rear corner of his desk. This signal simultaneously turns on a flashing lamp on a console at the instructor's desk and a lamp over the student's booth. If the instructor is at his desk, he simply presses a button on the flashing lamp and talks to the student through a hand-set telephone. The student hears the instructor over the same speaker from which the background music is fed. Separate volume controls allow the background music to be lower or higher than the conversational level. The students do not have hand-set telephones, so their hands are free for writing except when pressing the button to call for help. The figure on the next page shows the layout for the programed learning classroom at the Detroit Plant School.

On a magnet board alongside his console the instructor has a display of the room's layout with student names on small magnets indicating the booths which they are using. Therefore, the instructor knows the name of the student requesting help. Above the magnet board is a complete set of all the learning blocks and the panel books including the visual aids which are needed with each learning block. This arrangement of materials permits the instructor to have immediate access to the exact page of the program and the illustration which the student is working on. When the buzzer indicates a call for help, he simply notes which lamp is lit and proceeds directly to it to give assistance. The call for assistance may be canceled at the booth by simply pressing the off button.

The programed instruction course consists of 18 units covering the following topics:

Static Electricity
Current and EMF
Resistance, Conductance, and Ohm's Law
R Combinations, DC Power
Magnetism
AC

MICHIGAN BELL TELEPHONE COMPANY
DETROIT PLANT SCHOOL
LAYOUT OF PROGRAMED LEARNING CLASSROOM

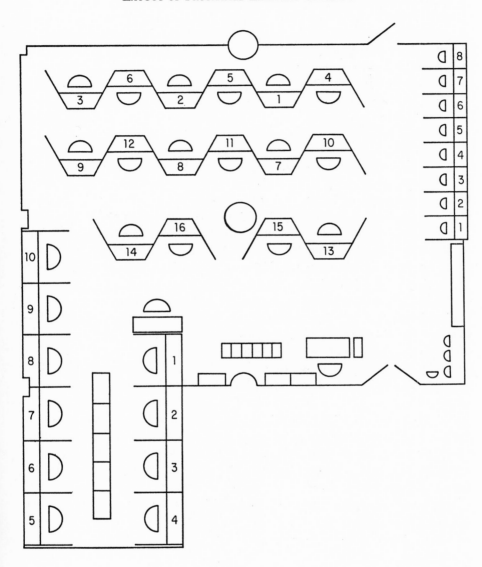

R Circuits

Meters

Inductance

Capacitance

AC Circuits (RCL)

Relays, Transformers

Electron Tubes (Diode, Triode)

Electron Tubes (Pentode)

Gas Filled Tubes

Varistors and Transistors

Transmission

Review

The classes begin at 8 AM and stop at 5 PM. A student works on the program rather continuously for seven and one-half hours with time off for lunch and a few short breaks. An effort is made to change the student's environment at specific points in the program by keeping each sequence or unit to a relatively small number of frames (between 200 and 300). After working on the reading and writing portions of the program for several hours, the trainee goes to the laboratory section of the classroom. Here he again uses the program, but about half of the laboratory portion is typed in a format similar to the programs used in the booth and the rest of it is presented on audio tapes so that the student will hear rather than read the instructions and questions. The laboratory programs are designed to present information in the form of actual components, visuals, and response requirements given either by printed programs or by audio messages from magnetic tape. The visuals are usually actual photographs, either black and white prints or 35mm color slides.

Following given groups of learning program units, the trainee takes performance criterion tests at five points in the program. These tests are in addition to the written tests which are provided after each unit. They are similar to the written tests in that the trainee must meet minimum criteria on each in order to continue to the succeeding programed unit.

Two hundred twenty students took the programed training between February 1963 and December 1, 1964, and of these, 182, or 83 per cent, passed with satisfactory criterion performance scores.

Montgomery Ward *

Montgomery Ward is currently using programed instruction in these areas: retail sales systems, retail merchandise mathematics, catalog correspondence training, "Effective Listening" for management training, and keypunch operator training. The company proceeded very slowly in introducing PI to its branches, has found it extremely effective and well accepted, and is investigating other areas where it might be used.

THE SALES SYSTEMS TRAINING COURSE AT MONTGOMERY WARD INcludes programed instruction in the operation of the six types of sales registers in use in the company's stores and in the writing of sales checks. The PI program covers cash, credit, layaway sales, and delivery.

The merchandise mathematics program includes training in figuring landed mark-up, landed cost, net sales, mark-up in inventory per cent, maintained gross profit per cent, and turnover. This program is a separate chapter in the company's *Department Manager's Manual*. Both the sales systems program and the merchandise mathematics program were written especially for Montgomery Ward by an outside firm.

The PI course on catalog correspondence training is "Improving Your Written Communications," by Scot B. Parry. The program is used to train correspondents in the catalog houses.

"Effective Listening" is a shelf program, published by Basic Systems, Inc., which uses a magnetic tape recording in addition to a programed book to teach the skills of effective listening. Before Montgomery Ward bought this program it was tested on two groups of management people in the home office. The plans are to give this training to participants in company-sponsored workshops and seminars.

"Keypunch Operator Training" is another shelf program, produced by Perceptual Development Laboratories, which utilizes an audio-visual adaptation

---

* Information and materials for this case submitted by Eleanor Rud, Training Materials Specialist, Montgomery Ward, Chicago, Illinois.

of PI presented by means of a special projector called a PerceptoScope. This program was also thoroughly tested in two catalog houses before it was bought. The results have been highly effective.

The initial consideration of the possibility of using PI at Montgomery Ward was instigated by Modern Teaching Associates, who wanted to try out, at a very nominal cost on an experimental basis, the desirability of PI in retail training. The training director at Montgomery Ward was approached and was willing to experiment. The moderate program was highly successful and convinced management that it should explore further. Following the validation of the program, a slide film with script and a pamphlet on programed instruction were produced for orientation purposes.

The following excerpts from the booklet, "A Guide for Using Programed Instruction in Retail Training," are illustrative of one portion of a rather concerted effort to keep the company management informed:

How to Use Programed Instructions
Programed Materials Available
Regional Training Manager's Responsibilities

● ● ● ●

Introduction

This Guide is intended to help you understand how to use programed instruction training material and how "programed instruction" can reduce training costs and time.

Programed instruction is designed for use in all stores. It can be used in pre-opening training for a new store and in training new hires in an existing store. More and more information will be programed in the future. Your thorough understanding of programed instruction is important, so study this Guide carefully.

● ● ● ●

When Used

Programed instruction will be used to train all new salespeople including extras.

Programed instruction eliminates the need for new people to have to wait for a scheduled training class. Immediate training can be given regardless of the number hired at any time.

● ● ● ●

Recommended Schedule of Training with Programed Instruction

Orientation

- Store's rules and regulations
- Benefit programs
- "You and Wards" slide film
- "Rule of Five" slide film
- "You and Plus Service" booklet (if a Plus Service store)
- "You and Professional Selling" booklet

Sales Register Training

Use "Programed Instructions for Sales Register Operations" (TR 181). This book includes:

- Reading the price tag
- Recording a sale on the sales register
- "No Sale" transactions

- Use of document envelope
- Correcting errors
- Counting change

Salescheck Writing

Use "Programed Instructions for Writing Saleschecks"—Part I (TR 182A) and Part II (TR 183A).

These books include:

- Employee discounts
- Charg-All sales
- Authenticating salescheck (sales audit stores)
- Setting up the salescheck book
- Lay-Away sales
- Delivery sales
- Store dock pick-up sales
- Correcting salescheck errors

Refund and Exchange Handling

Use "Programed Instructions for Handling Refunds and Exchanges" (TR 184).

This book includes:

- Refund and exchange policy
- Full refunds
- Even exchanges
- Uneven exchanges
- Setting up the refund voucher book

●　　●　　●　　●

TRAINER'S DUTIES

The programed instruction books are to be used in this order: TR 181, TR 182, TR 183, and TR 184.

Hand out only one book at a time. Be sure to also hand out a packet of supplies with TR 182, TR 183, and TR 184.

Only a few instructions are necessary. Explain that this is a new method of instruction and *is not a test*. Ask the employees to carefully read the page of instructions at the front of the book before beginning to work. The only other instructions that might be necessary in some stores regard the slight variations in sales registers. If the sales register pictured in TR 181 is *not* exactly the same as those used in the store, it will be necessary to explain the difference.

Check on the class occasionally. With programed instruction it is not necessary for the trainer to remain in the training room all of the time. Once brief instructions have been given, you may return to regular duties, checking on the class occasionally to answer any questions. This freedom will allow more time for on-the-floor inspection of training.

• • • •

SOURCE OF SUPPLY

The Regional Training Manager will maintain a supply of all programed books. A supply of each new programed instruction book will be shipped to the Regional Training Manager as it becomes available.

Additional quantities of any book can be obtained from the Retail Training Services Department, in Chicago.

REGIONAL TRAINING MANAGER'S RESPONSIBILITIES

The Regional Training Manager will be responsible for:

- Telling stores that programed instruction will be used in training new people.
- Giving instructions on the use of programed instruction.
- Distributing the type of programed instruction books each store needs and in the quantity needed.

SCHEDULING OF TRAINING

Length of Training Sessions

A change in thinking is necessary when scheduling training classes for programed instruction. The amount of time required to train sales register and sales check handling is just not as great as with standard instruction. In determining the amount of training to be given, reduce the length of time by *one-fourth* or *one-third* when using programed instruction.

A typical training schedule reflects two things:

- First, it indicates 12 hours of training in place of what would normally be 16 hours (or ¾ths of your usual training time).
- Second, it will require only one trainer in nearly all cases. So much less time will be spent in actual training that the trainer will not feel overburdened.

Since the reduction of training expenses is the most important feature of programed instruction, we *must* schedule shorter training sessions and fewer trainers.

The results of the programed instruction tests show conclusively that savings can be made, but only if we take advantage of the shorter time required for training.

It is strongly recommended that no more than 1½ to 2 hours be spent in general orientation. The cost of training is so high, and the retention of this type of information so low, that only the basic fundamentals of orientation and services should be given in pre-opening training.

Scientific studies show this most interesting information:

- At the end of a 1-hour lecture the average listener retains 50% of what he has heard.
- 48 hours after the lecture he retains 25%.
- After 17 days he remembers only 8%.

In addition, he tends to *add* in information, and to change emphasis on that retained. Knowing this, it would not appear economically sound to spend much time in lecture-type orientation meetings. The information you want the people to have can be put on paper and handed out—this will save time and money.

•   •   •   •

TIMING OF TRAINING SESSIONS

With programed instruction it will be possible to schedule training classes closer to opening date. This will reduce the number of dropouts and increase the retention of the new hires.

This "closer-in" training will also make more people available to the merchandisers for getting the store ready for opening.

Where it has been tried, such as in "new store" training, available data show that programed instruction has cut down training time from 16 to 12 hours (an average reduction of 25 per cent).

The management does not plan to develop any in-house programing capability. Future plans are to continue contracting for the development of custom-made programs. Management is convinced this is cheaper because it makes the services of experienced writers available without the growing pains of training an in-house staff.

The Home Office Training Services Department has one staff member who devotes full time to the subject of programed instruction. This person studies new training needs as they arise and recommends PI when feasible, contracts for services of outside programers, reviews shelf programs and recommends their use if suited to company's needs, and, in general, keeps up with the latest trends in PI. At this time, two programs are being written by an outside source: "Merchandise Mathematics for Control Buyers in the Catalog Stores," and "Order Writing in Catalog Stores." Shelf programs are currently being reviewed for possible use in the following areas:

- Interior decorating.
- Outside selling.

- Office cost reduction.
- Safety procedures.
- Interviewing.
- Supervisory training.

At present management has no firmly established criteria for selecting contract services. In its first experience with a programing agency, it agreed to allow the agency to develop the first program at a very nominal cost. This was mutually beneficial in that the company would be giving the programing house experience in the retail field. After the programing company had produced its first program, the one for the sales register, it simply negotiated and agreed on a price for the following programs.

The company plans to go to a variety of sources in the future for its programs and to ask for several bids on a job. The Purchasing Department asks for three bids on most outside purchases, but so far the Training Services Department has done its own contracting for PI. The department will ask for bids based upon a set of specifications.

To sell PI to the trainers who were to use it, a partially programed booklet, "What Programed Instruction Is," was widely distributed. The following samples of pages from this booklet are illustrative of its persuasive content:

PROGRAMED INSTRUCTION IS WIDELY USED!

- 1,500 companies are now using it.
- In four years it is estimated that all companies will be using Programed Instruction to some extent.
- There are between 500 and 1,000 programs now in use.

● ● ● ●

OF WHAT VALUE IS PROGRAMED INSTRUCTION?

Studies show . . .

A savings in *learner's time* of from 0% to 85%—
average savings 30%
A savings in *instructor's time* of from 0% to 98%—
average savings 80%

How does all this apply to Montgomery Ward? Well, Wards tested Programed Instruction, too.

Boulder, Colorado
Pre-Opening Training

Half the employees trained the regular way; half trained with Programed Instruction for . . .

- Sales Registers
- Wards Revolving Charge Account
- Time Payment
- Deliveries
- Lay-Away

•   •   •   •

So . . . how can you use Programed Instruction? It's easy . . . you just hand out the books and let the people train themselves. Well, not quite that easy—but it is easy.

No longer will you have to put an untrained person on the sales floor because there was no one to give the training.

You can now have a brief orientation session with your new employee, spend four or five minutes explaining the Programed Instruction books, and then let the employee complete the books at his own rate of speed.

You then have a well-trained employee, capable of handling any sales transaction with confidence, accuracy, and speed.

•   •   •   •

NOW . . . how do you get these Programed Instruction books that will provide you with confident, well-trained employees? This, too, is easy. . . .

Just let your Regional Training Manager know what type of register your store uses, and what type of credit plan you use, and how many books you need. Base your needs on the number of regulars and extras you plan to hire this fall.

Then he will send you the quantity you request.

•   •   •   •

How Can Programed Instruction Save You Money?

- Number of training hours reduced.
- Number of register and salescheck errors reduced—better accuracy.
- New employees able to produce more sales immediately.
- Requires little instruction time.

The concept of programing itself was extended in a film strip with a leader's guide to sell PI to all levels of company management as well as to trainers. The film was called "Programed Instruction vs. Standard Instruction." The following introduction in the guide illustrates its purpose:

NOTES TO LEADER:

Have enough copies of the Programed Instruction booklet on hand to give one to each person at the conclusion of this meeting.

For your background information: One of the most successful users of Programed Instruction is United Airlines. Their program designed to teach the city codes (LLH for Columbus, Ohio, ORD for O'Hare, Chicago, for example) is well known. These codes are difficult and prior to programing required 16 to 20 hours to master—PI reduced this time by 4 to 6 hours.

An example of an unsuccessful program was the attempt of a large department store to program "The Initial Customer Approach." There are too many variables in this sort of thing—the customer can lead you down too many paths.

Subjects which require logical, systematic steps to complete lend themselves very well to programing.

• • • •

—SCRIPT—

We are having this meeting so that you can become familiar with what has been called the greatest break-through in training since the invention of the printing press!

You have all heard of teaching machines—now Wards has adapted the teaching machine to training. Our "machine" comes in the form of Programed books (NOTE: Show book; do not pass out at this time).

Everything changes; with or without our inducing it, change occurs. If *we* don't make changes also, we will get left behind. So . . . in order to not get left behind, and indeed, to perhaps even get ahead, the Montgomery Ward Training Services Department has developed new programed training materials—for use by all Ward Retail Stores. Plans are now being made to expand PI to other company branches.

The terms "PI" and "programed instruction" will be used interchangeably throughout this presentation.

• • • •

Frame 1

PROGRAMED INSTRUCTION

WHAT IS IT?

"A program is a series of small bits (steps) of information presented in a logical order with each step requiring an active response."

Script

Programed instruction can easily be adapted to subjects which are either mechanical or can be broken down into small, logical bits.

Now, let's look at how PI, or programed instruction, is applied and upon what it is based. . . .

•   •   •   •

Frame 10

100 Studies Made in Industry

In 30 sample cases
(which were representative of the 100 studies)
reduction in learning time 0%—85%, average 30%;
reduction in instructor's time 0%—98%, average—80%

Script

Not only were these studies made, but we also made a detailed study of programing at Montgomery Ward. The Model 21 Sales Register and WRC and Time Payment were "programed" and put to a full test in a new Montgomery Ward store. These programs were for on-the-floor sales handling and were directed to selling personnel.

•   •   •   •

Frame 11

PI Tested in Pre-opening Training in Boulder, Colorado

Script

For this test the sales and sales audit personnel were divided into two groups. These groups were matched as evenly as possible according to test scores, previous retail experience, age, and sex. Dr. Chandler Screven from Modern Teaching Associates of Milwaukee, together with company training personnel, made the group assignments.

The two groups began training in what was almost a competitive atmosphere.

•   •   •   •

Frame 12

PI Pitted Against Standard Instruction

Script

Despite the fact that great care was exercised in setting up the groups, the contest wasn't really very even. The regular instructor had to work *very* hard, while the PI instructor had a pretty easy time of it. . . .

Not only did the PI instructor have an easier time of it, but the results were better and the training took less time.

Let's take a look at the amount of time required to conduct each type of training and compare the two.

• • • •

Frame 14

TYPE:
RESULTS
HOURS OF INSTRUCTION
(CHART)
(IDENTIFY WHICH BARS STAND FOR PI AND SI)

Script
Look at the large graph on the left. The blue line represents standard instruction. The hours shown on this chart are for comparable subject matters only—in other words, only the information contained in the PI books was compared with standard instruction. A stopwatch was used to determine exactly how much time was required. This was done to clock the students' time required to complete the PI books. The instructor's time spent teaching was also clocked and recorded.

As you can see, it took 11 hours to give the training in the regular way, and a little less than 8 hours, 7.97 to be exact, with programed instruction.

You will recall that industry figures showed a savings in training time of from 0 to 85%, with an average savings of 30%. Our training time savings of 33% in Boulder fit right into this pattern.

The smaller graph shows the figures for the store-opening extras. The results are virtually the same, with PI requiring one-third less time than SI. Extras normally receive less training than regulars because fewer subjects are covered.

• • • •

Script
Once again, look at the larger chart—the error difference was not great, but was in favor of programed instruction. The standard group had an average of 1.36 errors per test, the PI group an average of 1.13 errors per test. The smaller chart shows the error rate for extras with just about the same results. The SI group had an average of 1.41 errors per test, the PI group an average of .96 errors per test.

It is interesting to note that in some of the tests the standard groups had a better error performance than did the programed group—this indicated that the program was weak as presented and had to be strengthened.

The Boulder test showed that our programed instruction results tied in closely with the industry average—also tying in very closely was the saving in instructor's time.

As we saw above, the saving in instructor's time for the industry was zero to 98% with an average savings of 80%. Our Boulder test showed: . . .

●   ●   ●   ●

Frame 18

PI RESULTS
  IN COMPARABLE QUALITY
  IN LESS TIME
  GIVES IMMEDIATE TRAINING
    AND FREES INSTRUCTOR

The Boulder test proved that programed instruction does have a place in our training. Plans are now being made, or carried out as follows . . .

●   ●   ●   ●

Frame 19: Read from frame

FUTURE PI PLANS
  ● ALL REGISTERS
  ● REFUNDS
  ● CATALOG ORDER WRITING
  ● INVOICE RECORDS
  ● USCO
  ● SALES AUDIT
  PLUS OTHERS!

●   ●   ●   ●

Frame 20

TRAINING WITH PI

Script
Training in which programed instruction is used requires a change in our thinking in so far as the amount of time needed and the use of instructors (you may now only need one rather than two for new store openings).

In any training situation using PI the instructor needs only to give brief instructions on how to use the PI books. This will be particularly valuable in training new hires or extras—the personnel manager, (assistant) manager, store manager, or sponsor may continue with normal duties during the training. In the larger stores this will give the personnel manager more of an opportunity to actually check out training on the sales floor.

• • • •

And finally,

Frame 25

SAVINGS WITH PI

[Cartoon of $ sign and clock in background]

Script

With programed instruction it is as economical to train one person as it is twenty. Immediate training can be given, with no need to wait for a class or for someone to be free to conduct the training.

This makes PI equally useful in large or regular stores. In smaller stores, particularly, the new employee may receive a degree of training never before possible.

Some of the savings that are possible are:

1. Savings in training time and costs. The average training time required is reduced by one-third. Relate this to a new store having 300 people to be trained. With standard instruction, figuring $1.25 an hour salary, and 16 hours of training, the cost of training would be $6,000. Using programed instruction, these same 300 people could be trained for $4,000.

   This is a $2,000 saving!

2. Generally, one trainer for a new store can do what formerly required two.

3. Immediate and complete sales handling training can be given new hires, thereby saving many costly errors in recording sales.

Therefore—the conclusion must be . . .

• • • •

Frame 26

PI IS THE MODERN ECONOMICAL WAY TO TRAIN

National Institutes of Health *

Since July 1962 programed instruction has been used extensively at the National Institutes of Health, Public Health Service, Department of Health, Education and Welfare, Bethesda, Maryland, in training its employees, including M.D.'s and Ph.D.'s.

THE USE OF PROGRAMED INSTRUCTION AT THE NATIONAL INSTITUTES of Health (NIH) is actually a study in the increasingly sophisticated utilization of available off-the-shelf programs to train a variety of professional and administrative personnel. The professional staff at NIH includes over 1,700 M.D.'s and Ph.D.'s. The effort at NIH began on a shoestring. Richard L. Prather, an Employee Development Officer, held a demonstration to acquaint the various organizational divisions with this new educational technique, using the USI Autotutor.

Activity in programed instruction at NIH began when one branch chief agreed to send his subordinate supervisors to study an executive practices course on the Autotutor. Equipment was rented, and a memorandum was circulated announcing that the course would be available to other supervisors after it had been used by the branch chief's group. Many of those who responded were M.D.'s or Ph.D.'s.

The principle of self-pacing attracted attention at NIH because its training programs are often attended by a mixture of scientists and scientist administrators with M.D. or Ph.D. degrees and other employees without graduate education. Since the M.D.'s and Ph.D.'s might be expected to assimilate information rapidly, it was theorized that programed instruction could be employed successfully to conserve the time of the scientists.

Along with the teaching machine that was rented (and later purchased) from U. S. Industries, a program was selected entitled "Effective Executive

* Information in this case submitted by Richard L. Prather, Employee Development Officer, National Institutes of Health, Bethesda, Maryland.

Practices." This course was chosen because of general interest in management development. Each of the program's six lessons starts with basic management concepts and seemed appropriate for scientists who have moved directly from their professional specialties to supervisory and executive positions without having encountered the usual amount of minor supervisory tasks. The course is 502 frames long, it is programed by the intrinsic, or branching, method, and it can be completed by the average supervisor in three or four hours. The 46 managers in the test group included 26 who held either M.D. or Ph.D. degrees.

Attached to the memorandum announcing the course was a list of the topics to be covered. Since it was assumed that no one who felt completely proficient in the topic areas would take the course, managers were selected on the basis of self-nominations. Groups of six or seven managers were formed on the basis of physical locations and the machine was kept nearby for the one week each group was allowed to complete the program. As each group of managers started, a recording log was attached to the top of the machine to assist in monitoring the program. When a manager completed his time on the machine, he recorded the number of the image at which he stopped. When he returned the next day to continue the program, he had only to check the log and locate the image at which he had stopped. At the end of each week the machine was moved to another building to accommodate a new group.

After they completed the course, the 26 M.D.'s and Ph.D.'s (M-PD's) filled out a questionnaire. A summary of their responses follows.

- 24 of the 26 M-PD's indicated that the course was worth the time they had spent.
- 22 of the 26 indicated that the machine and program would be used further by their organizations if purchased by NIH. The other four did not respond to this question, which was indicated as optional.
- 23 of the 26 indicated that programed instruction was impressive and should be explored further for possible use in NIH educational tasks.
- 16 of the 26 indicated that a group discussion of the factors covered in the program would be welcome; 8 were opposed; 2 did not care.
- The M-PD's were asked to "cite one suggestion made in the program that was new to you and which you plan to use." Twenty-two mentioned some newly learned management technique which they planned to use. The remaining four received an early version of the questionnaire which did not contain this question.

The managers enjoyed the course and the concept of programed instruction, felt they were learning some useful management practices, and were glad the course could be accommodated to their work schedules. The following are some general observations:

- All M-PD's completed the course. They had chosen to take it and they finished without urging.
- When an M-PD missed an appointment on the machine, make-up time was arranged at his direction.
- Some of the Ph.D.'s worked on the machine before and after work hours and one worked on Saturdays.
- Early in the trial a rule was made: When a manager reached the end of a lesson, he was to stop regardless of how much time was left in his appointment. However, the managers did not stop but continued into the next lesson. Ultimately, the rule was dropped.

NIH eventually purchased an Autotutor, rented ten courses, and published a schedule so that employees could arrange to study with a minimum of red tape. These courses were also listed in the Civil Service Commission Interagency *Training Bulletin* and made available to employees of other Federal agencies. Other agency personnel did not participate, apparently because of the National Institutes of Health's suburban location. Many people from other agencies asked about NIH's experiences, however, and much guidance was provided to them.

During 1963 and early 1964, NIH also used some PI courses in the programed text format. About four copies of each of two programs—"Allergy and Hypersensitivity" (Pfizer) and "Routine Epidemiological Investigation of Food-Borne Disease" (Public Health Service, Communicable Disease Center)—were made available to professionals at NIH to acquaint them with programed instruction as an educational technique. Comments were very favorable. In addition, one student took an English course with satisfactory results.

The Human Development Institute (HDI) course in "Relationship Improvement" was taken by twelve persons at NIH in pairs, as instructed by the program. These employees had taken a general supervisory course in which human relations had been discussed briefly and the HDI course was a follow-up. Their final evaluation was only lukewarm. Letting each person select his own partner was not a good idea because the relationship of these pairs was already good and left little room for improvement. It was decided that the course would be better used by two new people who were to work together: They could accelerate the development of mutual trust and friendship by taking the HDI course.

Since the size of the training staff is relatively small at NIH, the time that can be devoted to programed instruction is limited. When requests for

PI began to demand too much time, a "lending library" system was adopted; those who couldn't be accommodated in the regular schedule were advised to rent their own machine and borrow the course. At one time recently, six Autotutors were being used with courses in computers, electronics, and management.

"Tailored" programs have had limited use at NIH. On the other hand, the GSA course on FEDSTRIP met with favorable student reaction and achieved high learning and good performance of necessary skills. It was designed to teach Federal employees the new GSA automated procurement system, and it has succeeded very well.

To date, NIH has spent approximately $4,000 on programed instruction courses, machines, and machine rentals. Employees, managers, and training staff are favorably impressed.

Off-the-shelf programs have been favorites. The usual procedure is for an NIH training officer to select a program which is designed to resolve one of the existing training problems, compare the course objectives with the training needs, go through the course, and then decide what *additional* training activity will assure that the training objectives are reached.

A study of comparative costs of programed and narrative tests is difficult to make because of the unique use of programed courses at NIH. Programed materials are being used to teach courses which were not offered in the past, primarily because of a lack of staff and time. The "automated" aspect of programed instruction has allowed NIH to present training courses while leaving staff members relatively free to handle other training matters. One very crucial comparison can be made, however. During the period June–December 1963, many employees were trained when regular lecture courses were not available. Training is an individual matter, and requests are often submitted for training which cannot ordinarily be offered for an individual or small groups; the cost would not be justified. Consequently, these employees would have to wait or do without. However, with programed instruction these employees can begin their training immediately and progress as their schedules permit. Thus far, the cost to NIH of the teaching machines and the 11 adapted courses has proved far less than the cost of an equal number of persons with other facilities. In addition, most of the programed texts have been given to NIH, and it has been able to try out these courses at no cost.

Northern Natural Gas Company *

Programed instruction at Northern Natural Gas Company has been limited to commercially available courses. It has not, that is, developed any in-house programs. The programs are presently administered by the Organization Development Section in cooperation with the library. PI has been enthusiastically received by the company's management.

ALL REGULAR FULL-TIME EMPLOYEES (APPROXIMATELY 4,500) OF Northern Natural Gas, its divisions, and its subsidiaries are eligible to participate in the self-instructional program. Any course is available free of charge if the employee completes it within specified time requirements. Unless circumstances warrant otherwise, if he fails to complete the course, he is charged for its full price (average cost: $10.05). Upon his completion of the course, credit for it is entered into his personal-history file.

The following courses are presently available to employees:

TITLE	PUBLISHER
Algebra I	Encyclopaedia Britannica
Algebra II	,, ,,
The Language of Algebra	,, ,,
An Introduction to Verbal Problems in Algebra	,, ,,
Arithmetic of Whole Numbers	,, ,,
Basic Mathematics	,, ,,
Introductory Calculus I	,, ,,
Introductory Calculus II	,, ,,
Plane Geometry	,, ,,
Solid Geometry	,, ,,
An Introduction to Sets, Inequalities & Functions	

* Information for this case submitted by Larry S. Geppert, Training Specialist, Northern Natural Gas Company, Omaha, Nebraska.

Analytic Trigonometry	Encyclopaedia Britannica
Trigonometry	" "
Whole Numbers & Numerals	" "
English 3200	Harcourt, Brace & World
Gas Laws	Holt, Rinehart & Winston
Basic Electricity	American Telephone and Telegraph
Introductory Statistics	TMI-Grolier
Fundamentals of Electricity, DC	"
Mathematical Bases for Management Decision Making	TEMAC

The following courses are presently under consideration:

Supply—Demand	ENTELEK
Theory of Income Determination	"
Reading Financial Reports	Basic Systems
Integers & Rational Numbers	TEMAC

The initial selection of courses is based on either reported needs or their apparent applicability to the company's operations. A course is first generally reviewed for content by the Organization Development Section. Next, someone on the staff who has completed the course evaluates its applicability, or selected employees (who may or may not be topic experts) review or complete and evaluate the course. Once the course is evaluated with positive results, it is purchased and appropriate quantities of it are placed in the library and publicized for use.

Employee participation during the past few years is as follows:

COURSES STARTED			COURSES COMPLETED		
1962	*1963*	*1964*	*1962*	*1963*	*1964*
302	186	184	98(32%)	144(77%)	121(66%)

In April 1963 the company injected the provision that the employee must pay for the course if he does not complete it in the required time. Completion experience as of August 1, 1964 was as follows: 279 started; 146 completed; 2 left the company without completing the course; 45 are not yet due; and 86 are overdue for completion.

Northern Natural Gas suspects that one factor which has affected completion results is curiosity about a "new" (and free) learning technique. Enthusiasm for the courses by those employees who were attracted by their novelty probably waned and caused the high rate of incomplete courses.

The following is a cross-section of employees participating in the program:

FIELD	OFFICE
Senior Storage Operator	Staff Geologist
Well Tester	Training Clerk
Maintenance Man	Stenographer
Engineering Aide	Production Engineer
Truck Driver	Statistical Typist
Master Mechanic	Reserves Engineer
Shift Engineer	Proration Engineer
Pipeline Repairman	Keypunch Operator
District Manager	Purchase Order Clerk
Welder	Draftsman
Compressor Repairman	Systems Engineer
Oiler	Auditor
Terminal Operator	Statistical Research Aide
Field Supervisor	Mechanical Designer
Meter Tester	Coefficient Clerk
Radio Engineer	Accounting Clerk
Dispatcher	Technical Clerk
Salesman	Project Engineer

The general consensus of participating employees toward the program and the individual courses has been favorable. Although they have been asked to evaluate and comment on the quality of the courses and their applicability, both actual and potential, to their work; how the courses could be improved; and so on, their evaluations have not yet been tabulated.

The decision to use off-the-shelf rather than in-house programs was reached because of (1) relative cost and (2) the quality of the courses available.

Management is relatively pleased with the amount of employee participation thus far, but more intensive promotion of PI is planned. Enthusiasm about PI is high, and good results are anticipated from its further use. PI is only one facet of the employee development effort, but it is increasing in importance. Northern Natural Gas Company has been invited by the Institute of Gas Technology of Chicago to participate in the promotion of PI in the gas industry.

Northrop Norair *

In the past two years Northrop Norair has produced 15 instructional programed courses, using more than 200 photos and 300 separate pieces of artwork. It found that exclusively verbal programs did not train in manipulative tasks. The case describes what Northrop Norair has called "A Working A/V System," which comprises the construction of programs, the system used to produce those programs, and the interface necessary to introduce the finished programs into the organizational structure of the company. The design and creation of one system led to a supporting production system, and that in turn pointed to a need to standardize all the training activities which are related to the original system.

NORTHROP NORAIR HAS A CONTINUOUS REQUIREMENT TO TRAIN nearly 3,000 employees, one or two at a time, in 24 different subject areas.

The usual procedure was to schedule the trainees in groups. Requests for training of employees would be held until a large enough group accumulated, making it economical to conduct a class. The lag between the time when Manufacturing requested training and when the Education and Training staff could satisfy that request was thought to be excessive.

In early 1963 the company decided to select one pilot course from all the training courses and program it for flip chart presentation. In the fall a four-step vestibule course was finished and in operation. It consisted of an assembly built by the student which required him to do the work he would perform in the plant. Each part of the assembly operation was shown by picture and presented step by step. After having completed this flip chart training and spending one month on the job, all men in the test group were rated from good to excellent by their supervisors. Other aircraft assembly courses were then programed for the same kind of presentation.

* Information for this case derived from interviews with R. H. Faulks, Programing Specialist, and L. H. Walton, Administrator, Education and Training, Northrop Norair; and remarks by R. H. Faulks during a film slide presentation to the Audio-Visual Education Association of California (AVEAC/DAVI) at its annual convention in Asilomar, California.

The vestibule program was designed to replace a 40-hour course. The course reduced the training time *to an average of 10½ hours.* This was a 75 per cent reduction and produced an $86 saving per new employee.

In addition to the structural assembly courses, a side experiment was being conducted in electronic assembly to investigate the possibility of presenting additional courses audiovisually.

Using its own "teaching machine," the A/V-4, Northrop Norair designed an experimental course to teach a new way of making solderless (crimp pin) connections. The trainee sits at a work bench which has all the equipment necessary to build an actual assembly. He activates a machine from which a recorded voice tells him how to accomplish each step of the assembly. The A/V-4 verifies how the assembly should look at each stage in a colored picture on a screen. At the end of each instructional step, the tape recorder automatically stops, allowing the student to do what is shown. Upon completing each step, the student presses a control button, and the machine continues.

The crimped pin course was reduced from eight hours of instruction by conventional teaching methods to *just over 45 minutes!* This phenomenal reduction in training time was not due solely to the audiovisual machine. The real time saving came from defining the behavioral objectives of the course and then programing to satisfy those objectives.

The results were so convincing that in February 1964 a tentative training system was presented to the manufacturing organizations. Under this system Education and Training assumed control of the trainee's progress from the time he entered employment until his release to the shop. A new employee takes the new, two-part, prehire indoctrination program which familiarizes him with (1) Norair's chief product, the supersonic jet aircraft that his working skill will help to produce, and (2) the retirement and fringe benefits he can expect as a member of the Northrop team.

If he is scheduled as a trainee, he next goes through a shop orientation program which covers items that he will be expected to know in order to do his best. He is informed of the degree of neatness and housekeeping that is expected of him. He is told about the way to work safely to protect himself and his fellow employees. He also learns about the kinds of material rework that are authorized and when it is necessary to get engineering approval. In essence, he gains a view of the shop atmosphere and of what will be expected of him.

If the new employee is skilled—that is, if he comes from another company where he did electrical work or if he has a background in electrical assembly —he bypasses the basic vestibule course and takes any one of the specific courses (see Exhibit 1). If he is unskilled, he starts the three-part vestibule

EXHIBIT 1

A Working A/V System

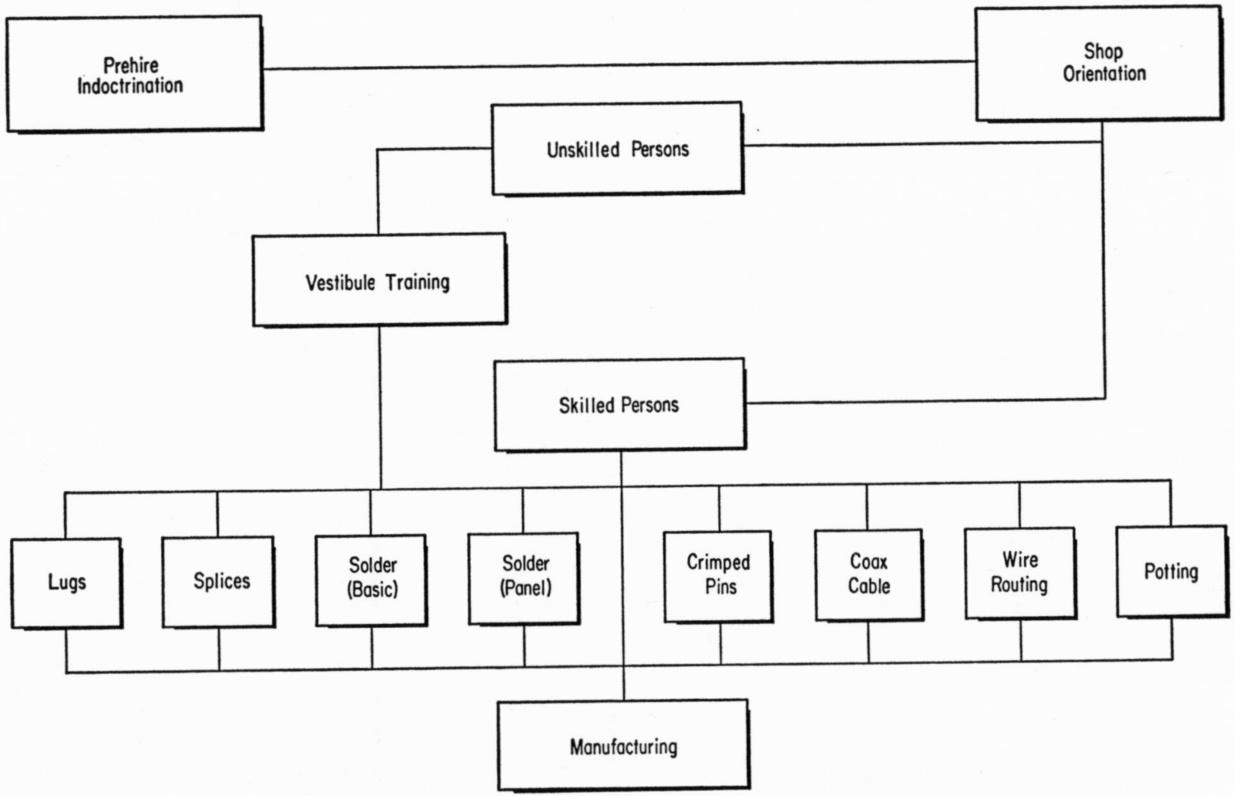

training course. This is a basic course designed to bring the skill of the new employee up to a level where he can take courses designed to instruct him in his specific work area.

The electronic three-part vestibule course is a springboard for all additional training. The first section introduces the program and shows the trainee exactly what he is going to build and how it will look upon completion of the program. It also introduces him to the assembly tools, by linking names with tools so he will recognize items that are generally used in the shop. The trainee gets a chance to pick up the tools and look them over; he is, in fact, encouraged to do so. It's not at all unusual to find a man opening and closing a tool over and over again until he is satisfied that whatever he is looking for he has found. The program also covers skills in measuring to one one-hundredth of an inch; recognizing, handling, and measuring wire lengths; and finally that basic of all basic skills, soldering.

While analyzing the workings of the audiovisual (A/V) system, the instructors found that when the new employee finishes the vestibule course, he is ready to take specific courses which teach the particular skill for which the company hired him. Because Manufacturing knows what skill is needed, it sends its request for his training many days before Education and Training receives the new man. All that is necessary is for the new man to complete subsequent courses which are conducted in the same manner as the vestibule (diagramed in Exhibit 1 on the preceding page), except that they are confined to particular aspects of assembly work; for example, the panel soldering course builds on the basic soldering capabilities of the trainee which he has obtained in the vestibule course and further shows him panel layout, ground and jumper wire assembly, component assembly, and wire routing, to mention just a few skills. When he completes a course, Education and Training issues a certification card which in essence says, "This man can do the job for which he has been hired."

This training system carries with it a degree of responsibility to both manufacturing and the trainee. The trainee must feel confident that he can do what is expected of him, while the shop must get people who can perform their jobs properly. The working A/V system satisfies both conditions.

Like bureaucracies which tend to reproduce others similar to themselves, the working A/V system generated another system to support its goal. Exhibit 2 shows the program production system which was generated to meet the programing demands of the working A/V system. Producing up to 42 hours of programs took many months of preparation, research, writing, and testing, so without a system to control the effort, the whole project would not have met the scheduled start date.

EXHIBIT 2

PROGRAM PRODUCTION SYSTEM

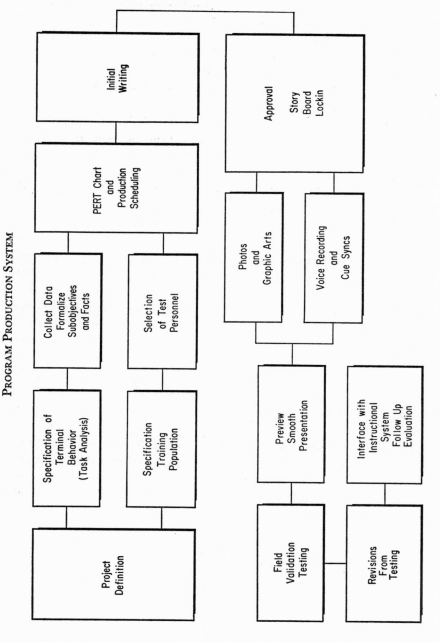

The program production system consists of four phases. Phase one is project definition, which essentially ties down the task to be programed by defining the problem and stating the training objective. This phase is the heart of the system and is the most time consuming and exacting. Ambiguous objectives and fuzzy definitions of expected student behavioral changes will lead to the wrong student responses and defeat the certification objectives.

The second part of the program production system is the initial writing phase with storyboard lock-in. Here is set down in script form the step-by-step sequence that will eventually become the audio portion of the program. Tentative pictures are blocked in, and the total package is given approval for the third phase, which develops a usable program by choosing the graphic arts, photos, and recordings to be included in the courses. The fourth and last phase is a field test in which the instructors find out whether what they have created really works. Many procedures of conventional instruction had to be eliminated in the search for a more standardized method of training.

All course projects are built to the same configuration, even to the same positioning, spacing, and size of the fasteners to be installed. This standardization increases the instructor's ability to judge the work being completed by the student. He need not look for errors in the design of the project or try to remember just how it was built and what kind of unique procedures had gone into its construction. By standardizing the training material for the student the instructor could standardize the grading. He merely checks different quality points on the project which are listed on an evaluation checklist. Unsatisfactory items are returned for rework and special instructor help.

Programed courses then have been Northrop Norair's solution to a pressing training problem. The need to be highly flexible and to conduct many courses at a time with a limited number of instructors, while still creating a method of showing the student a step-by-step building procedure, all had their influence, culminating in the use of an A/V system for training.

Pfizer Laboratories, Inc. *

Medical men are hard pressed to keep up with the developments in their field. Refresher courses and study of technical journals require more time than many physicians can spare. To help meet the need for more information in less time, Pfizer Laboratories, Inc., and Basic Systems, Inc., developed a programed course which was made available to physicians in 1962, with spectacular results.

In September 1962 "spectrum" published an article entitled "Can Undergraduate or Postgraduate Medical Education Benefit from Programed Instruction?" The article attempted to explain what programed instruction is and how it works, and it included a medical example.[1] An editorial in the same issue pointed out that—

> Some medical curricula have already been affected by programed instruction. Dartmouth Medical School, the University of Illinois College of Medicine, the Massachusetts General Hospital, the Columbia University College of Physicians and Surgeons, and the New York Hospital-Cornell Medical Center are among the many schools and teaching hospitals that have adopted it or are trying it out.

> That there is room for improvement of teaching methods all are agreed. Nowhere is the need for improvement more pressing than in medicine. In virtually every major branch, each year's research adds more knowledge than one can ordinarily assimilate in a lifetime of study.

After questioning how students today are to absorb a rapidly increasing body of medical knowledge and how busy physicians can keep up with new developments, the editorial concluded that—

---

* Information for this case submitted by Frances Waxman, Programing Editor, *Spectrum*, Pfizer Laboratories, Inc., New York City.

[1] *Spectrum*, September–October 1962, p. 73. *Spectrum* is a medical journal published by Pfizer Laboratories, Inc.

Of all recent innovations in education, the one that appears to hold most promise is programed instruction, which has been described as the first application of the science of learning to the art of teaching.

The *Spectrum* article introduced PI to the 225,000 physicians who receive the journal. It explained what PI is, presented some sample frames from a nonmedical program, and discussed its potential and limitations for medical education. The article also included a ten-minute programed sequence on how to read an electrocardiogram in myocardial infarction. The example was specially prepared by Pfizer and Basic Systems, Inc., to demonstrate how programing could be applied to medical instruction. This particular topic was selected to show the interaction of verbal and graphic elements; the sequence was pretested by a number of physicians and reflected their suggestions for improvement. The two frames in Exhibit 1 are from this EKG sequence. The originals are in color.

The physicians were asked to indicate their reaction to the idea of programed instruction for medical education by returning an enclosed postpaid reply card-questionnaire. The response was extremely gratifying. More than 30,000 promptly sent back favorable replies. Many returned their cards with long and enthusiastic letters. At the Rochester Conference on Programmed Instruction in Medical Education on June 26, 1964, Leon Summit, editor of *Spectrum,* told the conferees that after two years "these cards are still arriving, and though we long ago stopped counting, the total received to date is over 50,000. Only a handful of the replies have been unfavorable." Then he described his mixed feelings about this response:

> We had expected a good deal of interest, but this unprecedented response both startled and worried us. Could it be regarded as a blanket endorsement of medical programed instruction? Could the reaction to a sketchy three-page magazine article and a ten-minute example be taken as objective proof of the technique's value for medical education? Could a scientific judgment be based on so slight and superficial an exposure? How much of the enthusiasm for programed instruction was due only to novelty? How much of the response must be discounted as transient fascination with the latest do-it-yourself educational gimmick?

While admitting that novelty undoubtedly played a part in the response, he gave considerable weight to the "hundreds of thoughtful and lengthy letters [which] came from medical and other educators, people so accustomed to the flood of new educational devices and techniques that they were unlikely to fall prey to mere novelty." To Summit and his staff, this extremely favorable reaction had a special significance. It "affirmed the medical profession's need

EXHIBIT 1

SAMPLE FRAMES

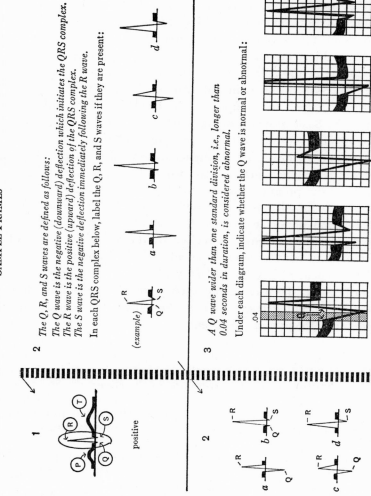

1

positive

2 The Q, R, and S waves are defined as follows:

The Q wave is the negative (downward) deflection which initiates the QRS complex.

The R wave is the positive (upward) deflection of the QRS complex.

The S wave is the negative deflection immediately following the R wave.

In each QRS complex below, label the Q, R, and S waves if they are present:

(example)

a   *b*   *c*   *d*

3 A Q wave wider than one standard division, i.e., longer than 0.04 seconds in duration, is considered abnormal.

Under each diagram, indicate whether the Q wave is normal or abnormal:

.04

☐ normal   ☐ normal   ☐ normal   ☐ normal   ☐ normal
☐ abnormal   ☐ abnormal   ☐ abnormal   ☐ abnormal   ☐ abnormal

a   *b*   *c*   *d*   *e*

for a good method of self-instructional review and the eagerness of physicians to try anything promising." The response to the article led to a commitment on the part of Pfizer and the editorial staff of *Spectrum* to carry out the promise that seemed implicit in the original article. This was to develop one or more programs on medical subjects for practicing physicians.

Basic Systems, under contract with Pfizer, began developing a course in allergy. The subject matter specialist was Murray Dworetzky, M.D., Physician-in-Charge at the Allergy Clinic of New York Hospital, and Clinical Associate Professor of Medicine at Cornell University Medical College. Dr. Dworetzky helped to set up the initial outline of the subject matter. Following this, Basic Systems, along with the *Spectrum* staff, developed a detailed sequential outline which was reviewed by a large number of general practitioners and allergists. These physicians were also asked to indicate the extent to which they felt such a course would be of use, interest, and value to them. After the program was drafted by Basic Systems and tested on a small number of physicians, it was revised, and the *Spectrum* staff had it field-tested by 50 physicians across the country and further reviewed by allergists. It was then extensively revised by the *Spectrum* staff. Following this revision, Pfizer felt the course was ready for publication.

The development of *Allergy and Hypersensitivity* depended on close coordination between the programing agency and the staff. This effort, however, was not without friction. As Leon Summit pointed out at the Rochester Conference, the programing agency

> ... was understandably jealous of its professional stature and leadership and resisted the intrusion of an editorial group that obviously had much to learn about programed instruction. As the client, the *Spectrum* group was equally jealous of its reputation for editorial excellence and deplored the resistance of a program-writing group that just as obviously had much to learn about editing and graphic presentation.

In addressing the Association of American Medical Colleges in Denver, Colorado, on October 17, 1964, Summit further pointed out that neither of the two groups "had appreciated the extraordinary difficulty of programing complex medical material to a high standard of quality. The pooling of *all* our talents was necessary to achieve maximum teaching effectiveness, and each individual's professional stature was enhanced rather than diminished by such collaboration."

In the development of the program the judgment of Dr. Dworetzky, as medical consultant and subject matter expert, was final since medical correctness and technical accuracy were paramount. Summit pointed out that once the programing agency, Dr. Dworetzky, and the *Spectrum* staff learned to work together and understood the need to do so, "ideas flowed much more freely, permitting more constructive blending of medical, psychologic, editorial, and graphic judgments." The friction, though sometimes intense, was extremely healthy. Out of friction, growth and sound solutions emerged. As Dr. Dworetzky aptly said, "We thus achieved excellence through mutual distrust." Although the process was expensive in both time and money and there was some apprehension about the merits of so vast an effort, the results were to make it all worthwhile. Eight months later, after agonizing months of intense work, days, nights, and weekends, the first edition of *Allergy and Hypersensitivity* went to press in June 1963.

The January-February 1963 issue of *Spectrum* contained a second article on programed instruction which was entitled, "The Response to Programed Instruction." This article presented a preview of the *Allergy and Hypersensitivity* program and indicated that other programs would follow. The readers were told that *Allergy and Hypersensitivity* and subsequent courses would be offered at no charge and could be reserved by returning the reply card enclosed with the issue. The article quoted an editorial on programed instruction which appeared in the *Journal of the American Medical Association* of December 1:

> Students, teachers, and society . . . have much to gain from [this] new tool of learning. . . . It promises to introduce a new degree of ease, effectiveness, and efficiency into the initial and continuing training of physicians. . . .
>
> The experience gained [through programed instruction] with the improvement of our textbooks may change ways of writing other books, to the lasting benefit of those of us who are too old to sit in classrooms, but not too old to learn.
>
> The new method constitutes experimental confirmation and refinement of a way of teaching known and practiced at least since Socrates—a reassuring example of age-old wisdom confirmed by contemporary science . . . an innovation in education compared recently to the development of printing in its significance as a new tool of teaching and learning.

The reader was presented with an outline of *Allergy and Hypersensitivity,* and the balance of the article was a preview of the first 21 frames. The frames that follow (Exhibit 2) are illustrative of the program, which has been described by Robert Horn of the Center for Programed Instruction, Institute for Educational Technology, Teachers College, Columbia University, as "the

EXHIBIT 2

SAMPLE FRAMES

2

antigen

antibody

---

3 The diagram below shows that an antigen-antibody reaction is involved in ☐ allergy only ☐ immunity only ☐ both allergy and immunity.

Antigen + Person → Antigen-Antibody Reaction →

Reaction of tissue cells → **Allergic reaction**

Neutralization of toxicity or infectivity of antigen → **Immune reaction**

The antigen-antibody reaction results in neutralization of toxicity or infectivity of antigen in ☐ allergy ☐ immunity.

The antigen-antibody reaction produces a tissue cell reaction in ☐ allergy ☐ immunity.

3

both allergy and immunity

immunity

allergy

---

4 Compare allergy and immunity by checking one or both boxes for each statement below:

	Allergy	Immunity
Person has antibodies.	☐	☐
Antigen-antibody reaction occurs.	☐	☐
Antigen-antibody reaction occurs on contact with antigen.	☐	☐
Antigen-antibody reaction results in tissue reaction.	☐	☐
Antigen-antibody reaction results in neutralization of toxicity or infectivity of antigen.	☐	☐

EXHIBIT 2 (*concluded*)

17 Examining the diagrams below, you would conclude that upon injection of an antigen such as a foreign protein, ☐ some ☐ all individuals will develop an antigen-antibody reaction..

The diagrams also suggest that anaphylactic shock will occur only if _____ occurs.

Person A	single bee sting →	Local toxic reaction	PAIN AND EDEMA
Person B	multiple bee sting by swarm of bees →	Local and systemic toxic reaction	MULTIPLE EDEMA AND SHOCK
Person C	single bee sting →	Local toxic reaction / Antigen-antibody reaction	PAIN AND EDEMA ANAPHYLACTIC SHOCK

18 Does a larger amount of foreign protein necessarily produce an antigen-antibody reaction?
☐ yes ☐ no (See PERSON B)

One important feature of allergy is the fact that an allergic reaction may result from the injection of a very small amount of foreign protein.

Only person _____ would be considered allergic to bee venom.

19 With equal doses of antigen, the intensity of the tissue response is greater when provoked by ☐ an antigen-antibody reaction ☐ a toxic reaction.

16
B

17
some

antigen-antibody reaction

18
no
C

most beautiful program from the standpoint of layout, typography, and illustrations." [2]

By June 1963, when the program went to press, 70,000 prepublication requests had been received in response to the preview article. Within only a few days after the article was published, 15,000 requests arrived in a single mail. The first edition of 100,000 copies (estimated total cost for development and publication: $100,000) was soon exhausted. Hundreds of suggestions and careful reviews were received. In essence, the first edition served as a professionwide field test. Based upon this, a second revised edition of 100,000 copies was printed and distributed (estimated cost for revision and printing: $30,000). Fifteen thousand copies of the program have been distributed in foreign countries. The program is currently being used in 74 of the 95 medical schools in the country. This more than justified the feeling of the *Spectrum* staff that all the time, money, and effort that went into the program were warranted and that the quality and quantity of this reaction could not be explained by novelty and faddism.

In its September-October 1963 issue *Spectrum* reported the response to the program. The introductory paragraphs of this report stated:

> Three months ago the first programed review of its type ever published —*Allergy and Hypersensitivity*—was mailed to some 70,000 physicians who had requested it.
>
> Several thousand physicians have commended both the course and the method of presentation. Almost without exception, they have found this a useful method for reviewing basic concepts and keeping up with some of the new developments in the medical and allied fields.
>
> These views have come not only from practitioners in every branch of the medical profession but also from residents, interns, and students, from administrators and educators in more than seventy medical schools, from medical research foundations, from representatives of many national and local medical organizations, and even from abroad.

The report described the results of the questionnaire that was included with every copy of *Allergy and Hypersensitivity*. The physician was asked to fill out the questionnaire when he had completed the program. A study of the questionnaires shows that the average completion time was five hours. Ninety-nine per cent of the general practitioners liked the course, and 100 per cent of the allergists liked it. Of all the recipients, 94 per cent indicated that the material in the course had practical value for them. When asked

---

[2] Robert E. Horn, "Innovation and Excellence in Programed Instruction," *Programed Instruction*, February 1965, p. 8.

whether, in comparison with the same amount of time spent on other forms of educational reading matter or instruction, they found this type of review of more, equal, or less value, 76 per cent indicated they found it of more value and 21 per cent of equal value. When asked if they would like to receive other subjects for review in programed form, 96 per cent said yes. Many physicians mentioned specific subjects.

The article pointed out that "such emphatic approval warrants the conclusion that programed instruction is a valuable technique for postgraduate study and for helping physicians in their effort to keep up with the flood of new knowledge."

The spring 1964 issue of *Spectrum* announced the next programed medical course to be published by Pfizer Laboratories: *Current Concepts of Thyroid Disease.* The preview article on this course quoted an editorial comment from the May 4, 1963, issue of the *Journal of the American Medical Association* that programed instruction could "no longer be ignored. . . . The theoretical core for this instructional method is the now well-established principle that the efficiency and effectiveness of learning can be increased if a learning task is broken into logical and sequential steps and the student informed promptly at the end of each step whether he has learned what he is supposed to learn."

As in *Allergy and Hypersensitivity,* the content development of *Current Concepts of Thyroid Disease* has been directed by carefully selected medical consultants. In this case they are Joseph J. Rupp, M.D., Associate Professor of Medicine and Director of the Division of Endocrinology at Jefferson Medical College, where he heads the endocrine and diabetes clinics; and Sheldon G. Gilgore, M.D., a former associate of Dr. Rupp, who is now Associate Director of Clinical Research at Pfizer and also Clinical Assistant Physician in Endocrinology at St. Vincent's Hospital, New York City. The program was begun in 1963 and published in April 1965. Prior to publication, there were more than 80,000 requests for copies, in response to the preview article. The program comprises 352 frames and requires five to eight hours to complete. It covers signs, symptoms, diagnoses, and treatment of hypothyroidism and hyperthyroidism; laboratory tests; thyrotoxic heart disease; and diagnosis and treatment of benign goiter and thyroid carcinoma.

Pfizer's future plans for the continuing education of physicians are ambitious, but they are well justified by the response to *Allergy and Hypersensitivity* (requests for 245,000 copies have been received since its publication) and by the interest that was shown, prior to publication, in *Current Concepts of Thyroid Disease.* On the agenda for publication late in 1965 and early 1966 are (1) *Physicians' Liability,* (2) *Fluid and Acid-Base Imbalance,* and (3) *Myocardial Infarction.* A program designed for medical technologists and technicians, *Immunohematology*, will be an overhaul of a program written for the Pfizer sales training department some time ago. It is being completely rewritten and reprogramed as a joint effort of *Spectrum* and Pfizer Diagnostics. For self-instruction of diabetic patients, a program on the care of diabetes is planned.

Another measure of Pfizer's activity in this field is the invitation it received from the University of California to present a three-day seminar–workshop in March of 1965 on programed instruction in the health sciences for the faculty of the university's medical, dental, pharmacy, and nursing schools. In preparing for this seminar–workshop it has developed materials which it hopes to make available to other schools that wish to conduct similar workshops.

Pfizer has received numerous requests from medical educators, medical organizations, schools, hospitals, and even publishers for assistance in developing courses in many fields of medicine and also in pharmacy, nursing, medical writing, and related fields. However, its response to these requests has been limited by the existing commitments of its small programed instruction staff.

Asked to cite some of the lessons his staff at Pfizer has learned from its experience with programed instruction, Summit offered the following observations:

> Our experience on *Allergy and Hypersensitivity* has shown that programed instruction, when it is well done, is a highly effective teaching tool. The volume of mail that we have received about the program has demonstrated this beyond any doubt.
>
> It pays to aim for excellence in the development of programed instruction. There is no substitute for quality and no short-cut to achieving it. It takes a great deal of hard work, usually much more than people anticipate when they first go into the development of programed materials. A good program results when qualified people are given sufficient time to do the job right. While target dates are important as guides, quality must be placed before deadlines, and a program should not be considered ready for large-scale reproduction until rigid tests prove it is ready.
>
> Unfortunately, the role of the subject matter expert has been generally underrated by organizations and individuals specializing in programed instruction. This is a major reason for the abundance of poor programed courses that have been published even though they are shoddy or at the very least inadequate. It is unlikely that a good program can result when either (a) the expert is not sufficiently qualified, (b) the expert does not fully understand programed instruction and his role in developing it, or (c) the programer minimizes the expert's role. The development of

a good program requires at least as much respect for content as for programing technique.

For senior management, it is worth spending time learning the components of good programed instruction, at least to the point where you can recognize what makes one program good and another bad. To achieve this goal, you do not have to be a behavioral analyst. But if you are not clear about what constitutes quality in programed instruction, it is possible to waste considerable time and money.

In evaluating programed instruction, whether it is material already available and being considered for use or new material that has just been drafted, it is necessary to be highly skeptical. If you appear to be soliciting favorable reactions from reviewers or students, you may get them even when they are unwarranted. It is better to emphasize that what you are looking for is not praise of the material but constructive criticism to help find its faults.

As in all good teaching, the simplest presentation is likely to be the most effective. This means simplicity in arrangement, writing, and format. Experience has shown that material presented well in simple, direct book format eliminates the need for teaching machines and gadgety formats and, of course, is much less expensive.

Good programed instruction is expensive, but it justifies its costs in terms of better teaching effectiveness and longer retention. With time and experience in developing programed materials, the cost can be reduced.

A good, closely coordinated team representing many different types of skills is vital to the development of good programed instruction. People with these skills are difficult to find. Good programers, good editors, and subject matter experts who understand the components of good programing are scarce. It is better to look for people with good potential and give them ample time and good training to develop these skills.

The Quaker Oats Company *

The use of an outside program development contractor can be highly beneficial, as we see emphasized in this capsule description of programed instruction in The Quaker Oats Company.

QUAKER OATS BECAME INTERESTED IN PROGRAMED INSTRUCTION IN 1959 when its training officials were "inspired . . . by Skinner's writings."

Its first effort was to utilize some early off-the-shelf programs. However, these programs were too general to meet specific job needs and it was decided that Quaker Oats would need to construct its own.

After a moderately successful effort in this direction, Quaker Oats concluded that the most feasible way to expand the program was to rely on an outside consultant rather than to enlarge the internal staff. This is the pattern that the company has continued to follow.

The first major effort was the development of 11 programed courses for use in training new salesmen in the Grocery Products Sales Department. The outside firm wrote the courses. The company training officials supplied the programing firm with complete information and with editorial critiques as it completed units in the rough. The courses were further tested and validated through a group of employees and finally printed and put into operation in February 1963.

Unlike many other users of PI, Quaker Oats has devoted nearly as much time and money toward the development of a "guide" to be used by field trainers in properly utilizing the courses as it has in the construction of the courses themselves. This was prompted by the belief that PI is a fine method of teaching basic knowledge, but it must be carefully supplemented by a patient trainer so that a trainee can convert knowledge into skills and simultaneously develop the proper attitude toward the company, its products, its accounts, and his job.

---

* Information for this case submitted by Clyde Harden, Sales Training Manager, The Quaker Oats Company, Merchandise Mart Plaza, Chicago, Illinois.

When this entire program of salesmen training by PI became operative over two years ago, management had to make a decision. Was its interest mainly in research, or did it lie mainly in training salesmen? Because of convenience and expediency, it chose to emphasize training over research into the effectiveness of training. Consequently, there are no statistical data to support its belief that the program is good, but it has bushels of sparkling testimonials from the field.

Quaker's experience suggests that, contrary to the opinion of some, programed instruction is *not* boring to the student if it is aimed at a specific skill which the student will subsequently have to demonstrate. Furthermore, programed instruction is *not* expensive—all of the direct costs for this program would be far less than those required to produce just one 16mm sound training film.

Currently the company is producing a series of self-study units for its experienced salesmen. These units will later be released to educational institutions and to the entire trade since they deal with subject matter of broad interest in the food industry. This program will be completed during the fall of 1965. The units will include a mixture of text and programed material with the most important matters reserved for the latter.

Schering Corporation *

Schering Corporation has used four programed texts: (1) "Griseo-fulvin Clinical and Technical Background," (2) "Diuretics and Anti-Hypertensives," (3) "Elements of Corticosteroid Pharmacology," and (4) "Phenothiazine Tranquilizers." The first three texts were prepared by Basic Systems, Inc., in cooperation with the medical staff of Schering Corporation. The fourth text was prepared internally by the Medical Services Department of Schering Corporation. In the past year the company has changed from objective tests to essay tests in order to challenge what conceptual learning might have taken place even though the tests per se did not contain this as an objective. The results have been gratifying although the average marks did go down from the high 90 percentile level to the high 80 percentile level.

SCHERING CORPORATION HAS MADE SEVERAL OBSERVATIONS RELATIVE to its programed instruction effort. It has found that (1) the duration of retention does not seem to be quite as long as with the conventional lecture method; (2) straight linear texts tend to become boring to the majority of the men, and they prefer one or two paragraphs of reading matter followed by six to twelve linear frames which reinforce the main facts. This variation has the added advantage that the paragraphs can be used for review.

Schering has also found that the use of additional panels in the back which contain drawings, charts, or graphs for the students' supplemental use, and on which the students then receive six to ten frames of linear text, can save 50 or 60 linear frames or up to six paragraphs.

At present the company is leaning toward shorter texts which cover only one aspect of a subject. The men seem less discouraged with these smaller texts than with several hundred pages of text which they must complete in a fairly short time, on their own, and then be tested on. The shorter texts

---

* Based upon information provided by Katherine H. Hain, M.D., Director of Medical Services, Schering Corporation, Union, New Jersey.

allow zeroing in on the most difficult aspects of a subject—the rest of which can be studied out of a text or backgrounder in the conventional manner.

The Schering staff has prepared seven five-minute programed texts on medical subjects for physicians. The titles of these programs, prepared for U.S. Industries teaching machines, are: "Mode and Site of Action of Thiazides," "A Simple Diagnostic Test for the Presence of Fungous Elements," "The Reticular Formation: Arousal and Emotion," "Differential Pathology of Rheumatoid Arthritis and Osteoarthritis," "Hay Fever (Seasonal Nasal Allergy)," "Urticaria (Hives of the Skin and Mucous Membranes)," and "Differential Diagnosis of Dermatologic Look-Alikes (Cases from Central America and the U.S.A.)." These programs have been exhibited before the American Medical Association and at meetings of other specialty groups. The company has had many requests from physicians, particularly in teaching institutions, to put these programed texts in book form for distribution.

The Schering staff was surprised at how much could be put into a five-to-seven minute program, at a graduate level. A multiple choice technique was used in which, if the wrong button is pressed, the learner must go back to read the original paragraph and look at the illustrations, if any, again.

Southwestern Public Service Company *

When Southwestern Public Service Company first became aware of programed instruction, E. W. Love, the training supervisor, was urged to attend a programed learning seminar at the University of Michigan. At this seminar he became convinced that programed learning could be a definite advantage for his company. Southwestern Public Service already had quite elaborate training programs for their field operating personnel and other employees. In the area of skills these consisted of linemen's vocational training courses and formal on-the-job apprentice training programs. It long ago became convinced that an electric utility employee must have a good basic mathematical background in order to pursue the more advanced phases of his training. Therefore, since mathematics was among the first subjects programed, it and a fundamental course in direct current were Southwestern's first ventures into practical application of programed learning in its vocational and apprenticeship courses. In the past two years it has rewritten and is still in the process of rewriting its vocational courses to insure more effective use of this type of training and to update and encourage more employee participation.

SOUTHWESTERN PUBLIC SERVICE FIRST USED PROGRAMED LEARNING IN its lineman's vocational training school during 1962–63. The company has been conducting this school for the past 12 years. Courses are given in company schools in Texas, Oklahoma, and New Mexico, and the average annual enrollment in the four-year curriculum is nearly 450 students. Until the 1962–63 school term, each of the four years of courses required 144 hours.

The average educational level in Southwestern's schools is that of high school graduate. A large percentage of the students, however, have had some college extension or advanced correspondence course training. The utility men involved come from all departments and job levels, with the majority holding titles in operation and distribution categories.

---

* Information in this case provided by E. W. Love, Training Supervisor, Southwestern Public Service Company, Amarillo, Texas.

Programed instruction reduced the first and second year courses ("Mathematics for the Lineman and Electrician" and "Fundamentals of Electricity") from 144 hours each to 80 hours each. Further refinement of the courses has made possible additional savings in classroom time.

During the 1962–63 school term, 158 men used the programed textbook at 19 branches of the lineman's vocational training schools. These men were in the first and second years of the four-year course. Seventy-seven first-year students used the programed textbook on mathematics for the lineman and electrician. Eighty-one second-year students used the programed textbook on electricity fundamentals.

Programed textbooks were used in connection with class work. Southwestern decided to use the programed text rather than the typical teaching machine, since, with the programed text, a great deal of class work could be done at home.

After programed textbooks had been used during the 1962–63 school term, instructors in the 19 schools were surveyed for their reactions. In turn, the instructors surveyed their students. These general conclusions were reached: (1) Nearly all the instructors were in favor of using programed textbooks and felt that this approach helped them teach more material. (2) All 19 instructors felt the programed learning textbooks could be used successfully in future vocational training program. (3) At the beginning of the course, most students liked using programed textbooks; at the end, they were still in favor of this approach and would like future courses to be taught in the same manner.

In addition to the vocational training schools, Southwestern has also started using programed textbooks in a separate training program for apprentice linemen. The use of programed textbooks on algebra and basic electricity has reduced the first-year line apprentice school from three weeks to two weeks.

Southwestern is now using the TMI-Grolier algebra course No. TT 501 in conjunction with textbooks which it has assembled. In the evening vocational math course each student is issued a programed text and a company textbook. He then spends 30 hours in the classroom, where he learns basic mathematics not covered in the programed text. The programed text work is done at home, but the instructor supervises progress. When the student completes the course, he receives a company certificate giving him credit for 60 hours, 30 of classroom work and 30 of homework assignments in the programed text.

In the lineman and substation electrician apprenticeship schools the same programed mathematics text is used. In this case, the apprentice is expected to complete several programed texts at home and to attend the vocational evening school. In addition, he receives a rather elaborate formal training course conducted on company time. Before he attends the first-year formal apprentice school, he must complete the TMI-Grolier programed algebra text No. TT 501. One of the regular vocational instructors is assigned to the apprentice and informally supervises his progress through the programed text. At the formal school the apprentice is given classroom instruction in the areas of mathematics not covered by the programed text. The same process is followed in the TMI-Grolier programed DC electricity text, which is used in the second year vocational schools for line apprentices.

Southwestern Public Service makes one other use of programed text in its vocational schools—in a second-year course in mechanics and basic vectors. For this course the student completes Basic Systems' program, "Vectors, A Programed Text for Introductory Physics." It consists of 16 classroom hours and 14 hours allowed for completion of the programed text. In the classroom the instructors teach basic physics and supervise the employee's progress through the programed text.

Reception by the students has been excellent. Experience has taught Southwestern Public Service that almost without exception progress depends upon the manner in which the instructor introduces PI to his class. When he has a good understanding of the purpose and possibilities of programed learning and is enthusiastic himself, his students will also be enthusiastic.

Very few of the vocational or apprentice instructors have had practical experience in education. They are usually field engineers, working foremen, or senior journeymen who are highly skilled in the specific area in which they are conducting instruction. Under these circumstances it is very important that the instructors have a thorough orientation in PI.

When programed texts were introduced, some instructors asked their students to do much of the work in the classroom. They soon discovered that they did not have enough time to cover related course topics, so now nearly all of the programed text work is done at home, and classroom time is reserved for specific questions by the student. Southwestern has also found that it could not hand an employee a programed text, even with a good explanation, and expect him to complete it on his own. It has therefore made a practice of minimum assignments for each evening vocational class. It has encouraged the instructor to give very short quizzes on these assignments. The students are also asked to bring their texts to class, where the instructor checks them to make sure that they have not fallen behind. Southwestern has found that it must emphasize the need for establishing definite study habits in relation to the programed text. It urges its students to set aside specific time for study, encouraging several short study sessions rather than one extended period of study.

As to retention, Southwestern's experience has been both encouraging and disappointing. It didn't find any unusual amount of retention, but it did find as much retention, and probably more, as with the conventional method of instruction. Much less classroom instruction was required and, therefore, retention benefits, although not startling, were satisfactory. Southwestern is convinced that retention relates directly to how much and how often a student applies what he has learned.

Southwestern's only use of PI in skilled employee training has been in the area of fundamental subjects. A definite problem lies in the fact that little programing has been done in its specific business. It could make good use of programed learning in, for example, basic transformer connections, capacitors, protective devices, and so on.

Since the training department is a one-man operation, company programing is impractical. Southwestern does not plan to prepare its own programs in the near future. E. W. Love, the training supervisor, feels that a highly specialized staff is the basic ingredient of such a project.

The cost of training varies with the number of students and type of school. In on-the-job schools the cost of programed texts can be compared to the wage, time, and living costs saved. However, cost control is secondary to effective training.

In each year of Southwestern's first two apprentice schools, it estimates a saving of about one week of working time, of room and board per student, and of instructors' time. However, its decision to use programed texts was not based on cost.

In its evening schools that use programed texts, it saves from 15 to 20 hours of instructor pay. Its employees also save from 15 to 20 hours of free evening time. Again, cost is not a very important factor, since as much training can be accomplished in less time where PI can be used, and a cost saving is the natural outcome.

Southwestern claims the following advantages in using programed learning: (1) more learning by students who are allowed to progress at their own capability rate and good retention; (2) time savings; (3) more uniform coverage of the educational material, which is important because the company's schools are geographically scattered; (4) greater interest on the part of the students; (5) lower employee turnover rate; (6) high degree of skill and efficiency; and (7) minimizing of expensive mistakes.

Sperry Polaris *

The Sperry Polaris training programs group in late 1962 completed an appraisal of a programed instruction course which it developed in cooperation with Basic Systems, Inc., to cover the optical alignment of the Polaris navigation subsystem.

THE FOLLOWING EXCERPTS FROM THE JOINT SPERRY POLARIS AND Basic Systems technical report, "Programmed Instruction for the Polaris Navigation Subsystem—Optical Alignment," describe Sperry Polaris' training mission:

In 1961 Sperry Polaris was established to manage the navigation subsystem programs for the Polaris submarine. In this capacity [it was] responsible for the following training programs:
New London crew training.
Dam Neck Guided Missile School.
Portsmouth Shipyard personnel training.
Charleston Naval Yard personnel training.
Mare Island Shipyard personnel training.
Shipboard training at sea.
Tender crew training.
Sperry Polaris field engineering training.
Sperry technician "in plant" training.
Subcontractor training.

The Sperry training support program for Polaris provided curriculum development and documentation, instruction for naval and technical personnel, Polaris navigation subsystem instructor training, training evaluation, and subcontractor coordination. These activities are enhanced by continuing technical inputs from the various Sperry engi-

* Information for this case based on (1) an interview with David J. Keller, Training Advisor, Sperry Gyroscope Company, Syosset, New York; (2) "Technical Report, Programmed Instruction for the Polaris Navigation Subsystem—Optical Alignment," Sperry Polaris and Basic Systems, Inc., January 31, 1963; and (3) David J. Keller, "Evolution in Industrial Education—The Product and the Systems Approach," unpublished report, October 20, 1964.

neering groups responsible for design, operation, and maintenance of the navigation subsystem.

Training activities include the preparation of technical manuals for equipment operation and maintenance and the evaluation of training requirements for present and future crew training. In addition, Sperry is developing audiovisual training aids for on-board training at sea and for fixed training installations on submarine tenders and shore stations.

Even though management at Sperry Polaris has felt that its conventional training procedures have provided an adequate teaching capability in the past, it decided to investigate the possibility of eliminating some of the disadvantages inherent in instructor-centered training. These disadvantages include the need for centralized training activity, fixed training schedules, and competent and highly skilled master instructors. Optimal development of the training functions at Sperry was inhibited by these factors. Training must often be conducted at distant shore installations, remote Sperry field installations, and on board the submarines and surface vessels. To satisfy these requirements large expenditures of time and manpower were necessary. It was emphasized that, "In addition, an unsatisfied requirement exists for the instruction of Polaris personnel needing only peripheral knowledge of particular tasks. No organized classes or training facilities are currently available for these personnel." The need for continual updating of reference material for the Polaris navigation subsystems is yet another training problem. The subsystems are complex, information comes from many sources, and changes are made frequently in equipment design. As a result, support information is not always updated, and it sometimes becomes obsolete. What is more, field personnel do not always make full use of reference material, which is a necessary training tool.

> Another significant factor in training complexity is the continually changing specification for maintenance training requirements. The procedures for equipment installation, operation, grooming, and checkout must be continuously monitored to determine necessary training inputs. Malfunction reports, patrol reports, spare requirements, and navigation center team tasks must be reviewed. Field material must be continually updated in accordance with survey results.

Sperry thought that PI technology would minimize instructor costs and achieve standardization and quality control over instructional procedures and subject matter content. This would virtually eliminate instructor variability and contamination in the learning process. Since self-instructional training requires little or no supervision, it is well suited to field training.

The program that was to be the vehicle to study these problems was developed jointly by the Sperry Polaris Training Programs Group and Basic Systems, Inc. Sperry developed the specifications, including the task analysis, terminal behaviors, and course outline; and Basic Systems wrote and tested the program. Exhibit 1 outlines the functions involved in the joint effort.

The 761-frame program was based upon Sperry-developed field training manuals and bulletins and instructor-prepared course outlines and examination. The program covered the following topics:

- General Coordinate Systems.
- The Polaris Coordinate System.
- The Optical Reference Unit.
- The Auto Collimator.
- The Alignment Periscope.
- Installation of the Optical Reference Unit.
- Flexure and Flexure Monitoring.
- The Theodolite.
- The Alignment of SINS.
- Checkout Procedures.

Ten engineers from the Polaris Field Service Group took the programed course, and nine engineers with equivalent education and experience took the conventional course, which utilized audiovisual procedures and supervised discussion periods. Both groups were matched on a 20-item pretest representing each subcategory of the final examination. Each man in the programed instruction group was given a copy of the course in a monitored classroom setting and told to proceed at his own rate. No instructor was present and no additional instruction was given this group. The conventional group was taught by a field training staff instructor who had broad experience and excellent professional skills. The instructor was allowed to use the information in the programed course freely and to make changes in the conventional course content at will.

Following the course, a final examination of 90 items was given to both groups of students, with these results:

	PROGRAMED INSTRUCTION GROUP	CONVENTIONALLY TRAINED GROUP
Mean final exam scores	88.9	90.7
Mean completion time	16.2 hrs.	20.1 hrs.

EXHIBIT 1

INTERFACE FOR PROJECT COORDINATION

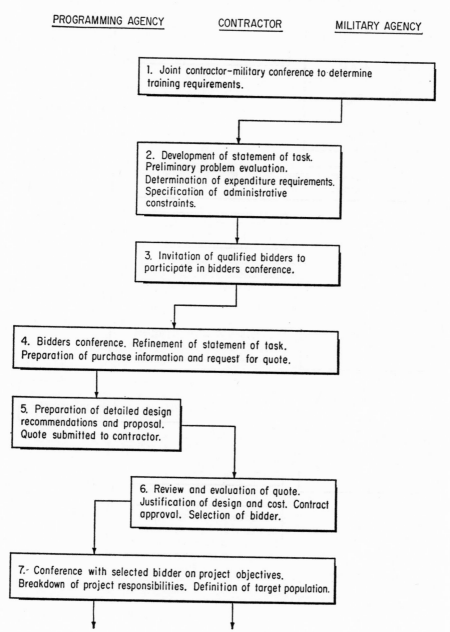

EXHIBIT 1 *(continued)*

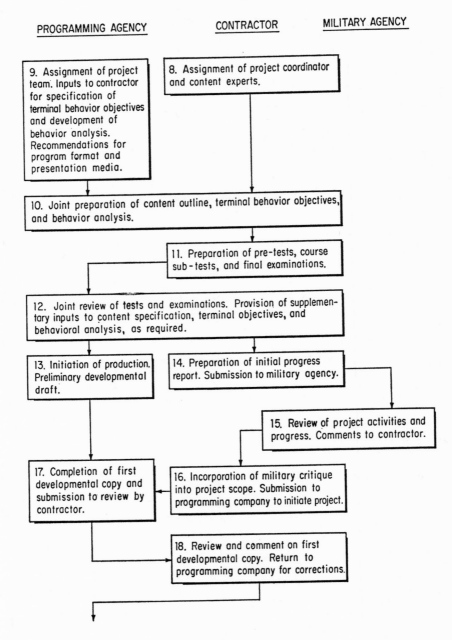

PROGRAMMING AGENCY   CONTRACTOR   MILITARY AGENCY

9. Assignment of project team. Inputs to contractor for specification of terminal behavior objectives and development of behavior analysis. Recommendations for program format and presentation media.

8. Assignment of project coordinator and content experts.

10. Joint preparation of content outline, terminal behavior objectives, and behavior analysis.

11. Preparation of pre-tests, course sub-tests, and final examinations.

12. Joint review of tests and examinations. Provision of supplementary inputs to content specification, terminal objectives, and behavioral analysis, as required.

13. Initiation of production. Preliminary developmental draft.

14. Preparation of initial progress report. Submission to military agency.

15. Review of project activities and progress. Comments to contractor.

17. Completion of first developmental copy and submission to review by contractor.

16. Incorporation of military critique into project scope. Submission to programming company to initiate project.

18. Review and comment on first developmental copy. Return to programming company for corrections.

EXHIBIT 1 *(concluded)*

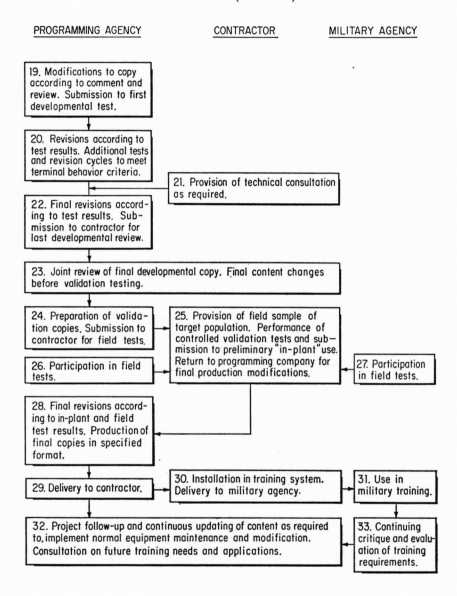

PROGRAMMING AGENCY   CONTRACTOR   MILITARY AGENCY

19. Modifications to copy according to comment and review. Submission to first developmental test.

20. Revisions according to test results. Additional tests and revision cycles to meet terminal behavior criteria.

21. Provision of technical consultation as required.

22. Final revisions according to test results. Submission to contractor for last developmental review.

23. Joint review of final developmental copy. Final content changes before validation testing.

24. Preparation of validation copies. Submission to contractor for field tests.

25. Provision of field sample of target population. Performance of controlled validation tests and submission to preliminary "in-plant" use. Return to programming company for final production modifications.

26. Participation in field tests.

27. Participation in field tests.

28. Final revisions according to in-plant and field test results. Production of final copies in specified format.

29. Delivery to contractor.

30. Installation in training system. Delivery to military agency.

31. Use in military training.

32. Project follow-up and continuous updating of content as required to, implement normal equipment maintenance and modification. Consultation on future training needs and applications.

33. Continuing critique and evaluation of training requirements.

The scores of the two groups did not differ significantly, but the programed instruction group completed the course in 20 per cent less time than the conventionally trained group.

Exhibit 2 is a sample of frames from the program.

The following student reactions to the course were expressed in the answers to an attitude questionnaire:

- All students thought they would remember the programed material as well as they do the information they learn in conventional courses.
- Seven students believed the program would have great value in field use, two thought it would be of little value, one was not sure of its value, and none thought it had little or no value.
- All students believed some supplementary training material was needed.
- Seven students said they learned more from PI than from textbooks, one said there was no difference, and two said textbooks were more efficient.
- Four students favored PI for major parts of courses, six favored more limited use, and none favored no use at all.
- Eleven students considered as disadvantages oversimplification, enforced study of every frame, and lack of time for reflection; five said the course offered maximum training with minimum expenditure of time and effort.
- One student was very enthusiastic about the programed course, eight were generally interested, and one was neutral.
- Students suggested that the course be used to supplement rather than to replace conventional instruction; that allowance be made for additional review; and that quiet, privacy, and more time be provided.

A systems approach to the training problems at Sperry Polaris is evolving from the study of the potential applications of programed instruction, as we can see in the following comments made by David J. Keller, Training Advisor for Sperry Gyroscope Company.

Consider the ramifications for developing a weapons system training program using a systems approach. The population to be trained has an educational range from no technical background to advanced specialized degrees. Among the specialists are some who have completed courses in core subjects, some who have taken special courses on particular equipment, and some who have had many years of practical experience in the field. The object of the training program is to bring these people to the functional level of a mission task—which is essentially to know the complex equipment and be able to perform in a variety of prescribed operating conditions.

Accurate statistical determination of an initial student population with a

EXHIBIT 2

SAMPLE FRAMES

92. After AP-5 is positioned so that mirror J is in the field of view of MTH-1, mirror J is adjusted until it is parallel in_____and_____ to within ± 5 sec. of mirror E.

This specification is (more / less)_____ accurate than the specifications for mirror G.

92. pitch
    train
    more

93. MTH-1 and AP-5 are used to adjust mirror_____ parallel to mirror_____ to within ± _____ sec. The_____ is used to position the heading gimbal on which the mirrors are mounted.

93. J
    E
    5
    gimbal clamp

94. Mirror J is adjusted until its_____ and _____ readings obtained with MTH-1 are within_____ of the readings taken off mirror_____.The mirror assembly on the _____ _____ is adjusted with the gimbal clamp.

94. pitch
    train
    ±5 sec.
    E
    heading gimbal

EXHIBIT 2 (*concluded*)

95. Off which mirrors are the following used to obtain
    readings ?
    1. MTH-1
    2. MTH-2 and AP-4
    3. MTH-2 and AP-8
    4. MTH-1 and AP-5

95. 1. E
     2. D
     3. G
     4. J

96. Refer to the illustration below and name the optical instruments used to obtain
    readings off the following mirrors: D, E, G, J.

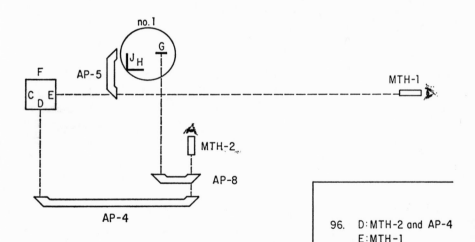

96.   D: MTH-2 and AP-4
      E: MTH-1
      G: MTH-2 and AP-8
     'J: MTH-1 and AP-5

wide spread of knowledge and background is of questionable merit in the real-world training situation. Some personnel testing may be undertaken, but in most cases acquiring deep background information takes a long time and the effort interferes with valuable productive time. When training and hardware are developed at the same time, there is a built-in allowance for identification and evaluation which better satisfies the need to determine individual levels. By "pulsing with" the various stages of hardware development, the training staff builds a capacity to ascertain and balance student levels rapidly by the time formal training takes place. Furthermore, a continuous and useful feedback is guaranteed throughout the life of the hardware and the training. This type of feedback loop is so sensitive that automatic response becomes a conditioned reflex of the entire training staff. Close identification also creates a climate or environment which is conducive to learning. Within this climate the training people can project their thoughts, assimilate product dimensions, and effect product changes, particularly in the area of simulation. In many cases "software" guidance is absolutely essential to the design of the hardware. This pulse identification in the time sequence of events gives both training and product a higher probability of success. The cost grade-off could be significant if it were possible to equate training and hardware in the original proposals and accounting of funds.

There is need for pilot research in the simultaneous development of training and hardware. Validated training programs coupled with a more aggressive training staff also effect cost reduction to vendor liaison and remote source activities. A great deal of time is wasted in long-distance communications with vendors. With "concurrency" in the development of training and hardware, the instructor can effectively assist company liaison and provide a signal flow between the product source and the remote facilities. For example, engineers, technicians, clerks, or salesmen at some remote installation or subsidiary plant may be using the product in addition to selling, distributing, and maintaining it. PI courses, developed by staff training and validated during the development of the product whose uses they are attempting to teach, can effectively be used to provide the necessary product knowledge at the remote outpost. In this respect PI serves several purposes in addition to teaching; it becomes a knowledge transmission device and a field testing instrument. This accomplishes two things. It raises questions and clarifies issues which are unforeseen before the field test, and it allows for feedback to training which may be transmitted to production in time to effect a corrective change. Many product deficiencies (previously uncovered by conventional post-product training) cost thousands of dollars which would have been saved if the problem had been detected earlier.

Routine task analyses are most effectively conducted when the training is closely tied to the hardware. Ordinal tasks for installing and testing equipment can be detailed step by step with much less time and effort. Thus the training staff is not forced to go back and "rediscover" the original methods used.

Title Insurance and Trust Company *

The Title Insurance and Trust Company is presently engaged in programing a 21-volume training series designed to instruct title officer trainees in the subject matter and procedures involved in insuring title to real property. The demand for and acceptance of the program have been high both with students and with the management responsible for training.

THE PROGRAMED INSTRUCTION EFFORT OF TITLE INSURANCE AND Trust Company, utilizing basically intrinsic (branching) programing techniques, is designed to instruct title officer trainees in the subject matter and title procedures involved in insuring real property ownership. The list of subjects is:

1. Community Property	12. Judgments
2. Joint Tenancy	13. Executions
3. Tenancy in Common	14. Notice of Completion and Mechanic Liens
4. Corporations	
5. Partnerships	15. Easements
6. Life Estates	16. Covenants, Conditions & Restrictions
7. Contracts of Sale	
8. Deeds	17. Courts & Procedures
9. Power of Attorney	18. Probates
10. Deeds of Trust & Mortgages	19. Homesteads
	20. Bankruptcy
11. Attachments	21. Oil & Minerals

Scrambled texts are being used throughout the California offices for on-the-job training programs. Other employees who wish to study the programs may do so on their own time, but are required to pass the same final examination if they wish credit for completion of the programs. Demand for and ac-

* Information for this study submitted by Winn L. Smith, Supervisor of Instructional Programing, Title Insurance and Trust Company, Los Angeles, California.

ceptance of this program have been high—both with the students and with the management responsible for training. The programed material is valuable as a review for experienced personnel as well as for training new employees.

Title Insurance and Trust Company has title plants in 34 counties throughout California. Including the northern California escrow operations, it has approximately 75 offices in California. Some of these offices have 200 or more employees; others have fewer than ten. The company can't always take employees off the job and bring them into a central office for training. By the same token, it is not in a position to send trainers to all locations.

In the process of becoming the nation's largest title insurance company, T.I. faced some other problems in training. Over the years, the company has been built up from a number of individual county operations. Many of the employees who were experts in the title field were nearing retirement age. In addition, expansion into new areas had increased the demand for trained personnel, drawing experienced employees into the supervisory and management ranks. Growth and expansion presented varying title practices, and it was desirable to establish uniform operating procedures. One problem, then, in addition to teaching the basic subject matter, was to teach employees how to follow procedures according to general company rules—hence the interest in programed instruction as a means for standardizing these practices.

T.I. looked to programed instruction with these basic problems in mind. The next factor it considered was time. In retrospect, Winn Smith, the Instructional Programing Supervisor, advises: "If your management is asking for a program last week, don't start to program. You can't do this job rapidly. Programing isn't a project that can be built overnight; it is a long, slow, and painstaking process."

The next factor to consider was cost. Even though it is expensive to undertake a programing project, management must look at the cost in two ways. First, consider the immediate cost in relationship to the reduction in training time. T.I.'s experience has been that its total training time can be reduced by approximately one-third. The second factor to consider is how long the program will be used. Mrs. Smith reminds management: "You should be able to prorate your cost over the period of time the program can be used, not just the budget for the quarter or for the year in which you are writing your program. If your program is suitable and usable for a longer period of time, the cost should be spread over this extended period."

T.I. anticipated that most of the material it was programing would remain generally unchanged for approximately 10 years. Some areas may require minor revisions, but the bulk of the program will remain useful for at least that period of time. While a great deal of money is being invested in the program, when the cost is spread over 10 years and when it is realized that it is reaching many geographic areas that have never before had an extensive training program, and that its content is consistent for all students at all locations, it is understandable why the investment in the project is justified.

Another area of serious concern at T.I. was whether to have the programs custom-designed by a contracting agency or to prepare them in-house. It recognized that using its own personnel would be expensive because of the training required and the difficulty in replacing the selectee. Further, taking people from its own organization would create a chain reaction of replacement, and it was already faced with a shortage of trained personnel—in fact, that was the reason for attempting the programing project in the first place. Also, when T.I. began its project, there were few professional programers available; there were none with knowledge of the title business. On the other hand, if it assigned a subject matter expert to a professional programer, it would double salary costs and would still have to provide replacements for staff vacancies. Furthermore, and this factor was highly significant, when the basic program was completed, the professional programer would move on to other contracts. Who would write the revisions necessary to update or expand the program in the future? Weighing these and other considerations, T.I. decided to use in-house programers.

Having decided to develop an in-house capability using its own personnel, T.I. next wrote a job description and job specifications. It placed heavy emphasis on writing ability—clear concise expression, knowledge of grammar, and organizational ability. The personal characteristics sought were (1) self-discipline, (2) high motivation, (3) patience, (4) ability to accept criticism, (5) self-confidence, and (6) creativity—*in that order*. Finally, it specified the need for technical experience in the title business, with knowledge of title language, procedures, and practices.

> Having finally described this elusive character—our next step was to find him. Beginning with the administrative vice president, we carefully described our needs to him, then to each of his division managers, who in turn passed the problem to their line managers. The managers were asked to recommend candidates for consideration in the programing project. We used this approach to overcome any possible reluctance to release qualified candidates to the detriment of their own staffing. By asking managers to submit their recommendations to their own division management, we were successful in avoiding this problem.[1]

---

[1] Remarks made by Winn L. Smith at the Annual Convention of the National Society for Programmed Instruction, April 1964, San Antonio, Texas.

When the candidates had been identified, each one was given the test for effective expression published by Educational Testing Service. Then each candidate was interviewed by the training director, who had attended a three-week programing orientation workshop some months earlier. The candidates selected for further consideration were asked to submit letters outlining their impressions of the proposed project and indicating whether they wished to participate in the program and why. Not all of the candidates accepted the challenge. Some were reluctant to give up present assignments for a project about which they knew little and for which they had no known experience or proven talent; others, for various reasons, did not wish to spend a month in the corporate headquarters for training. Finally a pilot group of four programers was selected.

In her advice to the conferees at the national NSPI meeting, Mrs. Smith pointed out that subject matter experts do not necessarily make good programers. At one phase T.I. used several attorneys as programers. Because the attorneys could not "step down" to the vocabulary level of a lay student, programing was difficult for this group. There were also editing problems because they tended to teach beyond the level necessary to accomplish the specific objectives of the program.

In selecting programer candidates, experience has caused T.I. to reevaluate the emphasis on writing skill and to place greater emphasis on the ability to analyze and organize material into a logical fashion. The person who cannot think in logical fashion, and who cannot collect massive quantities of material and sort out those points that are pertinent to the established objectives, has extreme difficulty in programing.

Because of problems in moving the families of programers selected from line operations for an assignment of approximately one year, the programers worked in their own offices in four separate areas of the state rather than in the corporate headquarters. However, T.I. is convinced that a programing effort should not be attempted on a decentralized basis. This condition has now been corrected, and T.I. feels that the decentralized operation of the programing effort was one major reason for delay in its schedule. Mrs. Smith comments: "The group needs to be together for moral support and for creative support. When one programer is having difficulty, he needs the ideas, the stimulation, and the consoling encouragement of his colleagues. And contrary to the opinion of some writers, he needs frequent contact with the editing staff."

There was no significant correlation between the results of the writing test and the success of the programers in program writing. But there was significant correlation between programing success and success in previous assignments. T.I. is not certain whether this is simply because the successful employee is highly motivated. There is no particular explanation as to why the correlation exists, but it does exist in T.I.'s experience. For this reason, Mrs. Smith suggests that management, embarking on developing an in-house effort, should be extremely cautious in selecting as a programer any individual who has not been successful in previous assignments. She comments: "If management asks you to take an employee who is having difficulty in his present assignment to see if *possibly* he can fit in this job—be careful! If the candidate is having problems in other areas of responsibility, he'll have bigger ones—for you and for himself—as a programer."

There was also correlation between identified development potential and success in programing. More significantly, successful programers have proved to be successful management personnel when they were returned to regular operations. The implication here may be that if you can select or identify good manager potential, by using the same techniques you may also be able to increase success in identifying programers.

The pilot group of programers was trained by an experienced programing consultant. The consultant conducted a four-week training workshop at the corporate headquarters. Subsequent programers were trained by essentially the same procedure, except that training was done by Mrs. Smith, a member of the pilot group and now the supervisor of instructional programing. The staff gained much experience from the original workshop. Success in subsequent training workshops stemmed from the fact that the new programers were now learning from and working with an instructor who had subject matter knowledge, who was familiar with the actual project in which they were engaged, and who had experienced similar difficulties in learning how to program.

The company feels the following factors are important in producing a successful programing workshop:

    a. The programers should be completely separated from all other responsibilities for the duration of the project—both the training period and the writing period. This is *not* a part-time job.

    b. The programers should be in an environment that will produce a cohesive unit. The training workshop should be conducted in an atmosphere that allows for discussion and idea development in the evening hours. The programers should be a team in every sense of the word.

    c. Programers should not receive material on the subject of programing in advance of the workshop. You may, if you wish, give them an overview, such as Klaw's article in 1962 in *The Reporter* entitled "What

Can We Learn from the Teaching Machines?" but nothing more than an icebreaker before you begin training.

d. Begin your workshop with a brief orientation on basic learning theory, the psychological principles, and the historical development of programed instruction. Indoctrinate the programer with the importance of establishing measurable objectives.

e. Start the programer writing almost immediately. Any simple assignment will do—something that does not require extensive research, but does require the development of objectives, the preparation of an outline, and the actual writing of frames.

f. Quite obviously, the student has only minimum programing knowledge at this point. That is exactly where you want him! Let him struggle; he'll be far more receptive to recommended programing techniques.

At the end of the first week of the initial workshop, the sample writing of each student was reviewed individually, and selected samples were reviewed with the group. The first official writing assignments were made after evaluating the strengths and weaknesses of each programer. The second week of the workshop was devoted to research and preliminary drafting of the course outline. In an effort to produce comprehensive outlines from which the programers could work without difficulty when they returned to their own offices, consulting assistance from line operations was provided in this phase. During the third and fourth weeks, each programer wrote the frame sequence (a series of identified teaching points required to meet the program's objectives, which is organized into a logical sequence for use in writing the program itself) for the first phase of the assigned subject and began programing. Copy was edited on an individual basis, with specific attention to the development of writing style and illustration, with constant review of the principles, philosophies, and techniques of programing. At the completion of the workshop, each programer was expected to submit approximately 25 frames of acceptable intrinsic material. When he returned to his own office, each programer had sufficient training to enable him to begin programing independently.

T.I. has made some major changes in its approach to the training phase: Programers are given their first official assignment before the workshop and are asked to research the subject thoroughly before training begins. By using this approach, more time is available for outlining and for preparing the frame sequence. The outline or frame sequence phase is the key to the success of writing the program. Utmost care should be given to extensive review of the outline, the frame sequence, and the pattern into which the frame sequence is organized. In an effort to anticipate and remove every possible difficulty in advance of the actual writing, T.I. called upon training staff, department supervisors, and recent trainees to evaluate the material and the sequence. Extremely careful analysis at this stage has paid dividends in later projects.

Finally, in using line personnel as programers, it is important that from the very beginning of the selection process, management consider what is to be done with the programer when the programing assignment is completed. If he is removed temporarily from regular operations, can he be returned to the organization without creating problems of salary, job classification, or work assignment? In general, the programer should be capable of being returned to operations at a level somewhat higher than when he was acquired for the program. The successful programer will have learned a great deal from the programing assignment—not only in the area of subject matter but also in writing skill. He will understand company organization, company policies, and company procedures far better than he did before the programing assignment.

At the NSPI conference Mrs. Smith was asked: "How do you know that your techniques will work—that your recommendations are worthy of consideration?" She replied: "A very significant thing is happening in our company. When a programing vacancy occurs, we no longer have to ask management to recommend candidates, we have a waiting list of qualified personnel identified by management to use—to train—and to return to them for assignment! Success in training good programers for good programing results permits us to give back good employees who produce good results in other assignments. And the proof is already in our favor."

The T.I. program is somewhat modular since segments of the 21-book series can be used by individuals who are not necessarily being trained for title examining. For example, the secretary to a title officer or an escrow officer needs to know something about the ways of holding title and the instruments that affect the title, but she does not need training in bankruptcy procedure or homestead law or easement examination. The required training can be supplied by selecting individual units from the series. Except in the case of Books 11, 12, and 13, each book acts as an individual instructional unit.

T.I. has designed a total training system based on job analysis, job specification, and analysis of the technical knowledge required for each job. The programed real property series is the foundation for technical training required for maximum performance at each job level and as preparation for additional job responsibilities.

By putting the books into scrambled text format, the series is readily available at all locations. In addition, a good many employees are studying the programs on their own time. These employees are not part of the formal training effort, but they are eager to learn, and the company encourages this desire.

The supervisor of instructional programing makes a monthly report to the department management outlining the current progress made on the project. Because of management's interest in the programing effort, this report frequently gets wider readership and closer scrutiny than might otherwise be normal for this type of report. A reader from the upper management noted excessive delay in the schedule for publication of one of the programed texts. He made the comment, "What takes so long? Aren't you ready to publish as soon as the programer has finished writing the program?" The flow chart on pages 363–365 reflects the steps that Title Insurance and Trust Company must complete before the program is ready for distribution. The chart begins when the programer submits a complete draft manuscript and, theoretically at least, retires from the picture. Apparently the chart made the point for the programing department. When the next book was delivered to the manager who had criticized the previous delay, he quietly commented, "So soon?"

T.I. has made some additional changes in procedure:

a. In selecting new programers, T.I. has added a logic test which has been successfully used in selecting computer programers. While the tested population is not large at this time, the test equates significantly with the programer's performance. The company has confidence in its experience with this phase of the screening process. At the present, it will not consider any candidate who does not meet minimum standards on the logic test.

b. All programing staff is now based at the corporate headquarters.

c. At the beginning of the project, the company felt it couldn't afford to team a qualified writer and a subject matter expert. Now it is using this team approach with a great deal of success.

> While at the beginning of this project we felt that the team approach to programing was more expensive than we could afford, we now recognize that this is actually less costly because of the time saved and the high quality of the basic manuscript. Programs developed in this manner require substantially less revision at the end of the legal-technical review. The subject matter expert, fully cognizant of the trainee's needs and the objectives of the program, is able to bring specific illustrations

WORK FLOW DIAGRAM FOR DEVELOPING SCRAMBLED INSTRUCTIONAL PROGRAM

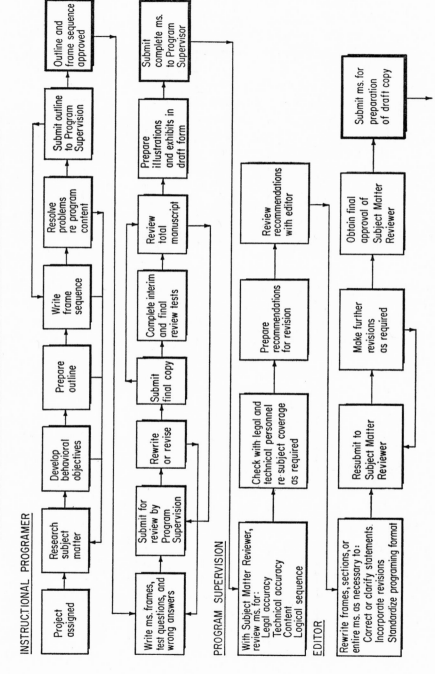

WORK FLOW DIAGRAM (*continued*)

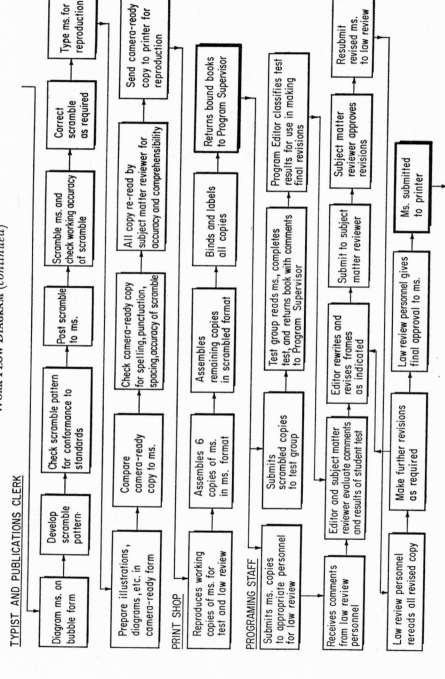

TYPIST AND PUBLICATIONS CLERK

Diagram ms. on bubble form → Develop scramble pattern → Check scramble pattern for conformance to standards → Post scramble to ms. → Scramble ms. and check working accuracy of scramble → Correct scramble as required → Type ms. for reproduction

Prepare illustrations, diagrams, etc. in camera-ready form → Compare camera-ready copy to ms. → Check camera-ready copy for spelling, punctuation, spacing, accuracy of scramble → All copy re-read by subject matter reviewer for accuracy and comprehensibility → Send camera-ready copy to printer for reproduction

PRINT SHOP

Reproduces working copies of ms. for test and law review → Assembles 6 copies of ms. in ms. format → Assembles remaining copies in scrambled format → Binds and labels all copies → Returns bound books to Program Supervisor

PROGRAMING STAFF

Submits ms. copies to appropriate personnel for law review → Submits scrambled copies to test group → Test group reads ms., completes test, and returns book with comments to Program Supervisor → Program Editor classifies test results for use in making final revisions

Receives comments from law review personnel → Editor and subject matter reviewer evaluate comments and results of student test → Editor rewrites and revises frames as indicated → Submit to subject matter reviewer → Subject matter reviewer approves revisions → Resubmit revised ms. to law review

Law review personnel rereads all revised copy → Make further revisions as required → Law review personnel gives final approval to ms. → Ms. submitted to printer

WORK FLOW DIAGRAM (*concluded*)

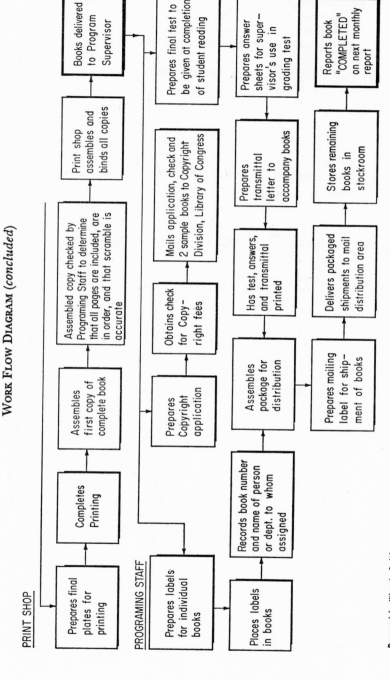

PRINT SHOP

| Prepares final plates for printing | → | Completes Printing | → | Assembles first copy of complete book | → | Assembled copy checked by Programing Staff to determine that all pages are included, are in order, and that scramble is accurate | → | Print shop assembles and binds all copies | → | Books delivered to Program Supervisor |

PROGRAMING STAFF

Prepares labels for individual books → Places labels in books → Records book number and name of person or dept. to whom assigned → Assembles package for distribution

Prepares Copyright application → Obtains check for Copyright fees → Mails application, check and 2 sample books to Copyright Division, Library of Congress

Prepares final test to be given at completion of student reading → Prepares answer sheets for supervisor's use in grading test → Prepares transmittal letter to accompany books → Has test, answers, and transmittal printed

Assembles package for distribution → Prepares mailing label for shipment of books → Delivers packaged shipments to mail distribution area → Stores remaining books in stockroom → Reports book "COMPLETED" on next monthly report

Prepared by Winn L. Smith
Supervisor, Instructional Programing
Title Insurance and Trust Company
Los Angeles, California

into the program that will simulate actual situations the trainee will face on the job. The writer, a skilled communicator with the student, can "translate" the technical information into a language that is readily understood by the reader.[2]

Based on present performance of programed instruction, T.I. management has approved the programing of six additional subject areas, four to precede and two that will supplement the 21-volume Real Property Series.

Students in the T.I. project must learn to relate specific conditions which vary with each title problem. The student must determine the appropriate solution, but in many cases, there may be more than one correct answer. The flexibility of intrinsic programing has proved advantageous in handling these situations. In a noncritical situation the student is taught how to make decisions, and how or when he has reached the maximum limit of his authority in the decision-making process. Success in this area is causing the company to explore the use of programed instruction at other training levels.

---

[2] Remarks made by Winn L. Smith at the American Management Association Orientation Seminar #8268-61, December 7–9, 1964, Los Angeles, California.

Trans World Airlines *

The story of programed instruction at TWA is, at this point, a progress report on an effort to apply a particular instructional system concept to improving the company's training procedures. Since the study is still in progress, the results are not final and conclusive, but the trends and the management frame of reference have been delineated, and the story of their evolution deserves attention.

THE TRANSPORTATION TRAINING DEPARTMENT AT TWA DECLARES that C. C. Tillinghast, Jr., president of the company, is convinced TWA's future success "will be determined by small margins in many things. TWA's success is based on the work and ability of its people, particularly those who train and supervise others." Since the senior management is likewise convinced that training contributes directly to the success of the airline, the Transportation Training Department felt that the key to developing the highest level of on-the-job performance was training to acquire initial knowledge and performance skills.

In trying to analyze how training could help meet the corporate objectives, the department undertook thorough evaluation of its present practices. The questions asked were these:

- What are the most efficient training methods to use in order to achieve our corporate objectives?
- What are we doing now?
- What should we be doing?
- How should we modify our present methods of training?

The first step was carefully to review current training practices and methods. At the same time it made a thorough investigation of the new methods of training being developed in universities, military agencies, and industry which offered promise of potential gains in effectiveness.

---

* Information for this case came from interviews with Robert Corrigan and Roger Kaufman and from prepared remarks by D. M. Crowley, Director of Ground Training, Transportation Division Training Department, Trans World Airlines, Kansas City, Missouri.

Its careful search brought into focus the concepts of programed instruction. Here, it felt, were training methods designed to produce predictable proficiency. In 1960 the department's members asked a critical question: "Are we doing this now in designing and presenting our courses of instruction?" Their answer to this question was twofold: Yes in intent; no in practice. They needed to learn more about programed instruction. They first heard in the late 1950's of Dr. Skinner's studies and, later, of the contributions made by Robert F. Mager in the field of programed instruction. Articles soon appeared on the subject in various books and magazines, and their interest was stimulated as they learned more about it.

In 1962 they contacted Peter H. Selby, Flight Training Supervisor, General Dynamics/Convair, who was writing a program on the KIFIS system. This was the first programed instruction training course developed specifically for airline flight crews. Their enthusiasm for programing was greatly enhanced as a result of this successful working example. Mr. Selby informed them of the Workshop for Programers which was being conducted by the University of Michigan.

They immediately formed a programed learning study group, consisting of nine management and instructor personnel, to determine how they should implement PI in their Transportation Training Department. Two delegates went to the NSPI Convention at San Antonio, Texas, on March 28, 1963. The second step was to evaluate the University of Michigan Workshop and decide whether the entire teaching staff should attend. These two men returned from their evaluation assignments most enthusiastic about the potential of PI methods. The top management approved the budget to send all of the TWA Ground Training instructor personnel to this course. Since then, many programs have been written for flight crews, cabin attendants, and airport terminal employees. These programs have been used to augment on-the-job training as well as home study in conjunction with classroom training.

In 1963 they felt that the same elements of written programed instruction could be transferred directly to classroom training. Some of the instructors call this application to the classroom "programed presentations"; others refer to it as the "group tutorial" technique.

During the fall of 1964 TWA Ground Training teaching personnel were asked, "Now we know how to train, but are we really doing what we believe in?" The answer given was: Yes in intent; partially so in practice. They had, in other words, made some progress. Their proposed method of achieving effective training was to design and implement one new program around which they would redesign and reshape all others. The model training program selected was for the newly purchased fleet of Douglas DC-9's. Implementation of this training will begin in October 1965, so they had one year to design and create a new perspective toward training.

This effort began with an introductory DC-9 course of instruction by the Douglas Aircraft Company at Long Beach, California. The instructors met, among others, Roger A. Kaufman, Head of the Experimental Training Methods, Advanced System. They discussed the plans Douglas had for using PI in the DC–9 training programs. They were carefully briefed by Mr. Kaufman on his work in instructional system design and implementation. They were informed that this concept of training demands answers to these questions: What about the organization and planning of the *overall* training program? What about the type of training aids that would be needed to achieve the defined learning objectives? What about designing and integrating all subjects within the total program to achieve the *total* on-the-job knowing and doing skills? To achieve effective learning, they were convinced that they must, from the outset, design for the complete scope of the training program.

Mr. Kaufman introduced them to the terms "open loop" instructional system and "closed loop" instructional system. "Open loop" represents the old conventional methods which are geared to the *instructor. He* plans, *he* organizes, *he* presents, and *he* tells the trainee group. There is little, if any, specific information about what the trainee can *really do* at the completion of the training program. There is little provision for directed and continued trainee response. In contrast, the "closed loop" instructional systems approach is designed for the *trainee.*

- It starts by specifying, in exact measurable "know and do" performance terms, *what* he is to be able to do and know at the completion of training.
- It requires a careful preselection of *only* relevant material and skills that represent the final objective.
- It provides for the design of instructional steps best suited to the progressive and *successful* understanding by *each* trainee, on the basis of his existing knowledge and background.
- It provides for *continuous, active response* by each trainee at each learning step.
- It provides for the *pacing* of instruction solely on the basis of *measured* trainee understanding.
- It provides for predictable trainee achievements which are controllable and measurable.

Of greatest significance to the TWA personnel, the closed-loop concept of instruction most accurately defines the model which they felt they had long believed in but have not been practicing in *all* their training programs. Its total application seemed to fit completely with their goals and requirements for upgrading TWA training programs.

The instructors were referred by Mr. Kaufman to R. E. Corrigan for further advice on where they could find a system to guarantee continuous and active response within the classroom. Mr. Corrigan is the inventor of the Tele-Test Teaching system. He was invited to spend several days in Kansas City discussing the closed-loop concepts with supervisory personnel and instructors in the TWA Transportation Training Department. They discussed the scope of the problems to be considered in designing an efficient instructional system for the DC-9 training program. They were convinced that this instructional-system approach agreed with their existing training policies and techniques, but it also assisted them further to raise their training standards. Mr. Corrigan also introduced them to the concept of deriving a "critical or optimal-learning path" as the basis for formulating and defining learning objectives. This "critical or optimal-learning path" requires the entire scope of management, instructional, and learning components to be integrated into a functional instructional system. This integration, together with a clear definition of the respective roles to be played by all instructors, is most essential. This "path" would specify the interactions required for every phase of training.

The members of the Transportation Training Department were convinced, after listening to Mr. Corrigan, that in TWA flight crew training the critical or optimal path would include Phase I-ground school, Phase II-flight simulation training, Phase III-flight transition training, and Phase IV-flight qualification on the line. Applying this model required them to:

- Define the trainee performance objectives for *each* phase in measurable, doing terms.
- Establish the prerequisite skills (knowing and doing) for advancement through the successive training phases (I, II, III, and IV).
- Determine the methods for controlling and measuring progressive trainee performance through *all* phases.

This path is based on acceptance of a common criterion by training managers in each of the four training areas. Applying this model within each training program required them to establish the steps to be carried out for selecting *only* "need to know" instead of "nice to know" subject content. It further required selecting the correct tools (media) and the best instructional technique (method) to produce the prestated performance skills required of the trainee.

Through this exercise they learned how to employ task analysis methods for defining and selecting only relevant subject content; the methods for translating these on-the-job performance specifications into functional performance objectives which are to be achieved by *each* trainee on the completion of training; and to plan strategies for defining and organizing the best sequence of instructional steps to produce predictable trainee performance. Of great significance was the realization by the training personnel that these methods were *not* foreign to their previous experience. They felt that they had been approaching this application in the past but without having the formal model for applying the correct order of steps and control required by the systems approach. As D. M. Crowley, the Director of Ground Training, has stated: "We listened; argued; hesitated; tried; and *we succeeded* in applying these methods of analysis and control with greater and greater assurance. We were in business!"

To assist in the clear understanding of the basic principles defining the closed-loop instructional systems approach, they developed a programed visual-aid sequence on this new look in TWA training. They applied what they had learned by validating this programed sequence; that is, by making certain it would produce the results they desired in achieving definable performance objectives. Several groups of supervisors and instructors worked out the design strategy and, on the basis of experience, the sequence was reshaped, rewritten, and tried again. Mr. Crowley is convinced that no longer would a course be accepted at TWA without performance validation.

Every instructor was later shown this slide sequence to insure a common understanding of the new look and the principles to be applied in designing, producing, and validating the DC-9 courses of instruction.

The full impact of the lessons learned and the design approach to the TWA problem pointed out the requirement for concurrence with the PI principles by *all* components of the instructional system. They began by achieving top management concurrence. They first established a closed loop between management directors from top to bottom. This insured that they were on the same "wave length," talking in common terms, and oriented to achieving common objectives.

The TWA Transportation Training Department plans to employ all appropriate tools to implement this outstanding instructional system. Selection and use of media (films, slides, programed lessons, programed texts, backlighted animated training aids, procedure trainers, flight simulators, airplanes, and so on) will be carefully integrated in group and self-instructional applications to insure controlled student response and reinforcement for learning effectiveness. And it will all cost less in the long run.

Union Carbide Chemicals Company *

Ten employees of the Union Carbide Chemicals Company, a Division of Union Carbide Corporation, were given the self-instructional Basic Systems program *Reading Engineering Drawings* by the Maintenance Training Director of the Institute Plant. Their performance confirms the experience of four representative industrial users, which have trained approximately 4,000 men to read engineering drawings through the use of the Basic Systems program. This suggests that Union Carbide can realize similar training and operating advantages.

THE FOLLOWING IS A SUMMARY OF UNION CARBIDE'S EXPERIENCE with programed instruction:

	AVERAGE	RANGE
Final examination score	92.3%	81–98.6%
Age	13.3 hours	12–19.5 hours
Self-instructional time	40 years	31–51 years
Experience	9.2 years	1–12 years
Formal education	high school	8–12 grades

A comparison of Union Carbide's evaluation with that of four other successful users of *Reading Engineering Drawings* indicates that similarly high and predictable results can be expected by Union Carbide through the wide-scale use of this program:

	4 COMPANIES GRAND MEAN	UNION CARBIDE CHEMICALS CO.
Evaluation sample	n=57	n=10
Experience	15.5 (data inc.)	9.2 years
Formal education	12 years	11 years

* Information provided by Dr. Irving Goldberg, Director of Training Systems Division of Basic Systems, and gathered from *Technical Report: Union Carbide Chemicals Company Evaluation Use of Reading Engineering Drawings*, The Training Systems Division, Basic Systems, Inc., New York.

Age (years)	41.2 (data inc.)	40.0
Self-instructional time	11.8 hours	13.3 hours
Examination scores	92.0%	92.3%

An evaluation of the four companies' experience is presented below:

	DU PONT	ESSO	CHRYSLER	CARNATION
Evaluation sample	n=30	n=7	n=10	n=10
Job description	Mechanics, operators	Operators, maintenance	Machinists, millwrights	Plant supervisors
Experience (years)	Data inc.	13.7	16.8	Data inc.
Formal education	12 years	12 years	11 years	14 years
Age (years)	40	45	42	Data inc.
Self-instruction time	12.8 hours	10.0 hours	12.1 hours	9.7 hours
Examination scores	91.2%	87.8%	94.2%	94.9%

The results from Esso, Chrysler, Carnation, and Union Carbide match those of Du Pont and suggest that the benefits reported by Du Pont can be enjoyed here through the wide-scale use of this course. Du Pont conducted a study to compare the effectiveness of programed instruction and traditional classroom instruction. This study convinced Du Pont's Engineering Services Division that PI could more economically and effectively satisfy Du Pont's plant operator and maintenance training requirements than could their traditional training techniques. The following data were developed from a closely matched sample of 30 men. A skilled instructor using traditional classroom facilities and techniques taught the same syllabus as was prepared in PI.

COMPARATIVE EVALUATION

	Programed Instruction	Conventional Classroom Instruction
Man-Hours of Instruction		
Minimum	11.5	17.0
Maximum	15.3	17.0
Average	12.8	17.0
Comprehensive Examination Scores	*Percentage*	*Percentage*
Minimum	87.2	72.0
Maximum	97.6	94.0
Average	91.2	81.2
Mechanical Aptitude Scores		
Minimum	300	307
Maximum	373	385
Average	344	340

On the basis of this comparative evaluation and Du Pont's subsequent field experience in training more than 3,000 men to read engineering drawings, Du Pont reports the following operating benefits:

a. Estimated savings of $90,000 in training to date; savings of $30 per man trained were estimated through 25 per cent reduction in trainee time and the elimination of the need for qualified instructors.

b. The training was accomplished with no interruption of work schedules.

c. Decentralized training, administered by supervisors, eliminated the transportation cost and the time loss that would be required by centralized classroom instruction.

d. Spoilage and down time on critical equipment were reduced because of uniformly high on-the-job skills.

Programed instruction results in several significant advantages for industrial training at Du Pont:

a. Performance levels are uniformly increased; note both the high level and the uniformity of the test scores of this evaluation.

b. Training time is reduced by one-third to one-half; see the Du Pont comparison with traditional training media on page 373.

c. The self-instructional aspect permits decentralized training, training with little or no job interruption, and reduced cost of training personnel and facilities.

In the Union Carbide evaluation these same benefits manifested themselves. The program allowed each trainee to proceed at his own best rate, and individual performance was not penalized because of differences in reading speed, study skills, or basic aptitude. A range of 12.0 to 19.5 hours of self-instructional time yielded a mean score of 92.3 per cent, with a range of 81.0 per cent to 98.6 per cent on a comprehensive final examination. This level of performance compares favorably with the grand mean (n=57) examination score of 92.0 per cent (range of 87.8 per cent to 94.9 per cent) produced by the four independent evaluations cited earlier.

The Union Carbide trainees' attitudes toward PI were an important factor in considering the utility of this program for wide-scale corporate use. A summary of these attitudes follows:

- All the trainees stated that PI is as successful or more successful as a training method than a teacher would be in the same amount of time.

- Eighty-nine per cent of the trainees indicated that they felt PI to be as successful as or more successful than traditional classroom instruction would have been.

At the same time, 89 per cent indicated that PI is less difficult than, or just as difficult as, traditional classroom instruction. These findings are typical of industrial experience with correctly administered Basic Systems programs. Perhaps the most revealing information provided by the attitude question-naire is the trainee preference for conditions of use. In response to the question, "Where do you believe most people would prefer using these materials?" 58 per cent of the men indicated that they would prefer home study; 34 per cent suggested that the programs be used on the job during slack periods; 8 per cent indicated a preference for individual program study integrated with on-the-job training. Significantly, none of the men stated a preference for using the programs in a classroom. When asked to make any additional comments they would care to, they showed great enthusiasm for the course. This pattern of use preferences suggests that the program materials would be best received and used by the men at home or during slack periods not conflicting with work schedules. The company's personnel and labor policies, however, should be considered in the former alternative since the economics of enabling the men to improve their skills at home is significant. This method of instruction also takes complete advantage of the administra-tive benefits of self-instructional materials in informal environments, and it should improve personnel relations by providing instruction under condi-tions acceptable to the employee.

United Services Automobile Association *

The United Services Automobile Association (USAA) is a fire and casualty insurance company that services officers of the Armed Forces. Its operation is worldwide and is handled entirely by mail from the home office in San Antonio. This case illustrates the application of programed instruction to the training problems of a company in a highly complex and competitive industry which is experiencing rapid growth. In a company in which 90 per cent of the employees are women, where employees are having increasing demands placed upon them, and in an industry where there are both an increase in job training time and a short labor market, programed instruction was turned to hopefully.

THE USAA HAS EXPERIENCED GROWING PAINS ALONG WITH THEIR concomitant problems. Its business has more than tripled (357 per cent) during the past ten years. It is the only fire and casualty insurance home office in the San Antonio area, so it can have no ready labor market. It has a high turnover among its women caused by pregnancies and husbands' transfers. The rate of turnover in the past three years has been as high as 34.9 per cent as compared to 20 per cent for other companies in the same city. As a result, USAA feels required to revamp its training program and upgrade the skills of its current employees.

Through the use of improved methods and electronic data processing, the company has gradually reduced the volume of lower-level clerical duties. It has not reduced its overall number of employees, but it has increased the number of jobs that require a higher degree of knowledge and technical accuracy. The following facts were used as a basis for its consideration of a revamped training program:

    a. High turnover rate versus local labor market.

---

* Information for this case submitted by Jean S. Moye, Personnel Director, United Services Automobile Association, San Antonio, Texas.

Overall Turnover	New Employees
1961—34.9%	594
1962—32.7%	640
1963—32.4%	764

b. Increased complexities of the casualty business by the addition of new lines—fire, homeowners, farm, boat, and so on.

c. Methods and procedures improvements by the introduction of EDP (7070 systems) and revised internal procedures.

These changes resulted in a shortage of qualified personnel, increased job complexity, and increased training time (from 6 to 24 months, in some cases).

The hidden costs of inadequate training were excessive. *One-third of the workforce was training another one-third of the employees.* It became imperative that productive employees be relieved of the burden of on-the-job training. With no foreseeable improvements in the local labor force and in view of the essential requirement to upgrade and retrain personnel, USAA decided to explore commercially available training resources such as formal insurance courses offered by the Insurance Institute of America and those of the Chartered Professional and Casualty Underwriters. In the search for ready-prepared training materials, information began filtering in about programed instruction. In 1962 USAA's managers began looking seriously into the possibilities of adapting PI to its training needs. It was impressed by the statistics showing a great reduction in training time. PI also offered an unprecedented standardization of training as well as a better use of the instructors' time. The experience the company had in 1961–1962 "with the machines and programs indicated that, while the material was slanted at a little lower level than we would have liked, training was accomplished with a higher level of final proficiency in a shorter period. Also, less time of the company training director, who was the instructor, was involved." [1]

In September 1962 the decision was made to explore PI. Supervisory and administrative personnel were enrolled in classes at two local colleges to acquaint them with the theory and techniques of PI so that they would be familiar with the concept when it was introduced into the company. Because of the rapidly changing nature of the casualty insurance industry, and because USAA anticipated further growth, it decided that any expenditure of money should be devoted to developing an in-house capability to produce,

---

[1] Jean S. Moye, "Training Programmers for USAA," in G. D. Ofiesh and W. Meierhenry (editors), *Trends in Programmed Instruction,* Department of Audio-Visual Instruction, National Education Association and National Society for Programmed Instruction, Washington, D. C., 1964, p. 114.

modify, and maintain PI courses. Another factor was the lack of programed materials in the insurance field. The most important factor in the decision probably was the strategic advantage in being geographically adjacent to Headquarters Air Training Command at Randolph Air Force Base, where some advanced programing design and development were in progress, and Trinity University, the home of the National Society for Programmed Instruction. These fortuitous circumstances gave USAA the opportunity to become knowledgeable about the most recent developments in the technology of PI.

Having thoroughly explored what was then known about programs and programers, USAA's management felt that it was bound to have a sufficient number of employees with the temperament and ability to form a workable programing unit. On the basis of advice from many authorities and from its own knowledge of its particular needs, the company decided to employ two consultants to help select programers and train them.

Competitive examinations were given to more than 200 interested employees. The personnel files and performance records of the top 35 were submitted to the consultants for review. From them 25 were selected for intensive training in a joint conference between the consultants and management. These 25 people came voluntarily on Saturday mornings from 8:00 to 12:00 for approximately eight weeks. The two consultants provided indoctrination and formal training, covering history, fundamentals, program writing, and program evaluation techniques. Following this formal instruction, presented in a conventional manner, the trainees were provided with practice in writing objectives, frames, and criterion tests. All the trainees had specific projects to work on, and the consultants worked with them on an individual tutorial basis. Their day-to-day work was not to be interrupted. Homework and additional study were done on their own time after working hours.

In January 1963 the consultants and the management jointly elected to establish the permanent programing unit. The training period did not end at this time, however. The consultants remained with the unit on an on-call basis for over a year and continued to advise management on additional projects and the use of off-the-shelf programs.

During the entire training period, from September 1962 to January 20, 1963, each programer wrote programs that incorporated material in which he was a subject matter expert. Many successfully tested and usable programs were produced. As their proficiency increased, the programers began venturing into lesser-known areas. It then became necessary to seek the assistance of subject matter experts in order to be assured that all programs were technically accurate. These technical experts provided the necessary information and edited the programs from the standpoint of accuracy.

Up to this point the programing effort had been scattered in various areas throughout the organization. The programs were helpful as far as they went. However, the consultants advised management that if USAA were fully to exploit PI technology, it had to concentrate its efforts on the training problems in a more confined area. Where to start? The programing unit was organized into a team as shown in the schematic diagram on the next page. After much consideration, management decided that it was logical for the team to start in the Fire Insurance Department, which handles fire, homeowners, and other allied lines. The growth of this department, which was organized in 1960, has been phenomenal. Because of this growth and the demand for experienced people by all companies, there was no labor supply and USAA had to train its own employees in these specialties.

The programers were divided into groups according to the team concept. One group interviewed and observed employees to determine how each job was performed and how one job related to another. The Fire Insurance Department, which has its own training staff, was currently conducting a class to train employees as correspondent analysts, jobs which require a working knowledge of the policy forms and coverages for the several lines of insurance handled in this department. They are responsible for the paperwork of rating and issuing policies. They must also be able to write clear and fluent letters. These classes were designed to run from six to eight months. The students begin by learning basic insurance principles, policies and coverages, company procedures, and the like. A portion of this material is being taught with USAA programed texts. The other group of four programers attended this class for about two months early in 1963. They gained firsthand information about the complexities of the job, and, what is more important, they learned about the areas in which the trainees were having the most difficulty.

Now came the job of evaluating the material gathered from the task analysis of the Fire Insurance Department and during the sojourn in the formal classroom. The most obvious need of both the productive employees and the trainees was for a knowledge of the routine internal procedures and how the work of one department is related to that of another. As a result the programed instruction staff devised an interesting and unique teaching tool. The lesson is entitled "Routing" and teaches not only where a piece of work or mail must go but why it must go there. The substance of the material is taught through a "programed lecture" in which the students respond orally. Pictorial cues are provided by means of a cartooned flip chart. The students

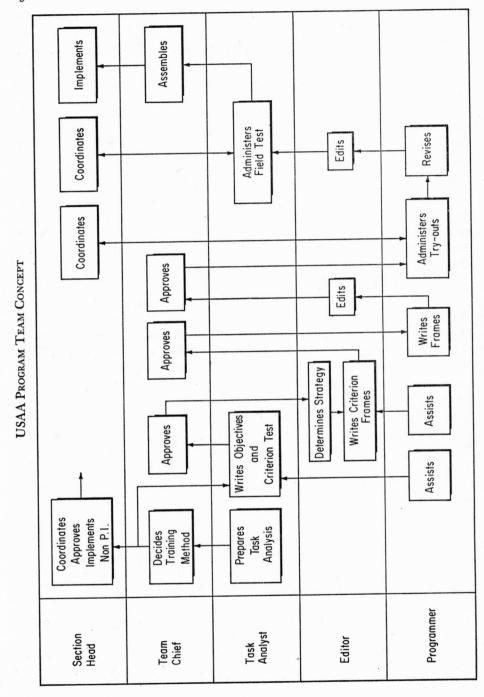

USAA PROGRAM TEAM CONCEPT

make notes on a printed flow chart that contains the essential cartooned cues. The lesson is made up of four units and six hours of classroom time. Test results and retention have been excellent. This program has since been adapted for use in other departments.

Also as a result of the task analysis and the classroom experience, the unit began programing some of the more difficult clauses in the various policies. This has led to programing the entire Household Goods and Personal Effects Floater Policy. The general insurance principles that are taught earlier in the class are tied to this policy where applicable. Thus the students gain a firm foundation upon which to build their knowledge of the other policies.

In less than two years the PI unit has produced about 70 usable programs. Some of them are for new employee orientation. For instance, an employee going into the Assigned Risk Department is given the program "An Introduction to the Assigned Risk Department." Similar basic concept programs teach new employees about the Automobile Policy Department, Comprehensive Claims, Terminal Digit Filing, the Rating Department, and so on. Some programs teach skills such as "How to Use the Rate Finder and Cancellator" and "How to Read an Invoice." Others teach basic insurance principles. Still others teach the student to decipher the technical language in an insurance contract.

The programers first learned the linear technique. They have since developed their abilities until the technique to be used depends upon the material to be taught. Now, a single program may contain one or all of several techniques, such as linear, branching, adjuncting, and nobbing. The programers have devised some techniques of their own—such as one they call "linching" because it is a combination of linear and branching on one frame. The programers have also found that functional illustrations used for cuing purposes increase learning. The standard set by the programers is high; 95 per cent of all students must achieve a criterion test score of 95 per cent.

The following list of programs developed by the in-house effort is representative of their scope and content:

USAA Programed Packages

I.   Automobile: Underwriting and Claims

    Auto Limits
    European Department
    Introduction to Assigned Risk
    Introduction to Comprehensive Claims
    Introduction to Rate Correspondence

Rate Classifications
Rating Definitions
Terminal Digit Filing
Differences Between Basic and Family Policy
Financial Responsibility
Insurance Terminology
Introduction to Claims
Junior Analyst's Rate Finder and Cancellator
Red Book
Why Purchase Automobile Insurance?
Your Deductible Interest

II. Homeowners

Additionally Acquired Property Clause
Definition of "Business Property"
"Insured" and "Residence Employee"
Homeowners Definitions
Introduction to the Household Goods Policy
Introduction to the Homeowners Policy
Nineteen Perils: Homeowners Policy
The Removal Clause
Basic Principles of the Fire Policy
Definition of "Fire"
The CPL Policy

III. General

Characteristics of Rate Making
Definition of "Fire"
Four Conditions of a Contract
Insurable Interest, Indemnity
Nineteen Perils: Homeowners Policy
Principles of Coinsurance
Six Methods of Handling Risk
Supplementary Payments: Auto Policy
Life Insurance Policies: Basic Types
Eight Characteristics of Insurance
Four Types of Reinsurance
Negligence
Pro Rata Liability Clause
Requisites of an Insurable Risk
Transportation Expense: Auto Policy

It is difficult to arrive at figures on costs on which management can agree and which will provide a basis for comparison. Except for the small consulting fees, the total expenditure was for salaries. The original ten programers are now six, and because of their increased skill and experience, this lesser number is completely sufficient for USAA's needs. After the original nine programers and one editor had produced seven usable programs and had 16 others in progress, the unit had to be reduced to six programers owing to budget limitations. Three members of the unit returned to their departments, remaining available on a standby basis.

The supervisors have significantly increased the extent and level of their understanding of USAA's training problems, and they have come to recognize that formal techniques exist for reaching training solutions. During the first year of intensive exploration of PI, "consultants and program representatives were concerned not to embark on projects so esoteric that the line organization and top management of the company would be unfamiliar with this technique and thereby possibly offer some resistance or hesitancy in either allowing programed material in their areas, or by not cooperating or proffering information and technical help." [2] Staff personnel and department heads were encouraged to enroll in the evening courses taught by the consultants which were offered in programed instruction at the two local colleges. Management felt that "in this way, they were not embarrassed, nor was their prestige in any way affected when they were included in general orientation classes with the program writers themselves. These staff people were assigned to the two universities, with the higher-level people in one course and the line supervisors and the department heads in a course at the other university." [3] Further to support management's orientation to and understanding of PI, an extensive library of materials was made available to all personnel through the company library and the training director's office. The programers have grown in skill and knowledge until they are now training specialists themselves. They no longer look at a task and ask, "How should this be programed?" Rather, they ask first, "How shall this body of knowledge be taught?" Using the skills learned in programing, they have embarked on an effort to develop entire courses that embody lesson plans, checklists, programed texts, programed lectures, manuals, flip charts, transparencies, color slides, and film strips, and they act as consultants to individual training units throughout the company. Programers are also gaining firsthand experience by instructing through PI courses in spelling, letter writing, typewriting, and other related subjects.

Management feels that major training benefits have resulted from the two years of exploration and experience in the field of PI. Management and the line employees are more aware of their training problems and more receptive

---

[2] *Ibid.,* p. 115.
[3] *Idem.*

to cooperating in finding solutions to them. Management feels that it has developed in the programers the capability of making a broad systematic approach to analyzing their job tasks from which will evolve training objectives and refinements which will enable them to decide which of many techniques should be used for the highest degree of learning effectiveness. Through PI the company is able to offer substantial relief to the supervisor in his training duties. The plan is to provide new employees, in a formal classroom or in home-study courses, with programed packages which will prepare them for their jobs in specific departments. It is hoped that they can come to their supervisor knowledgeable in fundamental and introductory skills. When the supervisor needs materials to upgrade the skills of his employees, the training director will provide them with programed packages which will minimize on-the-job training supervision. This will free the supervisors for other equally important functions.

> USAA feels the . . . program will greatly enhance the understanding of the role and effectiveness of the training director, the program writer, and the line supervisor, and, in addition, will hasten the time until the program becomes operational and of practical value to the company. This company is moving rapidly in the production and use of programs for training. It hopes to be in the forefront with those who are producing valuable, worthwhile, competent materials within a short period of time for the whole industry.[4]

---

[4] *Ibid.*, p. 116.

U.S. Industrial Chemicals Company *

The experience of this company with programed instruction has been random and limited. During the past year it has obtained courses in mathematics, statistics, and writing for individual employees at their request.

INTEREST IN PROGRAMED INSTRUCTION AT THE U.S. INDUSTRIAL Chemicals Company began with David S. Raymond of the Communications and Development Department, who read about it in personnel and training publications and in AMA's *Revolution in Training: Programed Instruction in Industry,* and then attended a PI workshop.

The company has not attempted to program any courses on its own because its population in any one job classification is not sufficient to justify the expense.

The company has a rather extensive supervisory classroom training program. This, coupled with a results-oriented appraisal system which stresses on-the-job training, has given its management people a pretty heavy diet of training. Some of its managers have expressed interest in more extensive training on some subjects in the program or in training on subjects not of sufficient general interest to be included in the program. To some of these people PI courses have been suggested.

One explanation for the limited use of PI is stated as being the extensive involvement with this formal management training program, which is now starting its third year. As a result of this program, however, an increasing use for PI is anticipated to supplement classroom programs.

USICC has been unable to locate any off-the-shelf programs which are closely tailored to its requirements. One solution is believed to be the combining of applicable sections from several related courses. The diversity of

* Information for this case provided by David S. Raymond, Communications and Development, Tuscola plant, U.S. Industrial Chemicals Company, Division of National Distillers and Chemical Corporation, Tuscola, Illinois.

teaching machines and formats has so far discouraged preparation of such a course.

If the company requires the training, it pays all the cost. If not, the employee is partially reimbursed for approved courses. Before he takes an approved course for which he is to be partially reimbursed, the employee must obtain approval from his supervisor, his department head, the Industrial Relations Department, and the plant manager.

The following procedure is used:

a. Permanent, full-time employees who have had at least one year of continuous service are considered for reimbursement for programed instruction upon recommendation from the manager concerned.

b. After completing one year of continuous service, permanent, full-time employees may receive retroactive payment for approved study satisfactorily completed during the first year.

c. The employee desiring to take a programed instruction course completes a written request and submits it to his supervisor, who forwards the request with his recommendation and reason to the department head. No commitment is made to the individual prior to actual approval. When the course applied for does not meet requirements, every attempt is made to counsel with the employee or suggest a course which would qualify. The department head forwards the application with his recommendation to the Industrial Relations Department, which verifies the eligibility for assistance and the applicability of the course before forwarding the request to the plant manager for his approval. If the plant manager approves, the Industrial Relations Department writes the publisher and orders the course, indicating that the employee is to be billed for the cost.

Approved courses of programed instruction are related to the employee's present work or to preparing him for greater effectiveness in the future.

USI reimburses eligible employees for half the expense of approved programed instruction courses after they have been completed. The maximum payment to an employee at the Tuscola plant is $50 in any one year.

Upon completion of a course, the employee fills out and gives to his supervisor a request for reimbursement and a receipt showing the amount paid for the course. The supervisor forwards the request with his recommendation to the Industrial Relations Department, which sends the approved request to Accounting for payment. Reimbursement checks are forwarded to the supervisor through the Industrial Relations Department for presentation to the employee.

The Industrial Relations Department maintains an up-to-date bibliography of available courses; provides counseling to employees and supervisors; reviews applications to insure that they qualify for assistance; and orders approved courses for the employees.

To date only three or four individuals who started a PI course have failed to complete it.

University of Illinois College of Medicine *

This report is about a study to determine the extent to which first-year medical students achieve knowledge and understanding of the physiology of body fluid metabolism when exposed either to programed or conventional instruction and the study time invested by each group in reaching this level of accomplishment.

THE UNIVERSITY OF ILLINOIS MEDICAL COLLEGE DECIDED TO USE branched programs instead of linear because "problem solving, rather than information storage and retrieval alone, seems central to education in medicine." Since neither branched nor linear programs in medicine were then available, it was necessary to create one before the study was undertaken. For approximately 30 months four programs were written by subject specialists on the Medical College faculty and programing specialists provided by ORME (Office of Research in Medical Education). This whole study was supported by USPHS Grant RG 8539. The first to be completed and studied, which was developed by Dr. Arnold Wolf with the assistance of Mr. Norman Crowder, was a physiology program in *Body Fluid Metabolism*.

Students who took the program were first-year students at the University of Illinois College of Medicine and two other state-supported schools. In each institution the class was divided into three groups matched on the basis of MCAT science scores. One group was instructed in a conventional lecture-conference format, a second was offered the same material in a printed program form, while the third went through the same program on a teaching machine. Each student was asked to keep a log of the time he devoted to study in the basic technique to which he was assigned and of whatever additional study materials and methods he selected.

At the University of Illinois Dr. Wolf, the senior author of the program,

* Information on this case submitted by Dr. George E. Miller, Director of the Office of Research in Medical Education, University of Illinois College of Medicine, Chicago, Illinois. Further information came from the University of Illinois, College of Medicine, Office of Research in Medical Education's *Report to the Faculty 1963–1964*, pp. 77–80.

also conducted the lecture-conference instruction, thus assuring comparable content for all groups. At the other schools, although the responsible faculty had been provided with the course syllabus well in advance and had agreed to the content covered, there were modest to marked deviations from this content in the final instruction they offered to their lecture-conference groups. These deviations did not, however, influence the basic exposure of groups assigned to the programed forms of instruction.

Two weeks after concluding the formal instruction all students in each school were given the same 31-item objective test designed to sample both recall and recognition of specific information as well as ability to solve familiar and unfamiliar problems and to analyze and interpret data.

Achievement scores showed no significant difference among the three groups in any school.

Mean Test Scores
(Highest Possible Score = 31)

	CONVENTIONAL INSTRUCTION GROUP	PROGRAMED TEXT GROUP	INSTRUCTION MACHINE GROUP
University of Illinois	20.2	21.0	21.8
School B	19.1	19.2	20.5
School C	21.3	23.6	22.5

The significant finding, however, was that in each school substantially less study time was required by those using PI than the conventional methods. The difference among the groups was statistically significant at the .05 level of confidence at Illinois and School C, but not at School B.

Individual Study Time in Hours

	CONVENTIONAL INSTRUCTION GROUP	PROGRAMED TEXT GROUP	INSTRUCTION MACHINE GROUP
University of Illinois	27.2	21.1	25.0
School B	24.0	19.8	20.4
School C	38.1	30.3	27.7

School C had a substantially greater study time investment because additional information was presented during the lecture-conference program, while those in PI groups had to acquire the same information by consulting other references. When the time devoted to programed text or teaching machine is isolated from the total, it is not significantly different in School C from the time devoted to this form of study by students at the other two schools.

An effort was made to capture the concept of efficiency of learning. Achievement and study time are combined in a ratio as follows:

Efficiency of Learning
Unit Achievement/Study Hour

	CONVENTIONAL INSTRUCTION GROUP	PROGRAMED TEXT GROUP	INSTRUCTION MACHINE GROUP
University of Illinois	.74	.99	.87
School B	.79	.91	1.01
School C	.56	.77	.81

The difference in learning efficiency between PI and conventional techniques is clear in all groups. Again School C has a less striking demonstration because of information covered which was not included in the achievement test.

On the basis of this study, it seemed reasonable to conclude that students could learn as much about this facet of physiology from PI as from the more conventional methods of instruction. PI appears to lend efficiency to the learning process. Some students, however, commented that they found the familiar conventional pattern more congenial to study as well as more effective.

University of Miami School of Medicine *

This study reviews the use of PI in the teaching of the freshman neuroanatomy course at the University of Miami School of Medicine for two academic years. Results and problems which developed and the rationale for revising the programed materials are discussed.

THE FRESHMAN COURSE IN NEUROANATOMY AT THE UNIVERSITY OF Miami School of Medicine has been taught in programed form during the past two academic years (1962–63 and 1963–64). The experiment was undertaken somewhat as an emergency measure. The School of Medicine was experiencing increasing difficulty in directing the students' attention to the essential concepts of this complex subject which is allotted a wholly inadequate amount of time in the curriculum. In 1962–63 the essential parts of the textbook (Ranson and Clark, *The Anatomy of the Nervous System*) were programed in branching form. The results were sufficiently good to show that an independent and more systematic sequence of concepts was needed and to encourage the School to undertake the task of preparing it. The second program is linear and provides much textual material in paragraph form as well as extensive references to several neuroanatomy and gross anatomy texts. The program was administered to the class in rough form in the 1963–64 year. The impact on the class was marked. The chief objective was accomplished in that the students mastered the major concepts with relatively little strain and spent their time mostly worrying about details which former classes never reached. With the examinations essentially unchanged, the number of final scores of 90 or above rose from 3 or 4 a year to 13. The class mean rose from around 72 to 76.

Two conspicuous problems emerged. The program appeared to help the good students more than the poor ones. Actually, it may have impeded the efforts of the less able students; the number of very low marks (20's, 30's, and

* Information for this case submitted by Frederic D. Garrett, Ph.D., Associate Professor, University of Miami School of Medicine, Coral Gables, Florida.

40's) increased slightly. In working with these students it appeared that, since they were unable to master the material, the actual effect of the program was to overwhelm them with a mass of incomprehensible exercises. The second problem appears closely related to the first and causes the School even more concern. The class as a whole, even the A students, while learning considerably more, appeared to enjoy the course less. In some way the spirit of the undertaking was lost, and the course became a monotonous series of uninspiring exercises.

The School is now engaged in extensive revision of the linear program directed toward sharpening the focus, weeding out redundant and otherwise nonessential material, and correcting the numerous infelicities which resulted from the haste in which the original was written. It hopes that this effort will both diminish the demand on the student's time and increase the esthetic appeal of the presentation to a point where the two problems encountered largely disappear. However, the problems may prove to be more deep-seated. There seems to be a current tendency among program writers to feel that PI is applicable only to preliminary surveys or restricted segments of complex subjects like neuroanatomy. The School's experience convinced it that this is untrue if one considers only efficiency in imparting information. But presentation of a complex subject seems to require a modification of the conventional approach which, while highly efficient (with an intelligent, strongly motivated, mature group), may be inherently unappealing. It has found it necessary to substitute rather large steps for the conventional Skinner small-step technique. This is partly due to the massive size which a small-step program would reach, but also the programers have come to doubt that broad concepts can be presented effectively in small steps. They feel that the Skinnerian approach often tends to teach words and diagrams rather than ideas.

The School has not had time to tabulate the error rate of student responses in its program, but casual inspection shows that it must be far above the conventional 5 to 10 per cent limit. The larger steps mean that using the program requires more effort, and the higher error rate means that it returns less satisfaction. If these drawbacks prove to be inherent in presenting complex subjects—that is, if future changes in the program (short of producing an unwieldy bulk or submerging the concepts) fail to resolve them—the School will have to balance the efficiency of the modified (large-step) program against its spiritually deadening effect. The choice might go to the less efficient but more comfortable textbook type of presentation.

Finally there is the possibility of another inherent problem which the School has detected in the reactions of its students. Under the peculiar conditions of the first year in medicine the very fact that the program achieves its purpose may lead to an adverse result. Freshman medical students work under a constant dread of failure. During the neuroanatomy course in 1963–64 the students' dread reached a pitch the School had never witnessed before. Part of the reason seemed to be that the program revealed to most of the students concepts whose very existence was ignored by former classes. The instructors' best efforts were ineffective toward assuring the class of the relative unimportance of these minor concepts.

University of Washington School of Medicine (Department of Pharmacology) *

The principles of programed instruction are being applied to the development of the self-instructional film system designed to supplement laboratory experience in pharmacology. Dr. Theodore C. West thought that through the self-instructional 8mm. film technique a system could be designed which would communicate practical data more efficiently and accurately than often is the case in conventional pharmacology laboratories for medical students. This particular programed instruction based system is a dynamic audiovisual component combined with a static visual component.

IN FEBRUARY 1963 THE UNIVERSITY OF WASHINGTON APPLIED TO THE National Fund for Medical Education for money to support a project designed to test the hypothesis that "laboratory instruction in pharmacology offers positive reinforcement of didactic material presented in lecture and text; the use of suitable motion pictures on a variety of pharmacology laboratory topics offers a superior means of achieving positive reinforcement."

In September 1963 the National Fund for Medical Education complied with the request, and the project was started.

The University's proposal involved developing (1) suitable short films in the laboratory, (2) a film projection system for self-instruction, and (3) a teaching machine with correlative material to accompany each film prepared.

The system which most nearly met the projection requirements is the Fairchild Mark IV fully automatic cartridge loading 8mm sound projector. It has a transistorized magnetic tape playback and was modified slightly to allow the designers to score their own narrations. The cartridge loading feature eliminated threading and rewinding. Its rear screen projection feature eliminated the need for maintaining a projection room. The Fairchild system is

---

* Information for this case submitted by Dr. Theodore C. West, Professor, Department of Pharmacology, University of Washington School of Medicine, Seattle, Washington.

lightweight and easily portable. It can be heard through a built-in speaker, a remote speaker, or headphones.

Films for this projector were produced on 16mm stock, processed, edited, and commercially reduced to 8mm, to which a blank magnetic strip was added. The 8mm films were mounted in the Fairchild FM-400 cartridge in the school laboratory and the narration was scored, either directly with microphone and recording amplifier or from a recording delivered to the projector from a magnetic tape recorder.

The production of the motion picture resulted from the joint efforts of the Departments of Medical Illustration and Medical Photography. The University of Washington Audio Visual Services supplied valuable technical assistance for development of the projection system.

A linear program was produced for each film which was earlier validated and developed on the basis of data acquired by putting the materials on a Mast Teaching Machine, which is a small rear screen projection system for linear presentation of materials.

Four films with programs have been prepared so far: (*a*) "Drug Modifications of Autonomic Function," (*b*) "Drug Action on Cholinergic Systems," (*c*) "Drug Action on Adrenergic Systems," and (*d*) "Adrenergic and Cholinergic Drugs on the Perfused Mammalian Heart." Currently in production are films on the pharmacology of neuromuscular transmission, pharmacology in anesthesia, and biological variation and the therapeutic index.

The School of Medicine is currently experimenting with translating the teaching machine program into pamphlet form, and the teaching machine program is being compared for its instructional value with the film program. The School is also attempting to study the relationship between the film and the teaching machine program by alternating the student from one system to the other every two or three minutes. The program provides a signal telling the student when to turn to the film and when to turn to the machine. This alternating sequence is continued as long as is necessary to learn the points the program is teaching. The program is meant to be dependent upon the contents of the motion picture. It supplements the film, but it may contain thought-provoking frames which demand a synthesis of the contents of both film and program. In addition, the program may present additional material within the framework of the general subject contained in the film.

Dr. West asked whether this approach to programed instruction can simulate or replicate laboratory experience. To what extent can the learning experiences of the students provide "a significant model of real experiences which it is expected the students will face later in their professional duties"? West asks, "Can the model experience be captured in an inanimate system of presentation?" And he answers as follows: "On motion picture color film are recorded the effects of autonomic drugs on the isolated, perfused heart of the rabbit. We capture the salient features of the preparation and the response of the heart to various drugs. We add a sound track. We now present such a film by means of a self-contained projection system. The film is less than ten minutes in duration, but it represents much more time of actual preparation. Is viewing it a laboratory experience? The data recorded on the film were actual data, first stored on magnetic tape and then played into an appropriate display system for filming. Does the viewer learn from the filmed experience? We try to insure his learning by interrogating him through the medium of programed instruction. The film, the program, and the student's response together form the total experience." This is undoubtedly an equivalent to a laboratory experience. The system is so designed that the display of information can be performed solely by the student, at his option. Dr. West maintains that "this is cinematic self-instruction in an area of practical pharmacologic knowledge. The system is complete when the film is combined with programed self-instruction for the reinforcement of the learning offered by the film."

Dr. West feels that the advantages of cinematic self-instruction as a supplement to, or substitute for, conventional pharmacology laboratory teaching include the following: (*a*) the complete predictability of experimental results, (*b*) the compression of long-term experiments to a few minutes, (*c*) the large number of laboratory experiences which can be filmed, (*d*) the convenient correlation of preclinical with clinical experiences, (*e*) the use of important laboratory experiences from other institutions, (*f*) the low cost of personnel, material, and time compared to that of conventional laboratory display.

Dr. West points to the following disadvantages: (*a*) a paucity of existing suitable filmed experiences, (*b*) the lack of *unpredictable* variations in pharmacologic responses which are lauded by many as important to student learning, (*c*) the lack of tactile, olfactory, and spiritual reinforcement presently associated with conventional pharmacology laboratory experiences, and (*d*) an aura of regimentation in the selection of laboratory instructional material.

Even though this system was developed to meet a specific need which was assumed to exist in the Department of Pharmacology, the implications in this study extend beyond this particular training requirement. It must be admitted that the traditional laboratory experience, while it is a real one and highly individualized, is a "cumbersome means of communicating a variety of pertinent experiences. Depth of learning is gained at the expense of breadth." Through this combined system an effort is made to increase breadth, even though some depth is sacrificed in the process. Certainly this particular approach should not be considered peculiar to the discipline of medical pharmacology. Cinematic self-instruction is suitable for many areas of industrial training.

Dr. West pointed out that the immediate challenge is production of significant economical film/programs in adequate numbers and variety. Already, he pointed out, Part III of the examinations of the National Board of Medical Examiners is presented partially in cinematic form. It should be a relatively small step to prepare analogous materials in a cinematic self-instruction package for a novel learning, review, or refresher purpose for continuing education in medicine.

A final feature of significance to international medical education seems worthy of comment. Because of the ease with which the sound track may be applied or erased, the cinematic self-instruction system should be especially attractive to schools and individuals from countries other than the United States. Since the sound track is separable, it is simple to supply a narration which is appropriate to the medical practices and language of the country in which the film series is to be shown.

Varian Associates *

This case reports a study carried out on a collection of programs written by Peter Pipe and Robert Kantor for Varian's Field Engineering Department. The case is of interest because of the implications in the study with respect to the trainee's entering attitudes and leaving attitudes and the concern that must be shown for them in planning in-house programing.

TRAINEES WHO ARE TO BECOME SALES ENGINEERS COME TO THE PALO Alto plant of Varian Associates for a three-month indoctrination training program in company product and policies. The trainees are graduate engineers with several years of experience. Usually they have specialized in some aspect of microwave electronics. Nearly all have what Peter Pipe refers to as a "near-expert understanding of some aspects of their job . . . plus several years of forgetting in other aspects of the electronics field."

Nine programs on microwave tubes and hardware were specially prepared for the trainees. Mr. Pipe indicates that he and Robert Kantor did not try to write a definitive work in any of the topics they programed. Instead they tried to insure that the programs would give the trainees a solid foundation on which to build during the rest of their training. In essence, their aim was to make sure that each man had, as a minimum, the key information he needed to ask meaningful questions when he was exposed to experts working in the factory. It was not too hard to write the subject matter objectives for this course, but they were not the only element of concern. After spending almost a month in the training program and in daily contacts with trainees spread over several months, the two men felt that "the trainees brought to the [training] a host of characteristic attitudes."

Characteristic of the entering attitudes were the following: (1) Trainees were skeptical of any instruction or instructional method that appeared new

---

* Information for this case submitted by Peter Pipe, Varian Associates, Palo Alto, Calif., and drawn from remarks by Mr. Pipe at the Second Annual Convention, National Society for Programmed Instruction, San Antonio, Texas, April 1964.

or easy. (2) They were defensive if placed in a situation where their competence might be questioned before their peers or before new or unknown supervisors. (3) They were impatient of any task that was not plainly pertinent to their training. (This was understandable, since they were away from their homes and families for three months.) (4) Their skills were highly divergent.

The programers felt that in order to adapt to these qualities and attitudes they had to provide for the trainees "a method of study which had some familiar features." Also, it was apparent that in order to overcome the skepticism of the trainees toward any method of instruction that seemed rather easy, some proof had to be provided of the merit of programed instruction. The threatening aspects of study had to be removed; that is, the programers had to create a situation in which no one would expose his ignorance before his peers or superiors. Further, the training would have to be directly and clearly relevant to the varying needs of the trainees. It also had to be highly adaptive to the individuals to accommodate their wide range of knowledge.

On the basis of these considerations the programers decided to provide the training in a book format, to give each student a copy of each program, to encourage him to read it on his own time, and to provide every trainee with a final criterion test *which he completed and marked for himself*. They hoped that a satisfactory score would demonstrate to the trainee that he had indeed attained the specified objectives of the program. And further, to adjust to the individual and idiosyncratic requirement of each student, they adopted a format which they called "criterion programing."

Criterion programing is defined as follows:

> We first tell the student the objectives and how we plan to get him to meet the objectives. Then begins the criterion program. The student is asked a group of questions at the criterion level. If he can handle the concepts at this level, he receives little further instruction on them; his responses are confirmed, and he is then exposed to criterion questions on further concepts, and so on, until he has either been tested and found sound on all the material to be taught or until he fails to perform adequately. The student whose performance is judged inadequate is given instruction in the concepts in which he failed, is tested on these concepts, and when *he* judges his performance satisfactory, he moves to the next batch of criterion questions.

The remedial "core material" is prepared on approximately six very carefully written and edited pages so that it is appropriate for the student and for the objectives. The programers attempted to make each page of the core or remedial material an entity in its own right. Therefore they normally presented a single concept on a page. They found that in some cases their explanation was not sufficient for some of the trainees, who wanted more information. So they added footnotes which directed the trainee to what they considered to be the best authority. Also, with each group of criterion questions, they gave the trainee the option of studying the core material or answering the questions. They attempted to eliminate for every student instructional materials which his experience made unnecessary and to adapt these materials not only to the level of instruction appropriate to the individual *but also to his attitude toward the instruction.*

Since the plan was to remove any threat from the student, including that inherent in testing, the programers did not provide statistics to demonstrate the success of the programs. The number of trainees was so small that it would not be useful for statistical evaluation, anyway. Therefore, the programers relied upon informal attitude surveys and direct observation of the trainees as they worked with the programs. From this kind of evaluation they concluded that the trainees' reaction was "overwhelmingly favorable."

In talking to the trainees and observing their behavior Pipe and Kantor noted, for example, that "a man who moves through the program with the alacrity that indicates proficiency, and who thus may be expected to see no more than a dozen pages in a given program, nearly always backs up and reads the whole of the core material after demonstrating his proficiency to himself." This seems to indicate that the subject matter, although relatively simple for this audience, was pertinent enough to hold its interest.

There was another interesting observation. The basic objective "was to help trainees ask meaningful questions when confronted by experts." It became apparent that the trainees' ideas on what they needed to attain this objective sometimes differed greatly from the experts' ideas on the subject.

> Most experts make the mistake of overestimating the beginner's knowledge, and some find it hard to believe that anything less than the definitive word is satisfactory for their particular specialty. This is not so strange. There is no real reason why the industrial, nonteaching expert should appreciate the difficulties of the nonspecialist; his job is to be an expert, not a teacher. But it presents a massive problem for the programer. He has great difficulty in getting the expert to generalize at the required level. And he can be assured that his finished product will not satisfy the expert. Nevertheless, we tried to be guided by our talks with the trainees. The outcome was a series of programs which might be regarded as "advanced remedial" material; interestingly, the programs cover material which in the formal classroom would probably have been covered only sketchily or even ignored as something "already known."

There is a lesson here, too, for the programer. It is that he should talk to his audience before he writes a word.

Mr. Pipe and Mr. Kantor began by trying to do something constructive about the negative attitudes with which students enter programed courses. They generalize these attitudes as: (1) threats of failure, (2) frustration, (3) boredom, and (4) discomfort. It is important, therefore, as their report illustrates, when designing instructional materials to establish a list of "attitude objectives" along with behavioral objectives. As well as avoiding the four negative entering attitudes listed above or making efforts to alleviate them the programer is urged to supplement these attitudes with efforts which will allow the student to demonstrate to himself that he is proficient; that when he demonstrates proficiency, he will be allowed to skip ahead; and that the proficient but doubtful students will have the option of calling for more practice. As Mr. Pipe urges, "Pledge that you will always try to keep away the shadows of unpleasant memories of the schoolrooms; try to provide your student with an informal atmosphere, give him credit for existence, pamper his preferences, and try to show how theory ties into the practice of his job or goals. Do something about these goals by getting out and talking to the student. . . . His adult attitudes and outlooks may tell you a great deal about how to shape your program."

Index

Date Due

9-22			
4-27			
DISCHARGED			